COMMUNITY, SPACE AND ONLINE CENSORSHIP

Community, Space and Online Censorship
Regulating Pornotopia

SCOTT BEATTIE
Victoria University, Australia

ASHGATE

© Scott Beattie 2009

All rights reserved. No part of this publication may be reproduced, stored in a retrieval system or transmitted in any form or by any means, electronic, mechanical, photocopying, recording or otherwise without the prior permission of the publisher.

Scott Beattie has asserted his right under the Copyright, Designs and Patents Act, 1988, to be identified as the author of this work.

Published by
Ashgate Publishing Limited
Wey Court East
Union Road
Farnham
Surrey, GU9 7PT
England

Ashgate Publishing Company
Suite 420
101 Cherry Street
Burlington
VT 05401-4405
USA

www.ashgate.com

British Library Cataloguing in Publication Data
Beattie, Scott.
  Community, space and online censorship : regulating pornotopia.
  1. Internet--Censorship--Australia.
  2. Internet--Censorship--Great Britain.
  3. Internet--Censorship--United States. 4. Internet--Law and legislation--Australia. 5. Internet--Law and legislation--Great Britain. 6. Internet--Law and legislation--United States.
  I. Title
  343'.09944-dc22

Library of Congress Cataloging-in-Publication Data
Beattie, Scott.
  Community, space and online censorship : regulating pornotopia / by Scott Beattie.
    p. cm.
  Includes bibliographical references and index.
  ISBN 978-0-7546-7308-8 -- ISBN 978-0-7546-8939-3 (ebook) 1. Obscenity (Law)--Australia. 2. Pornography--Law and legislation--Australia. 3. Internet--Law and legislation--Australia. 4. Australia. Broadcasting Services Amendment (Online Services) Act 1999. I. Title.

  KU4220.B43 2009
  345.94'0274--dc22

2009000627

ISBN 978 0 7546 7308 8
eISBN 978 0 7546 8939 3 (ebook)

Mixed Sources
Product group from well-managed forests and other controlled sources
www.fsc.org Cert no. SGS-COC-2482
© 1996 Forest Stewardship Council

Printed and bound in Great Britain by
TJ International Ltd, Padstow, Cornwall

Contents

1	Introduction: Classification Refused	1
2	'Protect me from what I want': Censorship and Internet Classification	7
3	Co-regulation and Symbolic Policy: The *Broadcasting Services Amendment (Online Services) Act 1999*	47
4	'Taking the Red Pill': Cyberspace, Jurispace and the Architecture of Regulation	89
5	Sexx Laws: The Spatial Strategies of Censorship	137
6	Censorship, Power and Regulatory Communities	191
Bibliography		*241*
Index		*275*

Chapter 1
Introduction: Classification Refused

In 2005, the Australian government introduced what it described as a 'new classification system' for films, video games and the Internet but which really amounted to little more than a new set of label graphics for the existing censorship categories which had been in use for many years.[1] These changes were hyped by extensive television and cinema advertising with the new slogan 'informing your choices'. A soundbite to which some critics cynically added 'by making them for you'.[2] According to the director of the Office of Film and Literature Classification (the OFLC), Australia's censorship body, these changes dramatically broke new ground and created a unique system of classification for Australia which ought to be emulated around the globe.[3]

Internationally, censorship of the Internet and other new media has created quandaries, public controversy and legal entanglements – so what is it about the Australian censorship system that makes it unique, a candidate for being held up as an exemplar? It is a system that has been variously described as the most effective in the world, the most draconian in the world and as entirely ineffectual. This book uses the Australian legal framework as a case study to illustrate some of the complexities of new media censorship faced around the world and the roles that theories of space and community have to play in this field.

Theoretical Framework

The *Broadcasting Services Amendment (Online Services) Act 1999* may not have significantly changed the Internet or the way in which Australians use Internet media and access adult content. The impact of the Act has been felt, rather, by regulators themselves in that it has opened for examination some of the foundations of media regulation. This book seeks to interrogate the Act and the legal and regulatory culture from which it arose via three interconnected conceptual sites: through

---

1 The classification categories had been in existence since 1982 and warnings, such as 'sexual themes', were originally derived from a government report, *Report of the Joint Select Committee on Video Material*, 1988, AGPS.

2 Australian games magazine *Hyper* has made this rejoinder several times, for example.

3 Clark D (2003) 'Film Classification and Harmonisation in Australia', speech delivered at *ShowCanada*, 30 April at 7.

space, through power and through the concept of community. The implications extend far beyond the Australian jurisdiction.

Spatial theory challenges the abstraction of liberal legal concepts, especially rule of law and jurisdictional maps. The work of Henri Lefebvre will be used extensively to examine the way in which law produces space and deploys strategies of spatial regulation. This theoretical position frames networks of power and engages with the governance of specific sites and spaces such as media spaces or sexual spaces. Lefebvre's work opens the way to examine spaces as discursive texts and to investigate the inscription of law on spaces and on bodies that occupy those spaces.

Spatial theory allows the examination of specific concepts such as law's textual 'jurispace' and the practices of regulatory fortressing. Jurispace is a type of regulatory space produced and occupied by law which connects with other regulatory networks and communities, in a complex variety of intersecting planes. Like cyberspace, jurispace provides a metaphorical parallel to physical space, connected to physical space at nodes and interconnected by networks of power.

'Regulatory fortressing' refers to practices of reification of jurispace, where the creation of more regulation becomes a regulatory object in itself. It can be argued that many laws engage in fortressing practices, particularly expressions of 'symbolic legislation' which are concerned with the integrity of their own regulatory frameworks and the colonization of unregulated space, rather than any empirically verifiable result.

The second conceptual site of investigation is power. Power is explored in order to challenge the simple mechanistic models of authority on which much legislative and law reform action is premised. Foucault rejects these 'top down' concepts of power and argues for a concept of power which is pervasive, circulatory and is based on a metaphor of fluid dynamics rather than mechanics. Simple models of positivist law based on social cause and effect cannot be sustained in the face of developments in critical theory of power. Space is an important concern for power when power is conceptualized as a flow and is deployed in networks.

Using Foucault's concept of power also allows the displacement of the state and law from the centre of an imagination of regulatory power. Nevertheless, the state retains an important role as a gatekeeper and holds strong ideological influence in many sites of power. The relationship between the state and power becomes important when the third concept is explored.

Community is the third site of analysis. Plato describes the idea of a community of citizens as a 'noble lie'; a deception or mere model necessary for the foundation of social solidarity.[4] Censorship legislation produces and imagines a particular kind of community; it reifies as truth what is really an abstract social construct.

---

4   Plato (1974) *The Republic*, trans Lee D, Penguin: London. See also Harden I and Lewis N (1986) *The Noble Lie*, Hutchinson: London and McDonald A (1998) 'The Noble Lie: Constitutionalism, Criticised', in Hirvonen A (ed.) *Polycentricity: The Multiple Scenes of Law*, Pluto Press: London.

The abstract community is persuasive in that it seems to prefigure the regulatory strategies which actually work to produce it. The legislative response to a diversity of communities and community spaces is the construction of a uniform and universal community, said to embrace all communities through practices of pluralism. Not all communities 'win' in the field of pluralism, some are validated, some are marginalized. The *Broadcasting Services Amendment (Online Services) Act 1999* and the censorship scheme it is connected to both treat community as an essentialist concept. Taking this approach, the only apparent difficulty seems to be determining what these community values actually are. Instead, this book calls for the concept of community itself to be problematized and reconsidered by the parallel explorations of concepts of space, power and multiple regulatory communities.

Regulatory practices shape content. Censorship's concept of the community is premised on 'the community member as complainant' which ignores the role of regulatory communities and community individuals in constituting, producing and reading media. The community imagined by censorship law is inexorably linked to the concept of 'complainant' (who is part of the community) and the interrogated media which is the subject of the complaint (constructed as outside of the community). The practices of censorship involve the classification of the object which is either rated and made compliant (brought within the community space) or 'refused classification' and exiled to the margins.

Chapter Breakdown

This book explores the concept of Internet censorship as a site of crisis for legal and regulatory theory, suggesting that spatial developments in theories of power and governance may assist in making sense of the issues raised by law. Chapter 2 establishes the environment in which Australian law reform occurred and compares the Australian censorship system (online and offline) to the comparable jurisdictions of the United Kingdom and the United States which have both had marked influence on the development of local law. This chapter also illustrates the major debates, moral panics and political issues which have developed around Internet content regulation.

Chapter 3 explores the Australian *Broadcasting Services Amendment (Online Services) Act 1999* in detail, describing its regulatory practices as well as the critique of the Act which has arisen in the media and through policy review. The contradictory critiques that the Act is both excessively draconian and completely ineffectual are further explored in order to sketch out the regulatory conditions under which the Act has been created and then analyzed. This case study illustrates the problems all regulators face when attempting to control Internet content in developed industrial nations.

Chapter 4 considers some of the arguments of critical legal geography as well the work of philosopher of space, Henri Lefebvre in order to lay the foundations of a spatial analysis of the Act. This chapter explores the relationship between cyberspace and law in order to illustrate the spatial deployment of law and to explore the models of space used in censorship law.

While censorship law permeates and governs the production of all media, debates around Internet censorship are largely occupied with pornographic media. Chapter 5 examines the practices of censorship in relation to pornography and explores the inter-dependent spatial deployment of these strategies. In particular Drucilla Cornell's concept of 'the Imaginary Domain' is examined, focusing on the nexus between public and private space and the governance of the obscene and the on/scene.[5]

Chapter 6 closes this book by asking if it is possible to replace a singular legal monolithic model of community with a concept of multiple regulatory communities. In exploring this argument this book surveys a range of cross-disciplinary critical material dealing with regulatory power networks, jurisdiction and legal subjectivity. While ethnographic investigation of actual regulatory communities is outside the scope of this book, three such communities are identified in Chapter 6 in order to apply some of these concepts and to argue for further research and discussion.

While the debates about pornography and censorship seem to be eternally irresolvable, the reason they are so persistent is that they are located at the convergence point of a great many social issues; of image and representation, identity and subjectivity, governance and freedom, citizenship and community. These are issues that the regulation of media technology has always revealed and the reception of new media accelerates the cycles of exposure and public debate.

Between the rock of draconian excess and the hard place of impotence, the law's regulatory culture may be able to reposition itself as the supervisor of regulatory space, mediating between other regulatory communities and managing sites of conflict. Rather than demonstrating the exhaustion of regulatory discourse, the problems faced by the Australian laws may just indicate the transformations which are occurring internationally and signify some future directions for research.

The neologism 'pornotopia' was coined in 1966 by Steven Marcus in his book *The Other Victorians: a Study of Sexuality and Pornography in Mid-Nineteenth Century*[6] and contains within its roots a reference to space via topos or 'place'.[7]

---

5   Pornography cultural critic Linda Williams describes practices of 'On/scenity', as a gesture by which a culture brings the private and hidden into the public sphere. She gives the example of the public investigation into President Clinton's penis as the transformation of an obscene/private concept into a public issue. Williams claims that on/scene practices involve the politicization of sexuality and the proliferation of sexual discourses by which 'sex speaks' in contemporary society. Williams L (1999) *Hard Core: Power, Pleasure, and the 'Frenzy of the Visible'*, University of California Press: Berkeley at 282.

6   Marcus S (1966) *The Other Victorians: A Study of Sexuality and Pornography in Mid-Nineteenth Century England*, New American Library: New York.

7   The word also references the word 'cornucopia' in representing a vast array and multiplicity of elements.

'Pornotopia' is a term that has been invoked by both sides of the pornography debate to variously describe the worlds as constituted by erotic media: as utopias of free excess or dystopic states of anomie. As we grapple with what cyberspace means for regulators and citizens, this seems a useful term to demonstrate that Internet media (sexual or otherwise) does not exist in a regulatory vacuum but rather in a network of individuals, communities, regulators and media spaces. The challenge in regulating pornotopia is to spatialize our ideas of law and regulation, to understand how the complex social networks constitute the spaces in which media is produced, consumed and controlled.

Chapter 2
'Protect me from what I want':[1] Censorship and Internet Classification

At the heart of the ambivalent operation of contemporary censorship law is the conflict between the positivist concept of law as a system of rules, and the impossibility of any set of rules being able to govern the flow of media images and words in any consistent and rational manner. The invocation of community values in censorship law gives an essential element of flexibility to the system's function, accommodating its inability to codify coherent and lucid rules, structures to govern the representations and images of the complex and chaotic tumble of media. No set of methodical criteria could hope to provide a scientific rationale – how many times can the word 'fuck' be spoken before a film becomes an *M*? What percentage of flesh can be revealed before a photograph can be described as showing nudity?

The socio-juridic concept of 'community' provides flexibility which allows rules to be applied, but for this to work it must itself be a rational and coherent concept. Censors need to provide consistency in administration of this role, or the entire system begins to look irrational.[2] Censorship and modern law do not sit easily together. Cultural critic Clive Bloom claims that the mechanistic models which have developed from industrial society are inconsistent with censorship as a regulatory strategy. He argues the regulatory language is impotent in the face of the complexity of media and the failure of the Meece Commission[3] was that it did not recognize the impossibility of mechanistic apparatus encompassing humanistic essence.[4]

Frequently, the concept of community values becomes conflated with assumptions about the harmful effects of violent or sexual media. Chapter 5

---

1 From the lyrics of 'Protect Me from What I Want', on the Placebo album *Sleeping with Ghosts* (2003).

2 The OFLC has been challenged on the inconsistency of its rulings. 'It's like having traffic laws saying that you can't drive "very fast", and then changing the speed limit from week to week without telling motorists.' Vnuk H (2003) *Snatched: Sex and Censorship in Australia*, Vintage: Sydney at 11.

3 Attorney General's Commission on Pornography (1986) *Final Report Vols 1 and 2*, Washington, DC ('The Meece Commission').

4 Bloom C (1988) 'Grinding with the Bachelor: Pornography in a Machine Age', in Day G and Bloom C (eds) *Perspectives on Pornography: Sexuality in Film and Literature*, St Martin's Press: New York.

will explore some of this contentious field and the impossibility of establishing scientifically verifiable, causal connections between reception of sexual media and social harms. Former censorship minister, Senator Alston, acknowledged the lack of scientific proof but defended censorship on the basis of the expectations, however misinformed, of 'the community':

> There is no conclusive evidence on any of this [...] it is not quantifiable [...] what you find is that [researchers] will say things like repeated exposure to unnecessary levels of violence may contribute to juvenile delinquency [...] so it becomes a matter of community expectations.[5]

In the late 1990s, the official classifiers of the Office of Film and Literature Classification (OFLC) Classification Board and Classification Review Board were all re-assessed and new classifiers were appointed with the government's stated preference for parents, especially mothers.[6] Senator Alston announced the removal of academics and experts from the OFLC Classification Board, claiming that they had become too comfortable and desensitized, they were to be replaced with others more representative of the community:

> If you have parents who are simply viewers [...] they are much more likely to give you a direct response from the heartland of Australia, rather than from an academic point of view [...] What you don't want is the experts or the so-called professionals who tend to become very cynical and particularly when they look at research.[7]

This period also saw the transformation of the relationship between publishers and the OFLC from one which was consultative, co-operative and professional (in which editors largely self-censored) to one based on surveillance and adversarial practices.[8] Former *Australian Women's Forum* editor Helen Vnuk has criticized the lack of specialist knowledge among the board: 'They won't necessarily have an understanding of sexuality and, in particular, minority sexualities.'[9] It is no coincidence that, at the time when Australia confronted the issue of Internet content regulation, the censorship paradigm was in the process of transformation – from debate of issues of free speech into questions of national identity.[10]

---

5   Guilliatt R and Casimir J (1996) 'The Return of the Wowsers', *Sydney Morning Herald*, 6 July.
6   Mills J (2001) *The Money Shot: Cinema, Sin and Censorship,* Pluto Press: Annandale, NSW at 115.
7   Guilliatt and Casimir, op. cit. fn. 5.
8   Vnuk H (2003) *Snatched: Sex and Censorship in Australia*, Vintage: Sydney at 7.
9   Ibid. at 174.
10 Mills, op. cit. fn. 6 at 116–7.

The *Broadcasting Services Amendment (Online Services) Act 1999* represents Australia's attempt to censor the emerging Internet media by extending the existing system of media classification and by endorsing industry codes of practice. Preliminary to a more detailed examination of the provisions of the act in Chapter 3, this chapter seeks to explore the background to the Act; the policy debates, political postures and media controversies which formed the foundation of the law reform process. Engaging with opinions and arguments, it becomes clear that a great many spatial concepts are tied up with not only the Internet component of the debate, but also in the censorship discourse generally which constructs 'the community' in specific ways. These constructions of space and law will become important in the discussion of spatial theory in Chapter 4.

In explaining the origins of censorship law concepts (such as obscenity, indecency and prurient interest) it will be necessary to engage in a brief overview of United Kingdom and United States censorship laws which were (and remain) strongly influential in Australia as a common law jurisdiction. Traditional and online censorship schemes from those two jurisdictions are examined in order to compare these to the Australian system of media classification and the Internet content regulation scheme which has become attached to it.

Finally, this chapter presents a brief overview of filtering and labelling technologies, which have been advocated as mandatory or voluntary tools of self governance. These related techniques have been suggested during both international and domestic law reform processes but have not been codified into mandatory law in any Western jurisdiction. The Australian scheme recommends filtering services to citizens but does not compel use.

Censoring Cyberspace

From the beginning of the year 2000, Australia has had in place the most comprehensive scheme of Internet censorship of any Western nation. In the early 1990s the institution of the censor may have seemed to be a fairly remote anachronism[11] but within a decade it had become a central feature in the everyday

---

11 Internationally, censorship was perceived to be receding throughout the twentieth century. The wake of various book trials which lifted bans on obscene writing, commentators declared, somewhat prematurely, 'the end of obscenity'. Rembar C (1969) *The End of Obscenity: The Trials of 'Lady Chatterley', 'The Tropic of Cancer' and 'Fanny Hill'*, Random House: New York. See also, in the Australian context, Coleman P (2000 rev. edn.) *Obscenity, Blasphemy, Sedition: The Rise and Fall of Literary Censorship in Australia*, Duffy and Snellgrove: Sydney. Compare Ellis who argues that the de-restriction process was not a triumph of liberation but of capitalism which realized the potential to sell controversy. Ellis R (1988) 'Disseminating Desire: Grove Press and "The End[s] of Obscenity"', in Day G and Bloom C (eds) *Perspectives on Pornography: Sexuality in Film and Literature*, St Martin's Press: New York.

experiences of citizens working, playing and living online. At the core of the political controversy surrounding the national censorship regulatory scheme are the abstract notion of 'community standards' – the yardstick of censorship and classification – and the role the state has in protecting and enforcing those standards.

This book concerns the new Internet censorship scheme, implemented under the *Broadcasting Services Amendment (Online Services) Act 1999*, and the context in which it operates. Among criticisms of the act[12] are its broad regulatory reach and, paradoxically, its regulatory impotence. The reception and operation of the legislation raises key challenges concerning the nature of regulation, the function of law and the manner in which regulatory apparatus intersects with society and the everyday experiences of citizens.

Conventional legal and regulatory theory is silent on the issue of space, presuming an even deployment of regulatory power across the jurisdiction of an authority. The regulation of the Internet is pre-occupied with spaces: cyberspace, the community, safe and dangerous places, neighbourhoods, erotic spaces and places, borderlines, domestic spaces, urban and suburban environments, mediascapes, spaces of childhood. Each of these is binarily constructed. In the same way that legality necessarily connotes illegality, each space is constituted and defined by what is excluded, the way in which the borders of the map are drawn.

Censorship or classification is itself an exercise in policing boundaries and imposing spatial taxonomies on media and human geographical subjects. Even with this plethora of spaces, legal and regulatory discourses are, largely, not informed by theories of space. One objective of this book is to make connections between regulatory and spatial theory, drawing heavily on the small but growing field of critical legal geography.

The censorship of new media forms just part of a revitalization of censorship polity generally and its spread to new territories of regulation. The mid to late 1990s saw censorship return to the Australian agenda under a federal conservative coalition in which Independent morals campaigner, Senator Brian Harradine, briefly held the balance of power in the Senate. The government agitated for the banning of films with increased frequency (including the infamous *Salo* (1975) which had just come off the restricted list), cabinet rejected an entire short list of candidates for the position of Office of Film and Literature Classification (OFLC) regulators, cable broadcasts of erotic material were curtailed, the television industry FACTs code was restricted under pressure concerning the *Sex/Life* television programme which was removed from air,[13] rules were amended to allow moral campaigners (instead of just the Attorney General) to challenge the classification of films and

---

12   See, for example, the EFA submission to the review of the Act, at http://www.efa.org.au/Publish/efasubm_bsa2002.html.

13   Chen P (2000a) *Australia's Online Censorship Regime: The Advocacy Coalition Framework and Governance Compared*, PhD Thesis Australian National University, at 82–3.

other media.[14] It is in this context that the Australian debate concerning the need, desirability and viability of Internet censorship took place.

The collision between new media hype and social scepticism of new technologies made for a volatile environment of media soundbites and political point scoring. Fearmongering was not limited to conservative parties, in the wake of the Colombine shootings, the then ALP Leader of the Opposition, Kim Beazley claimed that the uncontrolled growth of information on the Internet had a part to play in the massacre:

> There are opportunities now for people to put out good and bad propaganda, to be encouraging people to do dreadful things, to become totally egocentric, totally unprepared to assist their community with decent relationships.[15]

Most recently, the three year review of the Australian Internet censorship regime saw the Commonwealth Minister for Justice and Customs, Senator Chris Ellison, agitating for more punitive sanctions for child pornography, wider federal police powers and even an attempt to start a moral panic about suicide advocacy sites with an attempt to extend the prohibition regime in that direction as well.[16]

Internationally, the expansion of the Internet as a form of media and particularly as a site for the distribution of erotic material of various types saw a media frenzy, brief in duration but of lasting significance. Within the hysteria, the fear of uncontrolled spaces, terrorists, hackers and stalkers, the image of pornography looms large and frightening. Some examples of the rhetoric concerning Internet pornography can be found in media from around the Western world, many of which focus on children as unwilling victims of pornographic images:[17]

---

14 Marr D (2001) 'Daryl Williams QC at the Chauvel', http://libertus.net/censor/odocs/marr0110ag.html (viewed 7/4/03).

15 Statement on radio station 6PR, 22/4/99, quoted in Chen, op. cit. fn. 13 at 103.

16 Findlaw News Headlines (2003b) 'New Offences to clamp down on Internet child pornography', 7 April, via http://www.findlaw.com/news (viewed 7/4/2003).

17 The image of the child victim recurs through the Internet censorship discourse and throughout censorship generally. This image is connected to a spatial deployment of censorship in the geographies of childhood. The governance of adult media is frequently premised on the child consumer. In the Internet context, these concerns are linked to changes in media modes of transmission, particularly the interactive nature of new media which is difficult to conceptualize. Levinson marks the distinction between television and Internet as a point of crisis for regulators which is inadequately theorized in regulation laws. Levinson P (1997) *The Soft Edge: A Natural History and Future of the Information Revolution*, Routledge: New York at 159. Miller examines the spatial metaphors invoked and criticizes the use of the American colonial frontier metaphor (familiar in Western fiction and derivatives such as *Star Trek*) which has been used to 'soften the net up' for women and children who are constructed as victims who need the protection of law or regulation. She refers to the psychosexual metaphors used in this discourse, civilization's phallic intrusion into feminine natural space. Miller L (1995) 'Women and Children First: Gender and the

- According to British Labour MP, Frank Cook, cyber porn was 'tantamount to the injection of heroin into a child's school milk.'[18]
- Elizabeth Grice of the *Daily Telegraph* describes Internet pornography in the language of an epidemic: 'technology's HIV, a law-resistant disease that so far has no effective check.'[19]
- Similarly the *Evening Standard* describes the Internet as a 'heavily used red-light district, sending pornography into millions of homes.'[20]
- According to *ZDNet Australia* the web has created 'a world where sites catering to people's most primal fantasies are just a mouse click away. In some ways, peddlers of porn and other vices have become more insidious. After all, Web pages catering to fetishes of all stripes can be found at sites containing seemingly innocuous words such as "whitehouse", "Barbie" or "childrensbiblestories." What's more, once people stumble onto such a site – either unwittingly or intentionally – they are often trapped there by countless technological tricks including misleading metatags and a disabled back button.'[21]
- Infamously, Australian Senator Paul Calvert has stated: 'We are talking about the fact that you have only got to press P on the Internet and all this stuff appears free of charge in front of you and young children can access it.'[22]
- *The Australia Institute* claims that: 'For all of the hype, the information superhighway is principally a conduit for pornography.'[23]

In Australia, there has been limited public debate about the development of the Internet generally, perhaps because policy makers have been too preoccupied with the pornography issue.[24] This is an international problem, even some advocates of human rights and freedom have been conflated with paedophiles claimed to be exploiting the weaknesses of the permissive society. Anonymous remailler

---

Settling of the Electronic Frontier', in Brooks J and Boa I (eds) *Resisting the Virtual Life*, City Light Books: San Francisco. For an example of the use of this metaphor in the Australian context see Handsley E and Biggins B (2000) 'The sheriff rides into town: a day for rejoicing by innocent westerners', *University of New South Wales Law Journal*, v23, 257.

18   Calcutt A (1994) 'Exposed: Computer Porn Scandal in Commons', *Living Marxism*, 22 April.

19   Ibid.

20   *Evening Standard*, 11 October 1995.

21   ZDNet Australia (2001a) 'Taming the Web', 20 April, http://www.zdnet.com.au/newstech/ebusiness/story/0,2000024981,20216841,00.htm.

22   Paul Calvert, Liberal Senator for Tasmania, Senate Select Committee on Information Technologies (1999) *Senate Proof Committee Hansard*, 28 April, 74.

23   *The Australia Institute's* Clive Hamilton. Hamilton C (2002) 'Admit it: The left has lost its way', *The Age*, 14 May.

24   Nieuwenheizen J (1997) *Asleep at the Wheel: Australia on the Superhighway*, Australian Broadcasting Corporation.

operator Johan Helsingius was accused of being involved in the distribution of child pornography in the London *Observer*,[25] claiming that he and the Demon ISP were responsible for 90 per cent of paedophile material on the Internet. In fact, Helsingius' *Anon.penet* service was a not-for-profit service used for industrial whistleblowing and drawing attention to human rights abuses from inside police states. Furthermore, the technology used could not handle image files of a size useful in distributing pornography of any kind.

It is against the background of this panic, and related anxieties of child pornography, that the Australian Parliament passed the *Broadcasting Services Amendment (Online Services) Act 1999*, the Australian Internet censorship solution. It is a co-regulatory scheme which divides power and responsibility among existing media regulation stakeholders and an industry group, deferring to the abstract community standards for guidance. Increasingly the discourse of 'community' has been the site of conservative politics exclusion rather than any politics of inclusion.[26]

In 2003, policy 'think tank', *The Australia Institute*, published a series of reports[27] concerning youth access to pornography. These papers were reported in the media with an odd mixture of alarm and ennui.[28] The key claim of the report series was that 'Children are looking at Internet sites depicting images of incest, sex with animals, extreme fetishes and rape. The Federal Government and the regulators have become starry-eyed about the wonders of the information superhighway and have lost sight of the dangers to children.'[29] Given the political context in which the Act was passed, these claims seem to be at odds with the government's pro-censorship policy agenda.

---

25 Connett London D and Henley Helsinki J (1996) 'These men are not paedophiles – they are Internet abusers', *The Observer*, 25 August, 19.

26 Arguments about community and the necessity of sacrifice to community come in radical conservative critiques of bourgeois culture and cosmopolitan cultures of tolerance, individuality and 'reflexivity'. Dahl G (1999) 'The Anti-Reflexivisit Revolution: On the Affirmationism of the New Right', in Featherstone M and Lash S (eds) *Spaces of Culture: City, Nation, World*, Sage Publications: London.

27 Flood M and Hamilton C (2003a) *Discussion Paper Number 52: Youth and Pornography in Australia: Evidence on the extent of exposure and likely effects*, The Australia Institute: Canberra, Hamilton C and Flood M (2003) *Parents' Attitudes to Regulation of Internet Pornography*, The Australia Institute: Canberra, Flood M and Hamilton C (2003b) *Discussion Paper Number 53: Regulating Youth Access to Pornography*, The Australia Institute: Canberra.

28 *Sydney Morning Herald* (2003a) 'Kids drawn into vile web porn as '60s generation sits on its hands', 3 March (viewed online 4/3/03), *Sydney Morning Herald* (2003b) 'We've seen it all before, say teen surfers', 3 March (viewed online 4/3/03), *The Age* (2003a) 'Net porn traps unsuspecting', 3 March (viewed online 4/3/03), *The Age* (2003b) 'Regulations fail to protect children', 4 March (viewed online 4/3/03).

29 Per Australia Institute Director Clive Hamilton, *The Age* (2003b) 'Regulations fail to protect children', 4 March (viewed online 4/3/03).

This series of reports is worth examining, as it sketches out the broad contours of the content regulation debate and draws into sharp relief the difference between lived experience and the manner in which community spaces, particularly those around childhood, are manufactured and represented. Timed to coincide with the first review of the Australian co-regulatory scheme,[30] the reports suggest that, on the basis of empirical survey research, 84 per cent of boys and 60 per cent of girls had accidentally stumbled on hard core sex sites on the Internet[31] (38 per cent and 2 per cent respectively admitted to actively seeking them out).[32] Further, 73 per cent of boys and 11 per cent of girls had watched an X rated video, with 5 per cent of boys claiming to have watched them on a weekly basis.[33]

The most immediate problem with these figures is their sample group: the 'children' surveyed were 16 or 17 years old. The sample group was confined to these ages ostensibly for legal reasons, but renders generalizing claims about 'children' as a class inaccurate at best, dishonest at worst.[34] Comparable research from the *Crimes against Children Research Centre*, based on interviews of 1,507 youth aged 10–17 years found that 25 per cent had 'unwanted exposure to sexual pictures on the Internet' (most of which were simply nude images, only 32 per cent of this sub-sample had seen images of actual sex) and this group was mostly composed of older respondents (60 per cent were aged 15 or older, only 7 per cent were 11 or 12, none were 10).[35]

The *Australia Institute* reports go further, making frequent claims about the dangers of the Internet, and the psychological harms of pornography said to be backed up by 'studies' – none of which are ever cited. The reports do not have bibliographies and are not referenced. Chapter 5 explores these issues of media reception and harm and canvasses the range of anti-pornography and anti-censorship opinion.

The *Australia Institute*'s *Youth and Pornography* documents reveal some of the sources of anxiety concerning sexual material. While these reports express

---

30 Department of Communications Information Technology and the Arts (2002) *A review of the operation of Schedule 5 to the Broadcasting Services Act 1992*, September.

31 Flood and Hamilton (2003a), op. cit. fn. 27 at vi.

32 Ibid. at vi–viii.

33 Ibid. at v.

34 The methodology has also been challenged because of the small size of the sample, 200 respondents only: *The Age* (2003b) 'Regulations fail to protect children', 4 March (viewed online 4/3/03). The analysis of error in report is very unsophisticated, there is some acknowledgment that some respondents may have been reluctant to admit pornography use but no examination of how this might be gendered, and why some respondents may exaggerate their access.

35 Mitchell F J, Finkelhor D and Wolak J (2003) *The Exposure of Youth to Unwanted Sexual Material on the Internet: A National Study of Risk, Impact and Prevention*, Crimes Against Children Research Center, University of New Hampshire, http://www.unh.edu/ccrc/pdf/exposure_risk.pdf (viewed 20/5/03), also published in *Youth and Society*, v34(3), 330–358.

concern about 'psychological harm' of pornography, they frequently reveal this to be more a concern with 'non mainstream sex' or 'extreme and "deviant" sexual practices'.[36]

> Young people may be troubled or disgusted by images or accounts of non-mainstream behaviours, just as adults may be, given the range of sexual activity found on the Internet is broader than the range found in 'mainstream' society. Young people exposed to images of non-mainstream sexual behaviours may be more likely to accept and adopt them.[37]

This statement assumes a causal relationship between reception of media and behaviour, a relationship which has never been proven in any of the empirical literature. In addition, the report mentions a whole series of different sexual practices, grouping them together into one fearsome pornocopia. Intolerance of diversity is a prima facie posture, suggesting that those in the 'non mainstream' be forced to reflexively defend their position as different. There are some curious inclusions in the list of the most dangerous behaviours:

> Sexual behaviours involving rape, bondage, sadomasochism, transexuality, urination, defecation, and bestiality are widely regarded as harmful, immoral or unethical in and of themselves, and indeed some are criminal offences, and their portrayal may incite, eroticize and give legitimacy to such behaviours.'[38]

Later, the report adds multiple partner sex and amputee sex to the demonology of non-mainstream sex and claims that:

> Male–female anal intercourse is a second, almost mandatory, inclusion in pornographic depictions of heterosexual sex […] Australian studies [these are not referenced] suggest that this is a minority practice.[39]

The report then concedes that there is no evidence for this claimed causal relationship between media reception and re-enactment ('not yet' according to the report) but then suggests that a causal link is plausible.[40] It is unclear how tolerance and acceptance of difference necessarily leads seductively into re-enacting those different practices. The reports seem fixated with policing the line between mainstream and the Other – in which it vests the dark repressed fantasies

---

36 Flood and Hamilton (2003a) op. cit. fn. 27 at vii.
37 Ibid. at ix.
38 Ibid. at xi.
39 Ibid. at viii.
40 Ibid. at xi.

of the mainstream.[41] From a Foucauldian perspective it seems that censorship is concerned with more than just regulation of media: it becomes a political tool for regulating and normalizing behaviour.[42]

The *Australia Institute* reports demonstrate an unsophisticated understanding of media, its reception and use by an audience, particularly the role of fantasy and desire.[43] A causal relationship is presumed between representation and behaviour which no empirical study has satisfactorily proven.

The *Youth and Pornography* report recommends media literacy programmes as part of the solution. Elsewhere, these programmes are typically based on a non-censorious premise encouraging participants to learn effective self-governance and media exploration skills. Given the predilections evidenced in the *Australia Institute* reports the envisaged media literacy programme is less likely to involve

---

41 In Postcolonial discourse the Other is defined against the framework dominant Self which simultaneously excludes the Other and is fascinated by the difference of the Other. Said E (1978) *Orientalism*, Pantheon Books: New York.

42 The *Australia Institute*'s reports reflect the United States Meese Commission's concerns that pornography advocated 'unorthodox sexuality' and failed to cover topics such as love, marriage and sex as a form of procreation. The Attorney General's Commission on Pornography (1986) op. cit. fn. 3.

43 The concept of desire has become a significant poststructuralist site of study. Critical theory positions desire not just as an object but as an analytic process. Fuery P (1995) *Theories of Desire*, Melbourne University Press: Melbourne.

Human subjectivity is composed of a multiplicity of desires which are essential to the self's project of becoming.

Deleuze G and Guattari F (1987) *A Thousand Plateaus: Capitalism and Schizophrenia*, translated by Massumi B, University of Minnesota Press: Minneapolis at 238. Drawing on the work of anthropologist Rene Girard, Poyhonen and Reunanen argue that modern law creates the public space of community in order to stage the competition of mimetic desires, in the disguise of rationality and judgment. Poyhonen and Reunanen summarize Girard's concept of desire thus:

> Let us suppose that we are creatures haunted by desire, but we do not know what it is we desire. We must turn to other people in order to find an object that would satisfy our desire. These Others we meet function as the models for our desire, and our actions, directed by our desire, appear to be something we learn through imitation, through imitating the desires of other people. The things we strive for are always draw from some social context; our own private existence we meet as something empty, so we create models and idols in our minds and try to become similar to them. Otherwise our lives would not be the Living it is for the Others.

Poyhonen J and Reunanen S (1998) 'Law and Mimesis' in Hirvonen A (ed) *Polycentricity: The Multiple Scenes of Law*, Pluto Press: London at 98. For more of Girard's work see, for example, Girard R (1977) *Violence and the Sacred*, Johns Hopkins University Press: Baltimore and Girard R (1984) *Deceit, Desire and the Novel, Self and Other in Literary Structure*, Johns Hopkins University Press: Baltimore.

self empowerment and more likely to involve ideological engineering to 'help protect them from inappropriate and disturbing material, [to be] "inoculated" against [pornography's] negative effects through prebriefing or "cured" afterwards through debriefing.'[44] There seems little scope for autonomous subjects to make their own choices here and sexual identity is constructed in the reports as dangerously porous, liable to absorb new practices uncritically through 'copycat' behaviour.

The conclusion to the *Australia Institute* report is a remarkable piece of rhetoric, adopting for the moral crusader the mantle of the rebel, representing the pervasive moralizing discourse as a subaltern moral crusade against the mainstreaming of libertarianism:

> We believe that there is a widespread but subterranean recognition among the Australian populace that the pervasiveness of Internet pornography is a disturbing and potential dangerous phenomenon. But there is a peculiar reluctance to acknowledge these concerns and act on them. Australians who shared the broad liberal outlook that emerged in the 1960s and 1970s are hesitant to be associated with the out-dated and, in some cases, extreme views of the anti-porn lobby. As a result, liberal opinion in Australia has become subject to a new taboo that forbids serious discussion of the implications of the pervasiveness of pornography for our society and especially for our children.[45]

The *Australia Institute* report presents a model of community under siege, constituted and defined by resistance to non-mainstream deviant practices, the mere representation of which (or worse, tolerance of) threatens the coherence and integrity of the whole. This fictional community is one where conformity and media sterilization are the only defences against baleful 'outside' influences of *others*, creeping in through gaps and liminal spaces opened up by the Internet. This is the 'community' of abstract community values, of taking offence, of censorship.

Classification and Space

This book is concerned with the *Broadcasting Services Amendment (Online Services) Act 1999*, its context, and its effects. The administrative technology of classification, by state censor or by industry self regulation, is an important part of the regulatory discourse under the Act. The stratification of codes of representation across different age groups (defining what content is permissible for each) is a key tool in the constitution of autonomy and the social construction of the image of the child. This is a disciplinary discourse that seeks to govern through the internalization of regulatory schema rather than by exercise of force,

---

44 Flood and Hamilton (2003b) op. cit. fn. 27 at viii.
45 Ibid. at ix.

which is reserved for the most serious infractions euphemistically 'refused classification' and given an 'RC' status.

As a spatial practice, the practice of taxonomy is important to both urban space, human geography and regulatory discourse generally. Uniformity and consistency within taxonomic schemes is sought by border practices of exclusion and expulsion which are also expected to govern the individual through internalized standards and concepts of what is appropriate and inappropriate media.

The Internet is perceived as penetrating into the private spaces of home[46] in much the same way that reception of video cassette recorder technology created a moral backlash reaction in the 1980s.[47] Attempts to construct an Internet based moral panic[48] have yet to be entirely effective.[49] What is significant in the reactions to both video and Internet technologies is the spatial images used in the fear-based representations, especially images of the home, the street and urban locales. The Internet has been seen sometimes as a suspicious serpent, intruding into private spaces, bringing with it the corruption of 'the street'. At other times the Internet was fully conceived as a metaphorical street, a conduit in itself, with dark alleys luring children inside with dubious promises and inducements.[50]

It will be argued that understanding the spatial nature of both power and regulation, along with exploration of theories of space, provide guidance and means of navigating the uncertainty where spatial metaphors collide with regulatory practices. More spatially informed concepts of jurisdiction, regulation and society provide a method of examining and analyzing the sources of anxiety and the 'regulatory fortressing' that often occurs as a reflexive response to uncertainty.

'Regulatory fortressing' refers to a project of regulation that has the protection of the integrity of regulatory apparatus as its prime function, operating under a kind of 'meta-regulatory' impulse. Regulatory fortressing can occur despite any empirical proof of success or failure of the existing system, the regulatory apparatus itself becomes fetishized as the ends of regulation. Because lawmaking occurs in a mediated arena, without any readily accessible 'truths' to operate on, all regulation reflects some aspect of fortressing. It is argued that in the instance

---

46   Chen, op. cit. fn. 13 at 84.

47   O'Toole L (1998) *Pornocopia: Porn, Sex, Technology and Desire*, Serpent's Tail: London at 119–21.

48   For exploration of moral panics see Cohen S (1972) *Folk Devils and Moral Panics: The Creation of the Mods and Rockers*, Oxford University Press: Oxford; Goode E and Ben-Yehuda N (1994) *Moral Panics: The Social Construction of Deviance*, Blackwell: Oxford. The theme of moral panic is discussed in more depth in Chapter 5 of this book.

49   Chen, op. cit. fn. 13 at 93–5. For description of the sensationalism in the media see Reichel B (1996) 'New Directions in Censorship', *Artlines*, Issue 1(1), 1 and Shiff G (1997) 'Internet Censorship in Australia', *Metro Magazine*, No 108, 21 for a discussion of state government attempts at symbolic policymaking.

50   Examples of these images can be found in *Time Magazine* 'Cyberporn issue' (3 July 1995) and in Wakeley (1996) 'The New Stranger Danger on the Net', *The Age*, 14 May.

of Internet content, regulation fortressing becomes a problem because the impetus for reform is perceived gaps in the framework rather than any proven underlying social problem.

The consequence of regulatory fortressing is the construction of a regulatory system that is self justifying and exists as a perceived solution to a real or imagined social problem but in effect provides merely a disconnected image of regulatory coherence and inviolability. Often, the more impossible or fictional the problem, the fiercer and more irrational the regulatory fortress. Seeking to understand more about legal/regulatory space or 'jurispace' creates a method of conceiving of the regulatory fortressing phenomenon and the places in which it operates: the nexes between legal models of reality and other spaces – physical and virtual.

Common Law Jurisdiction Censorship Approaches

While the practices of censorship law have remained fairly consistent (texts are assessed for restricted content, then penalties applied by law), its ideological foundation has shifted from the nineteenth to the twenty-first century. Original theological concepts of blasphemy and sin were replaced by more secular notions of social harm. This is an excellent example of regulatory robustness (even to the extent of fetishization) where the regulatory structures can survive the dissolution of the original purposes for which they were erected by adaptation to new social conditions.

In this section two important common law jurisdictions will be examined, the United Kingdom and the United States. These two jurisdictions are significant as they gave rise to concepts which have been enshrined in the Australian legislation such as obscenity and community values. In addition, Australia defines itself legally and culturally in reference to these powers by imitation or by resistance.

Brief exploration of these two jurisdictions will be followed by a survey of the Australian classification system generally and discussion of criticisms levelled at the concept of classification as an administrative strategy. Lastly, the idea of filtering deserves some detailed attention. Mandatory filtering was suggested as one approach during the drafting of the *Broadcasting Services Amendment (Online Services) Act 1999*. The mandatory filtering approach proved controversial and has yet to be implemented in any Western nation. Australia rejected mandatory filtering, yet voluntary filtering still remains a key component in the self governance strategy.

In its comparative study of Internet censorship regimes around the world, Electronic Frontiers Australia (the EFA) has stressed how much more repressive the Australian legislation is than that of other Western nations which are governed purely by industry self-regulatory codes. Admittedly, in the United States this situation is as a result of the constitutional failure of control oriented legislation.[51]

---

51 http://www.efa.org.au/Issues/Censor/cens3.html (viewed 18/8/03).

These findings are at odds with the image of Australia as being 'in step' with the rest of the world, particularly the United Kingdom and the United States.

The EFA does not discuss the ways in which self-regulatory systems may in fact be more draconian, more intrusive and more pervasive than state centred regimes. The United Kingdom is held up by the EFA as a model of a more tolerant society,[52] yet the child pornography moral panics in the United Kingdom discussed in Chapter 5 reveal a culture of surveillance, reportage and paranoia which is, as yet, largely resisted in Australia.

Censorship in the United Kingdom

Censorship Generally

Laurence O'Toole, author of *Pornocopia*, describes Britain as the most censorious nation in the Western world,[53] a situation which has become further entrenched as all other European states (except Ireland) have entirely de-regulated their censorship schemes. British censorship rests fundamentally on the criminal common law offences of Indecency and Obscenity codified in the *Obscene Publications Act 1959*. These are supported by *Post Office Act 1953* (sending obscene materials through the mail), and the *Customs Act 1876* (importing obscene material).

Indecency is 'something an ordinary decent man or woman would find to be shocking, disgusting or revolting'.[54] Obscenity, on the other hand, threatens to 'deprave and corrupt', that is, to effect behavioural and personality changes. 'Whether the tendency of the matter charged as obscene is to deprave and corrupt those whose minds are open to such immoral influences, and into whose hands a publication of this sort may fall.'[55] These definitions encode paternalistic attitudes, immediately creating two zones or classes, of the autonomous regulator as subject and the corruptible regulatory object.

The United Kingdom obscenity and indecency laws, however broad, have had limited effects in everyday life. They rely on state (or even private) agents identifying obscene publications which usually happens in the process of locating and prosecuting peddlers. Each case is heard separately (those that make it to court) and each text judged individually. From the early twentieth century, changes in printing and media technology and the influx of overseas material created a mediascape which could not be contained by this process and bore only the faintest of regulatory inscriptions.

In the 1980s, the reception and rapid uptake of video cassette technology lead in Britain to a moral panic about 'video nasties', the cheap exploitation films which

---

52 Ibid.
53 O'Toole, op. cit. fn. 47 at 116.
54 Per Lord Reid in *Knuller v DPP* [1973] AC 435.
55 Per Cockburn CJ in *R v Hicklin* (1868) LR 3 QB 360 at 371.

capitalized on major media distributors' tardiness in embracing video technology, filling a market gap. Moral crusaders saw this influx of horror, soft porn and exploitation films as a social crisis. An important theme in the 'video nasty' debate was the vulnerability of the child in the home and the inability to control what 'other parents' allow their children to view.[56] A result of this was the establishment of the British Board of Film and Video Classification (BBFVC) and the *Video Recordings Act 1984* which made it an offence to sell or rent out videos which had not been classified by the Board, or which were in breach of the Board's classifications. The Board can refuse to give a certificate to a film deemed to be 'inappropriate':

> What sounds quite reasonable also actually amounted to a serious extension of censorship [...] In the long term, the Video Recordings Act installed pre-censorship [...] Statutory film classification smartly circumvented the system of legal test cases, the matter of shifting tastes and evolving cultural values in society [...] Now the offence was not having a certificate, with the content of the movie mainly irrelevant. In this way people were denied access to public juries to argue their case for freedom of expression.[57]

The BBFVC framework was the first scheme of its kind, the first to make lack of certification an offence in itself (rather than the nature of the publication) and was the model for changes to the Australian regulatory system.[58] Instead of a juridic model, the BBFVC model instigated a regulatory/disciplinary procedure, removing the process from the public eye and open court and instead vested it in a bureaucracy. In Britain most videos seized are destroyed without anyone watching them.[59] As yet this system only covers film and video, not print media which remain under the old scheme of obscenity and indecency law.[60]

Online Censorship

In the United Kingdom, the Internet remains largely unregulated by the state, except as an extension of existing offline regulation.[61] Under pressure from the police

---

56   O'Toole, op. cit. fn. 47 at 119–121.
57   Ibid. at 120.
58   Australian reforms occurred after the report: Australian Law Reform Commission (1991) *Film and Literature Censorship Procedure*, Report no 55, National Capital Printing: Canberra and were enacted in the *Classification (Publications, Films and Computers Games) Act 1995* (Cth).
59   O'Toole, op. cit. fn. 47 at 124.
60   Classification of books remains voluntary but magazines are classified under the *Classification (Publications, Films and Computers Games) Act 1995* (Cth) via the *Guidelines for the Classification of Publications* (1999).
61   For a survey of the United Kingdom and other jurisdictions see Electronic Frontiers Australia (2002) *Internet Censorship: Law and Policy Around the World*, http://www.efa.org.au/Issues/Censor/cens3.html.

and after a series of inflammatory media claims regarding child pornography and children's access to Internet pornography, the British industry formed the Internet Watch Foundation (IWF) a self-governing arrangement whereby ISPs agree to monitor their clients and report to the police.[62] The IWF members accepted the role of 'publishers'[63] rather than mere ISPs, a controversial status which means sharing responsibility for media distributed by clients and assuming a degree of control over clients' activities.

Because of their dependence on the state licensing of their business, ISPs are a more stable nexus of control than any model which regulates individual web authors or editors. The IWF's acceptance of the status of 'publisher' or 'broadcaster' (in contrast to mail or telephone providers which have no such responsibility) constituted a significant non-statutory extension the regulatory scheme. Additionally, the IWF endorses the future mandatory placement of the PICS labelling system (discussed later in this chapter) and promotes the classification of all Internet material, urging ISPs to force clients to self-rate through their service contracts.[64]

Censorship is by no means limited to formal state apparatus. In Britain (and Australia), libel laws can be used as de facto corporate censorship, to silence voices not resourced to fight litigation or simply to intimidate nervous British Internet Service Providers (ISPs).[65]

Censorship in the United States

Censorship Generally

Censorship is usually not a matter for state regulation in the United States which generally relies more on self-governance and censorship performed by industries rather than by government. The First Amendment to the United States Constitution provides a measure of protection for free speech from government intrusion[66] but

---

62 Ibid.

63 O'Toole, op. cit. fn. 47 at 269.

64 Note that non governmental censorship is not necessarily any less repressive than state mandated restrictions. ISPs may be even more censorious for fear of governmental action, or for completely different objectives. Consider the situation in the United States where a small news site (ostensibly protected by the First Amendment) was taken down by the ISP because it contained controversial news photographs of the Iraq war. Reuters News (2003) 'Net Censorship Debate Rages as POW Pictures Pulled', http://www.reuters.com/newsArticle.jhtml?type=InternetNewsstoryID=2446564 (viewed 1/4/03).

65 Verkaik R (2002) 'Libel laws used to curb web protests', Independent.co.uk, 18 December, http://news.independent.co.uk/digital/news/story/story.jsp?story=362634. In the United States, publishers, including ISPs, are protected as long as they are 'secondary publishers' where they have no control over contents.

66 Because of this protection, early censorship laws focussed on the mail system and prohibited sending obscene materials via mail rather than attack publishers directly.

this does not mean that a self-censorship regime will be less restrictive than a state imposed one. The history of the moralistic 'Hayes' production code of the Motion Picture Association of America (MPAA) (1930–68) and the informal communist black list are key examples of the wide reach of non governmental censorship schemes.[67]

United States law draws a semantic distinction between 'pornography', which is considered to be constitutionally protected free speech and 'obscenity' which is not.[68] Obscenity was described in the *Roth* case as anything 'utterly lacking redeeming qualities'.[69] The term 'utterly' leaves a large discretionary gap: regulation could be avoided

> ... if the defendants could summon up the briefest glimpse of something redeeming in their salacious piece of goods [...] Rather than tighten the situation by making clear what was considered prurient [...] the word 'utterly' opened things up.[70]

This allowed sexploitation film makers such as Russ Meyer[71] (following in the path blazed by Kroger Babb)[72] to provide a whole series of fictitious justifications for transgressive content. There, as elsewhere under regimes where such justification is permitted, issues such as plot requirements, psychological explanations, moral lessons, documentary and educational excuses, 'nature', health, nudism and

---

Kendrick W (1987) *The Secret Museum: Pornography in Modern Culture*, Viking Press: New York at 134.

67 *The Motion Picture Production Code (Hayes Code) 1930* regulated moral conduct in film and references 'the rapid transition from silent to talking pictures' as a point of crisis. It makes specific reference to Crimes Against the Law, Sex (forbidding representation of sex perversion, sex hygiene and miscegenation but allowing non-explicit rape), Vulgarity, Obscenity, Profanity, Costume, Dances, Religion, Locations (which governed representation of bedrooms), National Feelings, Titles, and Repellent Subjects.

68 *Roth v United States*, 354 US 476 (1957).

69 Ibid. at 504.

70 O'Toole, op. cit. fn. 47 at 8.

71 Exploitation film director Meyer made a film career out of 'pandering to prurient interest', typically of a sexual nature. His films include *The Immoral Mr Teas* (1959), *Wild Gals of the Naked West* (1962), *Lorna* (1964), *Mudhoney* (1965), *Motorpsycho* (1965), *Fast Pussycat! Kill! Kill!* (1966), *Mondo Topless* (1966), *Common Law Cabin* (1967), *Beyond the Valley of the Dolls* (1970), *Supervixens* (1975) and *Up!* (1976). Frasier DK (1990) *Russ Meyer – the Life and Films*, McFarland and Co: Jefferson, New York and Ross J (1993) *The Incredibly Strange Film Book: An Alternative History of Cinema*, Simon and Schuster: New York. See also the work of sexploitation director Doris Wishman, Ross, op. cit. at 76.

72 Kroger Babb was a film producer and pioneer of the 'roadshow' circuit, where cheap exploitation films were framed by morally edifying messages. Among Babb's most famous productions are *Marijuana: Assassin of Youth* (1937) and *Reefer Madness* (1947). Ross, op. cit. at 76–9.

physique allowed previously prohibited material to escape censorship.[73] Legal regulation produced new genres of sexual material, actively constituted by the laws themselves.

The *Roth* decision referred to the 'indigestible pit of hardcore' which lacked social importance. The decision allowed for the release of long suppressed literary classics and the notion of social importance politicized the text.[74] Contrary to hopes of libertarians, the *Roth* decision did not mean that standards were simply more liberal, rather, its notion of 'de-censorship' shifted the debate into the framework set by the censor/regulator and it reified the dichotomy between social value and 'worthless pornography'.[75]

In the 1970s, the United States obscenity test was further elaborated as 'the *Miller* test':

> Whether 'the average person, applying contemporary community standards' would find that the work, taken as a whole, appeals to the prurient interest; (b) whether the work depicts or describes, in a patently offensive way, sexual conduct specifically defined by the applicable state law; and (c) whether the work, taken as a whole, lacks serious literary, artistic, political or scientific value.[76]

The generality and flexibility in the framing of the *Miller* test worked against its certain application. While there were clear examples of purely prurient material, the general nature of the test exposed a broad spectrum of material in which serious value (or lack of it) was an uncertain issue. The introduction of community standards also failed to make matters more certain as it did not account for the broad variation of standards across the community and differences between localized communities in the United States, imagined geographically in places such as the 'liberal cities' and 'the Bible belt'.

What is interesting about the *Miller test* is that the constitutional protection of free speech drives a wedge between *good*[77] *constitutionally protected pornography and bad* obscene pornography, even though it is empirically difficult to distinguish between these binary categories. The legal invocation of 'community standards' at once creates an illusory image of certainty, an abstraction of homogeneity, which

---

73   Kendrick, op. cit. fn. 66

74   Williams L (1999) *Hard Core: Power, Pleasure, and the 'Frenzy of the Visible'*, University of California Press: Berkeley at 89.

75   Ellis R (1988) op. cit. fn. 11 at 38.

76   *Miller v California*, 413 US 15, 24 (1973): for an exploration of the *Miller* decision in the context of cyberspace, see Metcalf JT (1996) 'Obscenity Prosecutions in Cyberspace: The Miller Test Cannot "Go Where No [Porn] Has Gone Before"', *Washington University Law Quarterly*, v74, 481.

77   A further complication arises from *Ginsberg v New York*, 390 US 629 (1968) which holds that even constitutionally protected pornography must be distributed in a manner which keeps it out of the hands of minors.

delegates responsibility for enforcement onto localized authorities which are anything but uniform in outlook and values. Pornography industry news magazine, *Adult Video News*, describes the frustration this uncertainty causes:

> The point is, one of the bedrocks of the law in this country is supposed to be that the *law* tells you what you can and can't do, and if you've got any questions about it, you just go to the statutes and get the answer. A guy who walks into a bank, pulls a gun and says 'Gimme all your money' is a bank robber, pure and simple [... With pornography the] law no longer tells you whether you're breaking 'the law' or not. Now you have to spend thousands of bucks on attorneys who try to convince 12 good ol' boys in Pig's Knuckle, Nebraska that they'll 'tolerate' your product.[78]

The 'community standard' requirement has been imputed into Internet communication regulation, in prosecution of a Bulletin Board Service under federal obscenity laws relating to interstate commerce.[79] The legal abstraction of 'the community' has become of central importance to the censorship discourse (along with the related concept of 'offence') but this seems to be no more certain than before, a mere euphemism for state discretion.

It is important to realize that regulation also occurs through different regulatory channels and even in informal ways via use (even abuse) of procedures which make the business of publication more onerous. In the 1980s, invoking unproven claims about links between pornography and organized crime, the United States government used the RICO laws (Racketeering Influenced and Corrupt Organizations) to close down many adult video operations by seizing assets; relying on delays in proceedings to bankrupt a business before the matter was ever brought to court.[80] This resembles the government action in the *Steve Jackson Games* case[81] where the Secret Service sought to force a small independent publisher out of business by seizing its assets and creating a delay of three years before a trial date was set. This action was taken because the company published a fictional cyberpunk book which the Secret Service described as a 'manual for hackers'. Steve Jackson Games ultimately won but faced bankruptcy in the process.

Given sufficient impetus, even constitutionally protected rights can be circumvented by careful drafting or rhetorical argument. *New York v Ferber*[82] is the precedent which upheld legislative restrictions on depictions of minors in

---

78 *Adult Video News* (1996) 'Positive Legal Decision in Colorado, New York and More', September, 46.

79 *United States v Thomas*, 74 F.3d 701 (6th Cir. 1996).

80 O'Toole, op. cit. fn. 47 at 108.

81 *Steve Jackson Games Inc v United States Secret Service*, unreported decision of the United States District Court, Western District of Texas, Austin Division, 12 March 1993, archived at http://www.eff.org/legal/cases/SJG/decision.sjg (viewed 19/8/01).

82 458 U.S. 747 (1982).

sexual contexts, laws aimed at preventing child pornography. The court in that case recognized the legislation was overly broad and was concerned that it might infringe on what it considered worthy and serious literature, that it 'could apply not only to child pornography, but also to a *National Geographic* photographic essay on tribal rites, ancient Greek art, and textbooks showing the effects of child sexual abuse or genital mutilation.'[83] Even so the court set aside these concerns (and the potential constitutional illegality) to uphold the Act in the interests of protecting children from exploitation by child pornographers.

On the other hand, the *Ginsberg* principle which argues that a text will have a different definition of obscenity depending on the group to whom it is directed (such as children) has been challenged by critics, because it needs not prove actual harm. In describing all 'children' as a group, this principle ignores the differences within the group, between a very young child and a young adult on the verge of reaching majority.[84] One of the contradictions of censorship is the more it is specifically tailored to specific groups, the more abstract it becomes. Separating children as regulatory objects requires a denial of difference and the creation of an abstract image of 'the child'.

While the United States constitutional tradition resists state censorship, there are a great many different non-governmental systems of media classification and rating (such as the MPAA), each with different sources of funding, administrative bodies, modes of representation and objectives. In addition, there have been some suggestions that the civil litigation system might provide a kind of de facto system of censorship, permitting complainants to accuse the producers of pornography of complicit liability where it can be *legally* proven that harm was causally connected, such as a rape where the rapist was influenced by pornographic images.[85] Litigation such as this relies on the law recognizing that a causal relationship exists between

---

83 National Coalition Against Censorship (1999a) *Sex and Censorship: Dangers to Minors and Others?: A Background Paper*, http://www.ncac.org/issues/sex_censorship.html. It is relevant to note that even 'worthy' texts such as *National Geographic* can be read against the grain as erotic content, Lutz and Collins explore the folklore of secret perusals of *National Geographic*, a dangerous territory of forbidden desire and guilt. Lutz CA and Collins JL (1993) *Reading National Geographic*, The University of Chicago Press: Chicago at 172.

84 Heins M (1997) 'Indecency: The Ongoing American Debate Over Sex, Children, Free Speech, and Dirty Words', *Paper Series on Art, Culture and Society*, Paper Number 7, The Andy Warhol Foundation for the Visual Arts.

85 Bernstein A (1997) 'How to Make a New Tort: Three Paradoxes', *Texas Law Review*, v75, 1539; Wesson M (1991) 'Sex, Lies and Videotape: The Pornographer as Censor', *Washington Law Review*, v66, 913; Pacillo EL (1994) 'Getting a Feminist Foot in the Courtroom Door: Media Liability for Personal Injury Caused by Pornography', *Suffolk University Law Review*, v28, 123. These articles suggest that the torts system be used to regulate producers of pornography, making them liable where offenders enact fantasies from the text.

image and action and it has been argued that the influence of pornography in sexual assault might be similar to that of alcohol in drink driving cases.[86]

Beyond state regulation in the United States there are a variety of different self-governing codes which become less separable with convergent technology:[87]

- The *Telecommunications Act 1996* (USA) empowers the television ratings code of the Federal Communications Commission advisory committee and calls for manufacture of blocking technology such as the V chip under the umbrella of 'parents' power to choose'.
- The Motion Picture Association of America (MPAA) runs a self-regulatory classification scheme through its Classification and Rating Administration (CARA).
- The software industry gives rise to the Entertainment Software Rating Board (ESRB), the Recreational Software Advisory Council (RSAC) and the Software Publishers Association (SPA), each with different regulatory codes and practices, from external review (ESRB) to self-rating questionnaires (RSAC and SPA).
- The recording industry has a self-governing labelling system of 'Parental Guidance' under the Recording Industry Association of America (RIAA).

Interestingly, much of the focus of censorship discourse in the United States has shifted away from regulation of texts, toward issues of government funding of the arts.[88] Constitutional protection of free speech has caused moral crusaders to shift their focus to different avenues of control, attacking art projects which have sexual content by withdrawing financial support for arts sponsorship organizations.

Online Censorship

Published in 1995, Marty Rimm's infamous Internet porn scare article 'Marketing Pornography on the Information Superhighway: A Survey of 917,410 Images, Descriptions, Short Stories and Animations Downloaded 8.5 Million Times by Consumers in over 2,000 Cities in Forty Countries, Provinces, and Territories'[89]

---

86   O'Callaghan J (1995) '"Under the Influence": Pornography and Alcohol – Some Common Themes', *Akron Law Review*, Vol 29, 35.

87   Roberts D (1997) 'The Jurisprudence of Ratings Symposium Part I: On The Plurality of Ratings', *Cardozo Arts and Entertainment Law Journal*, vol 15, 105 at 133–4.

88   Stychin CF (1995) *Law's Desire: Sexuality and the Limits of Justice*, Routledge: London, Chapter 1 'Identities, Sexualities, and the Postmodern Subject: An Analysis of Funding by the National Endowment for the Arts'.

89   Rimm M (1995) 'Marketing Pornography on the Information Superhighway: A Survey of 917,410 Images, Descriptions, Short Stories and Animations Downloaded 8.5 Million Times by Consumers in over 2,000 Cities in Forty Countries, Provinces, and Territories', *Georgetown University Law Journal*, 83, 1849, also at http://www.TRFN.pgh.pa.us/guest/mrtext.html (viewed 10/8/99). This report was revealed to have included

seems to be a contemporary example of a moral panic, similar to the mugging panic and the perennial fear of various youth subcultures.[90] Rimm's article was, and still is, quoted in the media and has, through the power of statistics, seeped into popular consciousness, its methodological flaws notwithstanding.

Rimm claimed that 83.5 per cent of newsgroup image-based online traffic is pornographic. This was quickly conflated to 83.5 per cent of *all of the Internet* by clumsy re-reporting in the press, and it was presented to a larger audience through an influential story in *Time*[91] which itself was re and misquoted by fundamentalists and fearmongers.[92] Although Rimm's research has been debunked, these statistics still hold a firm grasp on popular understanding of the Internet and have spread memetically through the media.[93]

One reflexive response to this apparent crisis was the United States *Communications Decency Act 1996* (the CDA) which ultimately failed due to constitutional breaches. That act made it an offence whenever someone transmitted 'indecent' material to a minor but allowed a defence if the transmitter took 'good faith' steps to screen out children.[94] At the time, there was (as there is now) no practical way to do this on the World Wide Web, at least without paying for an adult verification service. The CDA applied to all speech, and the definition of 'indecent'[95] included much socially beneficial 'adult' material (such as health brochures). Many sites adopted the practice of including a warning page which asks users to verify their age. This was unlikely to have been sufficient, had the Act held up. Cyberlaw professor Larry Lessig describes the CDA as:

> A Law of extraordinary stupidity, it practically impaled itself on the First Amendment. [...] There were at least three problems with the CDA, any one of which should have doomed it to well-deserved extinction. The first was the scope of the speech it addressed: 'indecency' is not a category of speech that Congress has the power to regulate [...] Strike two was vagueness [...] Strike three was the government's own doing [...] it displayed a poor understanding of

---

misleading and false statements: Godwin M (1998) *CyberRights*, Time Books: New York at 206–59.

    90   Cohen, op. cit. fn. 48.
    91   *Time Magazine*, op. cit. fn. 50.
    92   O'Toole, op. cit. fn. 47 at 249.
    93   Godwin, op. cit. fn. 89 at 206–59.
    94   The *Communications Decency Act 1996* made 'transmission of any comment, request, suggestion, proposal, image, or other communication which is obscene, lewd, lascivious, filthy or indecent, with intent to annoy, abuse, threaten, or harass another person' punishable by $100,000 fines and two years imprisonment (Title V, Subtitle A, Sec 502, sec. 223, a1Aii).
    95   The definition of decency was defined to exclude 'obscene, lewd, lascivious, filthy or indecent' words or images, under title 47, section 223 of the *Communications Act 1934* (US), as it would have been amended by the *Communications Decency Act 1996* (US).

how the technology might have provided a defense [...] there seemed to be no way that an identification system could satisfy the statute.[96]

There is a suggestion that a core reason for the failure was that, given the technology of the time, providing an efficient way to verify identity was impossible and, that with time for the technology to develop, the courts may yet uphold an act in similar terms to the CDA.[97]

The intent of the CDA was to characterize the Internet as a form of broadcasting, a public and pervasive media form which is easier to regulate as broadcasting does not carry with it free speech protection. United States courts had already accepted regulation of radio and television because broadcasting is different to speech.[98] Once again, the 'child victim' was invoked to justify this exercise of state power, but this time it was not considered to be sufficient reason to violated constitutional rights.

The collapse of the CDA lead to the drafting of the *Child Online Protection Act 1998* (COPA), attached to a budget Bill, which targeted commercial sites, mandated use of access codes (already largely used through adult check organizations for pornographic material) and made it an offence to knowingly place material deemed harmful to children within easy access. This Act also breached the First Amendment's free speech protection[99] and was criticized by a congressional commission which recommended parental education and pornography industry self-regulation, and refused to endorse filters as a viable regulatory technology.[100]

The next act to follow was the *Children's Internet Protection Act 2000* (CIPA). This Act was aimed at compulsory filtering in schools and public libraries and has been criticized generally for its repressive nature and specifically because it 'accelerates the digital divide by forcing people who don't have computers at home to surf a filtered Web' in public facilities.[101]

Parallel to these laws, the *Child Pornography Prevention Act 1996* prohibits possession of digital images of sexual acts involving people who appear to be minors (regardless of actual age). This Act has also been challenged, especially since it would technically be illegal to own a digital text of *Romeo and Juliet*.[102]

---

96 Lessig L (1999) *Code and Other Laws of Cyberspace*, Basic Books: New York at 174–5.

97 Nesson C and Marglin D (1996) 'The Day the Internet Met the First Amendment: Time and the Communications Decency Act', *Harvard Journal of Law and Technology*, 10, 113.

98 O'Toole, op. cit. fn. 47 at 255.

99 ZDNet Australia (2001a) 'Taming the Web', 20 April, http://www.zdnet.com.au/newstech/ebusiness/story/0,2000024981,20216841,00.htm.

100 Commission on Child Online Protection (COPA) (2000) *Report to Congress*, 20 October.

101 ZDNet Australia (2001a) op.cit. fn. 99.

102 Ibid.

This act was struck down in *Ashcroft v American Civil Liberties Union*[103] because it breached the First Amendment. In doing so, the court challenged the Holy Grail of the regulation of both child pornography and pornography under moral and anti-pornography feminist positions, the contention that words and images *cause* deeds and thus become a locus for legal regulation:

> The normal method of deterring unlawful conduct is to impose an appropriate punishment on the person who engages in it ... The government may not prohibit speech because it increases the chance an unlawful act will be committed at some indefinite future time.[104]

In rejecting simplistic notions of media representations causing harmful behaviour, the Court's approach can be starkly opposed to the Canadian line of precedent, which accepts that pornography causes harm in the form of discriminatory messages and breaches of equality rights. It is worth briefly comparing the United States' position to developments in that jurisdiction. Canada's censorship system is similar in regulatory structure to that of Britain, but has evolved recently in a manner unique to that jurisdiction. The moral foundation of regulation has been replaced with a rights-based formulation which apparently keeps the entire regulatory apparatus intact, but which operates in a different ideological framework. In *R v Butler*[105] the court, drawing on the writing of Anti-Pornography Feminists such as Dworkin and MacKinnon,[106] found that while pornography was prima facie protected speech, it also contravened equality provisions in the *Canadian Charter of Rights and Freedoms*. The court held that, accordingly, criminal laws relating to obscenity did not violate the free speech provisions of the Charter and that the right to protection of equal status (which pornography was said to infringe) trumped the right to free speech.[107]

While the case has not been followed outside Canada, this rationale has proven extremely successful within that jurisdiction and has allowed for expansive readings

---

103   *Ashcroft v American Civil Liberties Union* 535 US (2002): Law Meme (2002) 'The Future of Virtual Kiddie PrOn and Other Notes on *Ashcroft v Free Speech*', 18 April, http://research.yale.edu/lawmeme/modules.php?name=News&file=article&sid=186.

104   *Ashcroft v American Civil Liberties Union* 535 US (2002).

105   *R v Butler* [1992] 1 SCR 452 (SCC).

106   For further exploration of these links see MacKinnon CA and Dworkin A (1997) *In Harm's Way: The Pornography Civil Rights Hearings*, Harvard University Press: Boston; MacKinnon C (1993) *Only Words*, Harvard University Press: Boston; Dworkin A (1988) 'Pornography is a Civil Rights Issue for Women', *University of Michigan Journal of Law*, Vol 21, 55; Scutt J (1991) 'Incorporating the Dworkin/MacKinnon Approach into Australian Law', *Inkwell*, Vol 5, 3.

107   Section 163(8) of the Canadian Criminal Code (R.S.C. 1985, c. C–46) holds that 'any publication a dominant characteristic of which is the undue exploitation of sex, or of sex and any one or more of the following subject, namely, crime, horror, cruelty, and violence, shall be deemed to be obscene'.

of the censorship powers, extending the prohibition to gay male and lesbian erotica[108] as demonstrated in the *Little Sisters*[109] case. Expressing his support for the *Little Sisters* decision to censor gay and lesbian erotic books and magazines, legal commentator Christopher Kendall challenges what he considers to be the facile counter-argument, that gay and lesbian pornography is not discriminatory because it subversively challenges gender stereotypes.[110] Rather, he finds only further reification of gender stereotypes:

> This publication [*Bear: Masculinity Without the Trappings*], like many others, promotes violence and aggressive, non-egalitarian behaviour. The theme throughout is hyper-masculinity found at the expense of some else's liberty and self-worth. Merit is found in degradation. Rewards attached to one's ability to use or be used. Equality, if at all, found only in reciprocal abuse.[111]

In examining the case law mutation from *Butler* to *Little Sisters*, it is possible to envisage further potential spread of the 'pornography as discrimination' legal meme. If degradation, rather than obscenity, is seen to be the core of the principle, violence can readily be censored under the same principle, especially the racialized violence of many action films. From that principle, any expression of violence or mere hostility could be restricted content, allowing the slow development of a broad reach of regulatory control which would be unthinkably draconian at the moment. Regulatory spread occurs through increments, virally as legal memes propagate themselves.

Academic author Carl Stychin's analysis of the *Butler* decision indicates a different view to Kendall's.[112] By framing pornography within the wider social and media context, Stychin illustrates just how important issues of subjectivity and representation are and how clumsy a legal prohibition solution is. He argues that pornography is not unique in its ideological issues, that the social environment is saturated with images of power, in particular in the related representations of

---

108   And little to no increase in prohibitions on heterosexual erotica. Busby K (1994) 'LEAF and Pornography: Litigating on Equality and Sexual Representations', *Canadian Journal of Law and Society*, vol 9.1, 165 at 185.

109   *Little Sisters Book and Art Emporium v Canada* (Minister of Justice), 2000 SCC 69, File No 26858, unreported.

110   Stychin C (1992) 'Exploring the Limits: Feminism and the Legal Regulation of Pornography', *Vermont Law Review*, 857.

111   Kendall CN (2001) 'The Harms of Gay Male Pornography: A Sex Equality Perspective Post Little Sisters Book and Art Emporium', *Gay and Lesbian Law Journal*, Vol 10, 43. This approach represents a tendency to read pornography monolithically and with a single authorized interpretation as to what it 'means'. Further, the same critique could be made of the representation of sport, war news, car advertisements and many other media forms. While these media representations raise issues for concern and debate, what is not substantiated is the necessity for invoking the violence of the state to regulate them.

112   Stychin CF (1995) op. cit. fn. 88.

masculinity, hierarchy, dominance and control. Stychin suggests that it is simplistic to impose a model of causation between image and result, and only through free expression may the full extent of this imagery be engaged and challenged.

The *Butler* line of common law has not been embraced outside Canada. The United States Constitution has prevented the spread of the 'censorship and causation' meme, through use of free speech protection as a trump against state action. In the recent history of United States censorship law there have been several significant national policy reports on the issues of pornography regulation. The 1985 Meece Commission[113] condemned pornography and was used as one of the justifications for the *Communications Decency Act* in 1996. In 2000 the Commission on Child Online Protection released a contrary report which advocated community education, parental management resources, industry self-regulation and the use of trade practices law to control unfair practices such as mousetrapping and pop up windows.[114] In 2002 the National Research Council made similar findings to the 2000 report.[115] Committee members did disagree regarding the effect that sexually explicit material had on minors but found agreement on that issue was unnecessary to suggest strategies of child protection focusing on empowerment and media literacy skills.

Technological innovations have been developed to respond to concerns about children accessing adult material. These have included the verification of identity via credit card for adult services, filtering and the development of labelling content rating standards[116] which are discussed at the end of this chapter. In keeping with the American censorship paradigm which displaces the state from the centre of censorship regulation, innovations of self-governance[117] and control by industry are perceived to be far more effective than government dictated action.

---

113 Attorney General's Commission on Pornography, op. cit. fn. 3.

114 Commission on Child Online Protection (2000) *Report to Congress*, 20 October.

115 National Research Council, Computer Science and Telecommunications Board (2002) *Youth, Pornography and the Internet*, National Academy Press: Washington, DC, http://www.nap.edu/books/0309082749.html, Executive Summary.

116 Resnick P (1999) PICS–Interest@w3.org, *Moving On*, http://www.lists.w3.org/Archives/Public/pics–interest/1999Jan/000.html, viewed on 13 May 1999.

117 It is important to remember that self censorship in United States is not unproblematic. AOL faced a angry backlash when it placed a ban on email from independent news source Znet which focuses on human rights issues, ostensibly because they believed email from Znet was spam. ZDNet Australia (2002a) 'Net censorship? AOL bans independent news source', 24 January, http://www.zdnet.com.au/newstech/ebusiness/story/0,20000,24981,20263129,00.htm.

Censorship in Australia: Film and Literature Classification[118]

Australia originally received the British concept of indecency[119] through its reception of common law generally. The United Kingdom tests of indecency and obscenity have been transformed over time to a single test based on being material 'offensive to current standards of decency'[120] and incorporated into law's production of the universal subject in a 'average man or woman' test[121] which underlies the 'community standards of decency' test.[122] In 1969, the High Court of Australia in *Crowe v Graham*[123] substituted a standard similar to the *Miller* test, that of offence against community standards. Offence was to be understood contextually, with regard to the audience to whom or among whom the matter was published, bearing in mind the age group and values of that audience. Although the test originally contemplated multiple regulatory communities, today in public discourse these have been conflated into a single community of reception and meaning and this transformation has been codified in the legislation.

Censorship is a politically sensitive term in contemporary Australian politics. The word 'classification' appears to have more positive connotations. Former Federal Attorney-General Daryl Williams insisted on a distinction between classification and the repressive political censorship of the past, declaring that political censorship no longer exists in Australia.[124] Former Federal Communications, Information Technology and The Arts minister, Senator Richard Alston has claimed that classification is not censorship.[125] The Internet content regulation scheme has been defended by the same semantic distinction:

> Claims that the new legislation is aimed at censorship are completely untrue. It merely applies to the Internet the same classification systems as apply to other forms of media.[126]

---

118   For a comprehensive overview of the Australian situation, see Griffith G (2002) 'Censorship in Australia: Regulating the Internet and other recent developments', *NSW Parliament Briefing Paper*, http://www.parliament.nsw.gov.au/prod/web/PHWebContent.nsf/PHPages/ResearchBf042002?OpenDocument (viewed 7/4/03).

119   *R. v Hicklin* (1868) LR 3 QB 360 established the 'deprave and corrupt test'.

120   *R v Close* [1948] VLR 445 at 463.

121   *Crowe v Graham* (1968) 121 CLR 375 at 379 per Barwick CJ.

122   Ibid. at 395–9 per Windeyer J.

123   Ibid.

124   Williams D (1997) 'From Censorship to Classification: An Address by the Attorney-General the Hon Daryl Williams AM QC', *E Law – Murdoch University Electronic Journal of Law*, v4(4), http://www.murdoch.edu.au/elaw/issues/v4n4/will441.html (viewed 7/4/03).

125   Altson R (1999) 'Regulation is Not Censorship', *The Australian*, 13 April, 55.

126   Department of Communications, Information Technology and the Arts, Press Release (untitled), 6 January 2000.

The history of censorship in Australia has been influenced by two environmental factors: the country's early status as a geographically remote colony of Great Britain and its island geography. With increasing cultural sophistication,[127] Australian censorship was liberalized and moved from outright prohibition to classification, based on the premise that mature audiences could make a decision for themselves, but should be free from unsolicited material.[128] The state remains the arbiter of classification but self regulation does exist.

Radio and television stations engage in censorship through internal procedures or self-regulatory groups such as the Federation of Australian Commercial Television Stations (FACTS) with limited oversight by the ABA through codes of practice under the *Broadcasting Services Act 1992*.

As Australia is a federal system, it should be acknowledged that the state governments hold power to implement their own censorship regimes, as well as allowing the Commonwealth cooperative scheme to exist.[129] Censorship at federal level is primarily the responsibility of the Office of Film and Literature Classification (the OFLC), which consists of a Classification Board and a Classification Review Board which hears appeals. Film and videos come to the OFLC already classified under self-regulatory systems, such as that of the United States. The OFLC examines and reclassifies material, occasionally departing from the existing classification.

The regulation of new media and the issue of technology and media convergence have brought censorship back on to the public agenda including a national report on the regulation of computer games and interactive media.[130] Computer game *GTA3* (2000) was banned in Australia, condemned for its realism and failure to impose a moral code on game behaviour. It was released in a censored form but uncensored copies are freely available via import from New Zealand or elsewhere.[131] The Board was concerned about game events generated by the interactive components of the game rather than scripted sections, troubled that there was the potential

---

127 Coleman P (2000) op. cit. fn. 11.

128 Australian Law Reform Commission (1991b) *Censorship Procedure*, Discussion Paper 47, AGPS: Canberra.

129 Classification (Publications, Films and Computer Games) Enforcement Act 1995 (NSW), Classification of Publications, Films and Computer Games Act 1996 (NT), Classification of Computer Games and Images Act 1995 (Qld), Classification (Publications, Films and Computer Games) Act 1995 (SA), Classification (Publications, Films and Computer Games) (Enforcement) Act 1995 (Vic), Censorship Act 1996 (WA), Classification of Publications Act 1991 (Qld), Classification of Films Act 1991 (Qld), Classification (Publications, Films, Computer Games) Enforcement Act 1995 (Tas), Classification (Publications, Films, Computer Games) Enforcement Act 1995 (ACT).

130 Brand JE (2002) *A Review of the Classification Guidelines for Films and Computer Games*, prepared for the OFLC, 11 February.

131 ZDNet Australia (2001b) 'GTA3 officially banned in Australia', 13 December, http://www.zdnet.com.au/newstech/enterprise/story/0,2000025001,20262360,00.htm.

for players to 'create offensive media' through their own choices to kill game characters regardless of provocation or moral justification.[132]

The objectives of Classification Board of the Office of Film and Literature Classification are spelled out in its *Guidelines for the Classification of Films and Videotapes* (2003):

(a) adults should be able to read, hear and see what they want;
(b) minors should be protected from material likely to harm or disturb them;
(c) everyone should be protected from exposure to unsolicited material that they find offensive;
(d) the need to take account of community concerns about depictions that condone or incite violence, particularly sexual violence; and
(e) the portrayal of persons in a demeaning manner.

In addition, s 11 of the *Classification (Publications, Films and Computer Games) Act 1995* requires the Classification Board to take issues of merit and community standards into account, thus importing the United States *Miller* test into Australian law. These include:

- the standards of morality, decency and propriety generally accepted by reasonable adults;
- the literary, artistic or education merit (if any) of the film;
- the general character of the film, included whether it is of a medical, legal or scientific character; and
- the persons or class of persons to or amongst whom it is published or is intended or likely to be published.

The classification and rating system establishes a taxonomy of media content involving a series of general categories; violence, sex, coarse language, drug use, nudity and adult themes (a catch-all term which includes horror and the supernatural).[133] Discretionary or evaluative terms such as *harmful*, *disturbing*, *gratuitous* and *exploitative* are used throughout the guidelines and disrupt the taxonomy of the guidelines. Discourses such as psychology (child development) and liberal humanism (artistic merit) are acknowledged in these guidelines but theories of media reception are not.

---

132 Classification Review Board (2001) *Review of GTA3*, 40th Meeting, 11 December.

133 However, the Guidelines define Adult Themes as: Issues dealing with aspects of adult life that are potentially harmful to minors or disturbing. Adult themes may include verbal references to and depictions associated with issues such as suicide, crime, corruption, marital problems, emotional trauma, drug and alcohol dependency, death and serious illness, racism, religious issues. Office of Film and Literature Classification (2003) *Guidelines for the Classification of Films and Computer Games*, OFLC: Canberra.

The regulations' glossary contains the following:[134]

Harm/ harmful	Causes developmental damage.
Exploitative	Appearing to purposefully debase or abuse for the enjoyment of viewers, and lacking moral, artistic or other values.
Gratuitous	Material which is unwarranted or uncalled for, and included without the justification of a defensible story-line or artistic merit.
Disturb/ disturbing	Causes emotional trauma.
Offensive	Material which causes outrage or extreme disgust to most people.
Treatment	The artistic handling of a scene or film especially with regard to style. In a *realistic treatment*, the material appears real to the viewer. It may be close to real life, and feel authentic. In a *stylized treatment*, the viewer is conscious of the unreality; examples include musicals, horror films, animation and fantasy.

Further exploration of the system of taxonomy implemented under the guidelines exposes the impossibility of the project, to reduce complex media images and meanings to a codified set of standards represented by mere words. The more community standards are defined, the more exceptions or variations become apparent, and the more ambiguous the standards become. These categories are, however, usually reasonably unproblematic as most of the media subjected to them have already been self classified and formed part of coherent genre products out of media industries. The problem in applying these to Internet media is that much of the material is not the product of an industry: it has none of these fixed starting positions. An examination of the guidelines' rating clusters further demonstrates these ambiguities which become ever more important when these guidelines are applied to the classification of Internet content:

MA rated[135]

> Minors must be accompanied by adults for MA rated film and video.
> Violence which has a high impact, is sexual or is realistic is permissible but neither should be prolonged, frequent or gratuitous. A greater amount of stylized violence is permissible than realistic violence.

---

134 Glossary of the *Guidelines for the Classification of Films and Videotapes*, ibid.
135 Material of this classification or lower (PG, G) does not fall within the Internet regulation scheme.

Sex may be implied with nudity as long as there is no 'exploitative detail'.

Coarse language may be used as long as it is not gratuitous.

Adult themes should be treated with discretion. Issues dealing with aspects of adult life that are potentially harmful to minors or disturbing. Adult themes may include verbal references to and depictions associated with issues such as suicide, crime, corruption, marital problems, emotional trauma, drug and alcohol dependency, death and serious illness, racism, religious issues.[136]

Drug use may be shown but not encouraged.

R rated[137]

R rated material is restricted to adults.

Material which promotes or incites or instructs in matters of crime and/or violence is not permitted.

Violence is permissible so long as it is not gratuitous, exploitative, sexual, frequent or 'real'.

Sex may be realistically simulated but not actually performed. Nudity should avoid obvious genital contact.

Coarse language which is strong, aggressive and detailed may be gratuitous, there are 'virtually no restrictions'.

Drug use may be shown as long is it is not 'gratuitously detailed' or encouraged.

X rated[138]

An X rating applies only to video material. X rated videos are legally available only the ACT and the Northern territory.

This rating describes sexually explicit material which includes real sex and mild fetishes (suggested sadomasochism and leather paraphernalia is permitted, coprophagia is not). No sexual violence or 'debasement'[139] is permissible.

---

136 In the 1997/98 period, in 68 per cent of films and 71 per cent of videos given the R classification, the reason provided was generic, unspecified adult themes – Graham I (1999a) *Blinded by Smoke: The Hidden Agenda of the Online Services Bill 1999*, http://rene.efa.org.au/liberty/blinded.html.

137 Under the Internet regulation scheme, R material hosted in Australia must be protected by adult verification technology.

138 Under the Internet regulation scheme, X material cannot be hosted in Australia.

139 Interestingly the terms 'debase' and 'abuse' do not receive definition, although several other terms refer back to them, as though the term was an objective given. Likewise the term 'abhorrent' is undefined.

RC rated[140]

> The RC rating represents banned material. Technically the material is not rated at all, a rating is refused and penalties are imposed for sale of unclassified material. This includes material containing paedophilia or offensive depictions of a person who is or appears to be under sixteen years of age.
> Material which promotes/incites crime and violence.
> Detailed drug use instruction.
> 'Practices such as bestiality'.
> Offensive or abhorrent fetishes.
> Incest fantasies or other fantasies which are offensive or abhorrent.
> Films that 'appear to purposefully debase or abuse for the enjoyment of viewers, and which lack moral, artistic or other values, to the extent that they offend against generally accepted standards of morality, decency and propriety'.[141]
> 'Films that [...] depict, express or otherwise deal with matters of sex, drug misuse or addiction, crime, cruelty, violence, or revolting or abhorrent phenomena in such a way that they offend against the standards of morality, decency and propriety generally accepted by reasonable adults'.[142]

The OFLC takes into account a wide variety of contextual issues when making its determinations. The Board's debates seem lively and even allow for dissenting opinions. A survey of the Annual Reports of the OFLC[143] reveals that many factors other than simply the moral rightness or wrongness of a text are taken into account. The list of factors below provides examples of how the rules can be applied, and an exploration of the zones of discretion and interpretation in which the OFLC operates:

- The relationship with 'real' material – including actual news or documentary footage may create a greater impact than a wholly constructed work.
- The use of absurd or black humour may reduce seriousness or may create a higher impact.
- 'Discretion' (in the sense of being discrete) is an important consideration in dealing with problematic material such as sex or violence. Implied, rather than directly represented, content is preferable.
- Stylistic or theatrical presentation may be a mitigating factor.

---

140 Under the Internet regulation scheme RC material cannot be hosted in Australia.
141 Office of Film and Literature Classification (1999) Guidelines for the Classification of Films and Videotapes (Amendment No.2), at 13.
142 From the National Classification Code under the Classification (Publications, Films and Computer Games) Act 1995 (Cth).
143 Graham, op. cit. fn. 136.

- Cumulative impact can be more important than individual incidences.
- The use of low-budget approach to production, acting and narrative mitigating against the extremity of some material (*Pink Flamingos*).
- A cheerful musical soundtrack was considered important (*Pink Flamingos*).
- A 'candid yet non-titillatory treatment of the topic of sex' was considered (*Chasing Amy*).
- The naturalistic use of coarse language decreased impact (*Chasing Amy*).
- 'Impactful verbal references to rape and murder' were as relevant as visual representations (*Blackrock*).
- 'The film does not present a fully resolved version of events, perhaps for the apparent purpose of encouraging viewers to contemplate the related issues'. It is uncertain from the report if this factor made the film more or less suitable for minors (*Blackrock*).
- The Board acknowledges where there is a targeted teenage audience (*Blackrock*).
- While the regulated material was not condoned by the film's narrative 'some impressionable minors may not see the anti-drugs, safe-sex messages which would be clear to adults in this portrayal of a teenage world without adult supervision' (*Kids*).
- An intelligent narrative is a mitigating factor (*Dead Man Walking*).
- The absence of 'instructional' representation of drug use acts to minimize the impact of drug-based narrative (*Trainspotting*).

These considerations challenge the stereotype of censors merely counting incidences of bad language or measuring centimetres of flesh exposed. However, in recent years this discretionary and interpretive process has become more politically charged, especially if a film or video is facing a potential RC classification. Civil libertarians and political commentators such as Peter Chen express concern that the term *classification* is merely newspeak for 'a censorship regime in an age when regulation and classification are words we prefer to use when society draws the line under material we want to see, but dare not allow ourselves access to.'[144]

Online Censorship

The Australian approach to Internet regulation has extended the reach of the Federal classification scheme and is enshrined in the *Broadcasting Services Amendment (Online Services) Act 1999*, is discussed in more depth in Chapter 3. The public policy consultation process undertaken preliminary to the Act's passage

---

144 Chen P (1999) 'Community without Flesh: First Thoughts on the New Broadcasting Services Amendment (Online Services) Bill 1999', *M/C: A Journal of Media and Culture 2.3*, at 2. http://english.uq.edu.au/mc/9905/bill (viewed 1/10/01).

drew heavily on American experiences.[145] While this approach imported United States moral concerns, it must not be forgotten that these include civil libertarian discourses which are influential, even in a jurisdiction, such as Australia, which does not have a constitutionally protected notion of free speech to draw upon.[146]

Beyond the federal Internet content scheme, there have been two state-based attempts to provide a system of Internet censorship which sit alongside existing criminal law provisions for prosecuting of child pornography.[147] New South Wales and South Australia are the two states which have passed legislation that makes it illegal to supply to anyone material online which is deemed unsuitable for minors, even if it is freely available offline, and these Acts have come under considerable criticism.[148] The *Classification (Publications, Films and Computer Games) Enforcement Amendment Act 2001*, the NSW legislation, has been passed but has not been proclaimed and has been the subject of public outcry and condemned by a government inquiry, the NSW Legislative Council's Committee on Social Issues, which recommended that the Act be repealed.[149] South Australia has opted for similar legislation, the *Classification (Publications, Films and Computer Games)(On-Line Services) Amendment Bill 2002* to similar outcry.[150]

Filtering and Labelling

Before the *Broadcasting Services Amendment (Online Services) Act 1999* is examined in more depth in Chapter 3, one last contextual aspect needs to be considered: the international trend toward adopting filtering technologies which restrict access to Internet content. Different types of filtering software function in different ways (for example, searching for words from a list of prohibited words or from a specified list of prohibited URLs) and at different sites (on the user's computer, the ISP's server or a national level) but each option involves an automated, mechanical process which censors material without the intervention of the user.

---

145 Chen, op. cit. fn. 13 at 96.

146 Yamaguchi I (2002) 'Beyond De Facto Freedom: Digital Transformation of Free Speech Theory in Japan', *Stanford Journal of International Law*, Vol 38, 109.

147 *Crimes Act 1900* (ACT) s92, *Censorship Act 1996* (WA) s60, *Crimes Act 1958* (Vic) s68–70, *Crimes Act 1900* (NSW) s578B–C, *Summary Offences Act 1953* (SA) s33, *Criminal Code 1899* (Qld) s228, *Criminal Code Act 1924* (Tas) s138, *Criminal Code 1999* (NT) s125B.

148 Australia (2001c) 'New Australian Net censorship laws condemned', 19 November, http://www.zdnet.com.au/newstech/security/story/0,2000024985,20261920,00.htm.

149 NSW Standing Committee on Social Issues (2002) *Classification Bill – Final Report*, 6 June.

150 ZDNet Australia (2002b) 'SA pollies debate Net censorship bill', 8 July, http://www.zdnet.com.au/newstech/security/story/0,20000,24985,20266592m00.htm.

While the Australian government rejected a mandatory filtering scheme, the philosophy of voluntary filtering underpins the Australian co-regulatory scheme and suggests user empowerment, self governance and faith in technology to provide an answer for technological problems. In opposition to the draconian image of state imposed censorship, the facilitation of voluntary filtering presents an apparently benign intervention as well as bolstering abstract models of community by suggesting individual and community empowerment. Australia's endorsement of filtering has led to it leading the world in web filter market growth, especially in the workplace.[151]

Closely related to the adoption of filtering technologies is the push for self-labelling (or classification) of material, either on a voluntary or compulsory basis. Various labelling standards have been suggested, such as PICs[152] or RSACi,[153] but there is yet to be any international consensus.[154] Labelling is presented by advocates such as the PICs group to be a reasonable and responsible technique of self governance, but this soon becomes burdensome when the practicalities of who is to do the labelling and how this is done are considered.

Both filtering and labelling techniques involve the extension of classification approach to places which it would be difficult for state censorship to reach. The bare exercise of state force is replaced by a more palatable regime of classification, particularly if self-regulation is allowed. However, filtering in particular has become controversial with high profile reportage such as when AOL banned access to the word 'breast' including material discussing breast cancer.[155]

In the late 1990s there was a short lived enthusiasm for technical filtering mechanisms which could analyse images directly and determine if an image was pornographic by the percentage of skin tone, such as *Eye-t* software. This approach was all but abandoned after it was discovered that it also filtered portraiture, pictures of pigs and tan-coloured suburban homes on real estate websites, but

---

151   ZDNet (2001e) 'Australian censorship leads Web filter market growth', 18 September, http://www.zdnet.com.au/newstech/enterprise/story/0,2000025001,20260515,00.htm.

152   The PICS (Platform for Internet Content Selection) standard was developed by the World Wide Web Consortium (W3C) in 1995 in response to the United States *Communications Decency Act*. http://w3.org/PICS.

153   The RSACi (Recreational Software Advisory Council) standard was based on a computer game rating standard but has been abandoned. The RSAC system was introduced as a way of dealing with the enhanced realism of computer games which arose out of high resolution graphics and digitized video content. In general it deals with the treatment of human or humanoid characters (and their sentience), the realism of violence, sexual content and language (including hate speech) – it was based on quite a different paradigm to PICS.

154   Roberts D (1997) 'On the Plurality of Ratings', *Cardozo Arts and Entertainment Law Journal*, vol 15, 105.

155   Harmon A (1995) 'On-Line Service Provider Draws Protest in Censor Flap', *LA Times*, 12 December.

failed to catch many pornographic images, especially where subjects were people with darker skin colour.[156]

All types of filters are known to make mistakes, to be over or under inclusive.[157] Filters have blocked the sites of anti-pornography campaigners, conventional artistic images, Amnesty International and United Nations reports, information brochures (for drugs, sexuality, HIV/AIDs), literature such as *Moby Dick* and *The Owl and the Pussycat*, tourism information of the Netherlands (containing the word 'dykes') and material written by people with names such as 'Dick' or 'Jenny' (due to the popularity of the exhibitionist 'Jennycam' website).[158]

In the United States, the National Research Council report condemned filtering solutions, 'technology solutions are brittle, in the sense that when they fail, they fail catastrophically.'[159] The Report challenges not only the function of filters but also their expense and the ease with which they may be circumvented. Instead, the report suggests sex education and media literacy as solutions, citing the comparatively more liberal experiences of European children and the lack of evidence that their potential exposure to media adult results in harm.[160] Similarly, the report of the Commission on Child Online Protection recommended public education, consumer empowerment and industry self governance (ISPs and adult industry) as the key elements of successful policy, after exhaustively evaluating and comparing technological options.[161]

Filters have also been challenged by civil rights advocates on the grounds that they operate as 'prior restraint' on free speech. Filters 'reflect a reductive view of human expression by reducing its value and meaning to decontextualized key words and phrases or broad subject matter', set up barriers and taboos, restrict

---

156   Rocks D (2000) 'Cyber Skin', *Business Week*, Issue 3667, p10.

157   See for example the list maintained at: Finkelstein S (2000) 'SmartFilter – I've Got A Little List', http://setf.com/anticensorware/smartfilter/gotalist.php (viewed 6/3/01).

158   Rodriquez F (2002) *Burning the Village to Roast the Pig: Censorship of Online Media*, A paper for the OSCE workshop 'Freedom of the Media and the Internet' 30 November 2002, p10; Heins M and Cho C (2001) *Internet Filters: A Public Policy Report*, http://www.ncac.org/issues/Internetfilters.html; CSIRO (2001) *Effectiveness of Internet Filtering Software Products*, report prepared for the Australian Broadcasting Authority, September.

159   National Research Council, Computer Science and Telecommunications Board (2002) op. cit. fn. 115.

160   Ibid. Chapter 6.

161   The report contains extensive exploration of the technologies is ultimately rejects and is a good resource of information on this topic. Commission on Child Online Protection (COPA) (2000) op. cit. fn. 100. For an Australian survey of just filtering technologies that lets the results speak for themselves, see Greenfield P, Rickwood P, Tran HC (2001) *Effectiveness of Internet Filtering Software Products*, CSIRO Mathematical and Information Sciences.

student research, replace judgments of teachers with those made by corporations and they exacerbate the digital divide between IT rich and poor.[162]

Without self-labelling, filtering does not work. Without legal compulsion, labelling will not be widely adopted. While mandatory labelling under a PICs system may not be constitutionally invalid in the United States,[163] it is practically unfeasible especially with dynamically created site content. Australia's Internet regulation scheme adopts something of a hybrid approach, effectively requiring R rated material to be self labelled or submitted for classification as well as being protected by age verification security.

Much of the filtering and labelling discourse anticipates technological developments which will make the process more feasible. Given that little has changed in this area during seven years this, however, seems unlikely.[164] Internet content creators are understandably reluctant to self label. Once content is labelled, it is very easy for a repressive government to annex this to a national censorship scheme.[165]

According to Irene Graham, Chair of Electronic Frontiers Australia,[166] compulsory labelling would result in much material being inaccessible because providers will be overly cautious in rating their material, either to offset complaints or because of limited resources and the difficulty of rating complex material (such as archived discussion groups):

> ... newsgroups discussions may become highly confusing. Imagine, if you will, the situation when half the participants in a particular thread are only reading the messages which are labelled [...] Consider also the situation when someone posts, for example, a highly racist message but rates it as not being racist because they don't think it is. Everyone could read that message. However when someone else attempts to follow it up, how would they rate their own message if racist text is quoted? Do they not quote any text, or do they rate their message at a higher level – resulting in those blocking higher rated messages only seeing racist speech?[167]

A similar difficulty arises from websites which are generated mechanically from databases by content management systems, allowing users to customize what material they wish to see. The regulation paradigm is based on the idea of web pages as discrete files, put together by a human author. Increasingly, automated

---

162 http://www.fepproject.org/factsheets/filtering.html.
163 Penabad C (1998) 'Tagging or Not? The Constitutionality of Federal Labelling Requirements for Internet Web Pages', *UCLA Entertainment Law Review*, Vol 5, 355.
164 Rodriquez F (2002) op. cit. fn. 158 at 11.
165 Ibid.
166 Graham I (2000a) *The Net Labelling Delusion: Saviour or Devil*, http://rene.efa.org.au/liberty/label.htm.
167 Ibid.

sites are used which, in response to a reader's request, will compile a collated set of results from a database, such as a news database. These pages cannot be rated individually (especially under a regime which requires you submit a URL to a rating authority) as they are generated on an ad hoc basis.[168] While the database itself might then become the site of regulation, this example demonstrates how shifts in technology are not recognized by the slow movement of regulatory apparatus.

Rights, Labelling and Liberalism

Much of the resistance to the apparently light touch labelling system of regulation comes from liberal resistance to self censorship on the basis of an auteur-centred approach to art. Graham suggests that 'labelling is of further concern when writers, artists and other content creators are *required* to judge and label their own material, thus forcing them to censor themselves in accord with values established by someone else.'[169] In addition, Quittner argues for the status of news media as a special case which ought not have to label, based on the pressure of deadlines and a public interest status:

> How would you 'rate' news sites, after all? News often deals with violent situations, and occasionally with sexual themes and even adult language. How do you rate that? Do you rate every story? On deadline? Or just rate your entire site off-limits, since sometimes you'll be covering treacherous terrain?[170]

Overall, arguments contain a cynicism about any effective automated system of content regulation. In a criticism of the RSACi rating system, Graham writes:

> RSACi does not distinguish between material with scientific, literary, artistic or educational value, and other types of material. A news report containing violent material must be rated under the same criteria as that [sic] applying to games or a novel. A web page providing information about safe sex or a photo of the Venus de Milo sculpture must be rated under the same criteria as that [sic] applying to pornographic material.[171]

This does raise the question as to *why* these texts are given a privileged status, and who is in the position to judge whether a text falls into which of these apparently discrete categories. The American Library Association makes takes a liberal approach when criticizing the labelling process:

---

168 Ibid.
169 Ibid.
170 Quittner J (1997) 'Empire State Censorship', *The Netly News*, 4 March.
171 Graham, op. cit. fn. 166.

Labelling is the practice of describing or designating materials by affixing a prejudicial label and/or segregating them by a prejudicial system. The American Library Association opposes these means of predisposing people's attitudes toward library materials for the following reasons:

1. Labelling is an attempt to prejudice attitudes and as such is a censor's tool.

2. Some find it easy and even proper, according to their ethics, to establish criteria for judging publications as objectionable. However, injustice and ignorance rather than justice and enlightenment result from such practices.[172]

Labelling is not yet officially part of the Australian co-regulatory system, but it may yet be mandated in the industry codes of practice. The governing state body, the Australian Broadcasting Authority (the ABA), has not yet established a policy commitment one way or another on the compulsory labelling debate. ABA Chairman Peter Webb states that 'There's no reason why you wouldn't label your site, and good commercial reasons why you would'.[173] Webb's comment implies a support for voluntary labelling, but this has been interpreted by the EFA as the first step toward a compulsory labelling scheme.[174] Ironically, the ABA voluntarily rated its own site with RSAC in 1996 and technical problems lead to the entire site (except the front page) being blocked by filters.[175]

Filtering and labelling technologies appear to empower members of the community and to allow self governance without the heavy hand of government intervention. In practice, as a part of media literacy everyone adopts their own filtering practices, in making media selections, choosing what sites to visit, which links to follow. The problem with technological filtering is that it is difficult to peek inside the black box, to see what the filter is actually doing in order to assess its effectiveness. These themes will emerge again in Chapter 3 as commentators critique the specific filtering options endorsed by the *Broadcasting Services Amendment (Online Services) Act 1999*.

Censorship: The Community's Scissorman?[176]

The difficulty of regulating Internet content is a subset of the problems faced by censorship generally. It demonstrates the impossibility of codifying community

---

172 American Library Association (1996) *Statement on Labelling – An Interpretation of the Library Bill of Rights,* http://www.ala.org/oif/labeling.html (viewed 27/7/01).
173 quoted in Graham, op. cit. fn. 166.
174 Ibid.
175 ABA Press Release (untitled) 14 Nov 1996.
176 The sinister figure of the Scissorman is drawn from Heinrich Hoffman's *Struwwelpeter* (1845) a moral text for children which involves violent punishment for the

standards, of reducing the complex social interaction of regulatory practices, individual choices and self governance strategies into a written code and then providing an apparatus to enforce these on resistant regulatory objects. While metaphorically rich, the concept of 'the community' is quite abstract and includes spatial practices are not apparent on the surface.

When censorship law uses an abstract and homogenous concept such as the community, along with legal/spatial practices by which that community is said to be constructed (for example, the pseudo-jury panel of representatives who form a Censorship Board), this model operates in denial of the difference and diversity of values throughout the population. Like law's 'reasonable man', the values of the community form a spatial enclosure, a denial of local practices and a political tool for marginalization of interests which do not conform.

Just who is excluded in the practices of censorship? Consumers and producers of sexually explicit or sexually explorative media certainly feel excluded and silenced, both by state practices and by more diverse moral practices (as will be discussed in Chapter 5). Queer and culturally diverse spaces are pushed to the margins, rendered invisible because they are different to the abstract community monolith. Censorship practices are political and deceptive in their appeal to the image of a 'normal' majority, an appeal which compels the individual to silence their own differences or face the same scrutiny and censure.

Spatial practices emerge again and again in the censorship debates, particularly where Internet content regulation is concerned. While censorship laws speak of broadly defined social consensus through its protection of community values, this is only achieved if diverse fragments of human geography can be fused together into an abstract image of wholeness and resistance can be moved into marginal spaces.

It is important to recognize that the regulatory practices include not simply those of the state, but also those of producers and consumers who define market niches, stabilize codes of representation and establish practices of access. So while human objects are homogenized, the media those objects consume is increasingly divided into spatial stratifications through classification and labelling. The spatial practices of censorship are complex and this book seeks to examine how these operate, taking the introduction of Australian Internet censorship as a point of examination, a break from tradition which has lead to re-assessment of the assumptions underlying the national system of classification.

---

transgression of community standards. The bogeyman 'Scissorman' cuts off the thumbs of a boy who sucks his thumb, a practice which may be a metaphor for masturbation.

Chapter 3
Co-regulation and Symbolic Policy: The *Broadcasting Services Amendment (Online Services) Act 1999*

Censorship law, in its invocation of community and its posture of defence of community values, is fundamentally concerned with the definition and expression of national identity. Can a multicultural society accept the singular and uniform notion of community that this seems to require? Can a national, jurisdictional territory (physical, electronic and even imaginary) be said to comprise a single homogenous and continuous public space?

This book argues that multiple regulatory communities are possible and are even contemplated within current regulatory thought. This runs against the grain of public censorship discourse, which posits a single and unified community which resists the incursion of Others and transgressive texts which must be expelled to the margins.

Nevertheless, this monolithic concept is disrupted by its own practices, particularly as these are codified in the *Broadcasting Services Amendment (Online Services) Act 1999*. The very fact that a censorship process exists indicates that community values are far from seamless and consistent. Part of the reason why pornography and violent media are expelled with such vigour is founded in the denial that producers and consumers are situated within the very spatial confines of the community. Historically, these subjects are identified, quarantined, pathologized, criminalized, demonized and marginalized by censorship practices.

Specific practices under the Act, such as the co-regulatory arrangement with the Internet Industry Association, explicitly recognize different regulatory communities, each with their own practices. Negotiation of spatial concepts and practices in the governance of cyberspace and the public space of broadcasting (which must be considered alongside the private spaces of communications technologies) all recognize a heterogeneity of regulatory spaces and different communities of citizens that occupy, move through and order these spaces.

Censorship practices are contradictory in that they both produce difference, creating argumentative discursive spaces, and then seek to deny and silence these spaces. The exercise of power by the creation of the Act constitutes communities of resistance in both the libertarian dissenters and the pro-censorship activists who call for more stringent controls. The apparent failure of Australia's Internet censorship scheme perhaps indicates not so much regulatory impotence but rather the friction and balance of power under which censorship law operates in contemporary Australia.

The Australian Internet content regulation scheme, enacted in the *Broadcasting Services Amendment (Online Services) Act 1999*, was germinated in an environment specific to the last days of the twentieth century. The Internet porn scare had subsided and was fairly low on the public agenda: in fact, issues such as fraud, privacy[1] and hate sites[2] were becoming acknowledged as more important concerns. Some conservative politicians and lobbyists maintained moral panic campaigns, however redundant these seemed to be in the public view.[3] The content regulation issue had been lost twice in the United States, and other nations around the Western world had settled for self-regulatory models.

Australia, a culturally and ethnically diverse nation, had resisted One Nation Party calls to 'middle Australia' for cultural homogeneity and Anglo–Australian values. Traditionally distrustful of moral regulators,[4] the only structural factors available for a content regulation scheme to build on were existing schemes of broadcast regulation and media classification. Therefore it became important to conceptually shoehorn Internet and other new media into these frameworks.

The scheme does just this by deeming the Internet to be a public broadcasting service (neglecting to discuss the difference between media transmission models[5]) and applying existing classification/censorship rules, at least the stricter end of the rules, for material rated *R*, *X* and *RC*. The major themes in the legislation

---

1 Australian Broadcasting Authority (2001) *The Internet at Home: A Report on Internet Use in the Home*, Sydney.

2 Human Rights and Equal Opportunity Commission (2002) *Race Hate and the Internet: Background Paper for Cyber-racism Symposium*, HREOC: Sydney.

3 Consider the lukewarm reception of the Australia Institute's reports, see Chapter 2.

4 Coleman P (1962, 2000 rev. edn.) *Obscenity, Blasphemy, Sedition: The Rise and Fall of Literary Censorship in Australia*, Duffy and Snellgrove: Sydney. Although Coleman ended the 2000 re-issue of his book (at 233) with this message, perhaps indicating a cultural as well as personal shift:

> This is a young man's book written some forty years ago on the cusp of the 1960s. In those distant days I was convinced that any restriction on any publication of any kind was an intolerable infringement of our freedom. I later lost this certainty.

5 Broadcast media work on the 'one to many' model. The Internet works on this basis but also allows for 'one to one' and 'many to many' models to operate. Livingstone KT (1996) *The Wired Nation Content: The Communication Revolution and Federating Australia*, Oxford University Press: Melbourne. The broadcast model has been challenged as inappropriate to apply to the Internet. Elkin-Koren N (1996) 'Public/Private and Copyright Reform in Cyberspace', *Journal of Computer Mediated Communication*, 2, 2. http://www.ascusc.org/jcmc/vol2/issue2/elkin.html. Part of the reason for this is that the structure and practices of the Internet resist definition as part of the public sphere on which the definition of broadcasting relies. Poster M (1997) 'Cyberdemocracy: The Internet and the Public Sphere', in Porter D (ed.) *Internet Culture*, Routledge: London.

are a politically and economically expedient co-regulatory model, the traditional invocation of 'community values' as a justification for censorship/classification, the construction of a model 'industry' to be involved in co-regulation and the connection of Internet new media to the metaphor of broadcasting (as opposed to publishing or telecommunications, for instance).

This chapter considers the Act in some depth and explores the critiques that it faces. Forecasting the remainder of the book, this chapter begins to sketch out some of the spatial practices in which the scheme engages, in terms of both cyberspace regulation and the spaces of censorship. The presumptions of the scheme, exposed by critics and lobbyists, challenge the flimsy framework of homogenous community that it is predicated upon and raise the potential for recognizing the diverse regulatory practices that already exist, situated in regulatory communities clustered and constituted around new media.

This chapter also concerns the spatial practices which are encoded in the Act. On the face of it, the Act, like other legislative documents, appears to be of universal operation, to be spatially neutral. The only direct references to space or geography made within the Act involve questions of jurisdiction. Within the jurisdictional territory the Act is presumed to have uniform operation, the regulatory network is presumed to be spread evenly, backed up by the ideologies of equality before the law and the rule of law.

On closer examination, there are several areas in which this regulatory uniformity is challenged. First and foremost, the notion of jurisdiction in cyberspace is far from simple. Even if an embodied notion of territory is considered (inscribing law to the bodies of subjects physically present in the jurisdiction) there are problems concerning the extraterritorial behaviour of those subjects – working with servers and data located internationally.

Second, the concept of community is directly contemplated by the Act but this is done in a contradictory manner. By integrating its operation with the classification and censorship system, the Act adopts censorship discourse's notion of community values – which depends on a unitary and monolithic model of community to support it. On the other hand, the co-regulatory parts of the Act embrace the standards of a smaller community division within the broader community, the 'Internet industry'. This practice recognizes the special constitution and values and at least one alternative regulatory community. This contradiction will be explored in this book and demonstrates a tension between the liberal ideology of unitary law and the pragmatist operation of multiple regulatory sites.

Finally, while the text of the Act appears to be neutral as regards media content, it is integrated with the existing OFLC procedures and guidelines and therefore engages with the spatial practices of censorship. When considering regulation of sexual content, censorship negotiates a specific kind of public/private divide: it considers the notion of publication (bringing a text into the public sphere), obscenity (things which 'should not be seen' in the public sphere) and complex issues of sexuality and identity (what is permitted in the privacy of the bedroom and what 'frightens the horses'[6]). By deeming Internet media as 'broadcasting', an activity which has a strong public character, a whole range of complex media behaviour and communities (each with its own constitution, identity and practices by which public and private are balanced) is homogenized into a single public practice.[7]

The Internet as a Broadcasting Service

The Australian approach to Internet censorship draws heavily on existing mechanisms of media control, effectively hybridizing the regulation of publishers (through the classification of media) with the control of broadcasters. The central administrative position given to the Australian Broadcasting Authority (the ABA) under the Act made it essential that the Internet could be squeezed, conceptually, into the ABA's area of responsibility. In 2006 the ABA was absorbed into the Australian Communications and Media Authority (ACMA) which regulates broadcasting and telecommunications. Both broadcasting and publishing statuses have proven to be important in order to establish a nexus of control over the socially stable category of Internet providers (rather than the person who provides the content who may be difficult to locate). It is essential to inscribe Internet service businesses with these metaphors, rather than the alternative metaphors of 'postmaster' or 'telephone provider' which would provide fewer opportunities for control. Traditional resistance to intrusion in these 'sacred' trust-based relationships has made them difficult metaphors to use in justification of coercive regulation. McLuhan's concept of 'rear view regulation' suggests that when regulating new technologies, it is necessary to use the metaphors of existing technology, and that the choice of metaphor can be vital in determining new media's future.[8]

Civil libertarian Danny Yee criticizes the broadcasting/narrowcasting metaphor imposed on the Internet by the scheme, which applies solely to *push* technologies.

---

6 This concept encapsulates Victorian attitudes to morality and discretion, attributed to stage actor Mrs Patrick Campbell (née Beatrice Stella Tanner); 'It doesn't matter what you do in the bedroom as long as you don't do it in the street and frighten the horses'; Knowles E (ed.) (2003) *The Concise Oxford Dictionary of Quotations*, Oxford University Press: Oxford.

7 For instance, a person might take a series of photographs and place them on a web server in order to share them with a (private) group of friends. If they make no efforts to publicize the site and do not use meta-tags which search engines might locate, there is no manner in which members of the public can readily access this site. Nevertheless this is considered to be broadcasting under the Act. Email, on the other hand, is considered to have a prima facie private character (using the mail metaphor) even though email can be sent to large lists, even lists which have subscription details posted in public places. Convergent media are not readily pigeon-holed into public and private models of activity.

8 Benedetti P and Detlart N (eds) (1970) *Forward Through the Rearview Window: Reflections on and by Marshall McLuhan*, MIT Press: Cambridge, MA.

He raises the important point that 'the Internet is not Television' but does not develop this further than expressing consternation at the assumptions made.[9] Of course, when considering convergent media the broadcasting model is even more arbitrary than it once was and the ideological foundations of state media control have not been adequately revisited. Instead, an approach of 'pragmatism' underpins the entire *Broadcasting Services Amendment (Online Services) Act 1999* scheme, of co-opting existing mechanisms with a minimum of fuss and expense rather than seeking to unpack fundamental issues of media, control, audience viewing practices and reader reception. Whether that approach, under the Act, actually functions pragmatically is another question.

Part of this low-key pragmatism has been the adopting of the velvet glove of classification instead of the iron fist of censorship which, particularly in the United States context, served to mobilize and focus resistance to censorship legislation. The Australian scheme seems reasonable because it adapts mechanisms to which its regulatory objects are already accustomed, merely extending some definitions to include the Internet as a form of new broadcast media.[10] The low impact approach also has the effect of placating regulatory stakeholders by dividing up the Internet pie between each of them as well as co-opting identified industry representatives and moral crusaders into state mandated regulatory organizations.

So far this approach seems to be a sensible extension of existing regulation, building structures which will have the minimum amount of impact on the regulatory order. But how, and by whom, is success to be evaluated? Regulation which is internally coherent and negotiates its place among existing stakeholders may nevertheless prove to be empirically ineffectual, to be an example of mere regulatory fortressing. Perhaps given the difficulty of establishing empirical benchmarks, internal regulatory integrity is all that can be hoped for.

The Act follows a string of formal and informal public debates around the issue of Internet regulation, inquiries and reports conducted by different authorities.[11]

---

9   Yee D (1999a) *The Internet is not Television*, http://www.anatomy.usyd.edu.au/danny/freedom/99/convergence.html.

10   For instance in the definition section, where ever the term 'broadcasting services' is used, the phrase 'and Internet services' is added (*Broadcasting Services Amendment (Online Services) Act 1999* Schedule 1 s3), and in the very title of the amending act where 'online services' is used to indicate that online media are merely a component of an overall broadcast category (*Broadcasting Services Amendment (Online Services) Act 1999* Schedule 1 s1).

11   Australian inquiries include Department of Communications and the Arts (1990) *BBS Task Force*, Senate Community Standards Relevant to the Supply of Services Utilising Electronic Technologies Committee (1997) *Report on Regulation of Computer On-line Services*, Australian Commonwealth Government: Canberra; the various reports of,the Senate Select Committee on Community Standards, Australian Broadcasting Authority (1996) *Investigation into the Content of On-Line Services*, Inquiry of the Senate Select Committee on Community Standards Relevant to the Supply of Services Utilising Electronic Technologies (1997), Department of Communications and the Arts (1997) *Principles for*

Part of the issue is, who 'owns' net regulation in Australia? Rather than opt for a complex approach to electronic media which acknowledges the diversity of self publishing and the relatively minor role of ISPs as facilitators, the tendency has been to deal with the Internet as a singular phenomenon (in keeping with the idea of homogenous community) with the ISPs in the role of the television or radio station.

This chapter begins with a description of the operation of the new revision of the *Broadcasting Services Act 1992* which came into effect on 1 January 2000 as amended by the *Broadcasting Services Amendment (Online Services) Act 1999*. Schedule 1 clause 10 of the 1999 Act constitutes an entirely new partition (Schedule 5) for the existing *Broadcasting Services Act 1992* into which this new regulatory apparatus is inserted.

The impossibility of Internet regulation is often cited by critics as the underlying reason for the perceived failure of the co-regulatory scheme.[12] Federal communications minister Senator Alston recognizes this but responds by a combination of pragmatism and semantics, quickly producing a folk devil to deflect the issue:

> The fact is our Internet content model is now regarded as one of the best [...] an example of how governments can get the balance right. The simplistic notion that because you can't achieve 100 per cent success in closing off any particular Internet site is a reason for not doing anything is not an acceptable explanation and I think everyone does expect us to do everything we can to control paedophile lists and bomb recipes and the like and most of the take down notices that have been issued have been of paedophile lists.[13]

The Government's claims of success have been challenged by civil libertarian organizations such as Electronic Frontiers Australia (the EFA), particularly in the light of Government changes to Freedom of Information legislation to put the decisions under the *Broadcasting Services Amendment (Online Services) Act 1999*

---

a Regulatory Framework for On-line Services in the Broadcasting Services Act 1992, The Senate Select Committee on Information Technologies (1998) *Self Regulation in the Information and Communications Industries*, as well as various drafts of the *Internet Industry Association Codes of Practice* (1996–present).

12   See Chen P (2000b) 'Pornography, Protection, Prevarication: The Politics of Internet Censorship', *University of NSW Law Journal*, v6(1), http://www.austlii.edu.au/cgi–bin/disp.pl/au/other/unswlj/forum/2000/vol6n1/Chen.html?query=percent7e+chen (viewed 6/3/01). Compare this position to claims that the first steps to Internet regulation are important regardless of impact, in Handsley E and Biggins B (2000) 'The sheriff rides into town: a day for rejoicing by innocent westerners', *University of New South Wales Law Journal*, v23, 257 at 259.

13   ZDNet Australia (2002c) 'Exclusive: Alston Hits Back', 27 November, http://www.zdnet.com.au/newstech/communications/story/0,2000024993,20270255,00.htm.

scheme outside the range of public scrutiny.[14] Ostensibly, these changes have been made to stop people from seeking out the offensive material which is the subject of takedown notices, but this does not seem logical if the material has already been taken down and current practice is to black out URLs on Freedom of Information (FOI) records in any event.[15] Even if the material has merely moved to international hosts accessed by the same URL, it is questionable if this infringement of open government is warranted. As academic commentator Peter Chen suggests, the fact that there have only been three FOI inquires, two of which were from the EFA, suggests that the FOI mechanism has not been used as a 'roadmap to illicit content' as the Government has suggested, but rather the changes to the law operate 'only to restrict a public interest advocacy group from undertaking democratically-valuable scrutiny of the act'.[16]

The Objectives of Regulation

The *Broadcasting Services Amendment (Online Services) Act 1999* contains express reference to objectives which are closely tied to existing notions of media regulation – classification of material, prohibition of certain material and the regulation of media 'broadcasters' as the beneficiaries of a pseudo-public status as gatekeepers of public information and opinion.

The new Internet content regulation scheme introduces Internet-specific objectives to the existing scheme of broadcasting regulation to:

- provide a means for addressing complaints about certain Internet content;
- restrict access to certain Internet content that is likely to cause offence to a reasonable adult;
- protect children from exposure to Internet content that is unsuitable for them.[17]

---

14   ZDNet Australia (2002d) 'EFA: Alston covering tracks on Net censorship failure', 22 July, http://www.zdnet.com.au/newstech/security/story/0,2000024985,20266815,00.htm. See also Chen P (2002) 'Australia: Where forward co-regulation?', paper presented at *Growing Australia Online*, 3–4 December, Canberra.

15   Martin L (2002) 'Opinion: Alston's X files: the secret truth about Internet censorship', *Sydney Morning Herald*, 21 January. In 2003 the Senate passed amendments to the freedom of information laws which would exempt the ABA from scrutiny responding to claims that information requests undermined the co-regulatory scheme as well as international efforts to stamp out child pornography. Findlaw (2003b) 'Amendments to Regulation the Publication of Prohibited Internet Content Passed by Senate', 11 September, http://www.findlaw.com.au/news/default.asp?task=read&id=16567&site=LE (viewed 22/9/03).

16   Chen, op. cit. fn. 14 at 6.

17   Broadcasting Services Act 1992 (Cth), s 3 (k)–(m).

Further, regulatory objectives of the Internet content regulation mechanisms are specifically addressed: these are defined in section 4(3) in the following manner:

> The Parliament also intends that Internet content hosted in Australia, and Internet carriage services supplied to end-users in Australia be regulated in a manner that:
> - enables public interest considerations to be addressed in a way that does not impose unnecessary financial and administrative burdens on Internet content hosts and Internet service providers;
> - will readily accommodate technological change; and
> - encourages:
>   - the development of Internet technologies and their application;
>   - the provision of services made practicable by those technologies to the Australian community; and
>   - the supply of Internet carriage services at performance standards that reasonably meet the social, industrial and commercial needs of the Australian Community.[18]

By defining objectives in this manner, the censorship objectives are contextualized and in some ways subordinated to practical issues of supply. Chen suggests that somewhat contradictory objectives underpin media regulation in Australia: supply of infrastructure, distribution of scarce resources and control/censorship.[19] It is worth noting the references to the Australian Community as a singular phenomenon which has some sense of agency (it has 'needs') but is undefined, implied to be self-evident.

At present the Internet Industry Association (the IIA) has adopted the 'professional body' role for pragmatic reasons,[20] but this may eventually lead to the IIA emerging as a state sanctioned authority similar to a law society or medical association, simply because it is easier to replicate these existing organizational roles than it is to develop new ones. Inevitably, this also contributes to the assumption that the Internet is primarily a *business* interest and the matter of Internet regulation is one of constraining businesses rather than private communications. This is in keeping with Government policy presuming communications to be fundamentally concerned with commerce. 'It is not surprising that the Government established the National Office for the Information Economy ("NOIE") rather than a National Office for the Information Society.'[21]

---

18   Ibid. s 4(3).
19   Chen P (2000a) *Australia's Online Censorship Regime: The Advocacy Coalition Framework and Governance Compared*, PhD Thesis, Australian National University at 74–5.
20   ZDNet Australia (1999a) 'Australia joins net censorship club', 26 May, http://www.zdnet.com.au/newstech/news/story/0,2000025345,20103417,00.htm.
21   Chen, op. cit. fn. 12 at 2.

As the new Act applies the film classification system of the Classification Board to the Internet, it also implicitly adopts the objectives of the Board, as spelled out in its *Guidelines for the Classification of Films and Videotapes (Amendment No.2)* and s 11 of the *Classification (Publications, Films and Computer Games) Act 1995* described in Chapter 2. These provisions install the dialectic between adult freedom and child protection and fall back on 'community offence' and 'the moral standards of reasonable adults' as the standards of adjudication. They contain specific reference to sexual violence, portraying people in a 'demeaning manner' and the artistic merits of the text.

Fundamentally the *Broadcasting Services Amendment (Online Services) Act 1999* scheme is based on the premise that the Internet can be and should be regulated, that the role is shared between state and an ill defined 'industry' and that the existing principles of media classification are the appropriate means and objectives of regulating this new media form.

The *Broadcasting Services Amendment (Online Services) Act 1999* creates two primary instruments of regulation – an industry code of practice and a complaints mechanism. The Act contemplates an industry-created code of practice which creates standards for controlling user access, backed up by the threat of a state imposed standard if the codes are unsatisfactory. The complaints mechanism is aimed at removing prohibited content hosted on Australian servers. While there are already mechanisms for police removal of illegal material (such as child pornography) and prosecution of those involved under other legislation at federal and state level, the *Broadcasting Services Amendment (Online Services) Act 1999* contains powers to remove a broader scope of material and penalize those who facilitate its publication.

The Act applies solely to Internet Service Providers (ISPs) and Internet Content Hosts (ICHs); that is, those who provide services which allow access to the Internet and those who provide resources for hosting Internet content (often the same providers do both but these sometimes are separate functions). The presumption is that these providers are 'businesses' rather than communities and the scheme does not extend to very limited private networks. While the end result may be the same as censorship, this Act establishes a 'business practice' zone of regulation rather than one based on individual media consumption.

Users and content providers are not touched by the direct operation of the Act, although a more restrictive environment in which their ISPs and ICHs operate will have a flow-on 'chilling' effect on free speech. The scheme also supports an artificially constituted 'Internet industry' and by implication a dichotomy of the Internet as either legitimate business/broadcasting or an Internet underground which all service providers, content providers and users fall into.

Regulatory Mechanisms and Practices

It is necessary to consider the specific mechanisms of the legislation in order to understand how abstract objectives are implemented through application of state power. The scheme mandates four primary regulatory techniques as well as the general moral/educative function of legislation. These are the takedown notice procedure, the endorsement of an industry code of conduct, the state sanctioning of filtering services and the provision of funding to a watchdog agency.

The Takedown Notice Procedure

Under the co-regulatory scheme, liability is imposed on Internet Content Hosts (ICHs)[22] and Internet Service Providers (ISPs)[23] to observe notices issued by the ACMA concerning prohibited content.[24] Liability is not imposed on those who produce or view content.

---

22 Internet Content Host is not defined under the legislation, but seems to imply some kind of permanence which may not cover those who unknowingly participate in the chain of data transmission: Scott B (1999) *An Essential Guide to Internet Censorship in Australia*, http://www.gtlaw.com.au/pubs/essentialguidecensorship.html viewed (27/9/99). The legislation makes no distinction between public and privately hosted networks (ibid.) – while the ABA is unlikely to receive a complaint or be able to investigate private networks, it does not excuse the legislation from a failure to contemplate this situation. Any data on a storage device is capable of being accessed; so, potentially, keeping something on your own hard drive would be considered 'hosting' as it could be sent as an attachment (regardless of other areas of Act which exempt email from regulation). 'The combined effect [...] is to place all Internet users at risk of an investigation by the ABA'; Johnson A (1999) *Key Legal and Technical Problems with the Broadcasting Services Amendment (Online Services) Bill 1999*, http://www.securitysearch.net/search/papers/bsaprobs.htm).

23 Internet Service Provider is defined extremely broadly and fails to consider the physical and technological nature of the Internet carriage services. (Scott, op. cit. fn. 22) ISPs need only take all reasonable steps to prevent access (cl 37 of the Act) whereas an ICH has no such protection, (cl 28 of the Act) given the broad non-defined assumptions about what a host is.

24 Internet content does not include 'ordinary electronic mail' (but does include a posting to a newsgroup) or 'information that is transmitted in the form of a broadcasting service' (cl 3 of the Act), an indication that the Act is designed to contemplate convergence with digital television. The definition of 'content' is extremely broad and the email exception was only added after critics highlighted the application of the Act to private correspondence. The inclusion of the ill-defined 'push' technology in this clause means that anything capable of being attached to an email (everything on your computer except emails) might be captured by the Act, whether it is actually online or merely located on a hard drive (Scott, op. cit. fn. 22). It may be suggested that this was not the actual intent of Parliament but this highlights a risk of eventual use and indicates a lack of technological expertise underlying the drafting of the legislation. The legislation does not contemplate de-centred technologies of distribution, such as the delivery of newsgroup content.

Where sites are hosted by an Australian ISP, content classified as *RC* or *X* is considered 'prohibited content' and *R* rated material must be subject to 'adult verification' or it will also be considered prohibited content.[25] It seems that the means of accessing content transforms the nature of the content itself, or at least the legal meaning of the content.

On international sites accessed through an Australian ISP, *RC* or *X* rated material is considered to be prohibited content.[26] *R* rated material on international sites is unregulated.

The ACMA is appointed as content policing body and must investigate complaints about prohibited content or potential prohibited content.[27] Decisions of the ACMA may be appealed to the Administrative Appeals Tribunal.[28]

A person who believes an ICH is hosting *prohibited content* or *potential prohibited content* may make a complaint to the ACMA which must then investigate it.[29] In addition, a person who believes that an ICH or ISP has breached an industry code may also make a complaint.[30] The complaint must be in writing but there is nothing in the legislation which requires the complainant to be identified apart from a requirement for Australian residence[31] (a clause which seems to preclude totally anonymous complaints) and a general requirement that the ACMA can require further information from the complainant.[32] The ACMA may also investigate on its own initiative.[33]

Investigative powers are conferred on the ACMA by the *Broadcasting Services Act 1992* Part 13, which are the existing powers of the authority, not modified by the *Broadcasting Services Amendment (Online Services) Act 1999* amendments. The final determination of the investigation depends on the local or international location of the site in question, as explained below. In either case, the ACMA may notify domestic and international law enforcement agencies of sites although the conditions under which this is to be done are not spelled out beyond the requirement that they be 'sufficiently serious.'[34]

---

25   Broadcasting Services Act 1992 Schedule 5 cl 10(1).
26   Ibid. cl 10(2).
27   Ibid. Schedule 5 Part 4. The Broadcasting Act 1992 Schedule 5 cl11 defines potential prohibited content as content which has not been classified by the Board but if it were to be classified 'there is a substantial likelihood that the content would be prohibited content'.
28   Ibid. schedule 5 cl 92.
29   Ibid. cl 22.
30   Ibid. cl 23.
31   Ibid. cl 25.
32   Ibid. cl 22(3)(e).
33   Ibid. cl 27.
34   Ibid. cl 40(1)(a), (8)–(10).

Content Hosted in Australia

If the ACMA is satisfied that an ISP is hosting prohibited content it must issue a 'notification of content' along with 'final take-down notice' (which is operationally an *order*, expressed in the more benign seeming term 'notice').[35] In the case where potential prohibited content is possibly *X* or *RC* rated and which is hosted in Australia, an interim take-down order may be issued until the content has been formally rated by the OFLC Classification Board.[36] *R* rated material hosted in Australia is considered below in the discussion of Approved Adult Verification Systems.

Penalties are set under the 'Online Provider Rules'[37] (discussed below) for failure to comply with interim[38] and final[39] takedown notices, presently A$5,500 per day.

International Content

If content is hosted outside Australia, the ACMA may notify ISPs through approved industry code procedures (or failing this by a *standard access prevention notice*).[40] Given the volume of prohibited content sites available internationally, to notify all Australian ISPs of each international site would be prohibitive, so in practice only the commercial publishers of filtering software are notified. Of course as this only applies to sites which the ACMA has received a complaint about or has discovered in its own Internet surveillance, most content is unregulated.

An ISP need not adhere to this notification procedure if the end user uses 'a recognized alternative access-prevention arrangement' (declared in writing by the ACMA).[41] This term is further defined[42] to include software filtering on the client's computer or a filtered ISP service. Just how the ISP is able to determine if their clients are using filtering software is not detailed, but the codes suggest they need only give clients an opportunity to purchase software, which need not be more than a mere advertising link.[43] Penalties for failure to comply are provided under the Online Provider Rules[44] at the same rate as other breaches.

---

35   Ibid. cl 30.
36   Ibid. cl 30(2)(a).
37   Ibid. cl 79.
38   Ibid. cl 37(1).
39   Ibid. cl 37(2).
40   Ibid. cl 40.
41   Ibid. cl 40(4)–(7).
42   Ibid. cl 40(6).
43   Internet Industry Association (1999a) *Internet Industry Codes of Practice*, December 1999 cl 7.9, Schedule 1: Approved Filters.
44   Broadcasting Services Act 1992 op. cit. fn. 25, cl 48.

Australian 'R' Sites and Approved Adult Verification Systems

The ACMA may, by written instrument, declare that an adult verification service has the status of *restricted access system*[45] which means *R* rated material may be hosted if access is limited by such a system.[46] The legislation introduces the concept of adult verification systems[47] which the ACMA can approve for access to *R* rated material, hosted in Australia. The legislation does not define these systems and leaves them to be determined by the ACMA. On 7 December 1999, the ABA (ACMA's predecessor) made a written determination of the minimum requirements for adult verification in a declaration which was tabled in Parliament.[48] In the process of deciding on these procedures, the ABA did consider existing identity and age verification procedures (financial institutions' 100 point identity checks, tax file numbers, documentary identification) and unsurprisingly found these to be unsatisfactory. According to the then ABA chairman David Flint, the declaration 'provides commercial certainty' and is 'consistent with Internet practices used throughout the world.'[49]

There are indeed existing adult verification practices used but these have developed out of commercial enterprises in the adult industry. So far, Australia is the only government to annex these systems as a part of a scheme of state regulation. Age verification services[50] require a payment of a membership fee in

---

45 *Restricted access system* is ill-defined under cl 4. It can be anything which the ABA declares to be so. It is unclear if this refers to content filtering, age check validation or both. Reference is made to a 'recognised alternative access prevention arrangement' under cl 40 (4)–(6) which applies solely to filtering software or services but this need not restrict the general reading of this term.

46 Ibid. cl 4(1).

47 *Adult verification* is a form of site security by which adults can gain access to a passcode for certain sites, usually in exchange for a fee. Age is generally verified by ownership of a credit card. Of course the passcode can be easily passed on to others but these commercial services are wary of abuse such as posting codes to newsgroups and revoke membership under these conditions. As yet, the only examples of adult verification system use are limited to pornographic sites. The increasing importance of the credit card as an identity document demonstrates a significant shift away from state control of identity and citizenship documentation.

48 Australian Broadcasting Authority (1999a) 'Restricted Access Systems Declaration (No. 1) made under the Broadcasting Services Act 1992', 7 December.

49 Ibid.

50 Some examples of adult verification systems include: Adultcheck (http://www.adultcheck.com), Freenetpass (http://www.freenetpass.com), Gaypassport (http://www.gaypassport.com), 4 Women AVS (http://www.4womenavs.com), Hentai Key (http://www.hentaikey.com), Male Ticket (http://www.maleticket.com), Age Ticket (http://www.ageticket.com), Certifier (http://www.certifier.com), Pro Adult (http://www.proadult.com), Mansights (http://www.mansights.com), Adults Allowed (http://www.adultsallowed.com), Sex Key (http://www.sexkey.com), Cyber AVS (http://www.cyberavs.com), Universal Gay Adult Sites (http://www.ugas.com), Free Gay AVS (http://www.freegayavs.com), Universal

order to gain access to affiliated sites via the provision of a username/password. The member's age is checked via credit card details. Part of the membership fee is sometimes passed on to sites using the age verification system, and there seems to be a variety of commercial permutations. There is also an important advertising impact of having a site indexed with an age verification service home page, or placed on its update list of newly added sites. This approach does not lend itself to other 'adult' content where consumers are unlikely to pay to see, such as a designer's online portfolio or a suicide advice page.

Further, the civil libertarians are concerned that the system is unfeasible. As the Project 1984 website emphatically states, 'PIN systems on porn sites will not work – as was proved with 0051 numbers. People do not want to be on a "pervert's database", risking breaches of privacy when they can surf overseas sites anonymously.'[51]

While the adult verification services are primarily of a commercial character, there is an important aspect of industry self governance and responsibility involved – keeping children away from material which content creators believe should be age restricted. Claims that the service is solely a profit making enterprise ignore the complexities of the commercial situation and the ethical practices of pornographic media creators,[52] all too easily demonized along with porn spammers.

Yee raises some difficulties with using 'restricted access' services: the technical features might not be available to small servers, the check process acts as a deterrent, search engines will not identify content and the complexity of rating a site which may have an *R* rating in different categories. 'The only sites that can work under such a scheme are those with "magnet" content, such as genuine pornography sites. Few sites with *R*-rated material will survive.'[53]

Endorsement of Industry Codes

The Act contemplates but only partially successfully implements a co-regulatory scheme which involves multiple state agencies and industry self governance.[54] The Internet Industry Association (the IIA), which has been 'deputized' as the industry representative body, sees its role in damage control, watering down the harshest aspects of the legislation, claiming that due to its arguments and involvement in

---

Passport (http://www.universalpass.com), and many more. Other adult sites charge for use and verify age for themselves through credit card details.

51 Quoted in Reynolds Technology (1999) *Project 1984*, http://www.rts.com.au/projects/1984.

52 While often the victims of stereotyping, the creators of pornographic media represent a broad spectrum of ethical responsibility and practice. McKee A, Albury K, Lumby C (2008) *The Porn Report*, Melbourne University Press: Melbourne pp 166–81.

53 Yee D (1999b) *The Effects on Content Providers*, http://www.anatomy.usyd.edu.au/danny/freedom/99/content–providers.html.

54 Chen, op. cit. fn. 24.

the policy process and drafting of the Act 'the Government knocked some of the sharp edges off it.'[55]

Obligations Imposed on ISPs

Beyond the investigative/policing role, the ACMA has also been appointed as the approval body for industry codes of practice.[56] This portion of the Act is interesting, as it is in many ways a tacit acknowledgment of the limits of regulation and the importance of other regulatory discourses in a world of de-centred control. It also recognizes the IIA as a regulatory community, an alternative to the monolithic 'community values' envisioned elsewhere in the scheme. Theory in the disciplines of sociology and criminology suggests that the best systems of control are voluntary where norms are internalized.[57] Even though the co-regulatory part of the scheme pays lips service to self governance discourse, it nevertheless seeks to submit the industry regulatory regime to the authority of the state, a move which undermines the efficacy of such systems.

The co-regulatory system shifts the burden onto ISPs to enforce the legislation and places power into the hands of bodies described as 'industry representatives'. The scheme allows for the creation of Internet codes (at least one, no more than two[58]) and, failing that, a state imposed set of Internet standards.[59] These terms are not defined precisely, and standards are described rather circularly as codes and standards developed under the Act.[60]

It seems that codes are created by 'bodies and organizations' (of a hybrid private/public character) and are voluntary unless the ACMA issues an order to comply. The term 'standards' seems to refer to the regulatory instruments imposed by the ACMA in the event that a code fails to appear or is deemed to be insufficient by the ACMA. This threat is held over the industry bodies and Part 5 Division 5 has extensive and complex mechanisms for the ACMA to take over the process of 'self regulation' (with some required public/industry consultation).[61]

Clause 60 lists matters which *must* be dealt with by industry codes and standards, for 'both sections of the Internet industry' (presumably ISPs and ICHs, although this is a rather narrow reading of what the 'Internet industry' encompasses).[62]

---

55   ZDNet Australia, op. cit. fn. 20.
56   *Broadcasting Services Act 1992* op. cit. fn. 25 Schedule 5 Part 5.
57   'Containment Theory' describes the process of norm internalization as 'inner containment' involving self concept, goal orientation, frustration tolerance and norm retention. Reckless WC (1967) *The Crime Problem* 4th edn., Meredith: New York.
58   *Broadcasting Services Act 1992* op. cit. fn. 25 cl 59(1) and (2).
59   Ibid.
60   Ibid. cl 53–4.
61   Ibid. cl 76–7.
62   Ibid. cl 56.

One immediate problem with the codes of practice concept is the process of identifying 'industry representatives'. Even merely counting on those who earn their livings from Internet service provision and content creation (which ignores the large numbers of Internet creators who are otherwise employed and contribute content in a personal capacity), it is impossible to establish who represents 'the industry'. This is a situation quite unlike the professions which are administered through licensing schemes. The assumption of a single set of representatives reveals the simplistic monocultural and commercial-oriented mindset under which the legislation was conceived and under which it is enforced on unwilling regulatory objects.

Of course, the Internet Industry Association (the IIA) was already positioned to assume the mantle of the voice of the Australian Internet because of its early formation and the involvement of its chair, Peter Coroneos, in the policy and law reform process. The IIA is an association of fee paying members who 'provide services on or to the Internet'[63] and pay on a scale according to their Internet related income. A person who does not earn an income from the Internet is nevertheless required to pay an annual fee of A$250, a pricing which excludes the most numerous voices on the Internet. While it is not unreasonable that an 'industry' body should focus on commercial and professional interests, it is wrong to make the assumption (as the legislation does) that this organization is 'the voice' of the Australian Internet community generally.

> The Internet Industry Association is Australia's national Internet industry organization. Members include telecommunications carriers; content creators and publishers; web developers; e-commerce traders; banks, insurance underwriters; Internet law firms, ISPs; educational and training institutions; Internet research analysts; and a range of other businesses providing professional and technical support services. On behalf of its members, the IIA provides policy input to government and advocacy on a range of business and regulatory issues, to promote laws and initiatives which enhance access, equity, reliability and growth of the medium in Australia.[64]

The objectives of the IIA similarly reflect the business orientation of the organization but include '5. to promote laws which facilitate unrestricted and open use of the Internet.'[65] This may be contrasted with '6. sponsor and co-ordinate the creation of independent organizations to service and regulate the Internet'[66] which seems to include regulation by bodies such as the IIA within the notion of free use; that is, 'freedom' is a concept challenged only by Government power.

---

    63   Internet Industry Association (1999b) *About the IIA*, http://www.iia.net.au/join.html.
    64   Ibid.
    65   Ibid.
    66   Ibid.

The IIA has been keen to represent itself not as a co-regulatory body as such but as a watchdog/user interest group. Sensitive about the 'censorship' label, the IIA's 'Guide for Internet Users' states 'The focus of the IIA's approach is on facilitating "end-user empowerment" by providing Australian Internet users with both the tools and information by which they can take greater control for content accessible via the Net'.[67] The organization is keen to emphasize that its role under the regulatory partnership is the soft rule of information and advice, not the hard rule of government.

The early development of regulatory culture is crucial: decisions can have wide impacts in the future. A comparative analysis of the invention and regulation of radio technology provides a salient lesson in the capacity of regulation to smother democratic potential.[68]

The Scope of the Internet Industry Codes of Practice

The codes actually comprise of three sets of principles, each corresponding closely to the source legislation:

> *Content Code 1: ISP Obligations in Relation to Internet Access Generally;*
> *Content Code 2: ISP Obligations in Relation to Access to Content Hosted Outside Australia;* and
> *Content Code 3: Internet Content Host Obligations in Relation to Hosting of Content Within Australia.*

The codes focus on the voluntary use of filtering software on the user's computer or the use of a filtered service, and continually emphasize the voluntary issue, without of course acknowledging the enforcement part of the scheme which is the responsibility of their government partners. This notwithstanding, the IIA points out its own elevated regulatory status, that the code is 'effectively law.'[69]

The Internet Industry Codes of Practice[70] provide, in summary:

- ISPs are responsible to provide information to their customers on their options for filtering and the complaints scheme of the ACMA;
- ISPs are likewise obliged to give information to content providers who use their hosting services regarding the law and their responsibilities;

---

67   Internet Industry Association (2000) *Guide for Internet Users: Information about Online Content*, http://www.iia.net.au/guideuser.html.
68   Spinell M (1996) 'Radio Lessons for the Internet', *Postmodern Culture*, v6:2, http://muse.jhu.edu/journals/postmodern_culture/v006/6.2spinelli.html (viewed 20/9/01).
69   guideuser.html.
70   Internet Industry Association, op. cit. fn. 43.

- ISPs should not provide accounts for users under 18 years of age without a parent/guardian's consent. This should be checked by a credit card, identification process, a notice on packaging which informs a young user should obtain consent or secure an undertaking of age/consent from the user in the registration process. This caters for a range of strategies, at different levels of enforceability;
- ISPs should provide subscribers with an *Approved Filter*, at a cost determined by the ISP, passed on to the subscriber. This can be done on an installation disk, online or a notice directing the user to a download site. The user's compliance does not seem to be surveilled. Allowance is made for commercial subscribers who use firewalls on their network, including an obligation for the ISP to provide advice;
- ISPs should encourage content providers to use a labelling system of rating;
- ISPs should have procedures to deal with complaints regarding the filtering of unsolicited email which advertises 'offensive' content but there are no obligations regarding spam mail generally;
- If the ISP becomes aware that another ISP is hosting prohibited content, they are obliged to inform that ISP by email, but there is no obligation to inform to the ACMA;
- If the ISP is given a notice under the Act regarding information on its server, it is obliged to comply (which it would be anyway, outside of these rules) and also to inform the customer that the conduct constitutes breach of the service contract (but there seems to be no obligation to go any further).

State Sanctioning of Filtering Services

Chapter 2 discussed the filtering/labelling debate which has divided Internet users internationally. The co-regulatory scheme embraces the concept of filtering as its primary thrust, relying on consumers to implement filtering as a technique of self-governance, keeping prohibited content (and other filtered content) from reaching their computers. The legislation is backed up by the IIA codes which are in turn supported by the legislation's 'online provider rules.'[71]

Schedule 1 of the industry codes provides a list of Approved Filters which may run on the user's computer or through the ISP's server. It is necessary for ISPs to provide access to filters (which can be a simple hypertext link on the ISP's home page), customers are not required to actually install or use them. The costs of filtering are passed on to consumers who must subscribe to the commercial service. The legislation provides dividends for Approved Filter suppliers; Australia

---

71 *Broadcasting Services Act 1992* op. cit. fn. 25 cl 79.

is said to lead the world in the growth of the lucrative filter market.[72] Nevertheless, it seems that most users do not use filters and are not interested in filtering their Internet service.[73]

Funding to a Watchdog Agency

As a part of its package of reform, the Commonwealth Government established Netalert, a Government corporation designed to be an 'independent' net surveillance body, with a A$3 million annual budget, to be based in Hobart. It is unclear what 'independent' means in the context of a Government corporation funded out of public monies. It was launched on 26 November 1999: its Board includes a high school principal (the chair), IIA senior representatives, a state librarian, a lawyer, a computer store owner, an OPTUS Policy manager and several representatives of lobby groups concerned with child education and welfare.[74]

Netalert's scope of operations include 'educating communities about managing access to online content', researching access management techniques and running national awareness programmes, and 'empowering parents'.[75] Initial claims that this body would monitor Internet material, operate a hotline and pass complaints along to the ACMA and police authorities[76] have not been realized, perhaps due to their politically controversial tenor.

At first Netalert's public profile was cautious. In connection with Netalert, the Department of Communications, Information Technology and the Arts also launched a glossy two page 'family's guide for managing access to the Internet' which provided little more than advertising for the ACMA complaints mechanisms.[77] More recent publications indicate a shift away from the watchdog role to more of a public information emphasis. In 2003 the Netalert website de-emphasized the role of censorship and dealt mainly with media literacy, user empowerment and strategies for managing spam and pop-up windows.[78] Suggestions on the website include keeping computers in open family spaces, introducing children to child-specific sites, use of security and anti-spam software, joining a user group and

---

72 ZDNet (2001) 'Australian censorship leads Web filter market growth', 18 September, http://www.zdnet.com.au/newstech/enterprise/story/0,2000025001,20260515,00.htm (viewed 2/2/02).

73 Wardill S (2002) 'Code to push Internet out of reach', *Courier Mail*, 13 May.

74 Department of Communications, Information Technology and the Arts Press Release (1999a) 'Internet Content Advisory Board Announced', 26 November.

75 Ibid.

76 Department of Communications, Information Technology and the Arts Media Release (1999b) 'Regulation of Objectionable Online Material', 5 October.

77 Australian Broadcasting Authority (2000) *Australian Families Guide to the Internet*, http://www.aba.gov.au/family (viewed 29/2/00).

78 see for example http://www.netalert.net.au/Files/00719_HowdoIstopPornandPopUps.asp (viewed 14/7/03).

'ensure grandparents, neighbours, babysitters and other family friends know your safe surfing policies, so they are part of the solution, not part of the problem'.[79]

The choice of a Tasmanian base of operations coincides with the fact that this is anti-pornography campaigner Senator Harradine's state (and, it has been alleged, the state locus for a disproportionate amount of Government employee access to pornographic material).[80] The fact that Netalert is explicitly funded out of 'Telstra social bonus funding' endorses this suggestion, given the political background of the scheme.[81]

Responses to the Act

The amendments to the *Broadcastings Services Act 1992* have drawn stern criticism from civil rights activists. Electronic Frontiers Australia (the EFA) has described the scheme as 'one of the most draconian Net censorship proposals the world has seen.'[82] Similarly, the head of the American Civil Liberties Union, Professor Strossen, criticized the Australian Act as 'draconian', comparing it to censorious practices in Malaysia and Singapore. Further, Strossen highlights the importance of freedom of speech by reference to the experience of Holocaust survivors and anti-Semitic policies.[83]

Critiques of the regulatory scheme can be divided into roughly five interconnected critiques: a rights critique, empirical challenges to its effectiveness, challenge to the definitions and metaphors used (which seem to suggest technical ignorance), the impossibility of the notion of 'community standards' and a specific challenge to the concept of filtering.

The Scheme Contravenes Civil and Political Rights

Restrictions on free speech rights are inevitably felt, first and foremost, by vulnerable groups, already struggling to protect their civil and political rights. The Australian Council for Lesbian and Gay Rights (ACLGR) criticized the co-regulatory scheme, arguing that it is likely to target queer sites, even those

---

79 Ibid.

80 See, generally, Taylor B (2000a) *The Bernadette List: Australian Government Viewing Porn*, http://www.prairie–dog.net/Blist.htm (viewed 22/4/00).

81 For details of the political situation, see Graham I (1999b) *The Debate: Government Control or Individual Responsibility*, http://rene.efa.org.au/liberty/debate.html (viewed 22/4/00).

82 Electronic Frontiers Australia (1999a) *Internet Regulation in Australia*, http://www.efa.org.au/Issues/Censor/cens1.html.

83 *Uninews*, 'Internet Censorship Laws Condemned', (Vol.8 No.30), 30 August 1999.

providing support services and health information.[84] The use of abstract community standards is a practice which reifies majoritarianism and excludes to the margins anyone who can be labelled as different in some way.

While there is no constitutionally recognized right to free speech in Australia, except for narrowly defined political speech,[85] freedom of speech is often taken for granted in its political culture, perhaps due to the influence of United States legal and popular culture.

The Internet censorship scheme has even attracted strong criticism from within the Liberal party. The South Australian branch of the party passed a resolution that home-based filtering by parents would be enough and that the legislation was unworkable, harmful to investment in the communications sector and should be repealed. According to Young Liberals SA branch president Angus Bristow: 'The legislation was "a sub-optimal solution, possibly even a negative solution", he said, and in some ways went against Liberal principles of light-touch government.'[86]

Most of the criticisms of the scheme posit a libertarian model of rights which is opposed to controls on communications media. This rhetoric of liberty was invoked by Howard Rheingold referring to the United States *Communications Decency Act 1996*:

> Democracy is what's at stake. It doesn't have anything to do with protecting children from pornography, because there are better ways to do that. It's about power to determine what people are allowed to say, write and believe. It's not about obscenity. We already have a decades-old body of case law about obscenity. This new 'decency' jive outlaws portions of the Holy Bible. People need to understand that this is not about sex, it's about the foundations of democracy. If citizens are not literate or don't have the freedom of open, uncensored public communications, they are incapable of self-government. Communication power is political power, because the power to influence the beliefs and perceptions of populations has proven to be the most effective political weapon of the century.[87]

Similar libertarian attitudes are prominent in the critique of the Australian Internet censorship scheme. Reynolds Technology's *Project 1984*[88] protested the construction of the *Broadcasting Services Amendment (Online Services) Act 1999*

---

84 ZDNet Australia (1999b) 'Gay community lashes Net censorship proposal', 5 May, http://www.zdnet.com.au/newstech/news/story/0,200002534,20103359,00.htm.

85 In Australia, free speech is limited to political broadcasting prior to an election. *Nationwide News Pty Ltd v Wills* (1992) 175 CLR 1, *Australian Capital Television Pty Ltd v The Commonwealth (no 2)* (1992) 177 CLR 106, *Lange v Australian Broadcasting Corporation* (1997) 190 CLR 520.

86 Quoted in Sinclair J (1999a) 'Net censorship under fire', *The Age*, 24 August.

87 Rheingold H (1996) *Democracy is About Communication*, http://www.well.com/user/hir/texts/democracy.html (viewed 27/7/01).

88 Reynolds Technology (1999) *Project 1984*, http://www.rts.com.au/projects/1984.

regulatory scheme by drawing comparisons to the totalitarian world of Orwell's novel, and by sending a copy of the novel to all Federal Members of Parliament. The *Project 1984* site does highlight a very pertinent point of intersection regarding the use of filters. First it quotes Orwell:

> By a routine that was not even secret, all letters were opened in transit ... Don't you see that the whole aim of Newspeak is to narrow the range of thought? In the end we shall make thought crime literally impossible because there will be no words with which to express it ... Every year fewer and fewer words and the range of consciousness always a little smaller.[89]

Reynolds Technology then goes on to suggest that the *Broadcasting Services Amendment (Online Services) Act 1999* amendments reflect a regime comparable to the 1984 paradigm in several ways: intrusion on private communications, the use of strawman problems (cyber threats and moral panics) and a bureaucratized regime. The most interesting of these critiques, however, is the parallels between the concept of filtering and 1984 Newspeak, control by the elimination of problematic words.[90]

Within libertarian discourse, frequent reference is made to 'the government's real intent', the legislation being depicted as a 'smokescreen'.[91] Graham, as with many of the libertarian activists, uses the conspiracy metaphor frequently, partially because of its historical importance in the liberal discourse of individual rights vs government oppression and partially because it is an effective rhetorical device to motivate public resistance.

> 'This legislation is about porn', they say. They are wrong. They have been blinded by a smokescreen. This legislation is about blocking the free flow of adult discourse on social and political issues.[92]

It is difficult to establish a singular clear agenda from the law reform process itself. The haste with which the legislation was passed has been a source of concern and critique, particularly the perfunctory nature of the public consultation process.[93] The legislation was passed through Parliament merely two months after being made available (to Parliament *and* the public), and the public inquiry by the Senate Select Committee on Information Technologies lasted a mere two and a half weeks from announcement to closure to final report (requests for extension of time were denied by Government).

---

89 Orwell G (1964) *1984*, New American Library, New York. This quote was selected and condensed by Reynolds Technology, ibid.

90 Reynolds Technology, op. cit. fn. 87.

91 See for example Graham I (1999a) *Blinded by Smoke: The Hidden Agenda of the Online Services Bill 1999*, http://rene.efa.org.au/liberty/blinded.html.

92 Ibid.

93 see, for example, Graham, op. cit. fn. 81.

Some commentators have suggested that the legislation was rushed through Parliament because the Government wished to obtain the vote of Senator Brian Harradine (who held the balance of power in the Senate prior to 1 July 1999) on its controversial Goods and Services Tax (GST) and sale of Telstra legislation. While this may in part be true, the Government had been threatening Internet censorship legislation for several years and has a record of increasing censorship of all media. It may equally well have been concerned about difficulties in passing draconian censorship legislation once the balance of power in the Senate passed to the Democrat Party on 1 July 1999 (the outcome of the October 1998 Federal election).[94]

This contention is supported by a Senate resolution on 30 September 1999, after the balance of power had passed to the Democrats, which acknowledged the criticism of the *Broadcasting Services Amendment (Online Services) Act 1999* amendments and called for the Government to address its concerns.[95]

Civil libertarians argue, further, that the legislation will not achieve its aims and may even worsen the problems that it claims to be addressing. Graham has also acknowledged the irony that target hardening may simply create a more challenging site of resistance:

> [The scheme is] highly likely to result in objectionable material becoming more readily accessible to children. If blocking technologies are used in an attempt to prevent adults accessing information, it is beyond doubt that circumvention technologies will become more widely developed, deployed, advertised and known, to both adults and children. The government would then be able to take credit for having 'done something' – encouraged the invention of a new and mildly challenging computer game.[96]

Of course the dilemma of power created resistance is not unique to the regulation of electronic media. The challenge presented in overcoming regulation is not in itself a reason to abandon regulatory measures per se. This perspective, however, acknowledges the fact that the very mechanisms of regulation can be the source of resistance and transgression has appeal in itself. This resistance is common across all regulatory fields (for example, criminal law or tax law) and the moral ambiguity of Internet censorship coupled with the individualist hacker culture results in regulatory mechanisms and technologies being seen as puzzles to solve rather than actual standards to believe in and internalize.

Exercise of power does not only produce resistance; it also asserts control and shapes the social fabric. Media and communications lawyer Brendan Scott is concerned about the 'police state' tactics used in the Act; the fact that complainants remain anonymous and invulnerable and that the ACMA is not required to notify an ICH of a complaint, an investigation or the result of an

---

94 Ibid.
95 Senate Motion 30 September 1999.
96 Graham, op. cit. fn. 91.

unsuccessful investigation. All show a lack of due process required under the liberal legal model of government.[97]

Many of the online protest sites adopt a similar posture, raising freedom of speech and urging protest and the lobbying of Parliament for legislative change. Sex entrepreneur and activist Bernadette Taylor's *Prairie Dog* site ('the cutest Internet watchdog') opts for a different form of resistance:

> Obviously it's important to lobby Govt (both ours AND foreign) ... and the EFA are doing a great job of this. However, personally I've never found that to be all too effective. I find that very few listen to opinion unless it supports them. My approach is somewhat different.
>
> This Bill relies on making ISPs do everything technically feasible to block offensive material ... so let's make it easy for you to make it technically *impossible* for them to block you. This can be done at both the user level and the web master level.[98]

Taylor's approach is two fold: to shame the Government and also to advise net users of technological methods of circumventing the legislation and developing more cautious Internet privacy management strategies. In the latter situation, one of the beneficial outcomes of a scheme of regulation is to force people to become more knowledgeable about the technologies which they use.

The shaming aspect of this strategy originates in Taylor's role as the web master of commercial pornography sites. Noting that many clients were accessing her sites from Government IP addresses, Taylor published a list of the IPs, the Government departments from which they originated but not the personal details of the individuals involved (each proxy could be accessed by a number of people within each department).

This move was not done to condemn the Government access to pornography but rather to illustrate the unworkability of the scheme by showing how the Government could not even regulate or monitor the conduct of its own members and employees, let alone the rest of the country. The move received local and international news coverage.[99]

The Prairie Dog list covers over 90 Government departments and is being continuously updated, even after the *Broadcasting Services Amendment (Online Services) Act 1999* amendments came into force. The list covers departments from all levels of Government (including Parliament House), from areas as diverse

---

97 Scott B (1999b) *The Dawn of a New Dark Age – Censorship and Amendments to the Broadcasting Services Act*, http://www.gtlaw.com.au/pubs/newdarkage.html.

98 Taylor B (1999) *Prairie Dog: The Cutest Internet Watchdog*, http://www.prairie-dog.net/.

99 Sinclair J (1999b) 'Sex sites and the gov.au connection' *Fairfax IT*, 7 June.

as Nuclear Science and Technology, the Bureau of Meteorology, Centrelink, DEETYA, even the DCITA itself.[100] Taylor notes that:

> I have made Senator Alston's office aware of this matter but his response was to say all these people are conducting research or came to the sites by accident ... well I can assure you that they aren't doing either judging by the viewing patterns!!![101]

While Taylor has kept the server logs, she refuses to disclose individuals involved, except under a compulsion by a subpoena. The response from DCITA has been less than satisfactory:

> A spokesman for the Communications Minister, Richard Alston, said that he could not see what her point was and suggested she should forward the list to the relevant agencies.[102]

Privacy rights are also threatened by the scheme. Graham challenges the use of a credit card as the foundation of an adult verification service on these grounds; the fact that a card number or password does not ensure that an adult is using the card (a borrowed or stolen card/code), the fact that adult verification services make a profit from the service 'a money making exercise for porn web site providers', the service is impractical and costly for those providing non-pornographic adult content, that consumers are unlikely to pay to view non-pornographic adult content and finally she raises privacy concerns.[103]

Other rights are likewise in jeopardy. Yee raises concerns that the legislation contains no protection for the rights of net consumers such as privacy, the freedom to read and the freedom to publish:[104]

> Especially worrying in this regard is the clause of the Bill (section [sic] 84) indemnifying service providers and content hosts from civil proceedings in respect of anything done to comply with the Bill's take-down or access blocking requirements.[105]

As already noted, the EFA has become increasingly concerned at the secretive practices adopted under the *Broadcasting Services Amendment (Online Services) Act 1999* scheme, as the Commonwealth Government has changed the Freedom of

---

    100   Taylor, op. cit. fn. 79.
    101   Ibid.
    102   Sinclair, op. cit. fn. 99.
    103   Graham, op. cit. fn. 92.
    104   Yee D (1999c) *Consumer Rights*, http://www.anatomy.usyd.edu.au/danny/freedom/99/consumers.html.
    105   Yee, op. cit. fn. 53.

Information laws[106] to exclude Internet censorship decisions from review.[107] This move was seen as inflammatory by civil libertarians and seems to reflect a certain squeamishness about the censor's role. The Administrative Appeals Tribunal shares these concerns and has criticized the ABA for its closed-government practices.[108]

The Government has also drawn attention to the moral aspects of the scheme with Senator Alston proclaiming that lesbianism was 'not normal'[109] and therefore outside of the concept of community. 'The Government, in alienating homosexuals and ignoring the concerns of the Jewish community regarding "hate speech" and the Internet, showed its predilection for slighting the views of "special interests", regardless of their legitimacy.'[110]

The Scheme is Ineffectual and Costly

> Apart from the questionable morality of the proposed legislation [...] The most glaring problem of all is that the legislation is unlikely to achieve its objectives of restricting and/or censoring Internet content.[111]

> The *Online Services Act* is a largely ineffectual and wasteful piece of legislation. Unnecessarily long and complex, it applies a regulatory model designed for oligopoly media models to a pluralistic communications medium.[112]

In the year 2000 the Internet censorship scheme saw only 67 takedown notices (from 22 complainants) with a total administrative and staffing cost of A$616,319.[113] This figure includes payment to OFLC of classification fees of A$85,040.[114] In the first six months of operations, Netalert spent A$255,430.[115] In 2002, the entire Internet regulation scheme came up for review with the publication of an issues paper by DCITA.[116] The paper describes some of the statistics by which the scheme was benchmarked:

---

106 Communications Legislation Amendment Bill 2002.
107 http://www.efa.org.au/Issues/Censor/cens1.html.
108 *Electronic Frontiers Australia v Australian Broadcasting Authority* (Q2000/979), 12 June 2002.
109 Rollins A (1999) 'Alston Brands Lesbians "Not Normal"', *The Age*, 26 May.
110 Chen, op. cit. fn. 12 at 3.
111 Johnson, op. cit. fn. 22.
112 Chen, op. cit. fn. 12 at 1.
113 Chen, op. cit.op. fn. 14 at 3.
114 Chen, op. cit. fn. 14 at fn. 13.
115 Netalert (2000) *Netalert Limited: Report for the Period 6 December 1999 to 30 June 2000*, Netalert: Hobart.
116 Department of Communications, Information Technology and the Arts (2002) *A Review of the Operation of Schedule 5 to the Broadcasting Services Act 1992*, Canberra.

- In the first two years of the scheme, the ABA received 937 complaints, two of which were found to be vexatious and in 168 instances insufficient information was provided by complainants;
- Of the remainder, 487 items lead to finding of prohibited content, 227 of these related to Australian sites;
- Filtering services were notified of 529 items;
- 492 items were claimed to involve child pornography;[117] and
- Matters were referred to state police in 132 instances, the federal police in 353 instances.[118]

It is unclear what constitutes an 'item' in this report – does a single URL within a larger site constitute an item or is the entire site contemplated? Does an 'item' cover more than one URL or one site? It is also unclear what is to be made of the five items which were defined as child pornography but not prohibited content.

The EFA provided substantial critique to the inquiry, in summary:

- The lack of practical, empirical evidence that the Act has achieved the purpose of making the Internet safer for Australian children;
- The expense of investigating/classifying overseas websites, when all the ACMA can do is notify filtering services which ought to already know;
- Concerns about the secrecy surrounding ACMA operations, and their refusal to provide a list of banned sites;
- Erroneous statistics;
- Misleading statements about child pornography;
- The differential regulation where material that is legal offline is illegal online;
- The OFLC costs for classification: a web page costs approximately five times the fee for an offline magazine;
- Restriction of online publishers' rights of appeal;
- The lack of information about successful prosecutions resulting from information given to police; and

---

117 This number 'bears no resemblance to numbers previously claimed in government reports', http://www.efa.org.au/Publish/efasubm_bsa2002.html. Previous reports include Minister for Communications, Information Technology and the Arts (2000) *Six Month Report on Co-Regulatory Scheme for Internet Content Regulation*, tabled September; Minister for Communications, Information Technology and the Arts (2001) *Six Month Report on Co-Regulatory Scheme for Internet Content Regulation: July to December 2000*, tabled April; Minister for Communications, Information Technology and the Arts (2002a) *Six Month Report on Co-Regulatory Scheme for Internet Content Regulation: January to June 2001*, tabled February; Minister for Communications, Information Technology and the Arts (2002b) *Six Month Report on Co-Regulatory Scheme for Internet Content Regulation: Reporting Period 4: July to December 2001*, tabled August.

118 Department of Communications, Information Technology and the Arts (2002), op. cit. fn. 116 at pp 8–10.

- The estimated A$2.7 million annual cost of the scheme, given its lack of proof of practical outcomes.[119]

The hosting aspect of the scheme can be easily avoided by moving sites to international servers, even if they retain their .au address. This issue arose soon after the legislation came into force, with the movement of Teenager.com.au to a United States server.[120] Sasha Grebe, a spokesperson for the DCITA, commented on the Teenager.com.au controversy:

> If this has been set up as an example of a flaw in the Government's legislation, it actually proves the opposite. [...] We set the legislation up to issue takedown notices to sites so they wouldn't be hosted in Australia. It's disappointing that people choose to do this, since the legislation attempts to bring the Internet into line with other media. It ignores the accepted norms, it ignores Australian standards.[121]

In defence of the incompleteness of the scheme, ABA Chairman Peter Webb has noted that 'our criminal justice system is a regulatory system which does not claim to be universally applied. We all know it doesn't bring to account every breach ...'.[122] Yet regulation within liberal legal systems is premised on the notion of universal application enshrined in the rule of law. These inconsistent legal geographies are explored in more depth in Chapter 4.

Webb's argument touches on an interesting aspect of regulatory theory – the incompleteness of regulation and need to embrace a certain amount of failure within all regulatory schemes. Caution, however, must be exercised. It has been argued that this kind of argument could lead to demands for new regulatory technologies to 'combat' the failure of the existing regulatory system.[123] The incompleteness of criminal justice regulation is used to establish an ideological beach head for 'law and order' campaigns to increase powers and remove rights on the basis of the system's own failures. Steinhardt, of the American Civil Liberties Union, discusses the potential for systems of self governance to be co-opted into strategies of target hardening, especially in the context of labelling:

> A lot of people in the industry believe they need to move towards this [self labelling] as a way to forestall further action by the US government [...] But the irony is that they are not going to forestall further government action. They

---

119   http://www.efa.org.au/Publish/efasubm_bsa2002.html.
120   Hayes S (2000) 'ABA fails to stop porn site', *Australian IT*, 8 June. See also Forbes M (1999) 'Porn sites head offshore to beat law', *Sydney Morning Herald*, 9 June.
121   Ibid.
122   ABA Chair Peter Webb quoted in Graham, op. cit. fn. 92.
123   Graham I (2000a) *The Net Labelling Delusion: Saviour or Devil*, http://rene.efa.org.au/liberty/label.htm.

are going to encourage it. They are going to create a road map for Congress for a system that requires by law that all sites be rated. Or that sites mis-rated be punished. And that is going to be a much more difficult constitutional question than any version of the CDA or son of CDA.[124]

If the Australian Internet censorship scheme is ineffectual, it is also costly. Costs of classification are paid for by the ACMA.[125] This has resourcing implications as well as income impacts on the Classification Board due to the sheer number of potential applications. This might also provide a site of resistance if the authority was to be flooded with complaints, imposing a considerable financial burden on the regulators, whether it is the OFLC or the ACMA which bears the eventual cost.

> Perhaps the most dangerous misconception about the Act is that it is a 'toothless tiger' in that, though it may be in place, it won't be enforced. This reaction has been fuelled in part by the perceived harshness of the Act in the Internet industry – if it is so bad, the thinking goes, it mustn't be intended to be enforced. [...] the legislation practically mandates the enforcement of its own provisions.[126]

Compounding its inefficiency, it has been argued that the principles of the legislation are legally flawed, making the wrong people liable for alleged misconduct. Scott compares the scheme to making the Post Office liable for materials sent through the mail, claiming that it is the legislative equivalent of 'shooting the messenger.'[127]

Danny Yee provides one of the most comprehensive set of anti-censorship resources and critiques of the Australian scheme.[128] Yee suggests that the legislation will cause 'collateral damage' by causing nervous ISPs to block entire areas of legitimate content rather than pay the stiff fines for allowing some prohibited content through.[129] Yee uses the example of an erotic stories archive, which contains stories of varying explicitness from tame to material which would be refused classification. The writers of the stories, along with the rest of the online community involved in similar pursuits, have developed their own tagging system, identifying the content type (rom – romance, nc – non consensual).[130]

This indicates that regulatory communities may exist independent of governmental regulatory culture. Much of the online erotic text material is comparable to material available in printed form without restriction in bookstores

---

124 Clausing J (1998) 'New Rules of Internet Content Fuel the Battle Over Filters', *New York Times Cybertimes*, 6 January.
125 *Broadcasting Services Act 1992* op. cit. fn. 25 cl 20.
126 Scott, op. cit. fn. 22.
127 Ibid.
128 At http://www.anatomy.usyd.edu.au/danny/freedom.
129 Yee D (1999d) *Classification and 'Collateral Damage'*, http://www.anatomy.usyd.edu.au/danny/freedom/99/classification.html.
130 Ibid.

and libraries (for instance the works of the Marquis de Sade are easily available offline). Yee suggests that the legislation is likely to cause panic responses with collateral damage falling across the spectrum, particularly where newsgroups are archived.

While the legislation attaches its enforcement provisions to service providers, Yee is keen to remind us that this has flow on effects for ordinary Internet content producers:

> Most Australian content-providers are not large corporations [... You] should picture an individual (perhaps a teenager with their own home page, a group of friends running a small online magazine (perhaps for fan fiction), or a small organization (perhaps providing resources and advice for the unemployed). There are hundreds if not thousands of such content-providers for every NineMSN or Fairfax.[131]

Further, Graham argues that the IIA does not represent these providers; it is:

> ... an organisation whose membership includes only 60 of Australia's some 700 ISPs according to the Telecommunications Industry Ombudsman in September 1999. The IIA is widely regarded as representative of the 'big end of town' rather than the many small to medium sized Australian ISPs.[132]

As a counterpoint to the mythological dichotomy of legitimate users (families and business) vs illegitimate users (pornographers and hackers), Yee suggests another (albeit also mythologized) group with a greater claim to legitimacy – the grassroots content creators who built the Internet.[133] Of course, these three categories are not discrete but Yee's claim produces a challenge to the myths of Internet control. The scheme encourages ISPs to surveil their clients and will disproportionately affect the small content providers who do not have the resources to grapple with censorship law.

Many of the critiques of the *Broadcasting Services Amendment (Online Services) Act 1999* scheme raise the issue of industry and economic development, claiming that the restrictions will inhibit the growth of the local Internet industry. Most of these claims are not elaborated and many seem to rely on the liberal capitalist ideal that freedom and development run hand in hand.

Scott's critique, however, raises explicit economic reasons for this impeded growth, based on a thorough understanding of the actual operation of the telecommunications and Internet service provision industry.[134] Latour's idea of

---

131 Yee, op. cit. fn. 53.
132 Graham, op. cit. fn. 94.
133 Yee, op. cit. 198.
134 Scott, op. cit. fn. 97.

conceptual 'black boxes' in technological policy[135] is important here: the complex technological and business arrangements underlying the provision of Internet service are usually sealed away unexamined and, in the absence of analysis such as Scott's, impede an understanding of how the *business* of electronic information provision actually operates.

> Forcing the content out of Australia also means that inbound traffic into Australia is increased. Australian carriers are currently forced to buy content from US carriers, but must give Australian content to US carriers for free. One of the justifications for this is that traffic is 70:30 in the US carrier's favour (exact figures vary). Recently this ratio has been gradually improving, putting pressure on US carriers to move to a fairer interconnection regime. At an APEC conference on Internet financing in Japan in [1999] US carriers were at pains to justify why they shouldn't pay for other people's content. Increasing traffic inbound into Australia knocks the leg out of Australian carrier's arguments for US carriers to play fair.[136]

Scott criticizes the inefficiency which arises from Act's ignorance of the 'underlying economy of the Internet' and finds three consequences at the level of carriage provision, not foreseen by the drafters, in summary:

- The Internet becomes more costly as international material will not be cached or mirrored locally. This covers not only restricted content but also content which will not be cached 'to be on the safe side'. Thus every time an Australian user requests access to international material, payment will have to be made.
- Forcing Australian content offshore will benefit the carriage provider Telstra whose access charges do not discriminate between local and international access. Smaller carriage providers offer differentiated rates to support local development, which will become less appealing as local content becomes less substantial.
- Unless a carrier owns the physical infrastructure of underwater cabling, they must purchase their carriage from overseas companies up to 12 months in advance. As more demand for foreign content arises, forecasting access needs becomes even more difficult than it already is. Large companies have much more market power to forecast their needs and to wear a shortfall or over-purchase.[137]

---

135 Latour B (1987) *Science in Action: How to Follow Scientists and Engineers through Society*, Harvard University Press: Cambridge, MA.
136 Scott, op. cit. fn. 97.
137 Scott, op. cit. fn. 97

The lack of consultation inevitably creates resistance from those who are meant to implement the scheme. Technical ignorance cannot be concealed beneath the black box which deems the Internet to be just a new form of broadcast media. Symbolic legislation may, even if it ineffectual, presume to have an educative role, but when it attempts to educate the community about what it only presumes to be community values, a conceptual flaw in the system becomes apparent.

Taking the three failings of the regime into consideration – low regulatory distance, lack of industry ownership and commitment to the co-regulation intention, and inadequate value of the current regime in addressing the variety of consumer concerns about the technology – the current approach is limited in its future viability. While technological incapacity for filtering and 'strong' regulation has been at the core of the critique so far, it is also important to attack the fundamental myth upon which the regulatory regime is based: that the co-regulatory system, in some way, actually reflects some form of community morals and standards of behaviour.[138]

The Scheme Displays Ignorance of the Technological and Media Forms it Aims to Regulate

'Many of the Bill's problems stem from an apparent misunderstanding of Internet technology and of how people actually use the Internet.'[139] A symptom of the failure to provide adequate consultation is the failure of the scheme to be properly grounded in an understanding of broadcasting, media or new technologies. This is a failure which strips it of credibility in the eyes of those who are immersed in Internet culture. Scott illustrates the different elements of broadcast media and Internet media, demonstrating the differences in media paradigm between the two:

> It is almost as if broadcasting and Internet are antonymous. Given the extreme divergence of characteristics, one might argue that the more experience a body has with broadcast regulation, the less qualified it is to deal with the Internet. Further, the justification for regulation of broadcasting is that an exclusive license over public property (the broadcast spectrum) is being given to a broadcaster for the purpose of conducting a business. There is no comparable analogy in the Internet space. There is no readily identifiable public property that is being appropriated for someone's exclusive use.[140]

If Internet content consists of an 'unmodified' film or computer game, the rating given to the original media by the Classification Board remains in force,[141]

---

138 Chen, op. cit. fn. 14 at 16.
139 Johnson, op. cit. fm. 22.
140 Scott, op. cit. fn. 97.
141 *Broadcasting Services Act 1992* op. cit. fn. 25 cl 12.

otherwise the site is referred to the Board to be rated 'in a corresponding way to the way in which a film would be classified'.[142] Once content has been classified, the board must not reclassify within two years.[143] Given the frequency of content change for many sites, this seems naïve. Even a relatively static site which does not change content substantially in two years would be very unusual.

The EFA has examined the difference between the film guidelines (which covers depictions, that is visual images), and the guidelines covering publications (based on descriptions in written text). The OFLC guidelines, read as part of the Internet censorship scheme, use the criteria for visuals depictions in the assessment of written descriptions:

> This unfortunately has the effect of creating a new form of thought crime, which is dependent on the thoughts and imagination of the members of the Classification Board/s. Whilst people who watch a film will see the same thing and there may be some justification for an assumption that it is likely to have a similar effect on many viewers, the same certainly cannot be said for reading textual information.[144]

Hypertext, in particular, is difficult to interpret in such a uniform manner. The difference in media is significant, deeming written text to be a film or video has significant consequences for much print literature.[145] Boyle points to the presence of a similar critique within legal theory, the legal realist hostility toward 'legal reification' (use of analogies to the point where these become things in themselves upheld by erroneous belief in the concreteness of legal representations).[146]

Drawing examples from across the field of electronic regulation, Boyle looks at the diversity of spatialized metaphors used to explain new media technology and proposed frameworks of regulation. These include public parks, shopping malls, Roman forums, a mail carrier, a community newspaper, a telephone company, a television station:

> There are advantages – in familiarity, evocativeness, and tradition – to this particular field of analogical reasoning. Nevertheless, it is hard to repress an occasional wish that the issue be framed as whether a specific type of regulation will help or hinder the creation or reproduction of a particular kind of society,

---

142   Ibid. cl 13.

143   Ibid. cl 14.

144   Electronic Frontiers Australia (1998) http://www.efa.org.au/Publish/publrev9805.html (viewed 8/5/99).

145   As demonstrated by the EFA in 'Application of Film Guidelines to Written Text. Example Classification Assessment, *Eat Me*, a best selling book by Linda Jaivin' at http://www.efa/org/au/Publish/agresp_apx1.html (viewed 7/4/03).

146   Boyle J (1996) *Shamans, Software, and Spleens: Law and the Construction of the Information Society*, Harvard University Press: Cambridge, USA at 111–3.

rather than being filtered through an additional layer of simile and metaphor. [... I]t would be unfortunate if we decided how to regulate the most important technologies of the next century by relying mainly on their formal resemblances to the physical environs or commercial settings in which the public information of the nineteenth century found its home.[147]

The technical limitations of the Australian Internet censorship scheme are not limited to the difficulties of classification and procedure. The technological architecture of the Internet has proven to be difficult to control and provides multiple opportunities to evade regulatory reach. 2600 Australia (an organization concerned with electronic security issues and policies) published a series of guidelines for avoiding the effects of Schedule 5. These guidelines only apply to those who want to *access* material outside Australia and they include a variety of technical and other strategies:[148]

- Use of an alternate proxy network outside Australia;
- Masking of web content before it enters the proxy network so that filters do not have a chance to monitor it;
- Encrypting content before it enters the proxy network;
- Use of an encrypted VPN ('virtual private network')/tunnel for streaming content which would escape the definition of the Internet under the Act;
- Distribution of content by means of a 'company' to its 'employees';
- Offering of on-demand point-to-point email access to content (a practice of the early, pre-World Wide Web Internet);
- Offering content through an IRC network, which can even be automated via an IRC transfer bot[149]; and
- Flooding the ACMA with legitimate, appropriate complaints thus increasing the cost of regulation to the point where it is no longer viable.

In a similar vein, more technological options of resistance are suggested by other commentators and cyberspace activists:

- A relaying proxy server provides one of the simplest ways to avoid censorship, circumventing local government restrictions as well as fulfilling the proxy's primary task in speeding Internet traffic;[150]

---

147   Ibid. at 113.
148   2600 Australia (2000a) *Evading the Broadcasting Services Amendment (Online Services) Act 1999*, http://www.2600.org.au/censorship–evasion.html (viewed 4 January 2000).
149   see http://iroffer.org/.
150   For a description of how to use a popular relaying proxy server in this way see Haselton B *Using Akamai to bypass Internet Censorship*, http://www.peacefire.org/bypass/Proxy/akamai.html.

- Mirroring of information, replicating information so widely and rapidly that it is impossible for censors to keep up with the spread of the media;[151]
- 'IP rotation' forms a technological solution, as many website censorship options rely on IP blocking, IP rotation automatically changing the IP address every few minutes;[152]
- Peer to peer applications such as *Triangle Boy*[153] and *Peekabooty*[154] that use peer to peer networks (similar to those in *Napster* and *Gnutella*) to share information fairly anonymously. Each client knows only the identity of the nearest partner in the network (who is likely to be geographically distant) which makes tracing information and infiltrating the network extremely difficult;
- Software such as peacefire.exe which disables filtering software.[155] Ironically, the United States proposed *Internet Freedom Act*[156] will, if passed, provide government funds to develop anti-censorship software to combat 'government censors and state persecution'.[157] Other items of software such as the *Camera Shy* project are meant to facilitate encryption at the browser level.[158]

Two points are apparent from the critique by 2600 Australia and Internet freedom advocates. First, what is evident is the readiness with which sites of resistance develop, particularly given the technical challenge involved in circumventing the regulatory measures (indeed this enhances the pleasures of resistance). In part, these pleasures revolve around the thrills of avoiding the 'repressive' laws and also in the organized resistance of sabotaging the ACMA bureaucracy.

Second, the fundamental contradictions arising from the legislation, stemming from its unsophisticated notions of media and attempts to force net content into 'broadcasting' are also obvious in the critique. In particular, the locations where Internet communications starts to overlap with or resemble telephone

---

151   Rodriquez F (2002) *Burning the Village to Roast the Pig: Censorship of Online Media*, A paper for the OSCE workshop 'Freedom of the Media and the Internet' 30 November 2002, p15.

152   http://www.xs4all.nl/~felipe/WWW.old/press/schneider.html.

153   http://www.safeweb.com/tboy_service.html.

154   See *New Scientist* 'Peekabooty aims to banish Internet censorship' 19 February 2002, ZDNet Australia (2001d) 'Hackers to unleash anti-censorship tool', 6 May, http://www.zdnet.com.au/newstech/security/story/0,2000024985,20220053,00.htm, and http://peek–a–booty.org/.

155   http://www.peacefire.org/info/about–peacefire.shtml.

156   Introduced on 2 October 2002 by US House Policy Chairman Christopher Cox and US House International Relations Committee Ranking Member Tom Lantos.

157   *Bipartisan, Bicameral Bill Stops Internet Jamming* http://policy.house.gov/html/news_release.cfm?id=111.

158   http://sourceforge.net/projects/camerashy/.

communications and other forms of 'live' communication challenge the simple definitions provided under the Act.

The mobilization of resistance to the Act has provoked at least one extreme Governmental response. A press statement made by the spokesperson of the Department of Communications, Information Technology and the Arts, interviewed by Sinclair, draws a broad range of grievances with activists and the information technology community:

> He dismissed the 2600 group and others who were providing information on getting around filters. '(Theirs' are) the sort of groups that go "ha ha, we'll do this to prove the legislation doesn't work and Richard Alston's an idiot, because we'll get around all the filters". Well, you have to say, they're a bunch of stupid twerps because we're not mandating any filters [... Further, the spokesperson] said that ISPs who advocated home-based filters should be providing them. Why don't (they) provide access to filters on their home page? Because they're too stupid to even think about it. Either that or they're just too lazy, or they have not real commitment to what they're talking about.'[159]

While it would an error to generalize a spokesperson's statements into formal policy, the conduct of the Government representatives in the public arena are an important aspect of the policy process as they shape the debate and seek to engage 'middle Australia' in fear of technology and isolate those critical of the scheme as others, outside of the general community.

The Impossibility of Invoking the Abstraction of 'Community Standards'

While the Australian Internet censorship scheme seems to be mostly ineffectual in achieving Internet media control, its symbolic power is in the continued reification of a fictional abstract community model, providing a mechanism to force undesirable elements to 'move along' and displace content to overseas hosts. The response to the scheme from members of the actual community has been lukewarm. Even with the possibility of a free trial of a filter service, the majority of Telstra Big Pond's 1.2 million customer base had not opted to download it.[160]

Clearly it is difficult to draw generalized assumptions about what 'the community' wants, demands or desires. A significant problem with the use of the OFLC classification system to regulate Internet media is that it uses the 'community attitudes' aggregate to classify material and limit access to it. Perception of 'community attitudes' is always subjective but the ratings standards create a false sense of security, deeming 'what most people think', while silencing dissenting voices.

---

159   Sinclair, op. cit. fn. 86.
160   Wardill, op. cit. fn. 73.

Those who do not agree with the community standard are by necessity a minority opinion and therefore less valid in the face of overwhelming community interest. The myth of community in the regulation of sexual media is explored in Chapter 5 which forms a vital link in the reconceptualization of regulatory models of community in Chapter 6.

The Scheme Endorses the Flawed Approach of Filtering

This critique is, in many ways, an accumulation of all four previous grounds, revisiting the issue of filtering already discussed in Chapter 2. Voluntary use of filtering technology is a key strategy of the scheme, yet it surreptitiously infringes the rights of those induced to use it (by being over-inclusive), is ineffectual and costly, is premised on technical ignorance of the Internet and reifies a problematic notion of community. These concerns seem to have presented a deal of anxiety to the regulators – the Government report on the evaluation of filters was only made available, on 5 January 2000, after a Freedom of Information application by the EFA.[161]

A related concern is the false security that parents may feel when using these easily circumvented filters, placing false faith in the technology and Government regulation. Graham argues:

> Of severe concern is that the legislation is very likely to give parents unfamiliar with the Internet, the very people it is claimed to be intended to assist, a false sense of security. It is highly disturbing that such parents may be led to believe that they can safely leave their children to play unsupervised in the streets of the online world, unlike they would do in the real world, because they're told the government has 'done something'.[162]

There are considerable problems defining adult content. The principle that sites containing adult content should authenticate the age of the viewer has a kind of basic logic but this is easily challenged by examining the breadth of the *R* category. Graham uses as an example the famous Vietnam War news photograph of a naked young girl, burnt with napalm – one which has had profound ideological impact on the way in which war is viewed. She asks if this photograph might disturb children; depict a child in a way likely to cause offence or outrage; or contain a high impact depiction of violence? All of these might be grounds for banishing the photo behind the walls of age verification, a significant detriment to the news and historical aspect of online information.[163] How are automated filtering services able to contend with issues of this complexity?

---

161   Graham, op. cit. fn. 91.
162   Ibid.
163   Ibid.

Automated filtering promises much but delivers little, many critics have highlighted the technical impossibility of a piece of software, however sophisticated, in determining meaning and context.

> How does a filter know whether the use of a word is legitimate or offensive? For example the word breast when used in breast cancer is a vital source of information that may be crucial to a person's informed choice. Yet when used in the context of big and voluptuous it may be deemed unsuitable for children. Whilst phrase filtering reduces this error marginally, there is no way possible a computer can decide on intent ... Something else to consider with the word breast is that when used to glorify porn it often appears on the page as a word typed onto an image ... not in the text at all ... so it will bypass the filter whereas [breast] cancer information will not.[164]

Taylor argues that once a comprehensive system of filtering is in place, it becomes simple to expand the list slowly and inexorably without legislative debate or even administrative gazetting – 'it wouldn't take much to add words like Labor, Green, Democrat or Communism to the filter'.[165]

Further, most filtering solutions are offered by companies operating out of the United States which, even in a co-regulatory system seems a remote agent to be making decisions which effect domestic polity and rights of free expression. 'It is ironic that, while the Commonwealth does not regard the US fourth amendment as acceptable for Australians, it considers US moral values to be entirely transposable into the Australian context'.[166]

The classification *R* evokes images of sex and violence, even though there are substantial other grounds for the rating including the broad 'adult themes' category which in the 1997/8 period accounted for 68 per cent of *R* rated films and 71 per cent of *R* rated videos.[167]

Much of the Internet censorship debate sees a false dichotomy between 'legitimate' business and pornography, especially where the sex industry operates quite legally under the current classifications system. Many advances in Internet technology have been driven by demands of the sex industry and its clients – including movie compression, streaming movies, credit card security and adult checks.[168] While the sex industry is not solely responsible for these technological innovations, it definitely contributed substantially.

---

164 Taylor, op. cit. fn. 97.
165 Ibid.
166 Chen, op. cit. fn. 14 at 6.
167 Graham, op. cit. fn. 91.
168 Think of it this way – your average user of online adult services wants four things. They need security if they're going to be putting credit card details into a Web form. They want privacy, from their personal details right through to a credit card statement that will *not* say '$49.95 billed to HotTeenSluts.com'. They want speed as most paid access to

The word-based lexical filtering approach has had a significant impact on Internet users and content providers who happen to fall into categories deemed sexual or adult but not directly concerned with erotic images. In particular, words such as 'gay' or 'lesbian' turn up frequently on filter lists, due to their perceived prevalence in pornographic sites. The ostensible expulsion of the erotic from heteronormative life involves a re-coding of the erotic, an embedding of heterosexist assumptions into social relationships. Sexual difference is, of its very existence, coded as erotic and draws the attention of censorship regimes. This is particularly true of transgressive or 'act-up' use of media which attempts to challenge the mechanisms of representation directly.

Labelling of 'deviant' sexualities is already a serious issue, with the label becoming a master status through which all behaviour and conduct is interpreted, the subject is hypersexualized. The web provides a safe non-judgemental space for exploring options, particularly for young or closeted people. The multiple identities of the net are also positive in exploring different personas, it can avoid the straight/gay dichotomy and therefore provide positive contribution to queer exploration and constitution of identity.[169]

Use of filtering services delegates a substantial censorship role to private, corporate interests. The notion of the 'private censor' has a place in American law, recognizing that constitutionally protected speech may nevertheless be regulated by private actors who own property in words and concepts. The phrase 'private censorship' comes from *Hughes Tool Co. v Motion Picture Ass'n of America, Inc.*,[170] a case which considered a scheme of moral regulation imposed by the Association through its control of 90 per cent of the theatres and the economic threat of barring advertising matter which had content subject to its prohibitions. The court found that the defendants had assumed a quasi governmental role and that its 'arbitrary, discriminatory and preconceived notions of public propriety' were an unconstitutional restriction on free speech.[171]

Concerns about private censorship also occur when film distributors re-cut their films in order to gain a lower rating under a film classification system, so as to best exploit a local market and its particular censorship laws. This action

---

adult sites depends on the person being 'in the mood' – having to wait will cool one's fire, so to speak. And it needs to be simple. These four requirements have forced the online adult industry to develop cutting-edge technology – all of which can be, and is, used in other non-adult industries.

Internet.au editor Nic Healy, interviewed in Vnuk H (2003) *Snatched: Sex and Censorship in Australia*, Vintage: Sydney at 56–7. See also Johnson P (1996) 'Pornography Drives Technology: Why Not Censor the Internet', *Federal Communications Law Journal*, v49(1), 217.

169   See Creed B (2003) *Media Matrix: Sexing the New Reality*, Allen and Unwin: Sydney and Altman D (2001) *Global Sex*, Allen and Unwin: Sydney.

170   *Hughes Tool Co. v Motion Picture Ass'n of America*, Inc 66 F. Supp, 1006 (S.D. N.Y. 1946).

171   Ibid. at 1022.

seems entirely in the private domain – the distributors are merely cutting 'their own' film – but this denies the economic and institutional environment in which films are made. The role of private censorship in Australia is explored again in the discussion of classification in Chapter 5.

In the context of the regulation of information, Boyle suggests that the public/private divide provides a de facto method of private censorship, of enclosing words within the concept of private property (as trademarks, copyright)[172] and enabling controls which would be impermissible if enacted by the state. He uses the examples of the United States Olympics Committee's litigation against the Gay Olympic Games use of the word 'Olympic'. Censorship had been effectively removed from the public domain and placed in private, corporate hands: 'There is no free speech issue because we are in the marketplace and not the polity'.[173] Another example of the fetishization of speech as property is demonstrated in the attempts by the Church of Scientology to silence critique of its doctrine by claiming discussions violated its intellectual property in its dogma and literature.[174]

While filtering may not enable the kinds of private control that intellectual property seems to convey, there are substantial and related issues of control as media forms (and legal/regulatory cultures) converge. The Australian Internet censorship scheme presupposes that filtering is effected through a neutral agent and that the voluntary choice to adopt a filter is necessarily an informed one. There a great many issues surrounding the concept, practices and implementation of filtering – a complexity which is obscured if the debate is reduced to simplistic oppositions of filters versus pornography.

Symbolic Policy and Regulatory Fortressing

An examination of the Australian Internet content regulation scheme reveals a clear need to explore further issues of space in both cyberspace and spaces of censorship, spatial concepts and human geographies which are implicit in the Act's invocation of the community and in assumptions made about pornography and representation of sexuality generally. More complex understandings of power, governance and jurisdiction require a complex model of the ways in which these discourses intersect, more sophisticated than the bare model of 'community values' as an assumed (or given) norm.

The structure of the co-regulatory scheme established under the *Broadcasting Services Amendment (Online Services) Act 1999* makes for particularly interesting exploration of contemporary theories of governance, particularly those that emphasis pluralist networks and the de-centred state.

---

172   Gordon W (1990) 'Toward a Jurisprudence of Benefits: The Norms of Copyright and the Problem of Private Censorship' *University of Chicago Law Review*, Vol 57, 1009.
173   Boyle, op. cit. fn. 145.
174   Project Clambake at http://www.xenu.net.

Chen's analysis[175] of the scheme emphasizes the role of policy networks but also questions the irrationality of the Act, challenging the abstract models which are drawn as 'a map of problematic social reality',[176] where these models as simulacra become regulatory objects in themselves. 'Not all policy can be seen to be founded on a 'rational' set of causal theory about the relationship between an identified social problem and the nature of the world as perceived by members of the policy subsystem.'[177] Faced with a lack of empirical policy outcomes, it would seem that the Australian Internet censorship scheme should best be analysed as a kind of symbolic policy.[178]

As symbolic policy, the Act has been challenged on the basis of its cost and the better educational uses to which those resources could have been put.[179] Edelman defines symbolic politics as the desire for a decision maker to appear active on an issue where they are in fact not, arising from two factors: the difficulty in empirically measuring public support behind lobbyists, and the difficulty of dealing with a perceived problem which may only occur in the future.[180] While symbolic politics may be born of cynicism, he suggests that they are nevertheless powerful influences on public action and a venue for government to engage in ideological engineering.

The creation of a symbolic but largely ineffectual scheme of Internet regulation has worked well with the Government's political strategy: allowing it to take a strong line to gain the support of conservatives, then concede to amendments during Parliamentary debate and thereby gain the acquiescence of the IIA.[181] This process produced legislation which did not impede electronic commerce but was symbolically 'family-friendly', and subsequent unrelated increases in Internet usage could then be cited as proof of the success of the approach.[182]

Just as this book was being finalized for publication the Australian Government announced a series of amendments to the censorship scheme. The *Classification (Publications, Films and Computer Games) Amendment Bill 2007* and *Classification (Markings for Films and Computer Games) Determination* propose an extensive set of standards for marking censorship labels on the packaging of films and video games, streamlines classification where a film has already been classified and

---

175 Chen, op. cit. fn. 19.
176 Here Chen, ibid., draws on Geertz C (1973a) *The Interpretation of Cultures*, Fontana Press: New York.
177 Chen, ibid. at 202.
178 Gustafsson G (1983) 'Symbolic and Pseudo Policies as Responses to Diffusion of Power', *Policy Sciences*, v15, 269.
179 Chalmers R (2002) 'Regulating the Net in Australia: Firing Blanks or Silver Bullets?', *E Law – Murdoch University Electronic Journal of Law*, Vol 9(3), http://www.murdoch.edu.au/elaw/issues/v9n3/chalmers93_text.html (viewed 7/4/03).
180 Edelman M (1971) *Politics as Symbolic Action: Mass Arousal and Quiescence*, Markham: New York.
181 Chen, op. cit. fn. 12 at 3.
182 Ibid.

distributors simply wish to add subtitles and makes a number of administrative changes to the organization. The *Communication Legislation Amendment (Content Services) Bill 2007* extends the reach of the Internet regulation laws to cover commercial providers of mobile services. Despite being heralded as innovations in press releases, none of these amendments significantly changes the operation of the scheme.

Leading into the 2007 federal election, both Labor and Liberal parties promised to 'get tough' on censorship. Liberals promised to make filtering available (which it already is) and Labor promised mandatory ISP level filtering, a proposal which has already been discredited as technologically unviable. There seems to be a great deal of cynicism in this debate with token gestures made to moral conservative groups but no real intention to change. It appears, at least for the immediate future, that the status quo will be preserved.

The Australian Internet regulation laws will do very little to pursue their purported aims of restricting access to pornography and other *RC* content, but their potential remains as symbolic regulation or to chill free speech. To understand this symbolic function we need to investigate the ideas of regulatory space, regulation of sexual content and community regulation in more depth.

The next chapters explore the creation of community as a spatial socio-legal construct and examine how this model engages with the Internet and adult media as sites of regulation. While the pluralistic notions of co-regulation and self governance hold some promise, the autocratic form of these adopted by the *Broadcasting Services Amendment (Online Services) Act 1999* means that the scheme is sabotaged by its own insistence on homogenous abstract notions of community. It fails to recognize both the attitudes of Australian citizens and the existence of the diverse and multiple regulatory communities in which these citizens are involved.

Chapter 4
'Taking the Red Pill':[1]
Cyberspace, Jurispace and the Architecture of Regulation

The Rule of Law is one of the key metaphysical 'foundation myths'[2] of modern law. This principle holds that law is everywhere and yet nowhere, an objective, timeless and placeless institution that provides the pervasive and universal 'power grid' for modern regulatory order. Through decades of work, the school of Critical Legal Studies has established a critique of Law's claims of ahistorical neutrality, yet the work of Critical Legal Geography has only recently begun.

In this chapter the research and analysis of Critical Legal Geography will be explored, together with the work of other geographers and philosophers of space (especially Henri Lefebvre) in order to gather a collection of critical tools necessary to disassemble the monolithic concept of community used in censorship law. The censorship of Internet media provides a further challenge to that monolith as the multiple and discontinuous spaces of cyberspace sit uneasily with law's limited spatial concepts such as jurisdiction. In order to understand the governance of new media spaces, it will be argued, we must examine the deployment of law in space generally.

Contested notions of community and community values emerge as strong themes in discussions concerning the *Broadcasting Standards Amendment (Online Services) Act 1999*. The legislation embraces what seems to be a simple notion of community, reflecting broadly held and consistent values. But, can any such model of community embrace the diversity of politics, values, beliefs and attitudes in contemporary multicultural society?

---

1   In *The Matrix* (1998) Neo, the protagonist, is offered the choice of two pills, a blue placebo and a red psychoactive that promises to open the gates of perception, reveal the prison of reality and expose the power structures of the underlying social order. 'Like Neo from *The Matrix*, the modern subject is eager to explore unknown territory and to make new discoveries, even if doing so involves the blurring of boundaries between the public and private, reality and fantasy.' Creed B (2002) *Media Matrix: Sexing the New Reality*, Allen and Unwin: Sydney at 4.
2   See Eriksson LD, Hirvonen A, Minkkinen P and Poyhonen J (1998) 'Introduction: A Polytical Manifesto' in Hirvonen A (ed.) *Polycentricity: The Multiple Scenes of Law*, Pluto Press: London.

The Rule of Law is predicated upon an unbiased operation of law across a jurisdictional space. Does this concept demand uniformity of culture and conformity as essential characteristics, or can it embrace multiple communities? Can Rule of Law tolerate a diversity of individuals and communities sharing a space in which autonomous individuals can freely engage in identity constitution? In short, does the integrity of the legal system demand a rigid framework of social conformity to support it? If diversity is permitted, are there limits to what the system can tolerate?

Regulatory space is not a void, not a terra nullius awaiting legal colonization. Prior to the state enacting laws, jurispace already contains multiple sites of regulation, regulatory apparatuses and communities conceived around regulatory endeavours. When law seeks to colonize this space it must negotiate a position among existing mechanisms or it will incur their resistance where intersections occur.

Specialized conceptual tools are needed to explore, discuss and critique the spatial practices of law. This chapter engages with the work of Henri Lefebvre in order to suggest ways of conceptualizing power and regulation beyond the simple causal models of positivist law.[3] Lefebvre's tools provide a guide for conceiving of regulatory space – primarily visually but also engaging with the other senses which define the sensation of space. Theories of cyberspace, virtual reality and cyberpunk literature also provide some concurrent guidance and present metaphors for describing and discussing the planes, intersections and junctions of spaces. The practice of working across the different technological spaces of virtual life suggests a method of simultaneously conceiving of multiples spaces, of superimposing images of regulatory space over the experiences and perceptions of everyday life.

Virtual Visions: Cybermagick, the Matrix of Power and the Hegemonic Order

The 1998 cyberpunk film *The Matrix* provides a vision of techno-mysticism in which a select few rebels could, by magickal hacking, transcend its two worlds – a virtual reality illusion of the contemporary world and the reality of the dystopian dark future which lay beneath it.[4] Key to the narrative was the ability to navigate

---

3   Legal positivists such as Hans Kelsen argue for a scientific or positivist approach to law. Kelsen H (1967) *Pure Theory of Law*, University of California Pres: Berkeley, CA. Positivism utilizes simple physical concepts of power as cause and effect, a simple dialectic between social problems and regulatory solutions. Law's use of scientific positivism, including Newtonian models of power, is extremely problematic. Minkkinen P (1998) 'Law, Science and Truth' in Hirvonen A (ed.) *Polycentricity: The Multiple Scenes of Law*, Pluto Press: London.

4   Margaret Wertheim locates cyberspace concepts of disembodiment and transcendence within a Christian tradition which sees the body and subjectivity separated.

between the two realities. This skill is represented in the dialectics between the dreamer trapped in the illusion who can see beyond the virtual world and the hacker from outside the system who can, by gazing into code (represented by the iconic screen of cascading green symbols) 'see' and modify the world constituted by the rules of software. The popularity of this film derived in part from its themes which echoed contemporary concerns of cyberculture.

Drawing on a variety of new age traditions; a simple interpretation the maya 'world of illusion' of Buddhism and Hermetic Magick's will to power, *The Matrix* posits a universe that ultimately is all about the code, the laws of reality and power comes from the ability to perceive and manipulate these systems of knowledge.[5] To perceive space as a construct gives the subversive agent a leverage point from which to defy the laws and rules of that space. Any reality, no matter how concrete it appears to be, is subject to production by coded systems of meaning, meanings which contain values and entrap those subjected to them.[6] In *The Matrix*, law and technology are conflated into an oppressive force of order which imposes both a space of control but paradoxically also creates the potential for resistance to that order.

In *The Matrix*, the technology of virtual reality is more than just a metaphor for space and power, but is also a metaphor for the importance of language and discourse in constituting both. Language and its role in the production of reality/space is also echoed in the themes of *Snowcrash*,[7] a cyberpunk novel which conflates language and code to an extreme model that allows neuro-hacking, a

---

Cyberlibertarian's 'electronic frontier' is ideology connected to the Christian metaphysical space. Wertheim M (1999) *The Pearly Gates of Cyberspace: A History of Space from Dante to the Internet*, Doubleday: Sydney.

5   Beys describes conflicts over online governance as invoking an 'anti-materialist kind of gnosticism', echoed in *The Matrix*. Bey H (1996) 'The Information War' in Druckery T (ed.) *Electronic Culture: Technology and Virtual Representation*, Aperture: New York.

6   While making postmodern gestures, the film remains firmly modernist in its insistence on a fixed reality underpinning the illusion of reality. It is worth comparing this to another virtual reality themed film of the same year, *eXistenZ* (1998) where no underlying referral reality could be fixed. *The Matrix*'s success comes in part from its greedy mix of themes and philosophies, churned together in the pop culture blender. Fusing Buddhist, Christian, Hermetic Magick and Marxist themes, *The Matrix*'s virtual reality has been created to serve the interests of the hegemony, an elite of conscious machines who feed off the bio-energies of humans trapped in the not-so-gilded cage of ideology. The revolutionaries of *The Matrix* aim to expose the ideological trap that the workers are ensnared in and liberate them, even if doing so dooms them to the harsher realities of the world outside the illusion. The forces of control have their own agents, who spend their time protecting the fragile illusion, even if they have to break its rules to do so. This philosophy seems to have touched a nerve among many in the audience, especially cyber libertarians. For more exploration of this film see Duncanson K (2001) 'Tracing the Law Through *The Matrix*', *Griffith Law Review*, v10(2), 16.

7   Stephenson N (1992) *Snowcrash*, Roc: London.

sophisticated form of neuro-linguistic programming similar to the concept of 'ghost-hacking' in *The Ghost in the Shell* manga/anime stories.[8]

Cyberpunk visions of virtual reality[9] open up discussion on the discursive nature of reality or, for present purposes, the relationship between code and the construction of reality, whether it be the computer code of cyberspace or the rules of legal space. It also suggests that there are substantial intersections between these spaces, sites where one can attempt to decode or at least attempt to map out these networks of power.[10]

Before the law, *The Matrix*'s rebel-hacker can not only perceive the encoded power relations which run through and constitute the production of 'reality' space but, when presented with those codes they can decipher the ideology embedded in them. While this messianic aspiration may not be shared by all who come to the law, it is a useful metaphor to begin exploring the spatial nature of law and, conveniently, the notion of law in electronic spaces such as the Internet. Unlike 'the One', however, the discursive features of the production of space means we can never find an enlightened, universal standpoint from which to speak.

The de-centring of control provided by the Internet is said to be the core of its power and also its threat to conventional governance.[11] For many libertarians the Internet is a key weapon against the control of big government. This notion is fraught with difficulties as the 'bottom-up' elements of disciplinary power do not disappear and may, indeed, become more pervasive in the absence of a centralized authority monolith.

Some commentators have argued that government anxieties about control are symptoms of progress – the death throes of a bloated system of laws, particularly in the field of intellectual property.[12] Yet others, particularly in the area of privacy,

---

8 Comprising of the manga; Shirow M (1995) *The Ghost in the Shell*, English edition, Dark Horse Comics: Milwaukee, OR; Shirow M (2005) *Man/Machine Interface*, Dark Horse Comics: Milwaukee, OR; and the anime incarnations produced by Mamoru Oshii; *The Ghost in the Shell* (theatrical film,1995) and *The Ghost in the Shell: Stand Alone Complex* (TV series, 2002).

9 McCafferey L (ed.) (1991) *Storming the Reality Studio: A Casebook of Cyberpunk and Postmodern Science Fiction*, Duke University Press: Durham.

10 While not explicitly referencing the film, Imken uses the term 'the Matrix' to reflect shifts in human geography, reflecting network collectivities and virtualities, impliedly integrating the movie's background concept into a more complex social model. Imken O (1999) 'The convergence of virtual and actual in the Global Matrix: artificial life, geo-economics and psychogeography', in Crang M, Crang P and May J (eds) *Virtual Geographies: Bodies, Space and Telations*, Routledge: London.

11 Lenk K (1997) 'The challenge of cyberspatial forms of human interaction to territorial governance and policing' in Loader BD (ed.) *The Governance of Cyberspace: Politics, Technology and Global Restructuring*, Routledge: London.

12 Barlow JP (1994) 'The Economy of Ideas', *Wired 2.03*, 84 and see the cyberlibertarian perspectives of the EFF (Electronic Frontiers Foundation), founded by Barlow and Kapor, http://www.eff.org.

see the potential for technology to encroach further and further on liberty,[13] providing new strategies for the instruments of control.

The discourse of space is an important organizing factor in the cybergovernance of Internet censorship. Rather than presenting a homogenous space to legislate and police, 'cyberspace' entails a multiplicity of different spaces and collectives, each with its own regulatory language, communities, and proclivities in relation to control.[14]

The concept of cyberspace is connected to discussions of virtual space and virtual communities which seem to disrupt social order, splitting the authentic/real from the electronic/mediated. This is not merely a recent issue, nor a product of the Internet. Science commentator Margaret Wertheim contends that television is the fore-runner of cyberspace as it accustomed consumers to a parallel world of virtuality.[15] Indeed, the reception of television in the home and the sharing of media have contributed to a blurring of the distinctions between adult and child audience in media regulation and have had deep ramifications for the censorship debate.[16]

Likewise, the Internet's destabilization of social and legal space may be seen as a part of a history of technology and media. In the 1950s, NBC president Sylvester 'Pat' Weaver declared that television would make the 'entire world into a small town, instantly available, with the leading actors on the world stage known on sight or by voice to all within it'.[17] Architectural commentator Lynn Spigel argues that television merged private and public space: through its strategic balancing of privatization and community involvement, television became a metaphor for the contradiction between the two spheres, between the privatization of spectacle and in fears of the possible disintegration of public space.[18] Television also contributed to the sanitization which was implemented through construction of suburban space, the purification of communal space by writing out the undesirables while maintaining the populist idea of 'neighbourliness'.[19] These transformations are significant for law, particularly for censorship law's use of 'community' as a regulatory structure.

---

13   Raab CD (1997) 'Privacy, Democracy, Information' in Loader, op. cit. fn. 11.

14   While such distinctions are ultimately arbitrary, I attempt to use the term 'regulation' in a more neutral context and 'control' in the sense used by WS Burroughs (Burroughs WS (1979) *Ah Pook is Here and Other Texts*, John Calder: London) and Salman Rushdie (Rushdie S (1990) *Haroun and the Sea of Stories*, Granta Books: London) to connote the self destructive drive toward regulation as an end in itself. Both regulation and control are dependent on each other.

15   Wertheim, op. cit. fn. 4 at 244.

16   Meyrowitz J (1985) *No Sense of Place*, Oxford University Press: New York.

17   quoted in Spigel L (1992) 'The Suburban Home Companion: Television and the Neighbourhood Ideal in Postwar America', in Colomina B (ed.) *Sexuality and Space*, Princeton Architectural Press: New York at 192.

18   Ibid. at 188.

19   Ibid. at 189.

Cybergovernance and Theories of Space

The term 'cyberspace'[20] directly imports spatial concerns into the regulation of the Internet, as does the concept of information networks or, for that matter, the cliché of 'the information superhighway'. Spatial metaphors provide the idiom through which electronic space is experienced and described[21] in popular and legal discourse.

The spatial aspects of cybergovernance are well demonstrated in the High Court of Australia's decision in *Gutnick*[22] and in the legal framing of arguments made by the disputants in that case. The Gutnick case concerned the jurisdiction of Australian courts to decide defamation claims made against the content of websites, the servers for which were located within the United States jurisdiction and viewed internationally. Affirming principles of existing Australian defamation and jurisdictional caselaw, the High Court upheld the plaintiff's entitlement to litigate in Australia, holding that publication occurs wherever someone 'reads' the material.

The *Gutnick* case is just one of a series of initial sorties to determine the question of 'who owns cyberspace?'[23] What is central here is not the tangled, and to some extent irreconcilable, web of jurisdictions, but the assumption that the Internet constitutes a spatial place, a territory[24] to be owned, conquered, colonized and civilized.

The ideological aspects of the *Gutnick* case are no less interesting than the legal ones. The case could be interpreted as a challenge to the presumed ownership of the Internet by the United States.[25] In many ways, the case was constructed by the litigant as a challenge to this presumption of sovereignty, as well as a challenge by the defendants concerning the sovereignty of Australian courts.

However, much of the *Gutnick* debate was framed not in terms of sovereignty, but in terms of individual rights and freedom. Dow Jones claimed that a decision permitting Gutnick's claim would open the way for decisions by other courts that did

---

20 'Cyberspace' means, literally, 'navigable space' (from the Greek *kyber* – 'to navigate'). Dodge M and Kitchin R (2001) *Mapping Cyberspace*, Routledge: London at 1.

21 Crang M (2001) 'Public space, urban space and electronic space: would the real city please stand up?' in Holmes D (ed) *Virtual Globalization: Virtual Spaces/Tourist Spaces*, Routledge: London at 76.

22 *Gutnick v Dow Jones and Co Inc* [2002] HCA 56.

23 In the United Kingdom see *Harrods v Dow Jones* [2003] EWHC 1162 (QB). In the United States see *Young v New Haven Advocate* 315 F 3d 256 (4th Cir. 2002).

24 Consider the term 'Electronic Frontier' which invokes Wild West and Star Trek – incidentally both very American mythologies. See also the use of the Western metaphor in Handsley E and Biggins B (2000) 'The sheriff rides into town: a day for rejoicing by innocent westerners', *University of New South Wales Law Journal*, v23, 257 at 259.

25 For an analysis of the economic pressure that the United States exercises over the Internet, see Scott B (1999) *An Essential Guide to Internet Censorship in Australia*, http://www.gtlaw.com.au/pubs/essentialguidecensorship.html.

not respect basic political rights, such as Iraq, to hear litigation against the websites of the 'free world' and thus chill free speech.[26] Of course the *Gutnick* decision is in no way binding (or indeed influential) on these 'other courts' and a successful judgment is always contingent on a defendant submitting to judgement or owning resources within the jurisdiction in which litigation takes place. The Dow Jones argument, delivered by 'human rights QC' and media figure Geoffrey Robertson, also invited the domestic courts to take exception to the presented dichotomy between freedom (United States law) and repression (Australian law, which was, after all, the only other body of law actually under consideration in this case).[27]

Dow Jones' simplistic reconceptualization of the Internet jurisdiction issue is interesting in that it describes electronic media ('the Internet') as being deployed in a space, one which falls into one jurisdiction or another one, but which cannot occupy multiple spaces simultaneously. Cyberspace would then seem to be an 'alternate reality', an extension of real world jurisdictions and a territory to be occupied, conquered if necessary.

In affirming their jurisdiction over the publication in question, the Australian courts recognized the heterogenous nature of electronic media publication – that it occurs in multiple jurisdictions simultaneously. Indeed, the same principles also apply to conventional media as the existing rules for jurisdiction contemplate with publication of defamatory material in international newspapers or other means of global communications. While the *Gutnick* case did not directly concern state censorship, its discussion of jurisdiction highlights the problems of space in cybergovernance theory.[28] The concept of jurisdiction is discussed again in Chapter 6 in relation to theories of regulatory power.

Unpacking the spatial component of cybergovernance involves coming to a more complex understanding of space and cyberspace. Much of the analysis in this book rests on the work of Henri Lefebvre[29] which will be considered in more

---

26 *Gutnick v Dow Jones and Co Inc* [2001] VSC 305. For analysis see Rolph D (2002) 'The Message, Not the Medium: Defamation, Publication and the Internet in *Dow Jones and Co Inc v Gutnick*', *Sydney Law Review*, v24, 263. William Alpert, the journalist who wrote the original article, has announced that he is seeking redress from the UN High Commissioner for Human Rights on the basis of free speech infringement. ABC News Online (2003) 'Author takes Gutnick decision to UCHR', 19 April, http://www.abc.net.au/news/newsitems/s835716.htm.

27 Given a background of critique of the United States imperialism and colonising power, it is unsurprising that the colonising subjects seem a little sensitive to these kinds of claims. See Ebo B (ed.) (2001) *Cyberimperialism? Global Relations in the New Electronic Frontier*, Praeger: Westport, CT.

28 The colonization of cyberspace and jursidictional territory markers might be compared to the inscription of law on public places through 'official graffiti' of regulatory signs and markers. Hermer J and Hunt A (1996) 'Official Graffiti of the Everyday', *Law and Society Review*, v30(5), 455.

29 Especially Lefebvre H (1991a) *The Production of Space*, Blackwell: Oxford (originally published in French, 1976).

detail later in this chapter. Lefebvre demonstrates how a certain way of looking at space, in terms of production and property, became naturalized to the extent that it is conceived of as a 'pragmatic' viewpoint. Critiquing the *Broadcasting Standards Amendment (Online Services) Act*'s use of community values involves broader challenges to law's assumption of spatial detachment while embracing theoretical traditions which expose the history behind law's apparent ahistorical neutrality[30] and the politics underlying the purportedly universal liberal legal subject.[31]

Legal Geographies

> Knowledge (both formal and informal) is unevenly distributed in space [...] as are ways of conceiving of the world. Similarly, the context that provides the basis for interpretation is a spatial, as well as a historical one. Put in reverse, a claim about the objective determinancy of law is not simply a claim about the stability of history [...] but can also be understood as a conditional representation of the geography of social life, whereby the geographic diversity of experience and legal understanding is totalized into one universal and placeless vision.[32]

While the notion of community used by censorship law may not be exactly placeless, 'middle Australia' is sufficiently abstracted from the everyday experiences of legal subjects to challenge its appropriateness. By claiming values of universal application, legal standards such as 'the reasonable man' or 'community standards' are geographical models constituted through and by power networks. Law resists and sometimes actively seeks to annihilate the concept of space in its discourse,[33] yet representations of space are fundamental to legal practices[34] and, particularly, the delineation and inscription of boundaries frequently has legal meaning.[35]

---

30 The school of Critical Legal Studies challenges law's professed objective transcendentalism by exploring the historical context of law. Blomley NK (1994) *Law, Space, and the Geographies of Power*, The Guilford Press: New York at 16. This involves two historical methodologies: a) Diachronic or Developmental histories – which attack formalism and b) Critical legal histories – which raise historicity of knowledge and practice. Both methods are used to destabilize legal knowledge's claims of closure.

31 Halewood P (1996) 'Law's Bodies: Disembodiment and the Structure of Liberal Property Rights', *Iowa Law Review*, Vol 81, 1331 (*81 Iowa L. Rev. 1331*).

32 Blomley, op. cit. fn. 30 at 41.

33 Mitchell D (2001) 'The annihilation of space by law: The roots and implications of anti-homeless laws in the United States', in Blomley N, Delaney D and Ford RT (eds) *The Legal Geographies Reader*, Blackwell: Oxford, UK.

34 Blomley N, Delaney D and Ford RT (eds) (2001) *The Legal Geographies Reader*, Blackwell: Oxford.

35 Ibid.

Nicholas Blomley's 1994 book *Law, Space, and Geographies of Power*[36] represents a gathering together of research threads pertaining to legal geographies, providing both an overview of the strands of research and an indication of where the field might be developing. He begins by comparing the work of Critical Legal Studies (CLS) scholars in exposing the historical undercurrents which shape law, despite protestations of historical neutrality. Likewise, he suggests that there are geographical factors which shape law in unacknowledged ways, denied by the myths of equality before the law and rule of law.[37]

Blomley draws from many examples of work which illustrate the geographical aspect of legal power. For example, Mathews and Phyne contrast the 'Hobbesian' Canadian national fishing laws (that presume that only state regulation can protect the resources from greedy exploitation and depletion), with the actuality of local and community informal regulatory networks which emphasizes fair access, distribution and environmental preservation and indigenous rights.[38]

While this example has clear critical historical aspects, particularly in the exercise of colonial power, the position of indigenous peoples and the construction of resources as property, these aspects also have strong geographical elements. Colonial power is spatially as well as historically exercised. The position of indigenous persons and communities before the law, opposing legal claims of universalism, chart the uneven spread of law across human geography. The isolation of resources as property (separate from general notions of environment) demonstrates the imposition of legal 'maps' of proprietorship over the experience of environmental space. Historical and geographical critique, to the extent that they can be seen as separate, augment and enhance each other.

Blomley's own work contains examples of the intersection between legal and geographic imagination including the geographical influence on Coke's common law project and its connection to cartographic ambition,[39] concepts of place in worker safety law,[40] policing of protests[41] and a study of law in concepts of locality and mobility.[42]

---

36 Blomley, op. cit. fn. 30.

37 Rule of law seems rational, benign, necessary – provides closure for 'value laden' social life Blomley, op. cit. fn. 30 at 9–10, Peller G (1985) 'The Metaphysics of American Law', *California Law Review*, v73, 1152–290.

38 Mathews R and Phyne J (1988) 'Regulating the Newfoundland inshore fishery: Traditional values versus state control in the regulation of a common property resource', *Journal of Canadian Studies*, 23(1,2), 158–76.

39 Blomley, op. cit. fn. 30 'Legal Territories and the "Golden Metewand" of the Law' at 67.

40 Blomley, op. cit. fn. 30 'A "Cabal of the Few?" Place, Federalism and Worker Safety' at 106.

41 Blomley, op. cit. fn. 30 'The Thick Blue Line: Rights, Movement, and the Struggle for Nottinghamshire' at 150.

42 Blomley, op. cit. fn. 30 'Moving, Leaving, and Arriving' at 189.

Many of these pieces of legal geographic research challenge the assumptions about spatial maps imposed by law, focus on regions in their own right and not as a derivative of macro structures and, (showing the influence of Foucault), reject the Hobbesian Leviathan model of governance in favour of a set of strategic relationships, tactics and strategies of power.[43] By cross fertilizing Critical Legal Studies with considerations from critical geography, new insight can be drawn on issues and controversies. Pue[44] provocatively suggests that geographically informed legal studies is by definition insurrectionist, making the entire enterprise appear quite exciting and far away from the politically impotent stereotypes instilled through high school geography.

Blomley establishes a preliminary framework for an exploration of the geographical characteristics of law, summarizing some of the key concerns of human geography (a conceptual division from physical geography) which should provide fertile collaboration with legal theorists. These include exploration of the dialectic between space and society (each producing the other), the idea of locality as a mediating structure, the relationship between geography and knowledge and the links between space and power.[45]

For the legal theorist, human geography can offer at least two approaches or methodologies.[46] The regional approach examines phenomena as discontinuous and regionalized. This is broadly compatible with comparative law, but entails an understanding that, even within a single society or culture, law is not a uniform phenomenon and is not evenly distributed. The impact analysis approach critiques political and disciplinary claims by seeking to chart the actual results rather than the professed intention.

However, both these approaches are flawed in that they reproduce conventional and problematic legal concepts – causality, interpretation and legal functionality, summarized thus:[47]

- Causality. The relationship between space and law is seen as a one way flow, either from law to space or space to law. This assumes that law and space are neatly divisible into two different concepts.
- Interpretation. Both approaches assume an unproblematic concept of what law 'is' and assume that legal texts have but one valid reading.
- Legal Functionality. Law is considered to be an abstract social engineering tool not as an ideological force.

---

43   Blomley, op. cit. fn. 30 at 44.
44   Pue WW (1990) 'Wrestling with law: (Geographical) specificity vs (legal) abstraction', *Urban Geography*, 11 (6), 566–85.
45   Blomley, op. cit. fn. 30 at 28.
46   Ibid. at 28–33.
47   Ibid. at 32.

Rather than rely on human geography as such, Blomley prefers to draw on critical geography to suggest a concept of 'critical legal geography' which conceives of law and space as inseparable and challenges the disciplinary institutions which seek to keep definitions apart. Invoking Kropotkin,[48] Blomley suggests that this spatial/legal concept must be connected to social life, the community and the environment.[49] Being critical of authority, the theorist must see state law as a geographic construct of power, but not the apotheosis of the law which it presents itself as. This requires close attention to the production of meaning and interpretation as well as acknowledge the fluidity of meaning, the 'elusiveness of interpretive determinacy'.[50]

Blomley suggests that this approach to legal geography can be found in the writing of critical geographer Gordon Clark[51] who challenges the 'reality' of consensual/integrated society:

> Essentially, he deploys a pragmatic geographic sensitivity against many 'foundational' accounts of law, including liberalism, the law and economics literature, and legal formalism. Such interpretive accounts, which treat legal disputes as problems of translation, are seen to be at best, naïve, and at worst, deeply conservative in their implicit characterization of society as integrated and consensual [...] they efface the moral pluralism and heterogeneity of social life [...] Society is not consensual, but is continually contested. Legal obligations

---

48   Kropotkin P (1885) 'What geography ought to be', *Nineteenth Century*, 18, 940–956. Kropotkin P (1886) 'Law and Authority', in Baldwin RM (ed.) (1970) *Kropotkin's Revolutionary Pamphelets*, Dover: New York; Kropotkin P (1903) *The State: Its Historic Role*, Freedom Press: London.

49   Blomley, op. cit. fn. 30 at 37.

50   Ibid. at 40. He notes this approach in literary theory; (Eagleton T (1983) *Literary Theory: An Introduction*, University of Minnesota Press: Minneapolis at 48; Mitchell WJ (ed.) (1983) *The Politics of Interpretation*, University of Chicago Press: Chicago) as well as within geography (Clark G L (1985) *Judges and the Cities: Interpreting Local Autonomy*, University of Chicago Press: Chicago). Within law he suggests that Stanley Fish's (Fish S (1983) *Is there a Text in this Class? The Authority of Interpretive Communities*, Harvard University Press: Cambridge, MA) approach to interpretive communities may offer some help.

51   Clark GL (1981) 'Law, the state and the spatial integration of the United States', *Environment and Planning, A*, 13(10), 1189–322; Clark GL (1985) op. cit. fn. 50; Clark GL (1989a) 'The context of federal regulation: propaganda in the US union elections', *Transactions of the Institute of British Geographers*, NS 14, 59–73; Clark GL (1989b) 'Law and the interpretive turn in the social sciences' *Urban Geography*, 10(3), 209–228; Clark GL (1989c) *Unions and Communities under Siege: American Communities and the Crisis of Organised Labour*, Cambridge University Press: Cambridge; Clark GL (1989d) 'The Geography of Law' in Peet R and Thrift N (eds) *New Models in Human Geography*, Unwin Hyman: London; Clark GL (1992) 'Problematic status of corporate regulation in the United States: towards a new moral order', *Environment and Planning, A*, 24, 704–725; Clark GL (1993) 'The legitimacy of judicial decision making in the context of *Richmond v Croson*', *Urban Geography*, 13(3), 205–229.

and rights are understood in radically different ways by groups at different social and spatial locations.[52]

Instead of the monoliths of law, Clark presents a morally pluralist terrain which, while shaped by the institutions of governance, is certainly more diverse in its experiences and ideologies than the 'official version' of State law.

The Project of Critical Legal Geography

While Critical Legal Studies provides the toolbox to examine the historical context of law, a Critical Legal Geography should provide a set of cartographic tools which critique law's relationship with space and the given-ness of the spatial maps implicit in legal and regulatory discourse.

These 'maps', representations of space, are produced by law in various ways and encode, then inscribe, aspects of property, identity and relationships in a manner which appears to practitioners to be neutral and pragmatic and is represented as such in legal ideology.[53] This legal mapping procedure is institutionalized by three elements – absence, hostility to spatial differences and providing law's own maps of social life, in summary:[54]

- Absence. The concept of Rule of Law denies a spatial component to legal discourse, aside from the problematic concept of jurisdiction (explored in more depth in Chapter 6). Law presumes the links between jurisdiction and territory to be a matter of history, to be accepted and not a matter for debate or analysis.
- Hostility to spatial differences. The Rule of Law and the concept of equality before the law deny the uneven inscription of law throughout space. Where uneven spread is actually acknowledged, this is simply perceived as a matter of the system breaking down (for example, poverty, gender discrimination or policing of dangerous spaces) rather than an acknowledgement that geographic variety is the usual situation.
- Providing law's own maps of social life. Superimposed over the experiences of those before the law, the simplistic legal maps of human relationships become truth rather than acknowledged as mere models or tools.[55] Concepts such as causation, motive or intention are filtered through

---

52 Blomley, op. cit. fn. 30 at 41–2.
53 Ibid. at 52 suggests that these 'deeply inscribed legal maps' include definitions of spaces (such as home/work), identities (employer/citizen) and concepts (public/private).
54 Ibid. at 53–6.
55 Lefebvre, op. cit. fn. 29 at 105–110 discusses the importance of reduction for analysis and also the danger of forgetting that your models are simplifications and lapsing into reductionism, where method becomes a mere veil for an ideology of homogenization.

legal channels of relevance and evidence to create functional accounts of complex and indeterminate situations. Relevant examples of research given by Blomley include the colonial practices of property law through re-naming a landscape,[56] the condition of homelessness under the privatization of collective space[57] and the regulation of queerness through the double geography of street and body.[58]

A critical legal geography might begin by describing and opposing these three practices and would seem to share a consistent outlook with postructuralism's concerns of local knowledges and conditions. Pue[59] suggests that the law's abstract view of conceptual space in its emphasis on 'general principles' and denial of heterogeneity merely compounds abstraction and produces geographically irrelevant 'facts' of social life. It may be possible to build more consistent connections between law and life, but the current legal framework, by insisting on its geographic and historical neutrality, fails to facilitate the flow of information and experience.

Producing Space: The Work of Henri Lefebvre

> Just as health is not found primarily in hospitals or knowledge in schools, so justice is not primarily to be found in official justice-dispensing institutions. People experience justice (and injustice) not only (or usually) in forms approved by the state but at the primary institutional locations of their activity – home, neighbourhood, workplace ... The notion of official law as a comprehensive monolith – and indeed as a system – are not descriptions of it but rather parts of its historical ideology. Legal regulation in modern societies ... has a more uneven, patchwork character.[60]

When considering the complex spatial relationship between the law of censorship, the notion of community values and the mediascape of the Internet, the work of

---

56 Carter P (1988) *The Road to Botany Bay: An Exploration of Landscape and History*, Knopf: New York; and Ryan S (1994) 'Inscribing the Emptiness: Cartography, exploration and the construction of Australia', in Tiffin C and Lawson A (eds) *De-Scribing Empire: Post-colonialism and Textuality*, Routledge: London.

57 Waldron J (1991) 'Homelessness and the issue of freedom', *UCLA Law Review*, 30, 395–424.

58 Goodrich P (1990) *Languages of Law: From Logics of Memory to Nomadic Masks*, Weidenfeld and Nicholson: London; Goodrich P (1998) 'The Laws of Love: Literature, History and the Governance of Kissing', *New York University Review of Law and Social Change*, v24, 183.

59 Pue, op. cit. fn. 44.

60 Galanter M (1981) 'Justice in many rooms: Courts, private ordering and indigenous law', *Journal of Legal Pluralism*, 19, 1–47.

Henri Lefebvre is useful in proposing a framework. Rather than dictate a rigid procedure, his published work provides a rough path, full of sidetracks, twists and panoramic 'shortcuts' which sets some general directions for the explorer of jurispace. This work is equally applicable to the study of cyberspace and, it will be argued, the intersections between the spaces of cyberspace and jurispace.

Using *The Production of Space* as the foundation of an analysis of skateboard culture, Iain Borden[61] describes the eight key features of Lefebvre's approach which can be summarized thus:

1. The approach is more a sensibility than a system. There is no patented set of methodologies, rather a way of encountering topics.
2. The process is political, aimed at gradually invoking total revolution, of the external system and the internal self.
3. Architecture is the locus of revolution, seen not as the project of city builders but as the 'possibilities machine' of those who live in it.
4. Space is ideological as well as material. The successor to our current concept of space is differential space where differences are not just recognized but also celebrated.
5. Time is part of the production of space. It must be rescued from the measurement and routine control of capital.
6. Everyday life is the site of increasing domination by capital but also the place from where resistance and revolution comes.
7. The human subject, especially the body, is the site of revolutionary activity especially in the reproduction of the self. Space and time are reproduced by the body.
8. Bodies are dynamic – they do something in the city and transform everyday life into a work of art. Actions produce meanings, relationships. Human history is lived and experienced. Spatial study should be applied and experiential.

The physicality and particular human geography of skate culture makes Lefebvre's approach extremely productive in Borden's work. These eight considerations are just as beneficial in an appreciation of censorship law with its spatial strategies of taxonomy, policing of public and private legal zones and invocation of abstract geographical concepts such as community. In particular Lefebvre's work might present a political opportunity to reclaim the concept of 'community' as an indicator of tolerance and a celebration of diversity rather than simply a conformist tool.

In an academic career that spanned most of the twentieth century, Lefebvre was persistently critical of overarching discourses of control such as 'Architecture' and 'Town Planning', specifically the way that these structures position their assumptions as natural and objective. A Marxist humanist, he also places his

---

61 Borden I (2001) *Skateboarding, Space and the City: Architecture and the Body*, Berg: Oxford at 11–12.

critique within a framework of historical materialism, extending the Marxist notion of production to encompass the production of spaces.

The Production of Space

It is useful to consider Lefebvre's *The Production of Space* more closely, particularly as it pertains to law and the regulation of cyberspace. Published in 1974, its scope is congruent with later developments in information technology, particularly the creation of the Internet, making the book especially relevant for present purposes.

Lefebvre begins by pointing out a general lack of engagement with space as a concept in most disciplines. He challenges several social theorists who make passing references to space but, Lefebvre suggests, the concept is significantly under-theorized. Taking the creation of Euclidean mathematical space as a starting point, Lefebvre sees divergence between the kind of space written about by academics and the spaces of everyday life. '[S]ocial space, and especially urban space, emersed in all its diversity – and with a structure far more reminiscent of flaky mille-feuille pastry than of the homogenous and isotropic space of classical (Euclidean/Cartesian) mathematics.'[62] Modernism's abstract re-interpretation of space presages the critical legal geography critique of law's expulsion of spatial particularity.

Far from being an empty, objective grid for containing objects of inquiry, space is produced and constituted through social practices and methods of representation. Lefebvre points to the work of Descartes as turning point from the original perception of space as a category, a description of perceptions, transformed into an abstract, absolute objective truth which pre-exists perception.[63] Descartes established a common language of space, but one which was elevated to the status of truth, rather than a mere means of representation.

Several analytical triads are key components of Lefebvre's project. The first triad conceives of three spaces: of physical space (the space of nature), mental space (the space of logical and formal abstractions) and social space (social practice, sensory space and products of the imagination).[64] These elements are often perceived as spaces which are disjuncted but which overlap significantly. Social space is usually not constructed in spatial terms at all. It is important to stress the unity and interdependence of these concepts as each derives meaning from the other.

---

62 Lefebvre, op. cit. fn. 29 at 86.
63 Ibid. at 1, Cartesian space is extremely important to mathematics, engineering and 3D computer modelling as a 'common language' to describe spatial disposition of objects along X, Y and Z axes.
64 Ibid. at 14.

Lefebvre challenges the modern nation state as his opponent, the gathering point of power and repression in society. The state's power is vested in its pervasiveness and its power to define what is normal, to frame debate. Lefebvre sees the state as a global phenomenon (irrespective of left or right political ideologies) which has spread its network of control through all aspects of social life, a 'monstrous excrescence transformed into normality'.[65] The state is not just the site of unilateral oppression; the rational regime of the state creates opposition, resistance and subversion.

Foremost among the state's machinery of control is the production of a particular kind of social space which supports is own existence (like the red weed of the Martians in HG Wells' *The War of the Worlds*[66]). This state created space is ideologically repackaged as a neutral, 'abstract' space. This social space, like others, is a social product, but it is concealed by the 'double illusion' of a) transparency and b) realism.[67] 'The rational is thus naturalized, while nature cloaks itself in nostalgias which supplant rationality.'[68]

The concept of power is Lefebvre's most significant point of dispute with Foucault. Lefebvre sees power as predominantly negative (in both senses of the word) and sees it as a part of repressive mechanisms of control, which sets up the state as a quixotic enemy. Rather than being inconsistent with Lefebvre's thought, Foucault's idea of power as a constitutive force (explored in more depth in Chapter 6) can be read alongside The Production of Space and actually refines Lefebvre's model of spatial production into a more elegant expression of the relationship between space and power.

Lefebvre invokes another conceptual triad to discuss the relations between production and the product, important tools that he returns to throughout the discussion. Social space is produced[69] by a combination of:

1. Spatial Practice. The techniques of the production and reproduction of meaning; for example, the separation of work and private spheres through daily routine.
2. Representations of Space. Texts and images connected to the relations of production. Signs and codes usually expressed verbally. 'Conceptualised space, the space of scientists, planners, urbanists, technocratic subdividers and social engineers.'[70]
3. Representational Spaces. These spaces involve complex symbolisms, the underground side of social life including art and music. 'Space as directly lived through its associated images, sensations and symbols, and hence the

---

65 Ibid. at 23.
66 Wells HG (2001 edn.) *The War of the Worlds*, Harper Collins: New York.
67 Lefebvre, op. cit. fn. 29 at 27–30.
68 Ibid. 30.
69 Ibid. at 33.
70 Ibid. at 38.

space of "inhabitants" and "users".'[71] Compared to the representations of space, these tend to be less coherent and non verbal.

Like the discipline of architecture, law carries with it its own spatial practices. Jurispace,[72] the social space of law, is produced by spatial practices which define zones of legality and illegality in criminal or civil trespass, or in obscenity laws' notion of a public place, imposing legal models on social space. Furthermore, the professional separation of lawyers as specialist technicians of law, the creation of courts and parliaments, law libraries, physical relics of reports and legislation all support an abstract space of law which is disconnected from everyday experience yet constructs itself as natural and objective.

Jurispace contains representations of space, such as those which create private property – co-opting systems of measurement, parcelling and the atomization of the environment and physical spaces. This occurs more abstractly in the legal networks of precedent, interpretation and enforceability which occupy a specialized inter-textual space. As the reification of professional training and expertise separates the lawyer from the layperson in practice, it also conceptually splits law from social space. Legal discourse seeks to isolate itself from the contamination of other spaces through self contained definitions and procedures which produce legal truths.

As a rationalist discourse, law's representational spaces are deeply submerged; however these remain possible locations of dissent. Law reconceptualizes narratives as truths, downplaying the facts of a case as merely the locus of grander abstract principles.[73] But, as with other abstract spaces, the very fact that the case facts are singled out, fragmented and reconstructed by law exposes the contradictions within the system of representation. The stories, lived experiences framed by other systems of representation, are not erased by being reframed into legal discourse and live on as a critique of it.

The censorship of the Internet is influenced not only by the spatial aspects of legal regulatory discourse but also by the production of cyberspace. Anticipating cyberspace, Lefebvre's categories aptly describe the intertextual media and communication landscape of the Internet. The various communications technologies and the uses to which people put them are spatial practices which

---

71   Ibid. at 39.

72   Boyle describes his exploration of the formation of law in relation to 'normative topography, the geography of assumptions within which issues are framed, possibilities foreclosed, and so on. This geography *matters*, because it excludes some options from consideration (excludes them even from being seen, perhaps), or prompts a hasty leap to judgement, or because it is one of the many forces shaping subsequent political struggles. But the process I describe is neither a giant conspiracy nor a deterministic and inevitable deep structure of thought.' Boyle J (1996) *Shamans, Software, and Spleens: Law and the Construction of the Information Society*, Harvard University Press: Cambridge, USA at 15.

73   Eriksson LD, Hirvonen A, Minkkinen P and Poyhonen J (1998) op. cit. fn. 2.

shape the form of the Internet with reference to its global scale, its immediacy and its networks. These practices suggest a model of the Internet as another space, coexisting with physical space but in which distance collapses and communications are transformed.[74]

The code of cyberspace, the programming languages, the electronic architecture of the technology; all contain representations of space – a space which is interconnected but mutable, always immediate, regardless of nation-state boundaries. The concept of hypertext moves electronic media beyond the model of individual files held on different computers, vast geographical distances apart to the idea of one large text, interconnected and sharing close spatial links through immediate (often imperceptible) shifts in physical location. At the same time that new media collapses electronic textual boundaries, it also imposes a strict barrier between wired and unwired spaces.[75]

Finally, the representational spaces of cyberspace have served an important role in the construction of cyberspace as a different world – a dark void space filled with glowing icons. The vision of science fiction 'cyberpunk' authors such as William Gibson has been influential on nascent Internet technologies and this has been recognized by technology theorists.[76] Technological innovations have been inspired by the fiction which in turn speculates on developments – the dialogue is drawn into a feedback loop.[77]

New media also challenge the cultural hegemony of law's existing representational spaces. The Internet is just one of several technological changes which has challenged hermetically-sealed theories of law and regulation. In the context of intellectual property law, Aoki examines globalization and trans-border information flows as having a distinctly geographical effect on the way in which law is transformed, resulting in significant effects on the interlinked notions of sovereignty and property.[78]

---

74 Castells M (2001) *The Internet Galaxy: Reflections on the Internet, Business and Society*, Oxford University Press: Oxford at 140.

75 These are like to begin collapsing as reception of wireless and bluetooth interconnective technologies allow the Internet to be more pervasive and less wired into the hardware. This emphasizes the digital divide in the information economy. Smith MA (2000) 'Some Social Implications of Ubiquitous Wireless Networks', *ACM Mobile Computing and Communications Review*, Vol 4(2).

76 Burrows R (1997) 'Virtual culture, urban social polarisation and social science fiction' in Loader, op. cit. fn. 11.

77 It is relevant to consider other science fictions representations of cyberspace as a place. Movie and television representations use particularly visual metaphors of representation. Consider *Johnny Mnemonic* (1995), *Cowboy Bebop* (1998), *Hack:SIGN* (2002), *Serial Experiments Lain* (1998), *Avalon* (2001) and, once again, *eXistenZ* and *The Matrix* (1998).

78 Aoki K (1996) '(Intellectual) Property and Sovereignty: Notes Toward a Cultural Geography of Authorship', *Stanford Law Review*, v48, 1293.

Lefebvre's conceptual triad has given fertile avenues for exploring the spaces of both law and the Internet. Later in this chapter the interface of jurispace and cyberspace will be considered in more depth, but this cannot be done until more parts of Lefebvre's theoretical framework are detailed.

Lefebvre and the Politics of Spatial Production

> Whenever a newspaper reporter characterizes an inner city neighbourhood as crime-ridden [...] or a forestry company casts its investments in a small single industry town as 'assets' in a larger portfolio, urban geographies are being drawn [...] Indeed alternative and oppositional geographies [...] can also be found, many of them opposed to the orthodoxy. If residents of poorer downtown areas resist their own invisibility, or insist on alternative 'maps' of their neighbourhoods (refusing to be case as 'beyond hope' or as simply 'in the way' of proposed redevelopments [...]) they are engaging in an important form of political struggle.[79]

Representation of space, in particular the creation of maps, is a political process. The size and complexity of the Internet has resisted any kind of topographical or typological mapping,[80] yet there are still broad brush strokes spoken of, about the legitimate (business) side of the Internet and its dark side, the spaces of hackers, pornographers and other 'deviants'.[81] The mainstreaming of the Internet has not expunged these shadows. One of the reasons why content censorship is such a politically hot issue is that it is one of the important sites at which this redevelopment occurs and boundaries are erected, like the gentrification of Times Square.

Political discourses, mass media and disciplines such as sociology contribute aspects of city maps (as the quote from Blomley above suggests) in a manner which is deeply ideological. As already mentioned, Lefebvre sets his targets on the modern state as the primary locus through which the control of space is implemented and the individual experiences of space are silenced. To an extent, this furthers Hobbes' demonization of the Leviathan of State and invokes anarchist and liberal fears of the concentrated power of the state. It may be argued that the state itself is a mere nexus, where multiple discontinuous control mechanisms condense together and are given expression through the technologies of regulation.

---

79 Blomley, op. cit. fn. 30 at 191.

80 Not that people did not try to construct comprehensive maps in the early days of Internet popularization. See for example Powell B and Wickre K (1995) *Atlas to the World Wide Web*, Ziff-Davis Press: Emeryville, CA.

81 Since the very beginning of the World Wide Web, the Internet has catered transgressive media, 'sick' humour and morbid images and popular sites such as Consumption Junction http://www.consumptionjunction.com continue this trend.

'The state' is a convenient mask, for diffuse systems and agents of control, to mobilize resistance around a central point, but a mask nevertheless.

Lefebvre suggests that the entire history of space involves a transformation from absolute (natural) space to abstract space – a process influenced by forces of production, the alienation of labour and creation of a commodity economy.[82] This is reflected in the enclosures of geography, property and the common law.[83]

In Lefebvre's analysis, abstract space is generated from centres of wealth and power. By abstracting space, institutions of power seek to transform peripheral spaces or exclude them altogether, through violence if necessary. While abstract space is not experienced in itself, it is imposed as a template on lived experiences as it is the 'locus and medium of power',[84] the power grid of the state. Formal and quantitative, '[a]bstract space functions "objectally", as a set of things/signs and their formal relationships.'[85] Abstract space erases differences, especially those of the body, through its supposed objectivity and concepts of bureaucratic equality.[86] Differences are expelled into the symbolic spaces where they must vie with other abstract symbolic forms that are repressive and authoritarian, like a phallic monument challenged by insubordinate graffiti. To Lefebvre, abstract space has no potential for pleasure and is the cause of adolescent rebellion, 'recovering the world of differences – the natural, the sensory/sensual, sexuality and pleasure.'[87] This rebellion is then channelled into repressive representational spaces of consumerism.[88]

> Abstract space is not defined only by the disappearance of trees, or by the receding of nature; nor merely by the great empty spaces of the state and the military [...] nor even by commercial centres packed tight with commodities [...] Its abstraction has nothing simple about it: it is not transparent and cannot be reduced either to a logic or a strategy [...] It has nothing of a 'subject' about it, yet it acts like a subject in that it transports and maintains specific social relations. [...] It sets itself up as the space of power, which will (or at any rate may) eventually lead to its own dissolution [... T]he abstract 'one' of modern social space and – hidden within it, concealed by its illusory transparency – the real 'subject', namely state (political) power [... L]ived experience is crushed,

---

82 Lefebvre, op. cit. fn. 29 at 46.
83 Blomley, op. cit. fn. 30 Chapter 3.
84 Lefebvre, op. cit. fn. 29 at 94.
85 Ibid. at 49.
86 Lefebvre's attitude invokes 'I am not a number, I am a free man', the primal cry of Number Six in the television show *The Prisoner*, influenced by revolutionary and situationist themes.
87 Lefebvre, op. cit. fn. 29 at 50.
88 This theme is picked up again in the next chapter, concerning the marketing of desire.

vanquished by what is 'conceived of'. History is experienced as nostalgia, nature as regret – as a horizon fast disappearing behind us.[89]

The state is the focus of Lefebvre's critique which implicitly includes the role of the law in imposing abstract notions of social relations and experiences, expressed as concepts such as equality, the values of the community, the 'reasonable man' test, all meshed into a placeless site 'before the law'. His critique extends beyond the formal power of the state and implicates the professions and disciplinary knowledges which contribute to this sale of 'the emperor's new clothes' as truth. Blomley critiques the discipline of law for not just ignoring spatiality of social life but in making it irrelevant, the 'centralisation narrative [...] has been one of continued disembedding of legal practice and legal knowledge from locality'.[90]

> The error – or illusion – generated here consists in the fact that, when social space is placed beyond our range of vision in this way, its practical character vanishes and is transformed in philosophical fashion into a kind of absolute. In face of this fetishised abstraction, 'users' spontaneously turn themselves, their presence, their 'lived experience' and their bodies into abstractions too. Fetishised abstract space thus gives rise to two practical abstractions: 'users' who cannot recognise themselves within it, and a thought which cannot conceive of adopting a critical stance towards it.[91]

Abstraction manufactures consensus through tacit non-aggression pacts, commonality of use and a system of property. The abstraction process is embraced in the logic of capitalism and the abstractions of liberal legalism, 'backed up by a frightening capacity for violence, and maintained by a bureaucracy which has laid hold of the gains of capitalism'.[92] While produced and constructed, abstract models are normalized through the 'modernist triad' of readability, visibility and intelligibility.[93] Within censorship discourse, the totalizing 'community' is just such an abstract contrivance, displacing local practices and experientially constituted communities and legitimating state control of media.

Ford suggests that homogenous, abstract space has an impact on law through the idea of jurisdiction, the locus of control being based on physical rather than human geography, which can be summarized in the following ways:[94]

---

89   Lefebvre, op. cit. fn. 29 at 50–1.
90   Blomley, op. cit. fn. 30 at 107.
91   Lefebvre, op. cit. fn. 29 at 93.
92   Ibid. at 52.
93   Ibid. at 96.
94   Ford RT (1999) 'Law's territory (a history of jurisdiction)', *Michigan Law Review*, Vol 97, 843 at 847.

(a) Spatial practices of jurisdiction present a control interface with no 'gaps', legal control is determined by checking the jurisdictional map. Physical location determines jurisdiction and there seems to be certainty. There seem to be no opportunities for authorities to dispute who is in control in a specific instance, even though territorial squabbles among regulators are actually quite common;[95]
(b) Jurisdiction obscures social relations and the distribution of resources;
(c) Jurisidiction presents social and political relationships as impersonal result of an abstract scheme. It presents itself as a kind of equality and may conceal decisions that are made on the basis of race, religion or some category. This recalls Anatole France's aphorism 'The law, in its majestic equality, forbids the rich as well as the poor to sleep under bridges, to beg in the streets, and to steal bread';[96] and
(d) Jurisdictional space is presented as conceptually empty (even though it impacts on other spaces rich in meaning) and the space is represented as an empty vessel for government control.

Through denial of spatial particularity, reification of theoretical models and endorsement of homogenous community standards, the institutions of law engage in practices of abstraction. Abstract space is essential to the constitution of contemporary legal space and it in turn contributes to an overall programme of control through expulsion of difference. Abstraction is, however, not just a one way street.

Abstract space carries in it the seeds of its own destruction tightly wound up within its own contradictions. Its unravelling is inevitable, to be replaced by what Lefebvre calls 'differential space' which rejects the homogeneity of abstract space and which positively embraces differences of all kinds. The foundation of this differential space lies in the uncontrollable diversity of representational spaces, which have been used but never mastered by abstract space.

Lefebvre is coy concerning the actual nature of differential space. His links to the Dadaists and Situationists and to the student revolution of 1969 suggested to him the existence of this space. Since the publication of *The Production of Space*, Lefebvre's work has become increasingly important in the critique of consumer culture, advertising and resistance to consumerism through art and culture jamming.

Differential spaces begin to emerge at the margins or in the liminal spaces which cut through other structures. These emerge 'either in the form of resistances or in the form of externalities (lateral, heterotopical, heterological). What is different is, to begin with, what is excluded: the edges of the city, shanty towns, the spaces of forbidden games, of guerrilla war, of war. Sooner or later, however, the existing

---

95 Ford, ibid., gives the examples that control over immigration or paying tax on oil deposits are referred to physical location.
96 France A (1894) *The Red Lily*.

centre and the forces of homogenization must seek to absorb and digest all such differences.'[97] Recent work on globalization suggests that this homogenization needs to be considered across national boundaries.[98]

Legal thought has been criticized for its tendencies toward centralization, abstraction and homogenization, its denial of spatial and local difference and diversity.[99] Critical Legal Studies scholars demonstrate that liberal legal ideology, despite all systemic claims to objectivity, rationality and coherence, is filled with contradictions and is committed to inconsistent aims and positions, such as the conflict between setting formal rules and relying on discretionary standards.[100]

One reason why the recognition of indigenous customary law is so controversial[101] is that recognition of dual jurisdictions challenges the totalizing power of the state, emphasizing the cracks which run through the apparently homogenous and uniform monolith of law. Regardless of actual consequences of customary law recognition, the ideological danger to abstract legal space is such that the legal system acts to contain and control sites of rupture, 'spackling' them over with the line of precedent which subordinates inter-jurisdictional recognition as a subsidiary part of the total sovereignty of common law. In other words it engages in regulatory fortressing to conceal its own contradictions.

Differential space emerges at the cracks in abstract space, where the contradictions cannot be contained. Lefebvre sees these contradictions as inherent in political power and that abstract space is a tool of that power ('power' he conceives as an oppressive phenomenon).[102] Differential space seems to originate in the world of 'signs and images', between real and unreal, bubbling up through the cracks and interstices of abstract space.[103] It is here that the body may find its way back to lived experience through a hybrid of textual reading (without seeing discourse as the ultimate object of inquiry) and existentialism. Central to the rise of differential space is desire,[104] the dialectic between Logos and Anti-Logos or Grand Desire (here Lefebvre invokes Nietzsche) – a spatial revolution of the

---

97   Lefebvre, op. cit. fn. 29 at 373.

98   Appadurai A (1990) 'Disjuncture and Difference in the Global Cultural Economy', in Featherstone M (ed.) *Global Culture: Nationalism, Globalization and Modernity*, Sage Publications: London.

99   Clark, op. cit. fn. 51.

100   Kelman M (1987) *A Guide to Critical Legal Studies*, Harvard University Press: Cambridge, MA.

101   Australian Law Reform Commission (1986) *The Recognition of Aboriginal Customary Laws*, Report no 31, AGPS: Canberra.

102   Foucault and Lefebvre can be read together, where Lefebvre refers to 'power' this should be read as Focault's concept of dominating power. Sharp JP, Routledge P, Philo C and Paddison R (eds) (2000) *Entanglements of Power: Geographies of Domination/ Resistance*, Routledge: London at 26.

103   Lefebvre, op. cit. fn. 29 at 389.

104   Here Lefebvre sketches tantalising links between desire and differential space, but unfortunately leaves this undeveloped.

self. 'The psychoanalytical account of conflict between a pleasure principle and a reality principle gives only an abstract and feeble idea of this great struggle.'[105]

Despite the commercialization, mainstreaming and censorship of the Internet, many of its pleasurable spaces remain. Cynicism of consumerism notwithstanding, it must be conceded that commercialization is responsible for some of the new pleasures which exist today via electronic entertainment media. Lefebvre sees the arrival of differential space as related to the rediscovery of the natural, of pleasure, difference, sensory/sensual and sexual experiences – of connection between people. In the context of the Internet censorship debate, it is important to see the dual nature of erotica/pornography as both the promise of the sensual but also repression through commodification and consumption. It is likewise important to avoid a false 'natural versus technological' dichotomy when discussing communications technologies that facilitate rather than determine content.

Lefebvre's Tools for the Exploration of Space

As conceptually rich as Lefebvre's work is, it requires new methods, new terminology and overall new approaches in the analysis of space. While not wishing to prescribe a totalizing methodology, Lefebvre does furnish the researcher with a set of conceptual tools and processes to start talking about space.

From the outset it must be acknowledged that the term 'space' is not used uniformly or consistently in *The Production of Space*. Frequently, it is a category used to disrupt or harass theoretical constructs of disciplinary approaches, grand narratives such as 'nation', 'society' or 'jurisdiction'. Incongruous and disparate elements can be connected together within spaces, montaged together: 'The history of space does not have to choose between 'processes' and 'structures', change and invariability, events and institutions.'[106]

Lefebvre explains what he describes as an 'anthropological' approach to uncovering the history of spaces, revealing the origins behind the façade of realism. Mental and social activities place pathways upon undefined space (like tracks in the wilderness); these become networks, patterns and eventually become defined. These networks eventually get ascribed meanings, names and boundaries (such as roads, cities, houses). These networks become encoded as representations of space and immersed in representational space.

A similar anthropology can be unearthed in the growth of the Internet as a general discontinuous phenomenon or through the genesis of specific inter-textual hypertext clusters.[107] Internet history begins with individual localized sites which become connected through links, then incorporates the invention of search engines

---

105 Lefebvre, op. cit. fn. 29 at 392.
106 Ibid. at 117.
107 Hypertext creates a space defined by links and motion, by border crossings. Shields R (2000) 'Hypertext Links: The Ethic of the Index and its Space–Time Effects'

and webcrawlers and continues to the rise in popularity of portals and content-managed sites produced by backend servers which create their own connections.[108] This history is not an abstract form of evolution; it must be explored within its social and cultural context, the everyday life of humans who give the technology meaning.[109]

In between Lefebvre's anthropological pathways are the 'holes in the net', marginal spaces.[110] This is not to say these are empty spaces or even uninhabited spaces. Depending on perspective, one person's well-travelled path is another's tangled thicket. The impulse of abstract space is to attempt to impose a homogenous map onto this complexity, usually for political purposes. For example, discrete but marginal communities arising out the consumption of erotica or gay subcultures, both spaces of the night,[111] are labelled deviant and excluded from a totalizing vision of society based on coherent community morality. This expulsion disciplines those in the marginal spaces, but also maps conformist morality onto the rest of the population.

The Internet has facilitated more spaces in the margins, localized centres of activity. Even if most people engage in stable and predictable communication patterns, centred on commercial sites, this has not diminished the grassroots activism of the Internet. Marginal and liminal spaces thrive in the shadow of the powerful communications hegemonists.

Lefebvre's wide ranging discussion involves broad and conditional acceptance of other forms of analysis such as historical materialism,[112] language and semiotics,[113] a threefold analysis of formal (contours, boundaries, limits, areas and volumes), structural (scale, proportion, dimension and level)[114] and functional elements,[115] examination of philosophical elements (being, nature, substance and matter)[116] and; decoding space using Barthes' methods.[117] Lefebvre does not

---

in Herman A and Swiss T (eds) *The World Wide Web and Contemporary Cultural Theory*, Routledge: London.

108 Hafner K and Lyon M (1996) *Where Wizards Stay up Late: The Origins of the Internet*, Touchstone Press: New York.

109 Levinson P (1997) *The Soft Edge: A Natural History and Future of the Information Revolution*, Routledge: London.

110 Lefebvre, op. cit. fn. 29 at 117–8.

111 Palmer BD (2000) *Cultures of Darkness: Night Travels in the Histories of Transgression*, Monthly Review Press: New York.

112 Lefebvre, op. cit. fn. 29 at 128.

113 Ibid. at 130.

114 Ibid. at 158.

115 Ibid. at 147.

116 Ibid. at 148.

117 Lefebvre (ibid. at160–3) adopts Barthes' (Barthes R (1974) *S/Z*, trans Miller R, Hill and Wang: New York at 18) five textual codes available when reading a text: knowledge, symbols, emotion, fugue, empiricism. To these he suggests we add analysis of body and of power.

propound any particular blueprint for research; rather he suggests how different approaches might usefully be adopted and integrated.

Lefebvre moves beyond traditional scholarship and encourages the examination of what were, at the time that *The Production of Space* was published, fringe areas of concern: the study of the body and its rhythms, its relationship to energies around it, its use and appropriation of rhythms, its rapport with the sphere of music.[118] Lefebvre's approach was many points of intersection with his contemporaries in the Situationists, particularly Debord's investigation of psychogeography.[119]

Some of the spatial terminology used by Lefebvre demands more clarification. Blomley suggests important distinctions between the concepts of space and place.[120] In his use, space simply refers to the recognition and location of spatial difference, a critical tool to challenge presumptions of homogeneity. Place, on the other hand, refers to the human understanding of a specific space in itself. Place focuses on the human 'boundedness' of social life and the recognition of the borders which, individually and collectively, define the sites of life. The concept of place includes location (a place's relationship to other places), locale (the local set of social relationships within that place), sense of place (the experience of a place and the representational map made by those who exist in it) and the historical becoming of place (the social process by which place is reproduced over time).[121]

When considering cyberspace, an analysis of space might recognize the geographical and social diversity of users and those excluded from wired society, against the presumptions of totalizing discourses such as jurisdiction or the mass media. Alternatively, conceiving of cyberspace as a place would examine the concept of electronic media as experiential spaces in themselves, as well as specific sites within the cyberspace concept as general as 'email' or as specific as 'the Dogpile website', or 'alt.movies.asian'.[122]

The production of space in electronic entertainment provides some further examples of difference between concepts of space and place. For exploration style games such as adventure games (and their online relatives, MUDs[123]) a sense of space is important as part of the pleasure, but also as a pragmatic strategy to distinguish different regions in the worlds described. Early text-based adventure games used simple name labels (for example, 'the stinky cavern') and allowed

---

118   Lefebvre, op. cit. fn. 29 at 205.

119   Bonnett A (1989) 'Situationism, Geography and Poststructuralism', *Environment and Planning D: Society and Space*, v7, 131.

120   Blomley, op. cit. fn. 30 at 111–2.

121   Ibid.

122   Batty suggests that each element of the Internet (each web page, each email message) should be conceived as a place, connected to others by networks and nodes. Batty M (1997) 'Virtual Geography', *Futures*, 29, 4/5, 337.

123   Multiple User Domains or the original, more arcane Multiple User Dungeons. These are shared storytelling spaces defined through textual interaction. Hafner and Lyon, op. cit. fn. 108.

specific pathways for movement, often compass directions linking each place to other locations (for example, 'a treacherous path winds to the east'). As the games and the technology became more sophisticated, graphic representations largely replaced these textual labels. First person representations of space became more commonplace, but these were initially limited to simple, featureless underground mazes. Maze games clearly established a feeling of space, but not much of a sense of place. Navigation requires a sense of space, but sense of place provides meaning and context.

With a new generation of games and game technology, sense of place became more important. One of the breakthrough games in this respect was *The Legend of Zelda: The Ocarina of Time* (1998) on the Nintendo 64 game console. Many adventure games used abstract maps to represent movement over large areas of land. *The Ocarina of Time*, while smaller in overall geographic area than some of its predecessors, modelled its entire Kingdom of Hyrule in detail from the (third person) perspective of the protagonist rather than as a mere topographical map. To travel from the woods to the castle, the player had to direct the third person avatar through a meadow, over a hill, across a plain – each filled with details. It was in this detail that the sense of place was experienced – in the sounds of the wildlife, the flow of water, the shapes of the terrain.[124] This experience was enhanced by the game's representation of time, albeit measured on an accelerated scale. In Hyrule the sun rises and falls, light and sound conditions change depending on time of day, as do the player's objectives and other game factors. *The Ocarina of Time* is a game in which the player may pursue game objectives diligently or may merely just explore without purpose and gain a sense of being in the spaces and places of Hyrule. The game has a deeply immersive sense of being in place and time, which outlasts the duration of the game. There are a vast number of players worldwide, each of them knowing the geography of the Kingdom of Hyrule, its sights and sounds, as well as, or perhaps even better, than they know their own neighbourhood.[125]

Many other electronic games also construct a strong sense of place, rather than opt for generic and clichéd images, the *Final Fantasy Series*[126] and the *Silent*

---

124 Senses that the electronic format does not presently support are sense of heat and cold, taste, smell and touch. In games like the horrific *Silent Hill* and *Resident Evil* series these omissions are fortuitous yet the user's imagination often suggests potentials, enhancing the experience and mixed pleasures of horror media. This indicates the importance of the reader's subjective space in constructing a sensory image of an electronic environment.

125 A sequel was published in 2003 on the Nintendo Gamecube platform, titled *The Legend of Zelda: The Wind Waker* (2003). This game disrupted existing players' sense of place by moving the narrative many years forward in time and presenting a Hyrule which is mostly covered by ocean and a small collection of islands. This disorienting strategy engages the experienced player in the game's narrative in an interrogation of history to discover what has happened to Hyrule in the intervening time.

126 *Final Fantasy 7* (1997), *Final Fantasy 8* (1999), *Final Fantasy 9* (2001), *Final Fantasy X* (2002).

Hill[127] series are key examples which market themselves on their highly detailed sense of place and have earned dedicated fanbases accordingly. Games like the neo-noir *GTA (Grand Theft Auto)*[128] crime series have had constant trouble with the Australian censors due to their verisimilitude in representation of violence and strong sense of realism in places of urban conflict.[129]

The technology of representing place and space has been extended by 'first person shooters' as well, which in turn developed online communities around the games such as the 'quake clans'.[130] With the popularity of online adventures (*Everquest*, *Phantasy Star*, *Final Fantasy 11*), computer games have become connected back into the MUD discourse, allowing people to explore vast online spaces together, build communities and communicate with each other.[131] Space, place and community are modelled, within the constraints allowed by the programming code which constitutes and constructs these virtual spaces.

Cyberspace is mapped as it is described and populated by virtual communities. The Internet provides challenges for ordinary cartographic assumptions that a) space is continuous and ordered and b) that a map is not a territory in itself, merely a representation of that territory.[132] Cyberspace geographers Dodge and Kitchin provide a comprehensive exploration of contemporary theories of Internet spatialization and consider that a variety of Internet cartographies and mapping tools might provide maps of Internet communications technologies, asynchronous media, synchronous social spaces and the imaginative mappings of cyberpunk fiction.[133]

Practices of mapping are governance practices, bound up with the establishment of power and regulatory structures.[134] Law has been heavily involved in the mapping

---

127 *Silent Hill* (1999), *Silent Hill 2* (2001), *Silent Hill 3* (2003).

128 *GTA 3* (2001).

129 Classification Review Board (2001) *GTA 3 Decision*, 40th meeting, 11 December.

130 Cassell J and Jenkins H (eds 1999) *From Barbie to Mortal Combat: Gender and Computer Games*, MIT Press: Cambridge, MA.

131 Often by competing with each other, but strategic contest is an engaging form of communication. Castronova E (2001) *Virtual Worlds: A First Hand Account of Market and Society on the Cyberian Frontier*, http://papers.ssrn.com/abstract=294828; Kim AJ (1998) 'Killers Have More Fun', *Wired 6.05*, http://wired.com/archive/6.05/ultima_pr.html, Lizard (1998) 'Kill Bunnies, Sell Meat, Kill More Bunnies', *Wired 6.05*, http://wired.com/archive/6.05/bunnies_pr.html.

132 Staple GC (1995) 'Notes on Mapping the New: From Tribal Space to Corporate Space', *Telegeography '95*. http://www.telegeography.com/Publications/mapping.html.

133 Dodge and Kitchin, op. cit. fn. 20. For a further example of the use of ethnographic methodology in mapping spaces of Usenet, see Smith MA (1999) 'Invisible Crowds in Cyberspace: Mapping the social structure of the Usenet', in Smith MA and Kollock P (eds) *Communities in Cyberspace*, Routledge: New York.

134 Reid E (1999) 'Hierarchy and power: social control in cyberspace', in Smith MA and Kollock P (eds) *Communities in Cyberspace*, Routledge: New York.

and colonizing of the imaginary spaces of cyberspace. Gaitenby examines the importation of legal frames of reference (of property, rights, social control and due process) into MUDs and MOOs in two primary ways: through operational rules (in the allocation of virtual resources) and interractional rules (codes of conduct).[135] It must be recognized that these practices are also colonizing practices[136] and critics are wary of the hegemonic power that the West holds in founding the culture and metaphors of cyberspace.[137]

Space and Everyday Life

> Space is social morphology: it is to lived experience what form itself is to the living organism.[138]

Lefebvre returns to the theme of everyday life frequently, as a site from which the totalizing ideology of abstract space can be challenged. Even the pure abstraction of law cannot totally expel life (contained in messy leaky bodies and relationships) from its models of the legal subject. Life and death, birth and disability all find their way into legal discourse as legal 'statuses', reconfigured to fit the discourse.[139]

---

135 Gaitenby A (1996) 'Law's Mapping of Cyberspace: The Shape of New Social Space', *Technological Forecasting and Social Change*, v 52, 135.

136 Ryan demonstrates the importance of cartography as a colonial strategy. Ryan, op. cit. fn. 56. In *Imagined Communities*, Anderson examines three interconnected technologies of colonialism: the census, the map and the museum. The census achieves the abstract quantification/serialization of persons. The map leads to the logoization of political space. The museum is an 'ecumenical' technology of profane genealogising. Anderson B (1983, rev. edn.) *Imagined Communities: Reflections on the Origins and Spread of Nationalism*, Verso: London.

137 Dyson E, Gilder G, Keyworth G and Toffler A (1996) 'Cyberspace and the American Dream: A Magna Carta for the Knowledge Age', *The Information Society*, No 12, 295–308 provide an example of the colonising ideology of which postcolonial critics are very wary:

> The bioelectronic frontier is an appropriate metaphor for what is happening in cyberspace, calling to mind as it does the spirit of invention and discovery that led ancient mariners to explore the world, generations of pioneers to tame the American continent and, more recently, to man's first exploration of outer space … Cyberspace is the land of knowledge, and the exploration of that land can be a civilisation's truest, highest calling. The opportunity is now before us to empower every person to pursue that calling in his or her own way.

138 Lefebvre, op. cit. fn. 29 at 94.

139 Cotteral R (1986) 'Law and Sociology: Notes on the Confrontation of Disciplines', *Journal of Law and Society*, Vol 13(1), 9–34.

In legal proceedings these concepts have been redefined as mere 'inputs' from society, fed into the legal process, a narrowly defined aspect of the process.[140]

Some scholars argue for the importance of law as a facet of everyday life rather than as a grand monolith or member of state superstructure. For Giddens,[141] ideology is reproduced by daily practices and, based on this, Blomley suggests that this is the way in which legal discourse filters our experiences, defines which wrongs and injustices we have to accept (such as poverty) and which are the valid subject of legal claim to justice (such as libel and assault in public places).[142]

Yet this 'everyday life' is merely the isolated, fragmented image seen from the window of the liberal legal individual. Everyday experiences are dynamic, located within the vital life of the collective or the community, through which the self draws identity and meaning. Legal scholar Nedelsky[143] is sceptical of law's atomism, of the barren and thin model of social life which it provides by placing the self at the centre and expelling the untrustworthy collective to the fringes. Where community is recognized under the individualist liberal scheme, it is totalized as an abstraction, an instrument of conformity tinged with nostalgia.[144]

Instead of disconnected and atomistic life we may seek to embrace a notion of law which is located within a sense of community or, rather, within multiple fragmented communities which shift and inter-connect depending on the context. On occasion, law reluctantly puts aside its universalizing umbrella to recognize that different communities exist,[145] but this is often done in methodologically awkard ways and all too often involves uncritical acceptance of stereotyped assumptions about culture, race and gender.[146]

A critical spatialization of law does not necessarily involve dissolution into irreconcilable fragments of conflicting communities and shifting values. It can begin with a simple acknowledgement of the situational nature of legal knowledge and a

---

140   Gordon RW (1981) 'Historicism in Legal Scholarship', *Yale Law Journal*, Vol 90, 1017.

141   Giddens A (1984) *The Constitution of Society*, University of California Press: Berkeley.

142   Blomley, op. cit. fn. 30 at 12.

143   Nedelsky J (1990) 'Law, boundaries and the bounded self', *Representations*, 30, 162–89.

144   The discipline of economics is another example of a abstract, virtual construct. These detached models and visions are imposed the experiences of producers and consumers. Miller D (1998) 'A theory of virtualism' in Carter J and Miller D (eds) *Virtualism and its Discontents*, Berg: Oxford.

145   The general rule of defamation law is that the standards of the community apply, yet on occasion the plaintiff's peers can be used so long as they form an 'appreciable' and 'reputable' section of the community, such as a religious or ethnic community, *Hepburn v TCN Channel Nine Pty Ltd* [1983] 2 NSWLR 682 at 694.

146   In Australia the case of *Mabo v Qld (No 2)* (1992) 175 CLR 1 and the line of authorities which follow it, demonstrate the ways in which stereotypes about traditional life can all too be easily reified in legal discourse.

critical attitude to the reception of precedent, to certainty and consistency as overriding objectives. The smooth administration of law involves the use of working models,[147] which are ways of understanding the social world and the behaviour of subjects before the law. These models occupy a legal constituted space, a jurispace, which is all too frequently represented as objective reality. The power of law and the institutions which support it allow this jurispace definition to extend beyond its initial purpose into other spaces of social life.[148] It is important that this legal modelling process be recognized and acknowledged if it is to form part of an accountable system.[149]

Space and the Geographies of Cyberspace

> well you're in your little room
> and you're working on something good
> but if it's really good
> you're gonna need a bigger room
> and when you're in the bigger room
> you might not know what to do
> you might have to think of
> how you got started
> sitting in your little room[150]

---

147 For instance the models of causation in tort law cannot be argued from first principles of physics and philosophy each time per Mason J in *March v E & MH Stramore Pty Ltd* (1990–91) 171 CLR 546. However this should not mean that the legal model supplants those other disciplines in other contexts.

148 To draw on the Torts example once more, the notion of 'duty of care' within negligence law models human relationships in particular ways, with reference to duty, breach, causation and (sometimes) proximity. Increasingly these standards are being mapped onto social life, particularly through the insurance industry's absorption of legal principles and its financial power to shape social behaviour through setting premiums. In Melbourne, the *Midsumma* queer street party was cancelled after the public liability insurance premium soared from A$5,000 in 2002 to over A$80,000 in 2003. *The Age* (2003c) 'Soaring Premiums Take their Toll on Festivals', 4 January, http://www.theage.com/articles/2003/01/03/1041566224854.html (viewed 6/1/03).

149 This, Trina Grillo argues, is a strength of the common law process over others that are not reported. She is critical of the manner in which mediators in family cases develop their own 'precedents' about what constitutes good and bad mothering – concepts which are never exposed to open reporting and discussion. Grillo T (1991) 'The Mediation Alternative: Process Dangers for Women', *Yale Law Journal*, v100(6), 1545. This approach was examined in Beattie S (1997) 'Is Mediation a real Alternative to Law? Pitfalls for Aboriginal Participants', *Australian Dispute Resolution Journal*, v8(1), 57.

150 Lyrics from 'Little Room' from the White Stripes album *White Blood Cells* (2001).

Cyberspace is conceptualized and described in different ways: as space, language, property, territories, jurisdiction, code, communities, network, systems, relationships, mythology and in other images.[151] Why is space such a compelling metaphor? Why have geometric and spatial images become so prevalent in representations such as science fiction and even the covers of academic books concerning computers and technology? The idea of cyberspace as a space in which networks of information, relationships and power exists is a useful one and allows one perspective on the sense of history and change which have shaped different regulatory strategies.

Representations of cyberspace are important, but it is also important to remember that Internet technologies in themselves represent space in particular ways, often in opposition to traditional geographical concepts. With synchronous communication, the limitations of timezone remain as a reminder of the physical distribution of globally diverse participants but in asychonrounous communication processes[152] the wired word appears to be without borders. The end to end (or 'e2e') architecture of the Internet protects the user from having to pass through gatekeepers which are all dealt with invisibly, adding to the illusion of borderless space.

The net, cyberspace, the Infobahn, the information superhighway, virtual communities – each uses a spatial metaphor to describe the relationships between people as being constituted in an otherspace.[153] This contrasts to the social practices around telephone and fax systems. A person using a telephone is unlikely to consider themselves as operating in 'phonespace'. This raises the issue as to why has the concept of cyberspace been taken up so quickly.

The choice of metaphor is significant. Chapter 3 has already suggested that McLuhan's notion of 'rear-view regulation' is important to the regulation of new technologies and has been applied in counter-intuitive manner in the *Broadcasting Services Amendment (Online Services) Act 1999* by deeming web pages to be film or video media.[154] In cyberspace regulation generally metaphors are chosen which suggest[155] regulatory strategies from offline space: an information superhighway

---

151   It is unhelpful to proclaim a single character of virtual geography – it is comprised of a heterogeneity of spaces and practices. Crang M, Crang P and May J (eds) (1999) *Virtual Geographies: Bodies, Space and Relations*, Routledge: London at 4.

152   Mitchell W (1996) *City of Bits: Space, Place and the Infobahn*, MIT Press, MA at 16.

153   Imken cautions us to be wary of 'Cyberpole' – the overdrawn opposition of the real and the virtual which exists in the rhetoric of both cyber-enthusiasts and detractors. Imken, op. cit. fn. 10.

154   'Rear view' regulation describes the use of past metaphors and regulatory structures to constitute debate concerning new technologies – such as the way the regulation of the telephone one hundred years ago was shaped by pre-existing structures regulating urban space and property. Stein J (1999) 'The telephone: its social shaping and public negotiation in late nineteenth- and early twentieth-century London', in Crang, Crang and May, op. cit. fn. 151.

155   And, it is suggested, create a position from which to critique offline strategies.

needs road rules, a virtual community a virtual bobby, a network needs gatekeepers. Interestingly enough, the notion of cyberspace as abstract space does not of itself suggest strategies which is perhaps why the abstract metaphor is often used in discourses which claim the impossibility of regulation and or promote the fear of cyberspace.[156]

There is a vast literature concerning cyberspace and much of it touches on the ways in which cyberspace is produced through language and discourse[157] and the relationship of the subject to cyberspace.[158] Technology theorist William Mitchell's influential *City of Bits: Space, Place and the Infobahn*,[159] introduces important architectural concepts to the cyberspace discourse. That book was published in 1995 at the height of cyber-utopian enthusiasm, when the liberational potential of the Internet was widely posited. Mitchell's concept of the architecture of the Internet remain important today, as information flows conveying power and public spaces are increasingly virtual resources.[160]

---

156   Cyberspace is often represented as an unregulated space, a new space in which 'distasteful' facets of contemporary society flourish, like pornography and hate speech. Squire SJ (1996) 'Re-territorializing Knowledge(s): Electronic Spaces and Virtual Geographies', *Area*, V28, 101. This is of course not a universal trend in the use of that term. The term is itself contentious. As Mitchell notes 'This word does not have a respectable technical pedigree, but was introduced by William Gibson in his 1984 novel *Neuromancer*. Many old computer hands detest it for the conceptual vulgarities that it has come to connote. But it has won out against all the plausible alternatives and has succeeded in taking possession of the semantic niche, so I shall use it.' *City of Bits* at 181.

157   When considering the dialectic relationship between the social and the technological, we must consider not just how the technology is socially constructed but also how society is constituted by technology. Bingham N (1999) 'Unthinkable complexity? Cyberspace otherwise', in Crang, Crang and May, op. cit. fn. 151; Bijker and Law (eds) (1992) *Shaping Technology/Building Society: Studies in Sociotechnical Change*, MIT Press: Cambridge, MA. Technologies cannot be considered in isolation; they must be considered in the context of 'landscapes of translation' in which they are encountered. Wakeford N (1999) 'Gender and the landscapes of computing in an Internet Café', in Crang, Crang and May, op. cit. fn. 151. Technology is hardwired with cultural traditions which determine form and content. Gunkel DJ (2001) 'The Empire Strikes Back Again: The Cultural Politics of the Internet', in Ebo, op. cit. fn. 27.

158   Chernaik argues for a materiality of cyberspace practices, these should not be conceptualized as virtual and ephemeral. Chernaik L (1999) 'Transnationalism, technoscience and difference: the analysis of material–semiotic practices', in Crang, Crang and May, op. cit. fn. 151. Virtual culture is embodied not bodiless as some have suggested. Stone AS (1991) 'Will the Real Body Please Stand-up?: Boundary Stories About Virtual Cultures', in Benedikt M (ed.) *Cyberspace: First Steps*, MIT Press: Cambridge, MA; Argyle K and Shields R (1996) 'Is There a Body in the Net?' in Shields R (ed) *Cultures of the Internet: Virtual Spaces, Real Histories and Living Bodies*, Sage: London.

159   Mitchell, op. cit. fn. 152.

160   Crang, op. cit. fn. 21.

Mitchell connects the study of cyberspace to the study of urban spaces and, significantly, introduces the idea of programming code as architecture, the concept that software constructs space.[161] In the context of legal regulation, the concept that 'Code is the Law',[162] has been adopted and elaborated by legal scholar Larry Lessig whose work is discussed the next section. Mitchell draws a broad set of connections between technology, governance and architecture:

> [R]eimagine architecture and urbanism in the new context [...] of the telecommunications revolution, the ongoing miniaturisation of electronics, the commodification of bits, and the growing domination of software over materialised form. They adumbrate the emergent but still invisible cities of the twenty-first century [...] It matters because the emerging civic structures and spatial arrangements of the digital era will profoundly effect our access to economic opportunities and public services, the character and content of public discourse, the forms of cultural activity, the enaction of power, and the experiences which give shape and texture to our daily routines. [... W]e can find opportunities to intervene, sometimes to resist, to organise, to legislate, to plan and design.[163]

This interdisciplinary awareness draws significant connections between law and other discourses, such as design and architecture. The notion of code as a regulatory instrument has impact on the way in which geography and architecture are perceived. Mitchell argues that new soft cities will fracture existing symbolic links between buildings and social function (for example, banks, work, home, shopping) and ultimately the idea of the city itself. Considering the impact that automatic teller machines (ATMs) and electronic banking systems have had on the notion of what constitutes a bank demonstrates the displacement of physical architecture and the increasing importance of cyberspace architectural concepts of code and security systems.[164] Likewise, the virtualization of architecture provides a challenge to the integrity of other social structures which use architectural representations such as the law courts.

In the world of code, human subjects are present as cyborgs connected to networks of information and power, structures in real and conceptual space:

> [T]he border between interiority and exteriority is destabilised. [... M]etaphysicians will be tempted to reformulate the mind/body problem as the mind/network problem. [... T]he cyborg soul [...] is no longer to be sought just on the wet side of the carbon/silicon divide.[165]

---

161 Mitchell, op. cit. fn. 152 at 5.
162 Ibid. at 111.
163 Ibid. at 5.
164 Ironically, perhaps, these changes have also acted as the site of resistance in the emergence of community banks as 'real' banks.
165 Mitchell, op. cit. 152 at 31.

While the cyberspace and information system aspects of this process are important, these should not be seen in isolation. Mitchell suggests that all spaces are constituted by code, by sets of rules, languages and discourses by which humans describe and construct their environment. According to Mitchell, law itself is a form of code and is inscribed on the city in spatial ways:

> Spatial cities, of course, are not only condensations of activity to maximize accessibility and promote face-to-face interaction, but are also elaborate structures for organizing and controlling access. They are subdivided into districts, neighbourhoods, and turfs, legally portioned by property lines and jurisidictional boundaries, and segmented into nested enclosures by fences and walls. For the inhabitants, crossing a threshold and entering a defined place – as an owner, guest, visitor, tourist, trespasser, intruder, or invader – is a symbolically, socially and legally freighted act.[166]

The debates surrounding the censorship of cyberspace occupy a diversity of regulatory environments and frameworks, each with their own codes of rules and systems of representation. Through Mitchell's observations and Lefebvre's spatial consciousness the regulation of cyberspace can be analysed as an inter-textual, physical and virtual architecture.

The Regulation of Cyberspace

As new media becomes more pervasive and wired spaces become accepted in the background of everyday life (at least for those on the privileged side of the digital divide[167]) cyberspace is becoming a principal site for social interaction, polity and virtual action.[168] The distribution of power in cyberspace and its relation to real space is still a nascent area of study[169] and systems of regulation and law have used traditional models as provisional measures. Keeping conversant with rapid technological change in communications media challenges the technicians who

---

166 Ibid. at 21.
167 See National Telecommunications and Information Administration (2000) *Falling Through the Net: Toward Digital Inclusion: A Report on Americans' Access to Technology Tools*, US Department of Commerce, October.
168 Terranova T (2001) 'Demonstrating the globe: Virtual action in the network society', in Holmes D (ed) *Virtual Globalization: Virtual Spaces/Tourist Spaces*, Routledge, London.
169 This is explored in much more depth in Jordan T (1999) *Cyberpower: The Culture and Politics of Cyberspace and the Internet*, Routledge: London. See also MacKenzie D and Wajcman J (eds) (1999) *The Social Shaping of Technology* 2 edn, Open University Press: Buckingham, UK.

administer the electronic systems,[170] let alone the regulators who traditionally lag cautiously behind innovations.

Issues pertaining to the jurisdiction of online transactions are governed by technically complex and uncertain forum and territory rules along with the complication of treaties which cross jurisdictional boundaries.[171] This uncertainty leads to difficulty in interjurisdictional enforcement:

> 'It's a whole bunch of gunslingers out there doing whatever they want', [Intellectual Property Lawyer] Norword said. 'It's not like you can send the US Marshals to Finland and shut things down. Nation states don't do a good job returning terrorists and kidnappers. Why would we think they should do a good job policing bald hair remedies sold online?'[172]

Despite this kind of cynicism, the enforcement of copyright (under the WIPO copyright treaty) and cybercrime laws have made inroads into regulating cyberspace, developments which may facilitate further regulation in other arenas.[173] In these areas of law foreign jurisdictions are constructed as problematic and foreign people as often perceived 'others', unregulated and dangerous.[174]

Among policy makers there is a perception that convergent technologies have eroded traditional legal boundaries.[175] Analysis of social activity online has often

---

170   Stefik M (1999) *The Internet Edge: Social, Technical and Legal Challenges for a Networked World*, The MIT Press: Cambridge, MA.

171   Jew B (1999) 'Cyberjurisdiction – Emerging Issues and Conflicts of Law when Overseas Courts Challenge your Web', Gilbert and Tobin Publications, http://gtlaw.com.au/templates/publications/default.jsp?puid=76; Burk DL (1997) 'Jurisdiction in a World without Borders', *Virginia Journal of Law and Technology*, Vol 1, 3; Johnson DR and Post DG (1996) 'Law and Borders – The Rise of Law in Cyberspace', *Stanford Law Review*, v 48, 1367.

172   ZDNet Australia (2001a) 'Taming the Web', 20 April, http://www.zdnet.com.au/newstech/ebusiness/story/0,2000024981,20216841,00.htm.

173   Ibid.

174   Critics are wary of the colonizing practices of the West, in 'cyberimperialist' technologies and through legal colonization. Some critics take a glum view of the information society Cyberimperialism reflects a new kind of imperialism driven by corporations instead of nations. Rusciano FL (2001) 'The Three Faces of Cyberimperialism', in Ebo, op. cit. fn. 27. Even the notion of decentralization can be perceived as a form of colonialism, a method of hegemonic domination. Gunkel DJ, op. cit. fn. 157 at 85. Others see developments in a more positive light. Glocalization in the information age can be result in economic decentring, cultural hybridization and political fragmentation, all of which resist cultural imperialism. Even the ubiquitousness of English, while it has worked as a force of cultural imperialism, has also resulted in the Creolization of the language and its vocabulary. Kraidy MM (2001) 'From Imperialism to Glocalization: A Theoretical Framework for the Information Age', in Ebo, op. cit. fn. 27.

175   Reidenberg JR (1997) 'Governing Networks and Rule-Making in Cyberspace' in Kahn B and Nesson C (eds) *Borders in Cyberspace: Information Policy and the Global Information Infrastructure*, MIT Press: Cambridge.

emphasized the creation of new conceptual spaces, communicative spaces in which online communities are constituted arising in newsgroups, chat rooms and other innovations.[176] These online communities have themselves been the subject of academic investigation, examining their rules, codes of behaviour, resources and negotiations.[177]

The concept of the Internet as a space raises concerns for the regulators of spaces adjacent or connected to it, particularly as the liminal cyberspace enters the home. Regulators are faced with deciding if cyberspace is a new frontier to be conquered, or a void in which no regulatory apparatus can survive. Certainly, in the early days of cyberspace, the challenges posed to conventional jurisdiction were heralded as the beginning of the end of repressive government:[178]

> The nineteenth and twentieth centuries were the centuries of government. For the first time, and brutally in many cases, government took control of both itself and the market. It became activist, focused on changing the status quo, antilibertarian. It could take control this way in large part because of the economies of its regulation and the diseconomies of escaping its regulations. Borders keep people in, and hence governments could regulate. Cyberspace undermines this balance. Regulation does not become more costly, but escape from regulation becomes easier [...] Effective regulation then shifts from lawmakers to code writers [...] We are just leaving a time when the code writers are a relatively independent body [and] entering a very different world where code is written within companies [...] If code is law, who are the lawmakers? What values are being embedded into the code?[179]

The image of cyberspace as an abstract, placeless non-space is challenged by the experiences of those who use new media in everyday life. In an exploration of Inuit web documents, Christensen demonstrates that identity is expressed and negotiated in texts which constitute a social and cultural space. Further, he argues that these new media practices are breaking down the 'walls of mystification' which model the online and offline worlds as separate worlds.[180] Globalization does not necessarily condemn local beliefs and abstraction can be resisted by local practices.

---

176   Kitchin R (1998) *Cyberspace*, Wiley: Chicksfer.

177   Smith MA (1998) *Voices from the WELL: The Logic of the Virtual Commons*, http://www.sscnet.ucla.edu/soc/csoc/papers/voices/Voices.htm (viewed 9/8/2000).

178   See Johnson and Post, op. cit. fn. 171. For a summary of this area, see Loader BD (1997) 'The governance of cyberspace: politics, technology and global restructuring' in Loader, op. cit. fn. 11.

179   Lessig L (1999) *Code and Other Laws of Cyberspace*, Basic Books: New York at 206–7.

180   Christensen NB (1999) *Inuit in Cyberspace: Embedding Offline Identity and Culture Online*, http://home.worldonline.dk/nbc/arcus.html (viewed 2/5/2001).

Internet commentator Peter Chen observes that with 'slight shifts of definitional paradigm [the regulation of] information flows (upon which late capitalism is becoming more dependent) [can be] located within the context of international law governing the flow of waterways' and riparian rights of access and fair usage.[181] The local can influence the global and the margin can become transformed into the centre.[182]

Libertarian dreams of cyberspace as a place of freedom beyond the reach of regulators have also been contested by regulatory technologies which harden the nexus between physical and virtual spaces, allowing users' physical location to be determined by IP tracking. These tools were developed by advertisers and enterprises whose operations are bound by individual American state laws (insurance and pharmaceutical companies) but could easily be used to 'erect geographic borders online'.[183] Practices which emerge from ordinary Internet usage can have dramatic effects if applied by regulators. Rapid technological changes such as these mean that the apparently ineffectual Australian Internet censorship laws might be transformed into capable regulatory apparatus at a future date.

These technological innovations demonstrate the importance of technology in the constitution and governance of cyberspace. New media lawyer Larry Lessig's *Code and Other Laws of Cyberspace*[184] picks up on Mitchell's concept of electronic architecture as regulation[185] and situates it within an exploration of regulatory power. Lessig suggests a model of regulatory power whereby four regulatory forces operate together: Law, Norms, Market and Architecture.[186]

As a conceptual model of regulation, Lessig's model allows the introduction of notions of architecture into legal theory which presently only recognizes a (limited) place for social and economic considerations. Social and economic factors are reconceived by Lessig in the forces of norms and market respectively. 'Architecture' is represented by physical architectural factors (a locked door), as well as systemic ones such as the code of the Internet and other regulated zones. Unfortunately, Lessig does not explore the architectural underpinning of law itself through the rules of construction and interpretation of the legal texts. The four factors are kept separate by Lessig, but some overlap is conceded and each is within government's portfolio of regulatory strategies.[187]

Lessig's four regulatory factors find ready application in cyberspace law. Laws provide sanctions for breaches of 'real world' legal standards such as copyright or

---

181 Chen P (1999) 'Community without Flesh: First Thoughts on the New Broadcasting Services Amendment (Online Services) Bill 1999', *M/C: A Journal of Media and Culture 2.3*, http://english.uq.edu.au/mc/9905/bill (viewed 1/10/01) at 2.
182 Appadurai, op. cit. fn. 98.
183 ZDNet Australia (2001a), op. cit. fn. 172.
184 Lessig, op. cit. fn. 179.
185 Mitchell, op. cit. fn. 152.
186 Lessig, op. cit. fn. 179 at 88.
187 Ibid. at 96–8.

defamation law. Norms govern behaviour through the responses of other netizens. Markets regulate through pricing structures. Architecture regulates through code – the hardware and software which determines what is possible and what is not possible. Lessig focuses on code as a key and under-examined area of regulation and a site which has potential for liberation or oppression. He endorses the open-source software movement as a forum for code that has transparent operation, which makes it more accountable than corporations such as Microsoft controlling the development of code.[188]

Rather than being fuelled by the revolutionary humanism of Lefebvre, Lessig's work is clearly dominated by a species of liberal legalism.[189] Nevertheless, his work has broad intersections with Lefebvre as it undermines the totalizing abstraction of law, with a consciousness that legal mechanisms are spread unevenly across Internet spaces and architectures. Unlike Lefebvre, Lessig does not seek to expose the contradictions of power (although his work may in fact accomplish this) and he does not seek to proclaim a revolutionary successor in differential space.

In Lefebvre's schema, each of Lessig's regulatory forces would comprise a social space, interconnected with the others. 'Architecture' has elements of physical space (a locked door) but requires the context of a social space to give it meaning (a lock means 'keep out', you are not entitled to break the door down). Laws, norms, market and architecture are all social spaces of themselves and in combination constitute a social space of regulation, jurispace.[190] While impracticable, Lessig's tactic in keeping law separate from the other factors is not unusual in legal theory:

> If identity is to be maintained, borders become places of danger and anomaly, not to be too often explicitly confronted. Indeed, the (common) law is not a 'brooding omnipresence in the sky' but law's operatives have to view it so because of the dangers of confronting law's terrestrial connections. Law cannot bear very much reality.[191]

Lessig seems to be inspired by Boyle's use of Foucault,[192] and shapes, perhaps in too arbitrary a manner, Foucault's notion of disciplinary power to fit his own regulatory model. The result is an odd hybrid mutant of Foucauldian liberalism which focuses

---

188 Ibid. chapter 8 generally.
189 Lessig acknowledges his bias towards constitutionalism as a form of governance. The international reader has to be content with numerous references to American law as the presumed norm and 'our' founding fathers. Nevertheless the scope of his writing applies to liberal legalism throughout the West.
190 Lessig's four elements are a good starting point but Jurispace is certainly constituted by many other factors and is spread across vastly different terrains, anchored by vastly differently distributed nodes of intersection with the physical plane.
191 Fitzpatrick P (1984) 'Law and Societies', *Osgoode Hall Law Journal*, v22, 115 at 127.
192 Boyle J (1997) *Foucault in Cyberspace*, http://www.law.duke.edu/boylesite/foucault.htm (viewed 27/7/01).

on the disposition of disciplinary power by institutions and suggests a strict boundary between legal, social and economic domains. Upholding the liberal legal notion of constitutionalism as an ideal, Lessig suggests that law and government are necessary to protect freedom and liberty. His moderate rhetoric indicates the audience to whom he is appealing, but also underpins the ideology of his claims:

> Our scepticism is not a point about principle. Most of us are not libertarians. We may be antigovernment, but for the most part we believe that there are collective values that ought to regulate private action. We are also committed to the idea that collective values should regulate the emerging technical world. Our problem is that we do not know how it should be regulated, or by whom. [... W]e are weary of governments. We are profoundly sceptical about the product of democratic processes. We believe, rightly or not, that these processes have been captured by special interests more concerned with individual than collective values. Although we believe that there is a role for collective judgments, we are repulsed by the idea of placing the design of something as important as the Internet into the hands of government.[193]

This approach is a useful starting point to examine legal change within the discipline's own terms. Lessig posits a gradual transformation of cyberspace, from an early architecture which made assumptions about liberty, free speech and anonymity to one where control is more and more possible. He ascribes these changes to the influence of two forces of 'social order'; code and commerce.[194]

Throughout Lessig's book and much of the other contemporary writing about cyberspace is a deep romanticism, a feeling of regret at the changes which have occurred with the commercialization and mainstreaming of the Internet. To some commentators this is nothing short of the betrayal of the utopian cyberspace dream;[195] to others it is akin to the process of losing freedom and gaining responsibility in 'growing up', that is becoming corporatized.[196]

The cleverness in Lessig's vision is the ability to fuse a model of regulatory apparatus with a notion of social space constituted by the abstract space of code and the ideology which drives it. Early cyberlibertarians[197] have represented

---

193 Lessig, op. cit. fn. 179 at 219.

194 Ibid. at ix.

195 See Coyne R (1999) *Technoromanticism: Digital Narrative, Holism and the Romance of the Real*, The MIT Press: Cambridge, MA.

196 McChesney R (2000) 'So much for the magic of technology and the free market: The World Wide Web and the corporate media system', in Herman A and Swiss T (eds) *The World Wide Web and Contemporary Cultural Theory*, Routledge: London.

197 See Dickinson T (2003) 'Cognitive Dissident: An Interview with John Perry Barlow', *Mother Jones*, 3 February, http://www.motherjones.com/news/99/2003/06/we_26_01.html (viewed 3/5/03) and Barlow's collection of writing at http://www.eff.org/~barlow/barlow.htm.

cyberspace as an empty regulatory space, of pure freedom. What Lessig reminds us, drawing on Foucault, is that even without government we are not free of governance.

Ultimately Lessig's weakness is that he remains in the shelter of liberal legalism and is not bold enough in extending his notion of law and governance. All too often governance and government are still too closely acquainted and government is fetishized, seen as a necessity for the protection of freedom and provision of accountability to the control mechanisms enshrined in architecture such as code.

Law demands more problematization than Lessig is prepared to give in *Code*, perhaps because of his narrowly constructed model readership. Critical legal theorist James Boyle, on the other hand, takes a more discursive view, taking cues from Professor Stanley Fish:

> [T]o understand law fully, one must see it as much more than a collection of rules, or even a collection of social effects. Instead, law should be seen as a complex interpretive activity, a practice of encoding and decoding social meaning that merges imperceptibly with rhetoric, ideology, 'common sense', economic argument (of both a highly theoretical and a seat-of-the-pants kind), with social stereotype narrative cliché and political theory of every level from high abstractions to civics class chant.[198]

One method of extending Lessig's analysis is to suggest that all social space is framed by architecture – this includes the code of programmers, the laws of government and the social networks of the communities.[199] Application of the umbrella term 'law' to all these coded systems might seem an exercise in legal colonialism, the annexation of other knowledges as subsidiaries of legal discourse. On the other hand, playing with definitions in this way may suggest a way to break down the monolith of law, to connect it back into the other systems from which it has sought to extricate itself in abstract isolation.

Lessig's analysis of code also fails to address the importance of interface. Mitchell notes how the GUI (graphical user interface) of the desktop computer functions in the same ways as physical library architecture, to arrange information and position the subject in relation to it – to define what is seen and what is unseen.[200] The mathematical interface of the Cartesian plane has become a conceptual

---

198   Boyle, op. cit. fn. 72 at 14.

199   Constitutional law professor JM Balkin adopts a similar position in this concept of 'cultural software' a metaphor for explaining reception of ideology using a critical toolbox which includes meme theory, linguistic viruses and heuristics. In doing so, Balkin suggests that ideology (including legal ideology) is like software, is discursive, textual and networked, in doing so he challenges the 'engine' model of power as force. Balkin JM (1998) *Cultural Software: A Theory of Ideology*, Yale University Press: New Haven.

200   Mitchell, op. cit. fn. 152 at 55.

interface for describing and organizing space.[201] What then of the legal interface? How does one conceptualize the user interface, beyond simplistic metaphors of the police officer or the court room? How is the experience of law in everyday life to be recognized?

Law is dependent on language. The code of language determines law. The socio/linguistic network is connected into 'code' of law through determination of meanings, especially those designed to create, in the interests of smooth operation, flexible slippage in the systems such as 'reasonable' or 'community values'.

Just as cyberspace is constituted by rules, by architecture which defines what is permissible, what is possible, social life is encoded just as virtual existence is. Some of these rules are formalized as legislation or case law; most are not. The legal space of jurispace represents a complex network of power, a turbulent system constituted by discourse. Legal theorists such as Lessig have, in analyzing the laws of cyberspace, opened a rift in the idea of monolithic abstract law. If it can be acknowledged that space is governed by the laws of its representation and encoding, does it follow that law is in turn governed by the spaces it has created?

The Impact of Cyberspace Governance on Conventional Legal Geographies

Beyond the physical networks of wires and electronics which constitute the Internet, cyberspace is also a social space. It is a space which is produced by many of the same social factors as the regulatory spaces which seek to govern it. While not isolated from forces of productivism and product fetishization, cyberspace is more than a mere consumer product or a commodified territory. It encompasses communities, relationships and power structures, including the regulatory ones:

> Social space contains a great diversity of objects, both natural and social, including the networks and pathways which facilitate the exchange of material things and information. Such 'objects' are thus not only things but also relations.[202]

Lefebvre discusses the difficulty posed in making maps of social space. The very character of the cartographic process depends on isolating a space from its context, on simplification and use of scale. In this discussion Lefebvre anticipates the

---

[201] Curry explains four main approaches to space: Aristotelian, Newtonian, Leibnizian and Kantian. Aristotelian space is static, hierarchical and concrete. A Newtonian concept of space imposes an absolute grid of reference on all space. Leibnizian space is concerned with the relationship between things in space. A Kantian approach to space sees space as merely a conceptual form imposed by human subjects. Curry M (1995) 'On Space and Spatial Practice in Contemporary Geography', in Earle C, Mathewson K and Kezer M (eds) *Concepts in Human Geography*, Rowman and Littlefield Publishers: Lanham.

[202] Lefebvre, op. cit. fn. 29 at 77.

Internet, giving the example of computer networks and posits the idea of a 'space peculiar to information science':[203]

> We are confronted not by one social space but by many – indeed, by an unlimited multiplicity or countable set of social spaces which we refer to generically as 'social space'. No space disappears in the course of growth and development: the worldwide does not abolish the local [...] The intertwinement of social spaces is also a law. Considered in isolation, such spaces are mere abstractions. As concrete abstractions, however, they attain 'real' existence by virtue of networks and pathways, by virtue of bunches or clusters of relationships.[204]

Further, Lefebvre insists that newly developed networks enhance, rather than eradicate, the spaces and places over which they are superimposed, pointing directly to worldwide communications networks (as of 1974):[205]

> Social spaces interpenetrate one another and/or superimpose themselves upon one another. They are not things, which have mutually limiting boundaries [...] Visible boundaries such as walls or enclosures, in general, give rise for their part to an appearance of separation between spaces where in fact what exists is an ambiguous continuity.[206]

This statement refutes any technophobic separation of the virtual from 'authentic' existence. To explain how these networks might be conceived, Lefebvre uses the analogy of hydrodynamics, where important factors are not boundaries but scale, dimension and rhythm.[207] 'Great movements, vast rhythms, immense waves – these all collide and "interfere with one another"; lesser movements on the other hand interpenetrate'.[208]

Spaces interconnect, attract, repel, exist in layers.[209] Layered spaces such as cyberspace are mapped onto physical space in a way which conceiving them as entirely separate spaces fails to do justice to. A similar phenomenon occurs with layers of jurispace which reflect, warp and compete with the physical spaces they are attached to.

---

203   Ibid. 86.
204   Ibid. at 86.
205   Ibid. at 86.
206   Ibid. at 87.
207   Ibid. at 87.
208   Ibid. at 87.
209   There is a multiplicity of virtual worlds which can be conceptualized as layered like onion skins or loosely linked like neighbourhoods. Heim M (1994) 'The Erotic Ontology of Cyberspace' in *The Metaphysics of Virtual Reality*, Oxford University Press: New York.

Further, a spatial approach challenges conventional assumptions about the static and stable nature of known objects. Lefebvre asks the reader to consider a house not as a stable set of structures, but a nexus in a complex network of conduits holding mobile energies (power, water, communications).[210] Social practice is determined by spatial images and representations. Like Neo's pseudo-Buddhist moment of transcendence in *The Matrix*, Lefebvre provokes the reader to go past the illusion of reality, to see physical matter as merely energy condensed into a temporary stable form.

The space of cyberspace is a space of flows, information networks and morphologies of connection and disconnection.[211] Perhaps jurispace is better conceived as a flow than as a static space. TW Luke argues that glocalization has seen the replacement of static notions of place with the idea of the flow. Access to flows as a source of power replaces domination, control and enclosure of space through juridico-legal sovereignty. However, xenophobic and nationalist responses also arise from the perceived threat posed by the decentring, despatializing and dematerializing results of glocalization.[212]

Considering the elements of spatial practice, representations of space and representational spaces together demonstrate a wild proliferation of cyberspaces emerging, each constituted by different experiences, identities and practices – lived by netizens and the real and virtual communities they belong to. Each time a user logs in to cyberspace they are building a new space, albeit on the foundations of their past experiences. In some ways this is reflected in the 'history' menu of the web browser, which constitutes a kind of fragmented self map each time the user logs on. If these records are viewed by an observer or perhaps a prying ISP,[213] a 'snapshot' image of the subject emerges – but one of many multiple identities an Internet user adopts across different media spaces and fluid communities.

Lefebvre would be critical of abstractions which suggest that the Internet is a single, consolidated phenomenon. The legal concept of cyberspace has been used in this way, allowing it to be conceived as a unified territory to be conquered or at least parcelled up among the jurisdictions. Some representations of cyberspace

---

210 Lefebvre, op. cit. fn. 29 at 93.

211 Castells M (1996) *The Information Age: Economy, Society and Culture Vol 1: The Rise of the Network Society*, Blackwell: Oxford.

212 Luke TW (1995) 'New World Order or Neo-World Orders: Power, Politics and Ideology in Informationalising Glocalities', in Featherstone M, Lash S and Robertson R (eds) *Global Modernities*, Sage Publications: London.

213 For a satirical take on this kind of interpretation see the *Onion* article, 'Web-Browser History a Chronicle of Couple's Unspoken Desires' (Vol 36, No 45, 14–20 December 2000). 'By simply opening Allen and Christine's Internet Explorer history folder, we find their innermost longings laid bare [...] From emotionally stunted, sexually frustrated Allen's frequent visits to porn and Camaro sites to childless Christine's frequent visits to baby-clothes sites, it's all there. [...] The dissatisfaction they hide from the world, and in most cases, each other can easily be found under the menu heading "Go" [...] a glimpse into an entire universe of unvoiced pain'.

indicate an empty space, a void awaiting explorers (followed by settlers).[214] But this void is already occupied, filled with shifting networks of social power. Like our consciousness, the Internet is built by discourse, not a vessel to be filled with it. The heterogenous experiences of multiple cyberspaces defy abstraction. The global and the local are fixed together as one can build a global network of correspondents, all obsessed about the minutiae of a single localized topic or theme.

If the institutions of law are to assert a place in virtual life, they need to do so in a way that is conscious of the indigenous laws and regulatory communities of cyberspace. The laws of jurisdiction, which will be revisited in Chapter 6, must be framed in a manner conscious of the regulatory communities that pre exist them, both online and offline.

Control, Space and Ideological Wetware

As illustrated in Chapter 3, the Australian content regulation debate concerns protection from dangerous spaces and the production of places such as home, community and an economically productive Internet. EFA Chair Irene Graham comments: 'Basically, we would say that you just do not give six-year-olds a computer and just let them use it. I mean, you do not let them go and run around Kings Cross. Why let them roam free on the Internet?'[215]

In its enforcement role, the *Broadcasting Services Act 1992* has a narrow geographical scope and relies on its power to deem ISPs and ICHs as 'broadcasters', broadcasting material within Australian borders. The Act also operates in support of a co-regulatory industry scheme and proposes ideological support for technologies of filtering that impact on the regulatory effectiveness to the choices of the individual (or their parent).

Implicit in the co-regulatory structure is recognition that the most effective regulatory mechanisms are those which are already internalized. The most effective way of protecting oneself from Internet porn is simply not typing explicit URLs like www.nakedhottwinks.com[216] into the browser and not following the links on sexually explicit banner ads and pop-ups.[217] This strategy is so simple that

---

214 Ryan. op. cit. fn. 56.

215 ZDNet Australia (2002e) 'Will NSW opt for Net censorship?' 11 March, http://www.zdnet.com.au/newstech/communications/story/0,2000024993,20263957,00.htm.

216 Not knowing the meaning of erotic slang (such as the gay expression 'twink') also provides a degree of protection, but not, unfortunately, if these terms have multiple meanings corresponding with other pursuits such as 'water sports' (that is, a urination fetish).

217 For the media-literature web surfer there are various technological solutions which may block banner ads and pop-ups, these are detailed on the Netalert site adopting an educative role. Netalert (2003) *How to Deal with Pornography and Pop-Ups on the*

it seems patronizing to express, yet it is strangely absent from many critiques of erotic Internet content.

The Australian Internet censorship legislation may have symbolic value. It can be regarded as 'an effort at managing perceptions; there seems to be a perception in some parts of the Australian community (especially among church leaders) that the Internet is an unsafe environment'[218] and perhaps not aimed at producing other, more tangible results. Indeed, Australian Federal IT Minister, Senator Alston specifically acknowledges that the purpose of the legislation is primarily about perceptions:

> I don't think anyone ever pretended that you were going to achieve perfection, any more than a law banning murder means that there are no more murders being committed. But if the principal purpose is to try and make the mainstream a bit safer, well I think it does achieve that. I mean it gives people a degree of comfort but does that mean that smart young kids can't get around it? No. But is that an argument for doing nothing? No.[219]

It is simple to dismiss regulatory fortressing as mere propaganda or a massive governmental confidence trick, but symbolic regulation is perhaps one of the most practical outcomes of state regulation. If regulation is already enacted through community regulatory networks (themselves too complex to be readily modelled and codified), perhaps the simplified but ineffectual legislative monolith provides a metaphor, a place from which to discuss the diverse strategies and practices of regulation. The very real danger is that the monolith becomes reified as the core of attention and the real everyday practices of regulation are expelled to the periphery. As de Certeau suggests in *The Practice of Everyday Life*:

> A society is thus composed of certain foregrounded practices organizing its normative institutions and of innumerable other practices that remain 'minor,' always there but not organizing discourses and preserving the beginnings or remains of different (institutional, scientific) hypotheses for that society or for others. It is in this multifarious and silent 'reserve' of procedure that we should look for 'consumer' practices having the double characteristic, pointed out by

---

Internet, http://www.netalert.net.au/Files/00719_HowDoIStopPornandPopUps.asp (viewed 14/7/03).

218 Rodriquez F (2002) *Burning the Village to Roast the Pig: Censorship of Online Media*, A paper for the OSCE workshop 'Freedom of the Media and the Internet' 30 November 2002, p9.

219 ZDNet Australia (2002c) 'Exclusive: Alston Hits Back', 28 November, http://www.zdnet.com.au/newstech/communications/story/0,2000024993,20270262,00.htm.

Foucault, of being able to organize both spaces and languages, whether on a minute or a vast scale.[220]

The Matrix provides a convenient, if insubstantial, example of the cyber libertarian culture which has permeated the Internet regulation discourse as well as most cyberpunk fiction. The emergence of the cyborg messiah is not just an embodied synthesis of technological power, but represents power in becoming a navigator of spaces and an engineer of the codes which constitute them. This revolutionary figure opposes caricatured forces of control, standing in for the discourses of legal abstraction and capitalist production. In the context of Internet regulation, the practices of censorship threaten to dislocate the subject's own experiences of regulatory communities, replacing them with a assemblage of abstract laws and media classification guidelines that point to an empirically unsustainable set of 'community values and attitudes' as their foundation.

In *The Matrix*, the freedom fighters are empowered by the transformation of their consciousness, their ability to perceive the textual nature of space and the rules of production on which its regulatory code is built. No longer bound by the prison of perceived natural reality, they are liberated (at some personal cost) to critique the fundamental power relationships by which that space has been constructed. Cyber-messiah Neo has the magickal potential to manipulate the rules by which reality is constructed, to take on the agents of control at their own game. The success of this film and other texts in the cyberpunk genre can, in part, be accorded to the differential space of resistance that cyberpunk fiction opens. While it appeals to the utopian technophile obsessions of its target audience, the genre also suggests that both the rules of reality (the production of space) and the laws of control (the production of legal space) may be defied by those equipped with the right mindset, the right ideological wetware. The regulation of the Internet is an issue close to the heart of many *Matrix* cyberpunk fans and one which reveals the contradictions of control.

> I know you're out there. I can feel you now. I know that you're afraid. You're afraid of us. You're afraid of change. I don't know the future. I didn't come to tell you how this is going to end. I came here to tell you how it's going to begin. I'm going to hang up this phone and then I'm going to show these people what you don't want them to see. I'm going to show them a world without you, a world without rules and controls, without borders or boundaries, a world where anything is possible. Where we go from there is a choice I leave to you.[221]

---

220 D de Certeau M (1984) *The Practice of Everyday Life* (trans Rendall S), University of California Press: Berkeley, at 48.
221 The One, (Neo the enlightened) at the end of *The Matrix* (1998).

Chapter 5

Sexx Laws:[1]
The Spatial Strategies of Censorship

Historically, legal strategies of prohibition have never been very successful. While censorship law has been transformed from bare moral expurgation into modern taxonomic practices of labelling and classification, its 'indigestible core' remains in the power to ban; in Australia, that is to inscribe a status of *RC* on an item of media. Beyond merely governing private consumption, censorship laws affect the governance of public space and public discourses which flow through those spaces – what movies can be shown, what images and stories can be displayed and exchanged and, ultimately, how we talk about those movies, images and stories.

Like censorship law, the town planning rules that zone adult stores and services are an example of the ways in which law is inscribed on physical space through various tactics: governance of morality in public spaces, the determination of red light districts and constitution of other marginal spaces.[2] This inscription is not just an exercise in expulsion. The Other of the regulated immoral subject defines the centre just as it is, itself, excluded to the margins.[3] Practices of Othering and expulsion are utilized in order to constitute, in whomsoever is left, 'the public' or 'the community' – a victim in which to vest moral offence and define social harm through exposure to Other influences.[4]

---

1   Can't you hear those cavalry drums/ Hijacking your equilibrium/ Midnight hags in the mausoleum/ Where the pixilated doctors means/ Carnivores in the Kowloon night/ Breathing freon by the candlelight/ Coquettes bitch slap you so polite/ Till you thank them/ For the tea and sympathy/ I want to defy/ The logic of all sex law/ Let the handcuffs slip off your wrists/ I'll let you be my chaperones/ At the halfway home/ I'm a full grown man/ But I'm not afraid to cry. Lyrics from 'Sexx Laws' from the Beck album *Midnight Vultures* (1999).
2   Ashworth GJ, White PE and Winchester HPM (1988) 'The red-light district in the West European city: A neglected aspect of the urban landscape', *Geoforum*, v19(2), 201–12.
3   Ogborn M (1992) 'Love–state–ego: "Centres" and "margins" in 19th century Britain', *Environment and Planning D: Society and Space*, v10, 287–305.
4   Bell D (1995) 'Perverse Dynamics, Sexual Citizenship and the Transformation of Intimacy' in Bell D and Valentine G (eds) *Mapping Desire: Geographies of Sexualities*, Routledge: London at 311.

Rather than effecting pervasive control, censorship seems to primarily operate by expulsion of examples of problematic media to the margins,[5] to unregulated spaces out of public view. The censorship system creates an uneven regulatory net and the invention of the Internet has torn the already worn fabric to tatters:

> Almost immediately after the ban on Ken Park was announced, people around Australia began downloading the film on their computers and passing copies to their friends –many of whom, no doubt, wouldn't have bothered seeing it if it had been cleared for general release at the cinemas.[6]

New media formations and the representation of sexuality and the self in those media have destabilized traditional boundaries between public and private spheres.[7] Creed argues that the negotiation between the centre and the margins is an essential element of media, particularly media of a transgressive kind:

> It could be argued that one of the functions of the media is to permit the individual to come into contact with those acts which threaten the norms of the day, to create a legitimate space for interchange before withdrawing and redrawing the boundaries established by the dominant social and cultural discourses of the day.[8]

Censorship law is a spatial practice, a form of governance by which media spaces are ordered and regulated. Because the Australian Internet regulation legislation directly imports the pre-existing censorship and classification scheme into its co-regulatory operation, it enacts legal inscription of these rules on cyberspace.

In doing this, state censorship power sets up an illusory binary between regulatory power and media. Based on a simple understanding of power, this model places power and expression in opposition to each other, an error which is replicated by both pro- and anti-censorship activists. Power constitutes the regulatory subject and censorship constitutes the media it governs.[9] Contemporary theories of regulatory power are considered in more depth in Chapter 6; for the moment it is necessary to suggest that censorship does more than merely exclude problematic texts from the public sphere. In its operation it defines the public

---

5 Foreign language videos and DVDs, for instance, often fall outside scope of the system. Griffith G (2002) *Censorship in Australia: Regulating the Internet and other Recent Developments*, NSW Parliament Briefing Paper, http://www.parliament.nsw.gov.au/prod/web/PHWebContent.nsf/PHPages/ResearchBf043003?OpenDocument, viewed 7/4/03, at 9.

6 Vnuk H (2003) 'X-rated? Outdated', *The Age*, 20 September at 8.

7 Creed B (2002) *Media Matrix: Sexing the New Reality*, Allen and Unwin: Sydney at 3.

8 Ibid. at 11.

9 This is a version of Foucault's proposition that power does not oppose and repress sexuality, it actively constitutes sexuality through discourses of control. Foucault M (1978) *The History of Sexuality Volume I: An Introduction*, Penguin: London.

sphere itself[10] – a mainstream of material – while it determines what is to be transgressive. An 'unregulated' *G* text, even though it is readily available, is just as regulated by censorship law and constituted by its regulatory taxonomy as an entirely banned text.

Censorship law, by imposing its own jurispace model of taxonomies on mediascape (which is already constituted by and through power, including legal power), requires the creators of media to engage in its discursive schema. Even where speech appears to be free, creators must justify the content of their product against the censorship array, they must inevitably speak in language of harm and dangerousness when positioning their content for consumption. Furthermore, if transgressive content (sex, violence, harsh language) is included, the media must communicate within censorship law's narratives of justification and artistic merit if it is to optimize its position in the framework. It is important to note that a more censorious position is not necessarily less commercially optimal. Regulation of restricted content, in part, creates demand through scarcity and commodification of the transgressive image.[11]

Censorship law draws on mutually reinforcing spatial strategies. Censorship as a practice involves reification of both the framework of taxonomic classification standards and also the abstract community whose values these are said to codify. The transmission of media involves a complex process of signification and reception, 'dangerous' content such as sexually explicit material or violence is merely the representation of these phenomena. When public discourse is predicated upon the description of the texts by the censor's reports rather than the texts themselves, discussion becomes removed from the initial context and inflected by further transmission and re-representation. Academic Simon Hardy[12] points to a similar problem when anti-pornography feminists such as Griffin[13] discuss the meaning of pornographic texts. By describing the text with presumption of a fixed viewpoint, the analyst is depicting their own readership rather than any objective

---

10 The more that regulatory and disciplinary practices seek to define sex, the more difficult it is to define what is obscene. Scrutinizing sexuality places it in the public sphere and it is difficult to then argue that it must be moved back into the private. Williams L (1999) *Hard Core: Power, Pleasure, and the 'Frenzy of the Visible'*, University of California Press: Berkeley at 95.

11 An example of the market power of censorship can be seen in the advertising for the film *Jules Jordan's Ass Worship* (2002) which bears a quote from Des Clark, the director of the Office of Film and Literature Classification 'In the BOARD'S view ... the film involves SEXUAL ACTIVITY accompanied by practices that OFFEND against the standards of MORALITY, DECENCY and PROPRIETY generally accepted by REASONABLE ADULTS ...' (emphasis added by the advertisers) followed with the advertising text 'So ... what's all the fuss about?'. Axis Media (2003) *Adult Catalogue Issue 104*, June/July, 1.

12 Hardy S (1998) *The Reader, The Author, His Woman and Her Lover: Soft-core Pornography and Heterosexual Men*, Cassell: London, at 59–60.

13 Griffin S (1981) *Pornography and Silence: Culture's Revenge against Nature*, The Women's Press: London.

meaning the text might have. The obviousness of pornographic images may be misleading, Day challenges the interpretation of the ejaculation shot as degrading and offers a psychoanalytic analysis of desire.[14] Creed describes the tension between opposing perceptions: on the one hand criticisms of pornographic gaze as inhuman or 'emotionally flat' and, on the other, arguments that pornography refuses to generate narrative involvement in order create a space in which the spectator can fantasize.[15]

The framework of Critical Legal Geography and space theory discussed in the last chapter provides a way of conceptualizing the operation of censorship law. In particular Lessig's description of Code[16] provides a manner of constituting regulatory apparatus which involves law but integrates other situational regulators. Censorship law's focus on the public sphere (where 'obscenity' literally means 'that which should not be seen'[17]) impacts on how public space is zoned which flows over into debates over the public character of the Internet, deemed by the *Broadcasting Standards Amendment (Online Services) Act 1999* to be public 'broadcasting'.

This chapter will focus on pornography as a predominant example of the relationship between censorship law's regulatory power and media. Throughout this discussion it is important to remember that sexually explicit content is only one type of regulated media and it is equally important that spatial explorations of depictions of violence, other adult themes and 'coarse language' be analysed at some later date.

This chapter aims to broadly examine the terrain of censorship and its history in order to locate spatialized concerns, particularly in the creation of the abstract notion of 'the community' and the regulatory fortressing which occurs around

---

14   Day G (1988) 'Looking at Women: Notes toward a Theory of Porn', in Day G and Bloom C (eds) *Perspectives on Pornography: Sexuality in Film and Literature*, St Martin's Press: New York.

15   Creed, op. cit. fn. 7 at 63.

16   Lessig L (1999) *Code and Other Laws of Cyberspace*, Basic Books: New York.

17   Pornography challenges hegemonic legal order by disrupting the orderly boundaries between public and private, bringing the obscene into the public sphere. Because of this, one important role of censorship law is the policing of the boundaries of public and private space. Even beyond mere representation of sexual acts, pornography continues to challenge this border. Porn star Houston, star of *Houston 500* in which she performed sexual acts with 500 men, has gone 'beyond naked' in her work, in her labiaplasty surgery (images from which were posted on the Internet) and in the Internet auction of her outer labia which were removed, sealed and placed on a marble plinth. Tom Hingston Studio (2003) *Porn?*, Vision on Publishing: London, Foreword by Mark Irving at 13–14. In the graphic novel *100%*, Paul Pope satirizes the increase of visibility (and viscereality) in sexual discourse by hypothesising 'gastro', a near-future variety of stripping performance in which the dancer's internal organs are made visible by a technology which scans her interior spaces and projects these images in lurid holographic detail. Pope P (2002–3) *100%*, v 1–5, Vertigo Comics: New York.

moral laws. This investigation involves a discussion of the connection between state censorship and the role of 'regulatory communities' such as anti-pornography feminism, anti-censorship feminism, civil libertarians and queer activists and intersects with law and cyberspace governance issues in the context of Internet censorship. While the censorship debate has broader ramifications, commentators have expressed the view that 'Regardless of any noble aspirations expressed by free-speech organizations ... this legislation is about porn.'[18]

Even if this argument is accepted, the category of 'pornography' is far from simple. Kendrick argues that pornography is not a thing, it is more like an argument, constituted by legal rules and definitions.[19] Lynne Hunt notes that there has been more written about the history of pornography regulation than of the history of pornography itself, and that pornography has 'always been defined in part by the efforts undertaken to regulate it'.[20] This reinforces the contention that sexual space is constituted by censorship and makes regulation and resistance a prime site for exploration.

Part of this exploration involves a mapping of the debate corning pornography and representations of sexuality, of the regulatory communities which shape media space and the discourses which flow between them. This book cannot propose a resolution to these debates, but seeks to understand how spatial concepts frame the debate and the role of censorship law as mediator and gatekeeper of public space. Law's adoption of reductionist and exclusionary spatial strategies involves problematic use of the concept of community. These spatial strategies are discussed in this chapter and include: the production of childhood; regulatory fortressing around censorship laws; the role of the censor as the gatekeeper to the public sphere; and the role of law in 'the Imaginary Domain'. It is the argument of this book that a more complex understanding of regulatory power allows for contemplation of multiple regulatory communities.

The mythology of a monolithic community requires a foil, a shadow against which it can define its bright spaces. In sharp contrast to the crowd of the majoritarian community stands the solitary pornohound. The spatial images are sharply contrasted, the sunny suburban places of the community are full of children, the dark urban spaces of pornography are a labyrinth of back alleys, seedy establishments with blinking neon signs.

The construction of dangerous spaces and dangerous practices is essential to generate appeal for the homogenized conformist space which has been given the label 'community'. What then is the fate of the communities as they are actually

---

18 Chen P (1999) 'Community without Flesh: First Thoughts on the New Broadcasting Services Amendment (Online Services) Bill 1999', *M/C: A Journal of Media and Culture* 2.3, http://english.uq.edu.au/mc/9905/bill (viewed 1/10/01) at 1.

19 Kendrick W (1987) *The Secret Museum: Pornography in Modern Culture*, Viking: New York.

20 Hunt L (1993) *The Invention of Pornography: Obscenity and the Origins of Modernity 1500–1800*, Zone Books: New York, at 41.

experienced by legal subjects? These are silenced, marginalized and rendered invisible by the totalizing homogeneity of the mythic community monolith, supported by the ideological framework of the state.

Into the Red Light District

How are sexual spaces described?[21] The networks of practices, power relations, texts and identities have been expressed, framed and constituted in many spatial ways. The red light district is just one of many metaphors used to conceive of a terrain, a space of sex. This has implications for the regulation and control of sexuality – if it can be bounded into a geographical area it can be contained, regulated, quarantined and sequestered. The construction of borders also denies the incidence of sexuality across all other spaces, it is apparently banished to marginal spaces but also flourishes in the flows of liminal zones. The creation of a 'gay part of town' provides a ready alibi, a denial that homosexual practices permeate society generally.

Erotic cultures are spatialized, particularly along spatial distinctions between public and private, night and day. In *Cultures of Darkness*, Palmer's extensive historical travelogue of the night, dark places are frequently associated with transgression, eroticism, specifically with the libertine political origins of pornography[22] and with the emergence of queer cultures.[23] Cornell cautions that what occurs in the dark is seldom without cost: 'we must always remember the dark side that will be with us as long as we are moral human beings.'[24]

But even Palmer's apparently sympathetic exploration is value laden and denies subjectivity to those engaged in the sex industry:

> Urban sex districts, strip joints, and prostitution come alive in the gaudy neon of night, where sex as simply cash-governed exchange relationship is enhanced by the obscurities of darkness, and desire is stripped of its humanity in the shadows of dimly lit street corners or the illumination of a seedy booth.[25]

---

21 Sexuality in space is an important theme in the work of erotic photographers such as Christien Sullivan, Anuschka Blommers, Niels Chumm and Larry Sultan. Vanina Sorrenti's work explores the body in space, the nude body on the border between public and private space. Tom Hingston Studio, op. cit. fn. 17.

22 Palmer BD (2000) *Cultures of Darkness: Night Travels in the Histories of Transgression*, Monthly Review Press: New York, chapter 4.

23 Ibid. at 13. See also Chauncey G (1994) *Gay New York: Gender, Urban Culture, and the Making of the Gay Male World 1890–1940*, Basic: New York, for an exploration of urban secretive queer spaces and the importance of the night.

24 Cornell D (1993) *Transformations: Recollective Imagination and Sexual Difference*, Routledge: New York, at 193.

25 Palmer, op. cit. fn. 22 at 75.

Ultimately, Palmer is sceptical of transgressive night spaces as a location for full revolution, but acknowledges their importance in mobilizing dissent and resistance, their defiance of scrutiny.[26] The freedom of the night is merely as respite and itself is dependent on the control of the day.

Spatial concepts of sexuality provide a landscape upon which censors operate, classifying and parcelling sex as though they were erotic town planners – policing boundaries and exclusions. As Foucault reminds us,[27] this power does not operate negatively, repressively; instead, it is actively involved in constituting the sexual subject in every way – building a framework of good and bad sexuality, healthy and unhealthy practices, valid normative romances and marginal seedy sites of resistance and forbidden pleasure. Exercise of power is not done in opposition to the margins, it produces the margins which, themselves, feed back into the power loop. Censorious power governs practices and identity through shame, control of public discourse and regulation of representation of the body. It constitutes resistant identities among those engaged in regulated practices. Censorship produces sexual space which in turn produces censorship.

Sexual censorship builds a regulatory fortress which aims to contain wayward sexuality by identifying, labelling and banishing bad texts which cause bad behaviour, rather like the Malleus Maleficarum's advice for hunting out demonic influences.[28] It is convenient regulatory myth to locate causation externally to the self and thereby render the subject into two objects of regulation – the passive body and the bad influence which operates on it.[29] The regulation of sexuality impacts on the laws of the body and its disposition in space – critical legal theorist Goodrich's work on the governance of kissing discusses the role of moral regulation in constituting public space.[30]

Like *The Matrix*'s codification of socio-juridic order as virtual reality, other metaphors exist to conceive of a uniquely sexual space. The term 'Pornotopia' was coined by historian Stephen Marcus, to describe the opulent fantasy worlds of erotic representation where social reality is banished at least for a moment in libertine bacchanals, dream worlds, each linked by common themes and codes of representation but distributed across a broad, lush landscape.[31] There is a related and equally evocative term, 'Pornscape'.[32] Irving uses the term 'pornoland' and

---

26   Ibid. at 453.
27   Foucault, op. cit. fn. 9.
28   Summers M (trans 1971) *The Malleus Malificarum of Heinrich Kramer and James Sprenger*, Dover: New York.
29   See Hardy, op. cit. fn. 12, Chapter 2 'Methods, Porn and Harm' for a critique of causal approaches.
30   Goodrich P (1998) 'The Laws of Love: Literature, History and the Governance of Kissing', *New York University Review of Law and Social Change*, v24, 183.
31   Marcus S (1974) *The Other Victorians: A Study of Sexuality and Pornography in Mid-Nineteenth Century England*, New American Library: New York.
32   Lasker S (2002) '"Sex and the City" Zoning "Pornography Peddlers and Live Nude Shows"', *UCLA Law Review*, vol 49, 1139.

argues that, like Disneyland, this space invites a child-like response in adults. It is a hyper-real world but its very unreality demarcates its boundaries with the real world.[33] Marcuse explored the terrain of phantasy in the unconscious, a critique of the repressive nature of the reality principle as a tool of state control.[34]

While many descriptions of erotic space seem Utopian, this is clearly a contested space. Challenges to the mythology of sexual liberation, from De Sade[35] to Dworkin[36] to Foucault[37] dispute the meanings of sexual texts and even what actually constitutes a sexual text. Even steadfast defenders of free speech may be squeamish about protecting some of the more distasteful images of pornography.[38] The term 'pornotopia' has also been used to describe a world of self indulgent onanism running amok, presented in the liberal dread that the sanctity of the public domain will be violated by the erotic, a kind of 'virtual reality' of images, of unchecked hedonism, a 'debauched dystopia'.[39]

The sexual space called *Videodrome* is described in the movie of the same name[40] which provides a cautionary vision, warns of the danger of getting lost in the voracious text and dislocated by the networks of representation. Here, technology and desire create an endless labyrinth, a mirror maze where identity and self are susceptible to metamorphosis, exploited by the unscrupulous using it to programme the viewer into a downward spiral of alienated representation and transgression.[41]

When censorship law did nothing but ban forbidden texts, the jurispace of censorship was divided neatly into the abstraction of binary spaces: the prohibited and everything else. Like the spaces of day and night, regulated objects are identified as controlled and dangerous spaces respectively.[42]

The shifts in regulatory culture from binary censorship to a diverse schema of classification occurred as disciplinary culture permeated society reflected in the

---

33 Tom Hingston Studio, op. cit. fn. 17, Foreword by Mark Irving at 5.
34 Marcuse H (1955) *Eros and Civilisation: A Philosophical Inquiry into Freud*, Beacon Books: Boston.
35 de Sade (1990) *120 Days of Sodom and Other Writings*, trans Wainhouse, Arrow Books: London.
36 Dworkin A (1981) *Pornography: Men Possessing Women*, Women's Press: London.
37 Foucault, op. cit. fn. 9.
38 'As for the company they keep, anti-pornography feminists observe that the allies of anti-censorship feminists include Bob Guccione, Larry Flynt, and many libertarian groups that are intolerant of any exercise of state power, including some exercises that are helpful to women, such as affirmative action', Wesson M (1991) 'Sex, Lies and Videotape: The Pornographer as Censor', *Washington Law Review*, v66, 913.
39 Collins RKL and Skover DM (1994) 'Changing Images of the State: The Pornographic State', *Harvard Law Review*, Vol 107, 1374.
40 *Videodrome* (1983) Director David Cronenberg.
41 Hardy's interviewees mention this feeling of alienation. Hardy, op. cit. fn. 12.
42 Palmer, op. cit. fn. 22.

constitution of childhood, family, autonomy and community. While it is feared that classification is nothing more than a more extensive form of censorship,[43] in practice it creates diverse and multiple forms of regulation. This indicates changes in the overall fabric of the social, the increasing importance of risk management, the permeation of disciplinary control,[44] regimes of warnings and consumer advice, that herald the rise of the risk society.[45] Tighter regimes of self governance are predicated on a changing state and a system of law which replaces liability based on moral culpability, with a form derived from assessment of risk and responsibility. Legal historian Alan Hunt is cautious about moral panic discourses, and suggests that the ubiquitousness of social anxiety is a key part of modern risk societies.[46]

Sexing Space

Censorship's practice of classification has clear geographical character in its uneven operation, use of spatial taxonomies and utilization of an abstract community model. Censorship of sexual content through classification practices attempts to project models of authorized and transgressive sexuality on the population and on physical space, in particular through the policing of the public and private division.

Censorship law, however, comprises only one of many ways in which space is sexed. Rather than a neutral, sexless stage for social drama, space itself produces sexuality in a number of ways which intersect or compete with censorship practices. This section will briefly consider some of the ways in which discourses of space, the body and sexuality intersect, preliminary to a discussion of the spatial practices of classification.

Critical geographer Smith argues that although the body is largely absent from geographic theory, the discourse of geography is saturated with the concept of the body; it is the basic unit of scale and the frame of reference from which the enterprise is initiated.[47] Similarly, geographer Mort suggests that sexual geographies have been neglected, under-theorized and deserve closer attention

---

43 Graham I (1999a) *Blinded by Smoke: The Hidden Agenda of the Online Services Bill 1999*, http://rene.efa.org.au/liberty/blinded.html.

44 Pro-censorship advocate Hamilton has suggested that imposing Internet censorship on the new media industry can be compared to seatbelt safety laws. Hamilton C (2003) 'Kids' exposure to porn must be curbed', *The Canberra Times*, 7 March.

45 Beck U (1992) *Risk Society: Towards a New Modernity*, trans Ritter M, Sage: London.

46 Hunt A (1999) *Governing Morals: A Social History of Moral Regulation*, Cambridge University Press: Cambridge, UK at 214.

47 Smith N (1993) 'Homeless/global: Scaling Places' in Bird J, Curtis B, Putnam T, Robertson G and Tickner L (eds) *Mapping the Future: Local Cultures, Global Change*, Routledge: London.

in research and practice.[48] While the body and sexuality are seldom articulated, these concepts are always present in spatial discourses such as geography and architecture, particularly when constituting public and private spaces.

> [W]alls, enclosures and facades serve to define both a scene (where something takes place) and an obscene area to which everything that cannot or may not happen on the scene is relegated: whatever is inadmissible, be it malefic or forbidden, thus has its own hidden space on the near or the far side of a frontier.[49]

Architectural critic Mark Wigley examines the hidden sexual history of architecture and finds that the design of the home itself produced sexuality in its separation of public and private spaces and its codification of regimes of surveillance and control of female sexuality.[50] The expulsion of sexuality is seemingly essential to the constitution of the Western city and urban spaces. Lefebvre was concerned with the production of erotic social spaces as is legal critic Lasker, who uses urban semiology to describe what she terms 'the pornscape' in which brothels and sex shops are separated from 'family centres':

> The context of certain land uses within the city – the juxtaposition of a use, the area surrounding the use, the architecture of the use and of those surrounding it, the access to the use, and so on – all create meaning and communicate the ideologies and oppositional relationships of the cityscape. The user of the city then reads the city, internalizes its codes and messages, and incorporates the connotations into her or his belief system for future reference, thus perpetuating or reinscribing such codes through future interaction with the city.[51]

Law inscribes space with public or private character. Kendrick describes the erotic murals of Pompei which once belonged in the public sphere but were locked up in secret museums by gentleman archaeologists. Using this analogy he describes the contemporary problem of pornography as one of mass consumption, of regulating that which was once reserved for the elite.[52] Similarly, Howell discusses the inscription of Victorian sexuality on public space, in the policing of prostitution

---

48   Mort F (2000) 'The Sexual Geography of the City' in Bridge G and Watson S (eds) *A Companion to the City*, Blackwells: Oxford.

49   Lefebvre H (1991) *The Production of Space*, Blackwell: Oxford (originally published in French, 1976) at 36.

50   Wigley M (1992) 'Untitled: The Housing of Gender', *Sexuality and Space*, Princeton Papers on Architecture: Princeton, NJ.

51   Lasker, op. cit. fn. 32 at 1182.

52   Kendrick, op. cit. fn. 19.

law in public parks and gardens.⁵³ Even the cinema is a 'geographically and culturally loaded space'⁵⁴ where public and private collide.

Geographer Mort describes the sexual networks which are spatially disciplined and mapped onto the city. He suggests that both sexual and physical space is regulated by tensions between morality and modernity.⁵⁵ The suggestion that sexual networks might be mapped raises the difficult methodological question of how to begin charting these spaces.

Hubbard, utilizing de Certeau and Benjamin, suggests a methodology which negotiates between the 'view from above' official geographies of the city (maps, reports, statistics, newspaper articles) and the 'view from below' of lived experiential accounts and practices of city-dwellers ('the hinterland between journalism, urban sociology, poetry and pornography, flaneurial accounts of the nooks and crannies of urban living').⁵⁶ Rather than privileging one over the other, Hubbard argues that the dialectic between the two provides insight into the sexual geography of the city. Rather than seek the illusion of 'pure representation', it embraces the contested and paradoxical nature of both ways of seeing.

Censorship law would seem to be an important organizing factor, distributing both official accounts of public/private spaces and creating transgressive spaces in which individual narratives occur. Pornography exists as both a site of transgression but also of conformity, replication of sexual normativity. Pornography can contribute to the abstraction of space in the commodification of sexuality and in the production of codes of representation such as 'the pornography industry', 'soft core' and 'Page Three girls'.

Challenging libertarian narratives, Marxist Lefebevre reminds us that in production and regulation, the erotic may become just another force of production, yet another alienated form of labour regulated not only by regimes of censorship but also by the market. His exploration of sexual space is distributed throughout *The Production of Space* and, overall, is pessimistic about the deployment of sexuality in media:

> Living bodies, the bodies of 'users' – are caught up not only in the toils of parcellized space, but also in the web of what philosophers call 'analogons': images, signs and symbols. These bodies are transported out of themselves, transferred and emptied out, as it were, via the eyes: every kind of appeal,

---

53 Howell P (2000) 'Victorian sexuality and the moralisation of Cremorne Gardens' in Sharp JP, Routledge P, Philo C and Paddison R (eds) *Entanglements of Power: Geographies of Domination/Resistance*, Routledge: London.
54 Mills J (2001) *The Money Shot: Cinema, Sin and Censorship*, Pluto Press: Annandale, NSW at 3.
55 Mort, op. cit. fn. 48.
56 Hubbard P (2002) 'Pulp Fictions: Mapping the Sexual Landscape', *Journal of Psychogeography and Urban Research*, Vol 1(2) formerly available at: http://www.psychogeography.cok.uk/v1_n2/pulp.htm, viewed on 26 February 2002.

incitement and seduction is mobilized to tempt them with doubles of themselves in prettified, smiling and happy poses; and this campaign to void them succeeds exactly to the degree that the images proposed correspond to 'needs' that those same images have help fashion. So it is that a massive influx of information, of messages, runs head on into an inverse flow constituted by the evacuation from the innermost body of all life and desire.[57]

Lefebvre's basic challenge to sexual space is that the operation of economic power and abstraction produces a kind of generic 'universal sex' through fragmentation of the body into parts, each separately conceived of in representational space through language (for example the separation of eye and genitals or the pornographic image of 'skin' from the interior self).[58] This fragmentation is experienced through representation but may be resisted by the body through lived experience, seeking unity and holism.

There is a danger that Lefebvre's Marxism leads him to focus on alienation and fetishization of an 'authenticity' which exists outside representational networks.[59] His critique is a useful analysis of modernist capitalist practices of commodification but it is only useful if read together with an appreciation of discursive social construction.

Lefebvre is concerned with the way in which abstract space has extended its dominion through emphasis on visualization, which breaks the body and body's experiences to mere fragments.[60] He asserts that natural (that is, bodily experienced) sexual relationships are built on a 'certain reciprocity' which is transformed into social reality through a process of abstraction (in marriage it is legalized as a commitment underwritten by authority) and thereby sexuality has undergone a 'dangerous modification':[61]

> [N]ature is replaced by cold abstraction and by the absence of pleasure […] the mental space of castration […] the space of a metaphorization whereby the image of the woman supplants the woman herself, whereby her body is fragmented, desire shattered, and life explodes into a thousand pieces. Over abstract space reigns phallic solitude and the self-destruction of desire. The representation of

---

57 Lefebvre, op. cit. fn. 49 at 98.
58 Ibid. at 204.
59 On a similar theme, Williams describes the 'money shot' of pornography as reflective of Marcuse's 'one dimensional man' and Debord's description of a society that consumes images more avidly than objects. She also connects to this feminist Irigaray's spectacularization/visibility of male power in which femininity lacks signification. Williams, op. cit. fn. 10; Marcuse H (1964) *One Dimensional Man*, Beacon Hill Press: Boston; Debord G (1967) *The Society of the Spectacle*, Black Spot Press; Irigiray L (1986) *The Speculum of the Other Woman* (Gill GC trans), Cornell University Press: Ithaca, NY.
60 Lefebvre, op. cit. fn. 49 at 309–12.
61 Ibid. at 309.

sex thus takes the place of sex itself, while the apologetic term 'sexuality' serves to cover up this mechanism of devaluation.[62]

In this space of abstract sexuality, the body is rendered into a series of organs of desire, isolated and interpreted through discourse, thereby transformed into a system of metonymic codes. Lefebvre points to the abstraction and representation of the body through advertising, 'where the legs stand for stockings,[63] the breasts for bras, the face for makeup [...] which serves to fragment desire and doom it to anxious frustration, to the non satisfaction of local needs.'[64] Through abstraction, capitalism's attack on the body results not only in aggression against the body itself, but also in the transformation of the body or its pieces into commodities to be sold or located in places of leisure or nightlife. In pornography the skin or body surface is an important saleable fragment.

Cautioned by Lefebvre and by feminist critics whose work will be examined later, it is impossible to conceive of the pornography censorship debate as the mere exercise of repressive state power over free expression as both concepts are mutually interdependent. The interconnected histories of censorship and pornography can both be conceptualized as the inscription of abstract space on the body,[65] a process which may yet allow the possibility of resistance at the site of everyday life and experience.

The body is not the only space site of regulation governed by censorship. Censorship has involved a process of mapping, dividing space, erecting fences between legitimate and dangerous zones – in physical space and media space.[66] Sexual spaces, whatever their nature (erotic media, sexual practices, bawdy talk,

---

62 Ibid. at 309.

63 The parts of a body, particularly a woman's body, become deeply coded beyond protects which are used on that part of the body. See also legs, fingers and keyboards in Jain SS (1998) 'Inscription Fantasies and Interface Erotics: A Social–Material Analysis of Keyboards, Repetitive Strain Injuries and Products Liability Law', *Hastings Women's Law Journal*, v9, 219. In Victoria the Transport Accident Commission (TAC) ran advertising campaign where billboards displayed the vulnerable form of a naked man in a communal shower (with only the caption 'If you Drink, then Drive, You're a Bloody Idiot'), his body standing in for sexual violation as an aspect of the threat of imprisonment for drink driving offences (TAC (1995), *'Prison' campaign*, November).

64 Lefevbre, op. cit. fn. 49 at 310.

65 Pornography is a genre which 'moves' the body as do genres such as thrillers, weepies and 'low comedy'. Dyer R (1985) 'Male Gay Porn: Coming to Terms', *Jump Cut: A Review of Contemporary Media*, V30 (March), 27. Pornographies are practices by which spectators discipline themselves to enjoy visual pleasure, produced in the imagination and felt in the body. Williams, op. cit. fn. 10 at 315.

66 Referring to Foucault's critique of the sexual liberation, Heath describes the expansion of sexual discourse as 'more knowledge/less pleasure', sex has become an almost disposable commodity, a quick 'fix'. Heath S (1982) *The Sexual Fix*, Macmillan: London at 3.

body spaces), become isolated, privatized, sequestered away from 'normal' spaces through shame and mortification of the body.

It is vital to retain a notion of space that allows for complex and interconnected social spaces and does not seek to isolate one space within hermetic borders. Alan Hunt urges theorists not to make distinctions between social, economic and moral realms as exclusive spaces, 'there is no "moral field", no place where "the moral" rules alone or even predominates. [...] Our conceptual distinctions are elaborated for analytical purposes only; in the real world they are always found in complex connection with other elements'.[67] One danger of a spatial analysis is that, if Lefebvre's advice is not carefully considered, each social space may seem discrete and disengaged. The cyberspace concept of hypertext is a good analogy for intertextual cultural spaces that are permeable, interdependent and fluid,[68] yet it is often represented as being isolated from the social spaces that produce it.

The fluid relationship between cultural and physical space has consequences for urban design, architecture, human geography and models of demographic distribution. Sometimes moral regimes are inscribed on physical space,[69] a process which Alan Hunt refers to as moral environmentalism, drawing on nineteenth century examples:

> [T]he provision of public parks as sanitised urban space was an environmentalist response to urban squalor and the street life of the poor, but they were soon perceived as dangerous because they provided a heterosexual social space that threatened middle-class children's future respectability. [...] Environmentalist campaigns resulted in municipal parks, bandstands, civic pageants, municipal art, playgrounds, garden cities and town planning. Such projects aroused enormous enthusiasm and great hope for their reformatory capacity. But no sooner were they in place than they elicited demand for moral surveillance and for regulation of parks, dance halls, skating rinks, ice-cream parlours, excursion boats and later movie houses.[70]

Notions of public and private space are also important for Lefebvre, connected to capitalist concepts of property. 'Prohibition is the reverse side and the carapace of property, of the negative appropriation of space under the reign of private

---

67 Hunt, op. cit. fn. 46 at 7–8. Hunt does use spatial language to describe moral regulation, as a 'domain' distinct from the field of political regulation (at 17).

68 Shields R (2000) 'Hypertext Links: The Ethic of the Index and its Space–Time Effects' in Herman A and Swiss T (eds) *The World Wide Web and Contemporary Cultural Theory*, Routledge: London.

69 Howell, op. cit. fn. 53.

70 Hunt, op. cit. fn. 46 at 131.

property.'[71] Under capitalism's regime, space is divided and specialized into zones of work and leisure and day time and night time spaces.[72]

To Lefebvre the sequestration of transgressive spaces is an essential part of the taxonomic practices of economic order. Of particular importance is the creation of the regulated 'red light' districts as objects of knowledge. Much in the same way that the bourgeois house effects the expulsion of the body through the separation of private from public space,[73] this is reflected in the creation 'of this peculiarly sophisticated form of exploitation. In these neighbourhoods, and during these hours sex seems to have been accorded every right; in actuality, the only right it has is to be deployed in exchange for cash.'[74] Censorship's image of 'the dark side' of the mediascape (including the Internet) is just as essential as the 'information economy' promotion of the corporate aspect – these maintain the illusion that these are separable realms where in practice libertinism is consumed and consumption becomes fetishized pleasure.

Classification as Governance of Space

If the erotic can be conceptualized as part of a spatial media terrain, then this terrain is the domain in which censorship law operates. The practice of classification is the cartography of media space, generating maps through the inscription of labels and the erection of boundaries. Australia's media and Internet content regulation regime covers many different grounds of classification, each of which has its own criteria for classification within one of the pre-established categories. In addition, these criteria allow mitigating circumstances which might shape the decision – a discursive dimension for debate and, in legal terms, an opportunity for appeal against a decision of the censorship authority.

> [A] ratings system should function the same way as a nutrition label which indicates the sodium content of a food. The label should be informative rather than judgemental. All too often, however, the viewer, like the prescription drug taker is ill-informed [...] However, the chemical components found in food and drugs are objectively quantifiable, whereas ratings are subjectively measured.[75]

The classification system is premised on the ability of a panel of censors to assess an item of media and place it within a taxonomic slot, weighing both aggravating factors and justification. Classification is presented as an information service,

---

71 Lefebvre, op. cit. fn. 49 at 319.
72 Palmer, op. cit. fn. 22.
73 Wigley, op. cit. fn. 50.
74 Lefebvre, op. cit. fn. 49 at 320.
75 Roberts D (1997) 'The Jurisprudence of Ratings Symposium Part I: On The Plurality of Ratings', *Cardozo Arts and Entertainment Law Journal*, vol 15, 105 at 133–4.

a purpose which is defeated by overly cautious broadcasters who use blanket warnings[76] for all conceivable sources of offence.

Self regulation is an important contributing factor within the censorship discourse and can have surprising consequences. The regulation of adult videos has unusual consequences in relation to corporate culture. Throughout the 1990s small video stores, largely family businesses, lost ground to large chains such as Blockbuster. However, Blockbuster's internal rules of self governance, its refusal to stock adult videos, has allowed the smaller stores which do stock such videos to stay in business in the face of the market dominance of the chain.[77]

The self regulatory discourse can in some ways be far more reaching than a power to censor. A censorial power excludes but it does so in a way that keeps the text intact (if unseen). Classification induces the modification, perhaps mutilation, of a text but the state is exempted of responsibility because it is the private 'owners' of the text who make the cuts. O'Toole argues that these standards are usually harsher than those used by customs on imported material:

> Due care and self-regulation is required. Any magazine published by the major porn publishers will be meticulously checked over by lawyers for any infringements of accepted levels of nudity, levels of spreadness in the 'crotch shots', angles of male tumescence. [... This has] over time encouraged a regime of self-censorship to emerge. You don't go to the trouble of commissioning a photo set, or printing up a magazine, only then to check to see what your lawyers [...] think. You do the censoring first.[78]

While censorship may be spoken of as a uniform phenomenon it might be better conceptualized as a site of activity involving different sets of practices and different regulatory communities. The state has a central role in this process, as a gatekeeper which can define public debate and reconceptualize other practices within its framework of classification. The entire strategy of classification is critiqued by Boyle, who challenges the process of 'typing' as a moral activity:

> [I]t is one of the fundamental methods we have for making – and avoiding – moral judgments. It is a fundamental way of making moral judgments because much of our moral discourse has the misleading form of a syllogism: I know that torture is wrong; the question is, 'Is this torture?' I know that free speech is to

---

76 For example, the Comedy Channel's generic warning statement reads '(M) Mature. Recommended for mature audiences, 15 years and over. Medium level coarse language. Medium level sex scenes. Drug use, horror, and adult themes', regardless of the actual content of the show which follows. Even children's show *PeeWee's Playhouse* was prefaced with this warning.

77 O'Toole L (1998) *Pornocopia: Porn, Sex, Technology and Desire*, Serpent's Tail: London at 172.

78 Ibid. at 140.

be protected; the question is 'Is this speech?' The moment of typing, classifying and defining becomes the moment of moral decision. It is a fundamental way of avoiding moral judgment for the same reason. The thing-like or 'reified' nature of categories can operate to obscure a moral issue, to resolve by pretheoretical definition an issue that would be troubling and painful if faced directly.[79]

Alan Hunt considers Foucault's 'dividing practices' to be an important aspect of moral regulation – the creation of a boundary between categories that not only privileges one side of the border, constructs people in the categories as subjects (to others and themselves) and legitimizes different treatment for different categories.[80] The old dichotomy of moral/immoral has been exploded along a multitude of axes, each of which draws a distinction between different types of content (sex, violence, language) and the classification of audience (*G*, *PG*, *MA*, *R*, *X*) and a range of justifications which modify the judgement (artistic,[81] moral value). Not only are the texts subject to this classification but so too are authors and readers through the regulatory schema. This subjectivity is internalized, sometimes manifesting resistance such as the creator or connoisseur of trash cinema who resists the 'art' justification.

Taxonomic Practices: Classifying Sexual Content

The visual metaphors for sex are more interesting than sex itself.[82]

All discourses of sexuality are inherently discourses about something else.[83]

Of all the classification categories, sexual content has some of the clearest criteria and codes of representation. An erect penis is a relatively stable signifier in Western culture. This is not to suggest that the classification process is simple or scientific in any way, but that the lines of the debate (such as the hard core/soft core binary) are more clearly established and commercially enshrined, compared to representations of violence or 'adult issues' where codes of representation are more ambiguous. Many creators, at least from the adult industry, are keen to self label as this positions their product in the marketplace.

---

79 Boyle J (1996) *Shamans, Software, and Spleens: Law and the Construction of the Information Society*, Harvard University Press: Cambridge, USA at 144.
80 Hunt, op. cit. fn. 46 at 8.
81 See Manchester C (1999) 'Obscenity, Pornography and Art', *Media and Arts Law Review*, v4(2), 65.
82 Photographer Larry Sultan quoted in Tom Hingston Studio, op. cit. fn. 17 at 1.
83 Simon W (1996) *Postmodern Sexualities*, Routledge: London at xvii. Simon, a student of Kinsey, adopts a sexual constructivist perspective which examines sexual scripts and analyses sex as something akin to drama, it is fragmented, a 'discontinous discourse on a discontinuous subject.' ibid. at 139.

There are rules governing explicitness of sexual material, especially at the 'high end' of *R*, *X* and *RC*, but less clear at the *G* and *PG* end. Generally, at that end, sex is said to be absent, but this is only when contemplating the most conventional and blatant forms of representation: issues of sexual dominance and submission tend to escape the censor's reach unless clearly dressed in black leather. Heteronormative representations are unproblematic provided they are expressed in a non explicit manner.

The dialectics of justification tend to be clearly established and fall into two strategies. Generally, sexual material is only excused if it is justified on scientific or artistic grounds. These definitions are largely uninformed by models of readership and reception and ignore the different uses and interpretations which a reader might adopt outside of the 'authorized' preferred reading.[84] Scientific justifications have tended to involve media pertaining to the distribution of birth control and family planning information.[85] There are established medicalized codes of representation which determine how media is to be coded 'scientific', although these were revisited in safe sex advertising in the post-AIDs era, many of which were considered to violate 'scientific' decency.[86]

Where artistic merit is considered, the perceived and arbitrary division between artistic erotica and non-artistic pornography is firmly entrenched in the debate.[87] Generally, the representational border is only tested from the 'artistic' side of the debate which pushes the boundaries of what is shocking.[88] Contemporary industry-produced pornography is content being just what it is (having a vested market interest in being so) and does not seek to establish for itself the status of art. It is this 'one track mind' which, pornography historian O'Toole argues, gets pornography into trouble as it offends the cultural hierarchies making the distinction – art is supposed to be non visceral 'it's supposed to make you lofty, not horny.'[89] Further, he offers this distinction:

---

84 See Hardy, op. cit. fn. 12 Chapter 6 'The Reader and the Author' for a discussion of reception theory in the context of soft core pornography. Other media may be co-opted for erotic use, such as the photographs in *National Geographic* – Lutz CA and Collins JL (1993) *Reading National Geographic*, University of Chicago Press: Chicago.

85 Eberwein R (1999) *Sex Ed: Film, Video, and the Framework of Desire*, Rutgers University Press: New Brunswick.

86 Hunter N (1993) 'Identity, Speech, and Equality', *Virginia Law Review*, v79, 1695 at 1709–10.

87 In the art/pornography partition, censorship discourse seeks to isolate sites of resistance and depoliticize expression, but this is doomed to failure. Kipnis argues that the separation of art from pornography was an important strategy in the segregation of the classes. High Art cannot be revolutionary as it maintains its distance from the materiality of everyday life. Kipnis L (1993) 'She–male fantasies and the aesthetics of pornography', in Church Gibson P and Gibson R (eds) *Dirty Looks: Women, Pornography, Power*, British Film Institute: London.

88 Tom Hingston Studio, op. cit. fn. 17.

89 O'Toole, op. cit. fn. 77 at 13.

Porn is the straightforward depiction of sexual fantasy, using an image system that has little room for working things out analogously or metaphorically. The fantasies might be complex, but they are nearly always full on. 'Art' works quite differently it is about deferral, the sublimation of bodily needs to higher planes of detachment. Thus 'art' is said to be improving while porn is mechanical waste. Plainly this denial of porn's complexity, the denigration of art that works on the body, is part of a larger political process. Art removing itself from porn's clutches is a class act. The arts represent escape from the useful, but also from the manual [... the] proletarian. [...] The mind gains hold over the body; the sublime evacuates the base. Art is not porn because it sublimates desire. Erotica is not porn, 'because they drink wine and the women have smaller breasts'.[90]

If a text is sexual and cannot position itself in relation to scientific or artistic merit it is restricted by the censorship scheme. The OFLC guidelines[91] are concerned with a variety of different factors: simulation, realism, frequency, nudity, fetishism, debasement, offence, abhorrence. These factors reflect a variety of different perspectives and are informed by different, perhaps conflicting, models of the role of media in society and the effect that it has on individuals. Some of the language is taken directly from anti-pornography feminist discourse, discussed later in this chapter. The inclusion of these concepts indicates a key site whereby the law acts as discursive gatekeeper and sets the boundaries of public debate.

The regulatory potential for exculpation through justification provides an excellent example of how law does more than merely regulate, rather, it constitutes the regulated object. Censors engage with the semiotics of the erection and hermeneutics of the 'wide open beaver', constituting a code of representation through inclusions and exclusions of regulatory inscription. The incidence of girl/girl action as a key element of heterosexual male pornographic fantasy can, in part, be explained by the fact that this practice was, at least initially, censored less often than heterosexual sex (due to the problematic erect male member) and thus increased in importance in the vocabulary of desire.[92]

In pornography this regulatory contortion reached what is perhaps its most remarkable moment in the late 60s, early 70s with 'documentaries' such as *Censorship in Denmark: A New Approach* (1969), *Sexual Freedom in Denmark* (1970), *Sex USA* (1970) and *History of the Blue Movie* (1970). Each of these films was a compilation of clips from other pornographic films with expert commentary by doctors explaining what was happening, cheekily suggesting that these films

---

90 Ibid. at 17. It is also worth noting some of the arbitrary ways in which the art/pornography distinction is code, for example, the difference between colour and black and white photography.

91 OFLC, (2003) *Guidelines for the Classification of Films, Videos and Computer Games*, AGPS: Canberra.

92 O'Toole, op. cit. fn. 77 at 69.

were actually serious scientific/academic inquiries.[93] Curiously, each of the films 'framed' the content by playing the films on a screen in the film, perhaps allowing the viewer to remove themselves one more step further away from the action.

From an applied regulatory perspective, the problem with permitting justification is that it further entrenches uncertainty.[94] Some censors argue that allowing exceptions may lead to an intolerable softening of community expectations. When *The Lovers' Guides* were released in Britain in the late 1980s and were accepted as justifiable sex education books, the head of the Obscene Publications Squad expressed dismay, claiming that these texts could make hard core material seem acceptable which would undermine the squad's justification for seizing material based on community standards.[95] In other words, changes in community values might undermine censorship's attempts to protect those already obsolete standards. Permissiveness is constructed as a threat to regulatory fortressing, whereby the integrity of the regulatory machinery is fetishized above any utilitarian or normative purpose of the regulation.

Police have used the fear of porno-anomie to argue for more discretion and broader powers. In an interview with O'Toole, one British vice squad member expressed perhaps typical attitudes when he suggested that strict words such as 'deprave and corrupt' should be replaced by 'upset, concern, annoy, discomfit' and that the purchase of obscene materials should also be made a criminal offence in addition to sale. Acknowledging that the market could never really be eliminated, the officer fell back on unsubstantiated claims that watching erotic materials would lead to a downward spiral: 'A lessening of morals really. You have satellite and cable now, legally showing soft core, but people always want more … cable soft core leads to hard core, leads to s/m and leads to snuff'.[96]

The concept of justification may compensate for the categorical inflexibility of the classification schema but it also forms a junction at which the presumed uniformity of community values might be challenged. How does an artistic or non-artistic context shape different kinds of values and expectations? How are these contexts constructed and why does 'art' provide justification unavailable to more popular media forms?

The recent history of Australian censorship demonstrates a pre-occupation with three kinds of restricted texts: hard core pornography, exploitation films involving depictions of sexualized violence and self-consciously artistic films which play off the first two categories. An examination of the Refused Classification[97] database of banned or censored films reveals several trends in both film making (specifically exploitation film making) and the censors' responses to these trends.

---

93   Ibid. at 70.
94   Ibid. at 9.
95   Michael Hames quoted in Thompson B (1994) *Soft Core: Moral Crusades against Pornography in Britain and America*, Cassell: London.
96   O'Toole, op. cit. fn. 77 at 126–7.
97   http://www.refused–classifcation.com (viewed 12/2/03).

The representation of sexualized violence is a prevalent, even the predominant, reason given for the banning of films. This emerges strongly from the genre of revenge–exploitation films[98] which culminates in the banning of the deconstructive *Baise-Moi* (2000). Further, cinema commentator Jane Mills argues that far from being liberating, the use of terms such as 'degrading' or 'dehumanizing' to prevent representation of rape 'can be read as a part of a masculinist displacement strategy which renders mute the woman's voice.'[99]

What is fascinating about *Baise-Moi* is its use of themes, explicit elements, even codes of representation from exploitation films (including the softer 'telemovie' strain) and hard core pornography to challenge the assumptions about subjectivity and agency in both.[100] Even the relatively mild art film *Dead Man* caused the censors consternation due to a minor scene of sexualized violence; the film was initially banned, then classified R on appeal.[101] There is a false (but generically reinforced) binary of representation between exploitation and art film and this is where much of the controversy of censorship seems to fall.

A discussion of exploitation films also establishes the importance of national cinemas, and the subgenres of exploitation or art film which are organized along national contexts of production and consumption. Rape revenge films, 'women in prison' films, zombie films and cannibal films have all enjoyed popularity in the Italian 'mondo' cinema and are disproportionately represented in the lists of films banned by the Australian censors. Likewise, Hong Kong 'Category III' films are frequently banned due to depictions of sexualized violence (*Raped by an Angel* (1993), *Demon Wet Nurse* (1992)) as are 'atrocity' films (*Man Behind the Sun* (1988), *Laboratory of the Devil* (1992), *Dr Lamb* (1992)). The Hentai genre of anime is similarly well represented in censor's lists such as the notorious *Urotsukidoji – Legend of the Overfiend* (1989) and *Urotsukidoji 2 – Legend of the Demon Womb* (1993). Inevitably the censors had trouble with the weird, brief lived, but enthusiastic Nazi sadism death porn genre: *Ilsa, She Wolf of the SS* (1974), *Greta – The Mad Butcher* (1977) and *Nazi Love Camp 27* (1977).

Many of the banned titles are easily available in ethnic or language specialist video stores. For instance, *Salo* (1975) is available in Italian language video stores,[102] *Dr Lamb* (1992) in Cantonese ones. Clearly censorious power is not evenly geographically or ethnically distributed and this puts an inflection on the

---

98   The 'in and out' history of the censorship of *I Spit on your Grave* (1978) marks the contours of the regulation of sexualized violence and the shifting interpretation of 'gratuitousness'. See http://www.refused–classification.com/Films_I.htm. (viewed 12/2/03).
99   Mills. op. cit. fn. 54 at 62.
100 It must be acknowledged that the line of analysis here, claiming the importance of *Baise-Moi* as a deconstructive rather than purely exploitative text, is a species of the 'artistic merit' discourse of censorship. This argument is one with which the Australian censors did not agree.
101 http://www.refused–classification.com/Films_D.htm (viewed 12/2/03).
102 http://www.refused–classification.com/Films_Salo.htm (viewed 12/2/03).

censorship process. The reception of video technology has made world cinemas (both exploitation and other genres) accessible as these films would not necessarily have the economic potential to support major cinema distribution. Censorship clearly defines 'Othered' minority groups in ways different to the ostensibly universal operation of law and the presumed uniformity of community values.[103] It was once believed that film festivals (including specific interest group festivals) were beyond the reach of censors but this was proven to be wrong when the 1995 Mardi Gras Film Festival faced the banning of *In a Glass Cage* (1986).[104]

The brutal image of censorship as coercive state power is a politically sensitive issue particularly as a metonym for totalitarian control. The previous Minister responsible for the OFLC, Senator Alston, protests the distinction between classification and censorship, drawing on semantic differences in the terms.[105] When a film has been refused classification by the OFLC and then recut by distributors for the Australian market, the label of 'censorship' can be partially avoided. The controversy surrounding the banning and re-editing of *Henry – Portrait of a Serial Killer* (1986) reflects this ambiguity: even though the Board claimed to have misgivings about refusing registration and being reluctant to specify cuts, it nevertheless did so.[106] Even Disney had to recut *The Hunchback of Notre Dame* (1996) to get a *G* rather than a *PG* rating.[107] OFLC head Des Clark, however, sees the role of the censor quite differently and denies that the OFLC has any power to make publishers modify content 'Really, it's just laughable that people say that we can influence people to modify the images'.[108]

In a disciplinary, highly regulated society such as Australia, one governmental response to the vexed power of the censor has been an attempt to make the censorship process more palatable by producing a model of 'community values' (which re-situates the locus of control away from the state) and by attempts to humanize the OFLC through publications and media promotion. The Classification Board and

---

103 Williams examines the increasing visibility of sadomasochism or gay practices in United States regulatory discourse, to the point where these are almost metonyms for a 'not normal' sexuality. One of the ironies of visibility or on/scenity is that it can make the practices and individuals more open to attack. Williams, op. cit. fn. 10 at 288.

104 http://www.refused–classification.com/Films_I.htm (viewed 12/2/03) 'The Office of Film and Literature classification has gone to some lengths to use state legislation to overturn the federal government rubric which until then had been thought to protect film festivals'. Mills, op. cit. fn. 54 at 59.

105 Alston R (1999) 'Regulation is not Censorship', *The Australian*, 13 April.

106 OFLC (1992) *Report on Activities* 1991–2, Canberra. It is significant that much of the cut material occurs in the 'cinema verite' film that Henry and his accomplice make to their victims, reflecting perhaps a higher level of realism than film artifice.

107 OFLC (1998) *Classification Board and Classification Review Board Annual Report 1996–97*, National Capital Printing: Canberra, also extracted at http://www.refused–classification.com/Films_H.htm (viewed 12/2/03).

108 Interviewed in Vnuk H (2003) *Snatched: Sex and Censorship in Australia*, Vintage: Sydney at 135.

Appeal Board member profiles furnished in the OFLC annual reports[109] gives an indication of the strategies used to make the censors seem less threatening and authoritative as arbiters of community values. These profiles include statements that the individual members are:

- 'Attuned to community expectations and standards';
- 'Engages a very wide network of contacts in diverse communities and is tireless in advocating tolerance, compassion and a "fair go"';
- 'links with members of [the] rural community';
- 'deep understanding of issues related to cultural diversity';
- 'Through her travels with her husband in recent years, she has come into contact with people of diverse cultural backgrounds [and] has always enjoyed mixing with people and listening to their views';
- 'has travelled extensively';
- 'a high level of contact with different sections of the community while in the police force [which] has given him a balance and understanding of the differences that exist within society and the tolerance to accept everyone for who they are';
- 'she believes that life is about a diversity of experiences as is evidenced by the range of successfully completed courses in such areas as communication, writing, fitness, directing, acting and creative thinking';
- 'worked as a researcher [...] bringing him into contact with people from a wide range of backgrounds';
- 'grew up in rural Victoria';
- 'worked with children and their families in urban, rural and remote communities';
- 'comes from a large country family and has three adult daughters';
- 'has always enjoyed mixing with people and listening to their views';
- 'experience in remote Australia has given him an understanding of sensitive social justice and health issues relevant to rural and remote communities';
- 'she is interested in current affairs';
- 'involved with such groups as Lions, Rotary, Young Farmers and the Women's Electoral Lobby';
- 'community activities have included doorknocking for the Salvation Army [...] and involvement in establishing and running a Neighbourhood Watch program';
- description of charity works, sporting club membership and previous government and administrative positions; and
- full reference to the number of children and grandchildren of each member.

---

109 OFLC (1999) *Classification Board and Classification Review Board Annual Report 98–99*, National Capital Printing: Canberra, OFLC (2002) *2001–2002 Annual Report*, National Capital Printing: Canberra.

These profiles seem intended to put faces to the faceless bureaucrats, to humanize the censorship authority. Instead, they reveal deep-seated anxieties within the censorship discourse about cultural sensitivity, credibility, charitable credentials, parenting status – in short about the authority to speak for the community and to define the boundaries of that community. Many of these criteria are argumentatively inert and imply a binary opposite which might also be used to argue for credibility, such as the rural/urban dichotomy.

While the concept of a Classification Board seems a democratic failsafe in the bureaucratic system, the process of appointment is not the comparable to the constitution of a jury.[110] In other ways, the censorship system makes occasional but under-theorized gestures toward the involvement of representative participants. In 1996 the conservative Commonwealth Attorney General proposed the establishment of 'community assessment panels' to double check the work of the censor. Between October 1997 and March 1998 three community assessment panels (Sydney, Brisbane and Wagga Wagga) reviewed nine films classified by the Board and in six cases gave the same rating, which was reported by the OFLC as clear proof of success with 'a high degree of correlation'.[111]

The discomfort with which the regulators perceive their task reflects, in part, the shifting ground on which the classification process operates. Civil libertarians might challenge censorship as a draconian exercise of moralist control, but this model denies the complex social environment in which regulation occurs. Rather than a return to moralistic Victorian values, the contemporary spatial practices of classification reflect a regulatory culture pre-occupied with management of risk and self-governance – spatial practices in themselves.

The secularization of moral regulation was achieved by a paradigm shift, the substitution 'offence of the community'[112] for the wrath of a paternalistic god. The transformation from old notions of blasphemy[113] and sedition were achieved by the creation of a new paternalistic myth in the shape of the community and sacrificial victims in the form of children and women who were to be degraded into sacred bodies, objects upon which the law operates.[114]

Because of this, media technology has long played a part in censorship discourse. While sensual images remained in the custody of the wealthy, they were unproblematic. With the possibility of mass consumption and mechanical reproduction, Victorian moral reformers feared the response from the uncultivated

---

110 Of course, the jury selection process has been challenged due to its failure to provide representation. Findlay M and Duff P (1998) *The Jury Under Attack*, Butterworths: Sydney.

111 OFLC (1999), op. cit. fn. 109 at 33.

112 *Miller v California*, 413 US 15, 24 (1973).

113 see Webster R (1990) *A Brief History of Blasphemy*, The Orwell Press: London, where he discusses Salman Rushdie's concept of a 'god shaped hole' left after the loss of faith (at 54).

114 Hunt, op. cit. fn. 46 at 204–211.

'common people'.[115] Arcand compares the emergence of pornography to the technology of the Walkman, whereby for a little cost anyone can experience the music of an orchestra, originally composed for the ruling elite.[116]

However, Alan Hunt contests the assumption that moral regulation is the ideological imposition of a cultural elite and powerful. Instead he finds the middle classes and women to be primary activists. Moral panics cannot be reduced to 'top down' models of control:

> [M]oral regulation movements form an interconnected web of discourses, symbols and practices exhibiting persistent continuities that stretch across time and place. The deep anxieties that are roused and stirred in moral politics involve the condensation of a number of different discourses, different fears, within a single image [... S]uch movements are not to be understood in isolation but as part of a shifting complex of projects of governance in which the long-run changes are not so much the shift from one target to another, but rather in the location of moral regulation within the field of governing others and governing selves.[117]

Hunt asks us to look past the anachronistic archaic trappings of much of censorship discourse and to consider moral regulation to be firmly entrenched in modernity, 'an ongoing anxiety about the governability of urbanized masses',[118] of a society where traditional control mechanism no longer seem to function and there is no stable model of social order. The rise of the social sciences and their concept of 'society' as a subject of inquiry has enabled a discursive shift, a secularization from 'offence to God' to 'harm to society'. Hunt examines the shift from notions of sexual purity to social hygiene in Britain and America[119] which involved the absorption of a medicalized concept linking morality with cleanliness.[120]

Therefore, the re-emergence of the censor in the public arena signifies not simply a regression to the moralistic past but the emergence of a new kind of moralism based on social harm. Anthropologist Clifford Geetrz[121] describes the

---

115   Ibid. at 118.
116   Arcand B (1993) *The Jaguar and the Anteater: Pornography Degree Zero*, Verso: New York.
117   Hunt, op. cit. fn. 46 at 9.
118   Ibid. at 12–13.
119   Ibid.
120   McClintock A (1995) *Imperial Leather: Race, Gender and Sexuality in the Colonial Contest*, Routledge: London. The 'unwired' spaces of developing nations have also been subject to the colonial gaze. Harpold T and Philip K (2000) 'Of Bugs and Rats: Cyber-Cleanliness, Cyber-Squalor, and the Fantasy-Spaces of Informational Globalization', *Postmodern Culture*, v11.1, http://muse.jhu.edu/journals/pmc/v011/11.1harpold.html (viewed 5/1/01).
121   Geertz C (1973b) 'Ideology as a Cultural System' in *The Interpretation of Cultures: Selected Essays*, Basic Books: New York.

invocation of traditional or community values as 'retraditionalism'. Alan Hunt expands this definition, suggesting that this complex notion involves both an attempt to find new justifications to reinstate traditional social relationships and an entirely new configuration of social and regulatory values.[122]

In the consumption of pornography, discourses of self governance are extremely important. Old notions of 'building character' by resisting temptation have been replaced by discourses of addiction and anti-social activity.[123] Hunt draws our attention to the moralization of tobacco through contemporary anti-smoking discourses tying together health and regulation of space by separation of smoking and non-smoking areas: 'These techniques and tactics come together to produce an intense moralization of tobacco consumption [...] which increasingly associates smoking with defective self-care and a lack of cultural sophistication'.[124] Moral issues surrounding pornography have been transformed by the same social, governance and spatial conditions that have resulted in the moralization of tobacco consumption.

Through the process of media classification, particularly in the regulation of sexual content, a contemporary kind of moral and regulatory order is implemented. This is achieved via the taxonomies of censorship and backed up by the abstract space of community in which these values are vested. A regulatory approach which focuses on the law as the single site of power, even if it acknowledges community input, ignores the importance of other regulatory processes and communities which exist and contribute to the code of erotic space. The jurido-centric approach constructs the media landscape as an empty container, devoid of regulatory power except for that which is invested and inscribed by law. The practices of censorship and pornography are engaged in the constitution of sexual spaces and the inscription of sexuality on the body and physical space.

The Spatial Deployment of Censorship Law

Censorship strategies are spatial in nature,[125] involving the civilizing and colonization of spaces. These include the policing of borders, the construction of

---

122 Hunt, op. cit. fn. 46 at 194–5.

123 See the issue of porn addiction of which Internet porn forms an important element: Irvine JM (1995) 'Regulated Passions: The Invention of Inhibited Sexual Desire and Sexual Addiction' in Terry J and Urla J (eds) *Deviant Bodies: Critical Perspectives on Difference in Science and Popular Culture*, Indiana University Press: Bloomington.

124 Hunt, op. cit. fn. 46 at 199.

125 In the context of electronic media, Pfohl examines the diversity of information flows in cyberotic geographies, invoking Sacher-Masoch as an archetypical erotic geographer. Pfohl S (1998) 'Theses on the cyberotics of HIStory: Venus in Microsoft, remix', in Broadhurst Dixon J and Cassidy EJ (eds) *Virtual Futures: Cyberotics, Technology and Post-Human Pragmatism*, Routledge: London.

pornography as a threat (often foreign in origin), invocation of fear of uncontrolled spaces, inscription of sexual zoning rules and taxonomies on human geography (such as the various age divisions, different sexual identities and sexualities). In this chapter, four primary strategies are examined: the production of spaces of childhood; the regulatory fortressing of censorship law; censorship law's gatekeeping of public discourse around pornography; and the policing of the Imaginary Domain.

The Production of Childhood

One of the express objectives of censorship is the protection of children from exposure to pornographic media as a safeguard against the harms which may result from it. Censorship law does more than just protect childhood, it also produces childhood as a regulatory object. Governance of childhood is usually primarily the responsibility of parents, but censorship, especially Internet censorship, is one area where the state claims a central role. Donna Rice Hughes, leader of the anti-pornography group Enough is Enough, favours government intervention because 'parents can't be expected to shoulder the entire burden.'[126]

One of the significant geographies invoked in the Western censorship discourse is the space of childhood.[127] Childhood spaces feature prominently in moral panics concerning children and Internet pornography, '[the media controversy] was an adult fairy tale of the 'nineties to rival Hansel and Gretel but with the added twist of something straight out of the 'eighties horror movie *Poltergeist*'.[128] While moral panics promote childhood as a stable and essentialist category, the social space of childhood is continually transformed – today's children are more dependent, spend more time in education, and yet youth consumerism is expanding as are demands for economic and personal autonomy.[129]

The child is represented in the Internet pornography issue not just as the victim of forced exposure but also the subject of predatory child pornographers, both real and imagined. In Britain, and elsewhere, there have been a series of controversies in which individuals have been named, pursued, even prosecuted for suspicions of child pornography possession, which have turned out to be family photographs or portraits.[130] This over-reaction is fuelled by the problems of context – how do

---

126 ZDNet Australia (2001a) 'Taming the Web', 20 April, http://www.zdnet.com.au/newstech/ebusiness/story/0,2000024981,20216841,00.htm (viewed 25/3/03).

127 And the presumption that the Internet (and television) form public spaces where children have free access. Marr D (2002) 'Opinion: The letter that dare not speak its name', *Sydney Morning Herald*, 2 January.

128 O'Toole, op. cit. fn. 77 at 260.

129 Hunt, op. cit. fn. 46 at 211.

130 'In the meantime, the bulk of *visible* police and judicial activity in the UK concerning child porn actually involves images of a non-pornographic nature – family

we decide if a specific representation of a child is innocent or not, especially if it contains nudity? The representation of nudity itself has become a more contested rather than a more stable signifier.

Contemporary public concern (and moral panic) concerning child pornography can be traced to a series of ten minute loop films and magazines produced in Denmark in the mid-1970s. These seemed to genuinely involve children and images derived from the films account for much of the child pornography seized today as virtually no commercially produced child pornography material has been created since.[131] It is difficult to establish a realistic picture of the incidence of child pornography as there is no sure way of ascertaining the age of models whether they be ostensibly adult or child. There is considerable scope within the term 'child', and a great deal of difference between the sexuality of a seven-year-old and a seventeen-year-old.[132]

Apart from the underground nature of child pornography production, empirical research is limited by legal considerations and the problem that much of the product which is known to be available exists solely as part of police sting operations for entrapment of potential offenders.[133] This uncertainty often manifests in fears of 'paedophile rings', a variation on criminal conspiracy theory, which serves to construct paedophiles as dangerous 'others'. When rare incidences of child pornography production are discovered, they can be used as examples to 'prove' that they are the tip of an iceberg of organized activity.[134]

The intersection between the spaces of childhood and pornographic media emerges as a justification for control of all sexual material, not just that which involves children or to which children have access. This convergence and amplification of moral strategies is described by Alan Hunt as an 'umbrella effect'.[135] O'Toole is cautious regarding the term 'child pornography' as it implicates pornography generally in recorded acts of child abuse.[136] Anti-pornography campaigns which ascribe victim status to women and children as generic categories not only demonstrate an unconscionable conflation of all women into one class of victim,

---

snaps, naturist images and art work' O'Toole, op. cit. fn. 77 at 224. See the Chard case (family snaps) at 217, Arthur Cotteril (naturist photography), at 237–8, Graham Ovenden and Ron Oliver (portraiture) at 239–43.

131   Schuijer J and Rossen B (1992) 'The Trade in Child Pornography', *IPT Forensics*, v4, http://www.ipt-forensics.com/journal/volume4/4_2_1.htm (viewed 27/4/98).

132   This scope is often exploited for shock effect, for example by The Australia Institute reports discussed in Chapter 2.

133   O'Toole, op. cit. fn. 77 at 221.

134   Williams L (1993) 'Second thoughts on hard core: American obscenity law and the scapegoating of deviance', in Church Gibson P and Gibson R (eds) *Dirty Looks: Women, Pornography, Power*, British Film Institute: London.

135   Hunt, op. cit. fn. 46 at 209.

136   O'Toole, op. cit. fn. 77 at 219.

but also taps into a history of infantilizing women and rendering them subjects of regulation, entrenched in law.[137]

As a spatial strategy, the emphasis placed on the child victim transforms part of the population into passive regulatory objects while undermining the credibility of the regulatory communities which exist around parenting.[138] In 1993 James Ferman, the Director of the British Board of Film and Video Classification, clearly stated the problem as he saw it: 'We can't have freedom for adults in this country, because we can't trust adults to protect children.'[139] Hunt sees these practices as problematic:

> Children had long been significant in moralizing discourses because the association between 'children', victimization and innocence was deeply imbricated in popular culture. They still figure as classic 'innocent victims' in an expanding range of scandals that revolve around abuse of power [...] Alongside and interwoven with the tensions that beset contemporary gender relations is a pronounced set of concerns about relations between adults and children, in particular between parents and their children. Unresolved and often unstable interpersonal relations are further compounded by a set of discourses involving both a sacralisation and a demonization of children. A profound paradox lies at the convergence of regulatory projects directed towards the 'protection' of the 'innocence' of children with a conjuncture in which the innocence of children has itself become increasingly problematic.[140]

While Internet pornographers and paedophile offenders certainly do exist, they have been elevated to mythological status as folk devils[141] of Internet regulatory

---

137 Brown W (1995) *States of Injury: Essays on Power and Freedom in Late Modernity*, Princeton University Press: Princeton.

138 Similarly, Bell argues that incest is vital to modern state power over populations, a nexus by which the family, previously protected by the public/private divide, was colonized by sexual and legal discourse. Infantile sexuality provides an important concern of social reformers from the nineteenth century onwards. Bell V (1995) 'Bio-politics and the Spectre of Incest: Sexuality and/in the Family', in Featherstone M, Lash S and Robertson R (eds) *Global Modernities*, Sage Publications: London.

139 (1993) *Right to Reply*, Channel 4 Television, 14 March.

140 Hunt, op. cit. fn. 46 at 204–211.

141 Using the term coined by Stan Cohen, in Cohen S (1972) *Folk Devils and Moral Panics: The Creation of the Mods and Rockers*, Oxford University Press: Oxford. This is not, of course, to deny the existence of paedophile offenders, more the emphasis which is placed on them as a justification for authoritarian exercise of power. Because of secrecy and the nature of the victims it is difficult to obtain proper empirical data about them and there may be a tendency to over-estimate, like the 'satanic day care' crisis of the 1980s. Nathan D (1995) *Satan's Silence: Ritual Abuse and the Making of a Modern American Witch Hunt*, Basic Books: New York.

discourse.[142] These Others present an enemy, a threat to structure the power of authority, a secret conspiracy. Children are simultaneously the victims of predators and vulnerable to exposure to dangerous images. All accompanied by the shrill cry of 'will no one think of the children?'[143]

Infantile sexuality is a serious and complicated field of study. The manufacture of innocence and the production of innocent spaces of childhood which occurs throughout the 'children and pornography' debates is based on a reification and fetishization of a notion of 'purity', a binary formed in opposition to vice which corrodes and corrupts this innocence. Instead of William Blake's complex dialectic of innocence and experience,[144] this approach posits childhood and sexuality as opposed concepts which exclude one another, locked in Manichean struggle.

The space of parenting intersects with the regulation of childhood, producing a confrontation between state and private power. It is frequently 'other people's families' which necessitate state intervention, the locus of the 'friend's house' or the permissive school or library where access to media is unsupervized, a metonym for anxiety about social control and parenting. O'Toole notes that central to the discourse of obscenity is a hierarchical strategy; speculating on the corruption of 'someone else' who, lacking the sophisticated and learned position of the legal scrutineer, may be depraved or corrupted.[145] This strategy depends on a denial of self and experience in order to assume a pretence of objectivity, a position of judgement outside of the production of the interlocutor's own sexuality. The child victim presents a ready example of such an Other.

The production of childhood is an important part of the constitution of adult legal subjectivity. It is a spatial practice which fetishizes powerlessness and reconceives complex social circumstances through an abstract framework based on legal inscribed notions of responsibility and autonomy. The population is regulated through abstraction and homogeneity, with an 'age of consent' in addition to media classification strata creating arbitrary fixed ages of autonomy, regardless of individual development and circumstances. A malleable and highly regulatable legal object is created in the place of a child's subjectivity. This exploration is not intended to deny that some children are victimized by sexual predators, but rather

---

142 In some discourses *pornography* and *child pornography* become virtually indistinguishable as parts of a single continuous concept. In many ways this recalls antipornography feminism's insistence that male gay pornography should be considered part of the ideological structure for the oppression of women. Stoltenberg J (1990) *Refusing to be a Man*, Meridian: New York at 53 and 132. The representational spaces of pornography are constructed as a uniform ideological monolith.

143 A rhetorical position which is neatly satirized in *The Simpsons*' Helen Lovejoy, the town busybody, hypocrite and moral panic engineer.

144 Blake W (1984) *Songs of Innocence and Experience*, Dover: New York (originally published 1826).

145 O'Toole, op. cit. fn. 77 at 13.

to examine the ways in which this harm is co-opted by censorship law through its production of childhood as a regulatory space.

Regulatory Fortressing in Censorship Law

Censorship law is premised on the self-justification of a set of community standards which are produced in a circular manner by its own practices. Forms of moral regulation are often described as symbolic legislation because the difficulty in proving their efficacy in positivist terms, operating as they do within a chaotic and discontinuous social discursive environment.[146] Chapter 6 will consider developments in regulatory theory which accommodate more flexible models of power and may obviate the need to resort to binary notions of effective/symbolic altogether.

Regulatory fortressing as a spatial practice circumvents these uncertainties by making regulation integrity itself the object of regulatory power. Arguments concerning the ineffectual nature of Australia's censorship law must be understood as part of greater discourses concerning the integrity of law, the knowability of regulatory objects and closure in regulation. In the absence of straightforward answers, regulatory fortressing construes regulation as sufficient in itself. In the censorship context, it is difficult to establish what role censorship actually plays and what role regulatory communities play and would continue to play in the absence of state intervention. Regulatory fortressing marginalizes these communities by deeming them irrelevant.

Overall, it seems that the Australian public favour the availability of sexually explicit material, including *X* rated videos.[147] Nevertheless, the Internet censorship laws assume a much less tolerant posture. Chapter 3 considered civil libertarian critiques of the dearth of empirical evidence that the *Broadcasting Services Amendment (Online Services) Act 1999* has been successful in its objectives. In utilitarian terms the Act is leaky, yet its jurispace model, isolated from its social consequences, remains intact. It is still good law 'on the books'. This regulatory integrity depends on the authority of regulatory language which is able to construct its own reality by deeming itself necessary. Even if a piece of legislation is proven to be empirically ineffectual, the notion of symbolic legislation provides regulation with a space of successful operation:

> Moral regulation movements are manifestations of an anxiety of freedom that haunts modern liberal forms of rule. Large urbanised masses live with no evident mechanism of unification and no shared values. Traditional authorities are no

---

146 Gustaffson G (1983) 'Symbolic and Pseudo Policies as Responses to Diffusion of Power', *Policy Sciences*, v15, 269.

147 Paterson K et al. (1993) *Classification Issues: Film, Video and Television*, Office of Film and Literature Classification: Sydney.

longer able to rule in the old way and social deference, whether of class, gender or ethnicity, is fragile. There is no 'natural' system of order. Formal education is conceived within a narrowing remit; projects of Durkheimian 'moral education', whether in schools or the media, have become attenuated.

[... T]he family is increasingly fallible, while increasing awareness of social diversity impedes state legislative efforts at producing a public realm capable of and committed to enforcing a moral order which is conceived as a necessary condition for social order. Any such state projects have first to create a sense of alarm and danger, epitomised in the state war against drugs, which itself undermines the sense of social and moral order.[148]

In the censorship discourse, regulatory fortressing is frequently expressed in a geographical manner, referring to national borders. Mitchell notes the importance of regulating flows of information for New Zealand as an island nation.[149] In the era of the stag movie, France became so well known for its stag films that 'French Film' became a euphemism for pornographic films.[150] In the United States, when second tier film houses relied on exploitation films, 'European' films were popular as they promised glimpses of flesh.[151] In Australia the liberal standards of the SBS broadcaster, screening 'world movies' late at night, has opened a transgressive space available in practically every home. From the 1950s through to the 1970s, the genre of Mondo films presented the foreign as a site of curiosities expressed in gory, exploitative and salacious material. One commentator remarks that Mondo cinema 'was like *National Geographic*, only the breasts moved.'[152] In each of these contexts the foreign 'other' is presented as an example against which normatively is measured and a challenge for censors to maintain the integrity of national and jurisdictional borders.

Britain's James Callaghan, Labour Home Secretary in the late 1960s, called for a halt to 'the advancing tide of so-called permissiveness' from Europe.[153] O'Toole finds clear links between the UK's censorious regime and its geography as an island: 'Being an island nation, not recently invaded, leaves some British people thinking that maybe we're superior to foreigners [...] Our army is better – the foreigners may start the wars, but we finish them [...] A picture starts to form, a familiar composite of paternalism, chauvinism and Puritanism.'[154]

---

148   Hunt, op. cit. fn. 46 at 215.
149   Mitchell W (1996) *City of Bits: Space, Place and the Infobahn*, MIT Press, MA at 148.
150   O'Toole, op. cit. fn. 77 at 66.
151   Ibid. at 66–7.
152   Ibid. at 67.
153   Haste C (1994) *Rules of Desire: Sex in Britain, World War I to the Present*, Pimlico: London.
154   O'Toole, op. cit. fn. 77 at 149.

The mediascape is not the only space shaped by censorship's regulatory strategies. The politics of censorship are connected to broader issues in legal and regulatory culture, especially where the integrity and coherence of the spatial concept of jurisdiction is under challenge.[155] Alan Hunt refers to the 'umbrella effect'[156] whereby diverse movements and trends are captured within a moral project. In the censorship example, xenophobic and nationalist discourses can easily be included within issues of moral regulation as condemnation of practices in other countries as potentially unregulated sites. Further, he suggests that nineteenth century concerns about sex, prostitution, homosexuality and masturbation are connected to economic and military imperialism and anxieties about vitality and 'adequacy' as a nation.[157]

The debate over *Broadcasting Services Amendment (Online Services) Act 1999* occurs amid deep-seated fears about the nation-state of Australia in its international context – here represented by the ungovernable wilds of the Internet. With Australia's geographical position in the Asia–Pacific region and its isolation from its cultural 'sponsors' (first Great Britain, now the United States), fortressed moral regulation provides a myth of connectivity to the cultural, economic and regulatory systems of the West and displaces the need to address localized conditions of multiculturalism. Complex social conditions are replaced by 'community values' through a form of regulatory fortressing which requires that values be developed within the discursive framework established by the regulatory scheme itself.

The Censor as Gatekeeper: Critique of Pornography

While many different regulatory communities may orbit around a certain issue, the regulator has an important role not just because of its coercive power but also because it acts as a gatekeeper to the public sphere. The role of the regulator involves a complex mediation of different claims and interests (including its own), and the power to set the public agenda is a crucial one. This power allows the regulator to define what matters are relevant and expel all others to the margins.

In censorship law, this gatekeeping power manifests in two primary ways. The general invocation of 'community values' acts as a generic hurdle, a concept under which interests must define themselves if they are to enter the debate (whether or not their voice is ever actually heard). Additionally, the classification guidelines contain definitions of concepts and descriptions of harmful media effects. These guidelines contain specific reference to the narratives of different regulatory communities such as anti-pornography feminism's argument that

---

155 The deployment of new media challenges simple models of jurisdiction in many ways. The connections between the legal model of jurisdiction and theories of space are explored in more detail in Chapter 6.
156 Hunt, op. cit. fn. 46 at 9–10.
157 Ibid. at 25.

pornography is degrading, or the psychological claim that viewing violence causes further violence. In this way, regulation positions and privileges interests in different ways.

The practices of regulation involve more than just the inscription of power on a regulatory object. One of the meta-functions of regulation occurs in shaping the public discourses which provide the impetus for regulation and also the discourses of regulatory power itself (which may involve regulatory fortressing). Regulation is deployed spatially in the regulation of an object and in the positioning in social space of interests and regulatory communities with reference to that object.

Lefebvre indicates that spaces are never entirely erased, that abandoned spaces are available for appropriation and use in different ways, like a hyena taking over the burrow of an antwolf. This kind of 'spatial ecology' is important to the complex connection of recurring themes and forms in the regulation of pornography. Generally, the pornography debate is represented by anti-pornography campaigners, a pornography industry, civil libertarians, experts (social scientist, media theorists) and the state which has a vested interest in exercise of power. None of these positions are stable and each involve discontinuous, sometimes inconsistent, ideologies and regulatory communities.

In practice, it is sometimes difficult to distinguish between critique and calls for censorship. While some key anti-pornography feminists such as MacKinnon and Dworkin see the power of the state as a key to social reforms,[158] others are suspicious of the state interest. Sara Paretsky reflects on the manner in which her own comments concerning *American Psycho* (that were, to ignore it and that people should not buy the book just in order criticize it) were reported in the press as the actions of a militant feminist book burner.[159] Imputing aggression into critique is not an unusual news media tactic, and feminist critics have been the subject of demonization through these media practices which Paretsky compares to the early twentieth century circulation of the anti-semitic hoax *The Protocols of the Elders of Zion*.

Within feminism, the anti-pornography discourse is resisted by anti-censorship feminist critics who are sceptical about the use of state power to reform social issues. King is concerned that once radical concepts are codified into law, the very radical interests who proposed them lose control over how their ideas are applied and interpreted.[160] Cultural theorist Linda Williams suggests that censorship

---

[158] MacKinnon C (1989) *Towards a Feminist Theory of the State*, Harvard University Press: Cambridge, MA; Dworkin A and MacKinnon C (1988) *Pornography and Civil Rights: A New Day for Women's Equality: Organizing Against Pornography*, Minneapolis; Dworkin, op. cit. fn. 36.

[159] Paretsky S (1994) 'The Protocols of the Elders of Feminism', *Law/Text/Culture*, v1, 14.

[160] King L (1985) 'Censorship and law reform: will changing the law mean a change for the better', in Burstyn V (ed) *Women against Censorship*, Douglas and McIntyre: Toronto.

prematurely forecloses debates on issues of sexuality and representation in which women ought to be assertively engaged.[161] Marxist feminists such as Segal[162] and Wilson[163] express frustration with the entire pornography debate and consider the pre-occupation with representations of oppression to be a significant retreat from engagement with material conditions of exploitation generally, of which the sex industry is merely an example.

The anti-pornography feminist position is often summarized in the famous polemical quote: 'Pornography is the theory; and rape is the practice'[164] and rhetoric such as Dworkin's claim that pornography is 'Dachau brought into the bedroom and celebrated.'[165] For some anti-pornography feminists, censorship is certainly on the agenda, either directly through the co-option of state censorship apparatus[166] or through civil products liability, litigation aimed at making pornographers liable for harms claimed to be the consequences of their product.[167] An expansive regulatory posture can quickly be conflated with other regulatory issues – one reason why the Internet regulation and pornography debates have been so closely connected. MacKinnon was quick to endorse Rimm's claims that a major proportion of the Internet was pornographic and likens the Internet to a 'Trojan horse'.[168]

The anti-pornography feminist discourse is aimed at challenging three assumptions about sexual representation, specifically (but not limited to) pornography. The first is the assumption that mere images do no harm. Anti-pornography campaigners argue that pornography's visual extremity does harm in a sense intelligible even to liberal concepts of harm, arguing for causal links

---

161 Williams, op. cit. fn. 10.

162 Segal L (1987) *Is the Future Female? Troubled Thoughts on Contemporary Feminism*, Virago: London; Segal L (1993) 'Does pornography cause violence? The search for evidence' in Church Gibson P and Gibson R (eds) *Dirty Looks: Women, Pornography, Power*, BFI: London; Segal L (1994) *Straight Sex: The Politics of Pleasure*, Virago: London.

163 Wilson E (1992) 'Feminist fundamentalism: the shifting politics of sex and censorship' in Segal L and McIntosh M (eds) *Sex Exposed: Sexuality and the Pornography Debate*, Virago: London.

164 Morgan R (1980) 'Theory and Practice: Pornography and Rape' in Lederer L (ed.) *Take Back the Night: Women on Pornography*, William Morrow: New York.

165 Dworkin, op. cit. fn. 36 at 121.

166 Dworkin and MacKinnon, op. cit. fn. 158 and see *R v Butler* (1992) 89 DLR (4th) 449.

167 Bernstein A (1997) 'How to Make a New Tort: Three Paradoxes', *Texas Law Review*, v75, 1539; Wesson, op. cit. fn. 38; Pacillo EL (1994) 'Getting a Feminist Foot in the Courtroom Door: Media Liability for Personal Injury Caused by Pornography', *Suffolk University Law Review*, v28, 123. These articles suggest that the torts system be used to regulate producers of pornography, making them liable where offenders enact fantasies from the text.

168 MacKinnon CA (1995) 'Vindication and Resistance: A Response to the Carnegie Mellon Study of Pornography in Cyberspace', *Georgetown Law Journal*, v83, 1959.

between it and a range of violent harms. The second assumption is that 'sexual liberation' of itself has liberated and empowered women. Instead, some feminists argue that sexual liberation has expanded the repertoire of control and opportunities for oppression of women.[169] The third assumption, implicit in liberalism, is the political notion that private matters ought to be beyond regulatory influence.[170]

All of these claims were incorporated into Canadian law in the case of *R v Butler*[171] which, in a rare example of judicial notice of social theory, endorsed MacKinnon's claims that pornography caused harm and was therefore not protected by the right to free speech. Ironically, feminist and gay and lesbian authors, performers, artists and scholars were the first and foremost penalized by exercise of power under this line of authority.[172]

Anti-pornography feminists have successfully forced the issue of pornography onto the public agenda, where previous calls for debate had been ignored. The effect of this critique 'has been to force us to confront the pervasiveness of pornography and the way in which it has become completely enmeshed in our social reality.'[173] The stridency of much of the argument has inevitably also created sites of resistance, required many of the hidden and liminal practices around pornography to be brought into public examination in order to assess the claims made against it.

O'Toole's *Pornocopia: Porn, Sex, Technology and Desire*[174] presents an example of mobilized resistance. By compiling a framework from criticisms which have been directed at anti-pornography writers, he sketches the terrain of resistance and challenges anti-pornography feminism on seven grounds:

First, he challenges pornography critics to produce proof of the empirical data on claims that pornography is responsible for sexual violence. O'Toole suggests that the reasoning linking pornography and rape merely creates convenient excuses for sexual offenders seeking to blame someone else for their actions.[175] Kutchinsky examined the removal of restrictions on erotic material in Denmark during the

---

169   Dworkin A (1987) *Intercourse*, Secker and Warburg: London.

170   Assister A (1989) *Pornography, Feminism and the Individual*, Pluto Press: London.

171   *R v Butler*, op. cit. fn. 166.

172   Plank T (1997) 'Expanding the Feminine Sexual "Imaginary": A Response to Drucilla Cornell's Theory of Zoning Pornography', *Women's Rights Law Reporter*, vol 18, 215 at 220. See *Glad Day Bookshop v The Queen*, Toronto 619/90 (Ontario Court, General Division), 14 July 1992 [unreported].

173   Cornell D (1995) *The Imaginary Domain: Abortion, Pornography and Sexual Harassment*, Routledge: New York at 126.

174   See generally O'Toole, op. cit. fn. 77 Chapter 2 'The Porn Wars'.

175   Ibid. at 40, specifically critiquing MacKinnon's argument that Thomas Schiro was unable to perceive the wrong that he had done because of pornography resulting in diminished responsibility, MacKinnon C (1993a) *Only Words*, Harvard University Press: Cambridge, MA. at 20. See also O'Callaghan J (1995) '"Under the Influence": Pornography and Alcohol – Some Common Themes', *Akron Law Review*, v29, 35.

late 1960s and found a reduction in rates of sex crime.[176] Similarly, Baron found an inverse relationship between availability of pornography and indicators of gender equality across the United States.[177] The British Home Office report[178] in 1990 similarly found no links between pornography and violence, a report that the government suppressed and almost managed to bury completely.[179] Cornell goes further and challenges the entire causal model which draws a straight line from representation to consequence, because it 'is difficult to use such a model in the complex, symbolically ridden world of sexuality.'[180]

Second, Pornocopia challenges the claims to uniform experiences of pornography, of women exposed to it (whether involuntarily or as willing consumers) and those working in the industry as model/actors and as entrepreneurs (sometimes both).[181] Cornell points to Ona Zee's attempts to unionize the pornography industry and director Candida Royale's profit sharing and mandatory-condom set as examples of women contesting and challenging stereotypes of women as victims,[182] and men as mere biology, lacking any ability of self determination.[183]

Third, O'Toole challenges the idea of pornography as a homogenous phenomenon. 'It is not possible to take such a diverse entity and call it a singular thing, available to be read in a singular way, and always resulting in a negative experience.'[184] An example of this approach is Dworkin's claims to a universal reading of erotica, that gay men and transsexuals ought to be conflated with women as 'victims' of pornography and that gay and lesbian pornography ought to be censored in the same way as heterosexual texts.[185]

Fourth, O'Toole disputes some of the terminology used such 'sexist', 'degrading', 'dehumanizing', 'objectifying' and the manner in which they are deployed. He suggests that these terms are used as though they were empirical facts rather than judgements and that this approach eliminates space for debate. O'Toole

---

176   Kutchinsky B (1990) 'Pornography and rape: Theory and practice? Evidence from crime data in four countries where pornography is easily available', *International Journal of Law and Psychiatry*, v 14, 47 These findings were challenged on their empirical credibility in Court JH (1984) 'Sex and violence: a ripple effect', in Malamuth NM and Donnerstein E (eds) *Pornography and Sexual Aggression*, Academic Press: London.

177   Baron L (1990) 'Pornography and gender equality: an empirical analysis', *Journal of Sex Research*, vol 27(3), 363.

178   Howitt D and Cumberbatch G (1990) *Pornography: Its Impacts and Influences, a Review of the Available Research Evidence on the Effects of Pornography*, HMSO: London, commissioned by the Home Office Research and Planning Unit, UK.

179   O'Toole, op. cit. fn. 77 at 112.
180   Cornell, op. cit. fn. 173 at 101.
181   O'Toole, op. cit. fn. 77 at 54–5.
182   Cornell, op. cit. fn. 173 at 97.
183   Ibid. at 125.
184   O'Toole, op. cit. fn. 77 at 15.
185   Dworkin, op. cit. fn. 36 at 62.

invokes cultural and literary studies to propose that meanings are never fixed.[186] Other media texts are not free from the challenge of objectification. Romance fiction may contain just as overt objectification of the female subject.[187]

Fifth, O'Toole takes issue with some of the decoding of media, especially of sadomasochistic imagery which is construed by critics as non-consensual violence.[188]

Sixth, O'Toole raises concern about the political alliances made by anti-pornography feminists in the course of their campaign. These include alliances with the new right, traditional moral agents and the 'long spoon' attempt to co-opt state power. Author Anne Rice is concerned that feminism can be hijacked by conservatism, 'If two Baptist ministers from Oklahoma came up with their arguments, they would have been immediately laughed out of the public arena. They got away with their nonsensical arguments because they were feminists and because they confused well-meaning liberals everywhere.'[189]

Finally, O'Toole contests the effectiveness of the policies which merely drive the pornography industry underground and do nothing to change public attitudes. He argues that state power merely provides an illusion of a regulatory effectiveness, a 'quick fix'.[190] In saying this, he uses a fairly basic model of state power and does not consider the symbolic effect of state action – both in setting 'standards' and in creating resistance to enforced rule.[191]

The framework of this debate demonstrates that there are difficult issues at stake, which cannot be reduced to an assessment of pornography under a harmless/harmful binary. It is beyond the scope of this book to engage thoroughly with the social issues of pornography or to suggest solutions. Rather, a spatial analysis of regulation is concerned with the different ways in which that debate can be framed in the public sphere. Regulatory power spatially deploys the issues, positions the participants in the debate with relativity to the community, contextualizes different interests and legitimizes some voices.

By its nature, legal regulation is a reductionist practice which is premised on producing manipulable models of social issues and providing simple, universal

---

186   O'Toole, op. cit. fn. 77 at 27–8.
187   Assister A (1988) 'Romance Fiction: Porn for Women?' in Day G and Bloom C (eds) *Perspectives on Pornography: Sexuality in Film and Literature*, St Martin's Press: New York.
188   A few critics have sought to contextualize the 'violence' of sadomasochism by describing the consensual rules under which sadomasochist play is enacted. Ehrenreich B, Hess E and Jacobs G (1986) *Re-Making Love: The Feminization of Sex*, Anchor Books: New York.
189   Novelist Anne Rice quoted in Strossen N (1996) *Defending Pornography: Free Speech, Sex, and the Fight for Women's Rights*, Abacus: London.
190   O'Toole, op. cit. fn. 77 at 38.
191   A good example of resistance is the 'Refused Classification' website which records and describes films censored by the Australian OFLC. http://www.refused–classifcation.com (viewed 12/2/03).

and abstract maps of social relationships. The inscription of regulatory status on a particular text reduces its complex intertextual relations to a single classification standard, with some allowance for warning indicia.

Feminist legal theorist Cornell is disappointed that the public debate surrounding pornography is drawn too easily in facile clichés:

> The pornography debate portrays its contestants within sex and gender stereotypes, its contending figures drawn in the broad outlines of a Harlequin romance. Rapacious men with libidos of mythological proportions heartlessly brutalise innocent women as the hopeless victims of their lust, while the anti-pornography feminist poses herself as the sacrificial victim, the barrier to a tide of male sexuality that threatens violence. Bold freedom fighters ride out, drawing their lances against the oppressive feminists, the purported enemies of these brave warriors.[192]

Reductionism is not solely the province of law. In order to create space for more complex positions within a debate, Cornell suggests a reconceptualization of the public sphere – the topic of the next section.

Sexual Representation in the Spaces of the Imaginary Domain

As the pornography debate has developed over time, the critical terrain has shifted from primarily social science oriented approaches, focussing on issues of causation and harm, to critical perspectives informed by cultural studies, exploring issues of representation and reception. In examinations of both soft core[193] and hard core[194] pornography, discourse analysis has been used in order to explore complex issues of authorship and readership, the position of subject and object and the depiction of pleasure. In part, this trend has been generated by the deadlock in the debate and the failure of social science to provide convincing empirical evidence one way or another regarding causation. Studies informed by critical theory have promoted an understanding of the multiplicity of meanings in pornography and the relationship with social space that is shared with other discourses, including regulatory and cyberspace discourses.

Exploring this social space, Drucilla Cornell seeks to re-invigorate liberal concepts of free speech by fusing a Kantian/Rawlsian model of liberty with Lacanian psychoanalysis and a critical geographical posture, producing a strangely cohesive

---

192 Cornell, op. cit. fn. 173 at 95.
193 Hardy, op. cit. fn. 12.
194 Williams, op. cit. fn. 10 which challenges assumptions about degradation in the depictions of genitals, ejaculation and other external signifiers of internal, invisible pleasure.

and very appealing mutant hybrid. In *The Imaginary Domain*,[195] Cornell posits a social space of the same name, a space of becoming which must be protected by a just society. Central to Cornell's thesis is the problem of offence – how are 'feelings of being offended' to be conceptualized and under what conditions does this crystallize into a harm upon which the justice systems ought to act?[196]

Cornell's theoretical model re-conceives offence as something more substantial and useful than mere moral outrage or feelings of disgust, which could be generated in the overly-sensitive or prejudiced by otherwise harmless behaviour. This approach has some broad sympathy with the Australian censorship scheme but indicates a more sophisticated re-conceptualization of 'the community'.

Instead of opposing binaries concepts of free speech versus the harm that may be done by that speech, Cornell conceptualizes a representational domain where speech and other forms of media are deployed. In this domain, speech may augment a person's project of becoming,[197] and it may result in the degradation of others' becoming (these are not necessarily exclusive). Departing from the anti-pornography feminists, Cornell uses a very specific definition of degradation which involves inscribing on a person a status label (such as one based on sex or sexuality), and treating that person as 'unworthy of personhood, or at least as a lesser form of being'[198] on the basis of that status. This definition is much more rigorous than simply asserting that sexually explicit images are essentially degrading.

Key to Cornell's project is the replacement of problematic liberal concepts including privacy, atomistic individualism and universalism. Instead of the liberal legal concept of privacy, she suggests a social space of becoming, some of which must be private and some of which must be public. The public character prevents the compulsion to 'closet' which is a feature of traditional liberal models of the public/private divide. Against the grain of radical feminist thought, Cornell seeks to hold on to a kind of liberal concept of individualism embodied in a self who becomes. While sceptical of universalist claims, she still seeks to retain a concept of justice, if not universal then at least built on a contextually sound network of relationships.

---

195 Cornell, op. cit. fn. 173.

196 To use but one example, one person may be offended by child abuse, another by extra-marital sex. Leaving aside any 'objective' assessment, both these people may, subjectively, experience the same amount of offence. The traditional liberal approach might be to look to the possible harm of those individuals actually involved (the child victim or the consenting fornicators) rather than focus on the offended subject. Increasingly with pornography, the ideological space constituted by the 'offence of others' is being used as the site of regulation, see *Miller v. California*, op. cit. fn. 192.

197 What we think of as 'individuality' and 'the person' are not assumed as given but respected as part of a project, one that must be open to each one of us on an equivalent basis. [For a person to do this] she must first be able to imagine herself as whole even if she knows that she can never truly succeed in becoming whole or in conceptually differentiating between the 'mask' and the 'self' – Cornell, op. cit. fn. 173 at 4–5.

198 Ibid. at 10.

Cornell builds a concept of equality based on 'minimum conditions of individuation' which involve '1) bodily integrity, 2) access to symbolic forms sufficient to achieve linguistic skills permitting differentiation of oneself from others, and 3) the protection of the Imaginary Domain itself.'[199]

Through the Imaginary Domain, the struggle for justice and equality, at least as far as sexual identity is concerned, is shifted to a social space whose own rules must be protected by the law generally. This model allows recognition of offence, but it is not automatically construed as harm unless it violates the rules of fair play in this space. Instead of a state-based monolith, Cornell's model allows for a multiplicity of legal and social spaces, with significant planes of intersection.

Cornell attempts to define degradation in a way that both protects minorities and also offsets the moral minority strategy of co-opting anti-discrimination and hate-crime law to protect their 'right to hate':

> The presence of a transsexual in a restaurant does not deny equal personhood to anyone. Nor does a lesbian couple holding hands. The homophobic spectator may be offended, he may even find his restaurant contaminated by the presence of the transsexual. But the presence of a being whose 'sex' violates his own sense of propriety of public space does not degrade him as a person. He is left in his freedom to be heterosexual [...] If he, for example, feels that his sexuality is dependent on its power to reign as the norm, then the very acceptance of transsexuality and transvestitism attacks his conception of his sex and the exercise of his sexuality. His happiness is undermined. But his worthiness to be happy is not challenged.[200]

The social space of the Imaginary Domain therefore comprises a network of selves connected by social relationships and behaviours. Each individual needs a 'buffer zone' of protection around the self, to allow it to engage in the process of becoming. This zone is in part private (and needs to be protected from intrusive laws) and it also has a public character which, so far as it does not attack another self, should be allowed the same space for development.

Rather than pornography itself, it is the pervasiveness of heterosexist representations which are the problem. These images are so widespread that they become naturalized as a 'truth' of sexuality and become a barrier to alternative voices being heard.[201] Cornell suggests a zoning of public space which places explicit sexual images behind barriers. This strategy is aimed at retailers and goes beyond merely behaving discreetly (putting explicit images at the back of the store/art space rather than in the window), it encourages an attitude of shared public space. Expressly rejecting a 'public morals' approach, Cornell invokes the Imaginary Domain and seeks to restrict images which encroach on others in unreasonable ways:

---

199   Ibid. at 4.
200   Ibid. at 11.
201   Ibid. at 148.

> No woman should be forced to view her own body as it is fantasised as a dismembered, castrated other, found in bits and pieces [...] She should not [...] be forced to see her 'self', her 'sexed self' since a woman's self is always sexed, as reducible to an object, and thus inherently unworthy of personhood.[202]

Significantly, Cornell sees this 'psychic space' as embodied, and suggests that the protection of the Imaginary Domain is part of the protection of bodily integrity under a liberal system of rights.[203]

Ultimately, Cornell's Imaginary Domain represents an attempt to salvage the most useful components from liberalism (especially its notions of rights and justice) from postmodern nihilism or the endless mirrors of multiple subjectivities. In the free speech discourse it represents an attack on the solipsist concept of 'offence' by which liberal concepts of harm are invoked to trump other rights, such as the homophobe who is offended by gay people 'acting up' in public, or a person who is 'offended' by what people do behind closed doors. The Imaginary Domain is a strategic space where competing projects of self becoming can negotiate. This space should be contested by women as well as men who, while privileged, are also constituted by patriarchy and need space to explore their sexuality.[204]

Cornell's approach is compatible with strategies of media literacy, for children and adult learners. It has been suggested that 'acceptable use policies' might be a tool for media literacy, for developing responsible habits in children, 'how to recognise good information from bad, good decision making, and self-protective behaviour.'[205] Because the Imaginary Domain is, in part, a mediated space, skills in decoding representation and positioning media texts become crucial tools in the protection of civil rights.

The process of representation is very important for activists who ascribe a certain meaning to pornography, for the industry which has a commercial interest in satisfying an audience and for censors who attempt to distil complex texts to simple ratings. Media literacy skills must involve the four key practices explored below: judging realism,[206] decoding signifiers and fetishes, framing new media and assessing the harmful consequences of media reception. It is unclear from the OFLC Board profiles how much media literacy training members are required to have or actually receive.[207]

---

202 Ibid. at 103.

203 Ibid. at 105.

204 Cornell D and hooks b (1998) 'Dialogue: The Imaginary Domain: A Discussion Between Drucilla Cornell and bell hooks', *Women's Rights Law Reporter*, vol 19, 261.

205 Free Expression Project white paper 'Identifying what is harmful or inappropriate for minors', http://www.fepproject.org/factsheets/mediaviolence.html (viewed 18/5/03).

206 Mills demonstrates that representation of realism is a complex process and it does not necessarily follow that more detail, more blood equates to more realism. Mills, op. cit. fn. 54 at 82.

207 The OFLC's re-classification of *Salo* (1975) indicates problematic and subjective media analyses, including as the claim that in the representation of Fascism 'the metaphor was not clearly established'. OFLC (1999b) op. cit. fn. 109.

Representing Realism

The representation of realism[208] provides significant difficulty for censors, especially since it may be an aggravating factor in one context (hard core pornography) and a mitigating factor in another (realistic violence with an 'anti-violence' message). Realism in sexual representation is defined by a problematic (and heteronormative) judgement as to whether the actors are actually performing a 'sexual act' or merely simulating it.[209]

Violence in particular is represented by a complex array of signifiers which may represent realism in different ways. Where violent media is concerned the intent of the auteur becomes all important, a news broadcast is considered much more generously than an exploitative 'mondo' film.[210] Reality television programming has eroded any certainty this division may once seemed to have.[211]

---

208 In a recent discussion paper, the OFLC has provided this definition involving the representation of realism:

As a general rule the strength of elements, for classification purposes, is indicated in the following relativities:

- Depiction is stronger than description;
- Real is stronger than simulation;
- Simulation is stronger than implication;
- Implication is stronger than suggestion;
- Suggestion is stronger than reference.

OFLC (2001) *Review of the Classification Guidelines for Films and Computer Games – Discussion Paper*, http://www.oflc.gov.au/PDFs/rev_class.pdf.

209 OFLC (2003) *Guidelines for the Classification of Films and Computer Games*, AGPS: Canberra.

210 Films that using confronting real footage, or faked footage edited together for shock purposes. Banned examples include *Savage Man, Savage Beast* (1975), *Faces of Death* (1978), *Faces of Death 2* (1981), *The Last Savage Part 2* (1982), *Sweet and Savage* (1983), *The Savage Zone* (1984), *Mondo Sexualis* (1985), *Death Scenes* (1989), *Inhumanities 2 – Modern Atrocities* (1989), *The Amazing Shocking Asia* (1997), *Executions 2* (1997). For analysis of this genre and the prevalent use of faked footage, see Kerekes D and Slater D (1995) *Killing for Culture*, Creation Books: San Francisco. The genre, including the tamer titles which are available here such as *Mondo Cane, Shocking Asia* and *Shocking Africa, Brutes and Savages*, reinforce a spatial reading of the developing world as a site of dangerous violence which threatens to corrupt via the vector of the video cassette.

211 *Inhumanities 2 – Modern Atrocities* (1989) was a compilation of newsreel footage of death and disaster, most of which had already been shown on television. The censorship board refused classification on the grounds of prolonged and relished depictions of violence and cruelty, without documentary or artistic value:

The depiction of atrocities in bona-fide news programs could, in our view, be justified (within limits), especially when events were of topical interest. But the repetition and concentration of such depictions ran the risk of trivialising events

Decoding Signifiers and Fetishes

In addition to a consideration of realism, censorship also involves complex decoding of symbols in judging what is represented in a particular text. Sexual fetishism involves representation of sexuality through representation of a symbol which might have otherwise non-sexual connotations.[212] Nudity, for instance, becomes a symbol of sexuality, concepts which can become conflated in public discourse. Events such as the censorship of art galleries, scandals over parents' photographs of their children, restrictions of sex education, removal of information on breast examination from 'family time' television, prosecution of book stores for leaving Jock Sturges books where children can reach them, prohibition of breast feeding in public places – all represent a sequestration of nudity and depictions of nudity from the world of children and from public space.[213] Ironically advertising becomes even more sexual and pervasive in public space, as long as it plays by the rules of bodily depiction.

Framing New Media

New media carries new challenges as representational codes read in one media form may not be readily transferred to new media such as websites or computer games. The EFA[214] has been actively challenging changes to the OFLC Classification Guidelines[215] including attempts to further enclose the control over computer

---

and desensitising viewers' reactions [...] What ought to be normal and humane responses to the suffering of others [...] is diminished by familiarity and over-exposure (OFLC Report on Activities 1990–1991).

212   Of course there are entire categories of sexual media devoted to specific fetishes. The Australian censorship rules are unique in their detailed discussion of fetishes, the word 'fetish' is not itself used other jurisdictions. http://www.efa.org.au/Publish/oflc2001.htm. Fetishes are problematic for censors due to the incompleteness of representation; in particular, the inability of mere words to describe what is sexual and what is not. Fetish media disrupts a normalized view of sexuality and sexualizes objects and practices which in other contexts do not necessarily carry a sexual meaning. However, a readership can always import meaning. A diversity of readership significantly broadens the scope of texts which could be considered to have sexual meaning.

213   National Coalition Against Censorship (1999a) *Sex and Censorship: Dangers to Minors and Others?: A Background Paper*, http://www.ncac.org/issues/sex_censorship.html.

214   OFLC (2001) *Review of the Classification Guidelines for Films and Computer Games – Discussion Paper*, http://www.oflc.gov.au/PDFs/rev_class.pdf and EFA Submission http://www.efa.org.au/Issues/Censor/classifrev01.html.

215   The review of the computer game classification scheme was restricted by terms of reference which did not allow challenges to the idea of classification per se, but which was able to critique the arbitrary and somewhat abstract nature of classification categories. On the issue of community standards it is noted 'that there does not exist a single community

games and interactive media. Interactivity is a difficult concept which has yet to be comprehensively theorized and it is difficult to establish whether interactive components increase the impact of media.[216]

New media often present content in a non-linear manner, a practice which demands an understanding of multiple readerships. The Australian censors have expressed great anxiety about interactive media, fearing the DVD technology would remove context and allow a view to 'dispense with all the action and just look at the sex'.[217]

Issues concerning subjectivity in pornography are likely to become even more contentious as virtual pornography[218] becomes more technically feasible, less resource intensive and more pervasive. This issue has already arisen in the fear of 'virtual child pornography', criminalized under the United State *Child Pornography Prevention Act 1996* which was overturned in *Ashcroft v American Civil Liberties Union*[219] in 2002.

Assessing the Harmful Consequences of Media Reception

Media reception involves one of the fundamental issues of representation – the effect which a particular type of media has on its audience. Of particular concern are harmful behaviours or attitudes read from the media which the audience may then replicate. Different arguments have been used to explain the causal connection; modelling bad behaviour, psychological conditioning, ideological programming and/or that the media simply enforces a dangerous hegemonic structure.

---

standard, but rather a range of standards depending on the particular sub-community one considers,' but this is frustratingly left unexplored.

Brand JE (2002) *A Review of the Classification Guidelines for Films and Computer Games*, prepared for the OFLC, 11 February.

216   Bensley L and Van Eeenwyk J (2001) 'Video Games and Real-Life Aggression: Review of the Literature', *Journal of Adolescent Health*, Vol 29, 244; Emes C (1997) 'Is Mr Pac Man Eating our Children? A Review of the Effect of Video Games on Children', *Canadian Journal of Psychiatry*, Vol 42, 409; Durkin K and Aisbett K (1999) *Computer Games and Australians Today*, OFLC: Sydney.

217   Dickie J (1997) 'Challenges for Classifiers', paper presented at the conference: *Violence, Crime and the Entertainment Media*, Australian Institute of Criminology, 4–5 December at 3.

218   The ability to create computer generated, yet realistic looking, images is a great source of anxiety to regulators. This regulatory discourse ignores a history of erotic illustration and animation including pornographic anime. CGI Porn provides potential for interaction, a dynamic medium in which the consumer can substitute their own acts, scripts, angles (even impossible ones) and scenarios, much like current game players modify the models and 'skins' of their game avatars. Law Meme (2002) 'The Future of Virtual Kiddie Pr0n and Other Notes on *Ashcroft v Free Speech*', 18 April, http://research.yale.edu/lawmeme/modules.php?name=News&file=article&sid=186 (viewed 20/11/02).

219   *Ashcroft v American Civil Liberties Union* 535 US (2002).

The 'philosopher's stone' of social science research into media harm has been the claim that causation can be proven, that links between media representation and harmful behaviour or more abstract mental harm can be proven as a matter of objective methodology.

The 'media violence' area of inquiry has resulted in some two or three hundred reported experiments, observations and correlation studies, none of which has proven their hypothesis in a scientifically convincing manner.[220] Nevertheless, these studies are often cited, frequently in an adulterated form, in public discourse as proof of causation.[221] The relationship between viewer is too complex and there are too many extraneous factors to consider to ever make judgments on correlations of simple data.[222] Even if the social science theories were accepted, reducing these into practical regulatory codes and legal remedies is an impossible task.[223] In the context of sexually explicit material, similar research has also failed to prove causation of psychological or behavioural harm from exposure.[224]

---

220 For a review of this area of research see Freedman J (2002) *Media Violence and Its Effects on Aggression: Assessing the Scientific Evidence*, University of Toronto Press: Toronto; Brown M (1996) *The Portrayal of Violence in the Media: Impacts and Implications for Policy, Trends and Issues in Criminal Justice No 55*, Australian Institute of Criminology: Canberra; and more generally the Free Expression Policy Project website which includes an extensive bibliography, http://www.fepproject.org/factsheets/mediaviolence.html (viewed 18/5/03) or the libetus.net site on violent media, http://libertus.net/censor/studies.html.

221 Consider the un-referenced allusions to these studies in The Australia Institute reports in Chapter 2.

222 Kellerman J (1999) *Savage Spawn – Reflections of Violent Children*, Ballantine: New York.

223 Seiden J (2001) 'Scream-ing for a Solution: Regulating Hollywood Violence; An Analysis of Legal and Legislative Remedies', *University of Pennsylvania Journal of Constitutional Law*, v3, 1010.

224 Heins M (2001) *Not in Front of the Children: 'Indecency', Censorship, and the Innocence of Youth*, Hill and Wang: New York; Linz D, Malamuth NM and Beckett K (1992) 'Civil Liberties and Research on the Effects of Pornography' in Suedfeld P and Tetlock PE (eds) *Psychology and Social Policy*, Hemisphere: New York; Carol A (1993) *Fake Science and Pornography*, Libertarian Alliance: London; and generally The Free Expression Policy Project (2001) *Identifying What is Harmful or Inappropriate for Minors: White Paper Submitted to the Committee on Tools and Strategies for Protecting Kids from Pornography and their Applicability to other Inappropriate Internet Content*, http://www.fepproject.org/whitePapers/NRCwhitePapers.html, (viewed 3/3/02) which contains extensive references to other research or the equivalent and wide ranging libertus.net pages on the pornography controversy http://libertus.net/censor/pcontrov.html (viewed 3/3/02), the research into erotica and harm http://libertus.net/censor/studies2.html (viewed 3/3/02), and debunking fallacies and urban legends http://libertus.net/censor/fallacies.html (viewed 3/3/02). See also Hardy who rejects the concept of causation altogether and instead pursues a methodology based on discourse analysis. Discourse analysis depends largely on the reception of media and is unlikely to support coercive solutions in the same way that a causal analysis does. Hardy, op. cit. fn. 12.

Pornography in the Imaginary Domain

This brief consideration of four of the elements of representation – realism, symbolism, medium and reception – indicates that media literacy provides a foundation for a discussion of censorship and pornography. Cornell's concept of the Imaginary Domain reinvigorates the deadlocked legal censorship debate by opening another space of contestation and integrating media analysis tools into the framework of its interconnected public and private representational spaces.

Cornell is not alone in stressing the importance of media analysis skills. Williams' influential *Hard Core*[225] argues that pornography must be read as discourse and situates misogyny as a result of women's exclusion from discourse production rather than as an essential generic component of pornography.[226] Similarly Hardy's analysis of soft core pornography in Britain[227] uses discourse analysis to explain the genre's modes of authorship and reception. The politics of pornography must be contested in the Imaginary Domain and it is unlikely that legal strategies of prohibition will provide adequately sophisticated strategies of contestation. Feminist author Angela Carter argues that:

> Pornographers are the enemies of women only because our contemporary ideology of pornography does not encompass the possibility of change, as if we were the slaves of history and not its makers, as if sexual relations were not necessarily an expression of social relations, as if sex itself were an external fact, one as immutable as the weather, creating human practice but never part of it.[228]

Pornography can be analysed as a discourse with its own genre, means of production and consumption, modes of representation and challenges for readership. Ethnographic study of consumers indicates that pornography is something that readers learn to read and that this process is far from straightforward.[229] Some

---

225 Williams, op. cit. fn. 10.

226 Jessica Benjamin suggests that women should engage with erotica through the exploration of 'Intersubjective space' – the space of exchange in which one experiences a self of self. Rather than sex being something which is done to a passive female body by an active male one, Benjamin challenges the ascription of agency solely to the penis. Departing from pornographic imagination in the signification of sexual pleasure through the 'money shot', she situates sexuality in the space of the interior (which is an extension of intersubjective space) is part of a woman's sense of being rather than experienced as a lack or a passive object. Benjamin J (1986) 'A Desire of One's Own: Psychoanalytic Feminism and Intersubjective Space', in de Laurentis T (ed) *Feminist Studies/Critical Studies*, Indiana University Press: Bloomington at 92.

227 Hardy, op. cit. fn. 12.

228 Carter A (1993) *The Sadeian Woman: An Exercise in Cultural History*, Virago: London at 3–4.

229 See Hardy, op. cit. fn. 12 Chapters 4–6 which cover, respectively, Text, Reception and Impact. A rough comparison may be presented in the reading of another visual medium,

pornography aficionados, even famous pornography director John Stagliano, have admitted to being made uneasy by initial experiences of hard core pornography: 'It made me uncomfortable, too many bodily functions, too many close ups of fucking.'[230] This suggests that the ideological field is far from pre-formed and is open for contested readings and dialectical change.

The crisis in representation is nowhere more apparent than in the regulation of child pornography.[231] Currently existing websites with names like 'Nude Boys World' and 'Sunny Lolitas' provide eroticized images of children, occupying a borderline between legal and illegal material.[232] Often the images can be said to be offensive only in a certain context, that context too often being the pre-judgement that the person under inquiry is a paedophile. Images of nudity, revealing underwear, flirtatious poses, even images which are innocent in other contexts, can be montaged together with other sexual images. According to criminal profiler Detective Sergeant David Minzey, child sex offenders tend to keep retail store clothing catalogues rather than child pornography.[233] These images derive their power to offend from meanings that the viewer themselves imports, whether the spectator is a paedophile, a police officer or a censor.

> There is a dread of the power of the image in Western culture. This dread underlies a lot of discussions of child porn, especially theories of escalation. The escalatory model suggests that a person may come across images of child nudity and might as a consequence develop paedophilic tendencies. This version of events figures human sexuality as deeply unstable, and pornography, particularly child pornography, as a highly toxic substance that can cause people to develop desires they would never have felt otherwise.[234]

---

anime film and television texts. When first exposed to the medium, many (including those who go on to become serious fan 'otaku') may find the large eyes, exaggerated emotions and moments of 'superdeformed' craziness to be odd, distracting or even unappealing. Over time, the viewer learns to read the medium and these signifiers are naturalized. Visual media are never read without first learning the rules. Drazen P (2002) *Anime Explosion: The What? Why? And Wow! Of Japanese Animation*, Stonebridge Press: Berkeley, CA.

230   O'Toole, op. cit. fn. 77 at 210.

231   In 1999 a National Coalition Against Censorship panel in New York 'explored some of the tensions and contradictions in adult responses to children's sexuality and the ways in which these responses are socially constructed.' The panel challenged the historical discourse in which children were defined as innocent and passive and yet sexually desirable, examined the depiction of young bodies in marketing and challenged the lack of evidence in the contention that images cause sexual abuse. Further, they suggested that anxieties and censorship inhibited meaningful research concerning childhood sexuality. National Coalition Against Censorship (1999b) 'Issue #73: Children's Bodies: What Are We Afraid of?', http://www.ncac.org/cen_news/cn73childrensbodies.html (viewed 1/7/00).

232   Scheeres J (2002) 'When Kid Porn Isn't Kid Porn', *Wired News*, 8 May, http://www.wired.com/news/business/0,1367,52345,00.html (viewed 9/5/02).

233   Interviewed in Vnuk, op. cit. fn. 108 at 193.

234   O'Toole, op. cit. fn. 77 at 231.

Censorship law is largely uninformed by cultural theory and is premised on the protection of the community (abstractly conceived) from the contamination of toxic media such as pornographic which emerge somehow external to that community space. Cornell's theory of the Imaginary Domain is one important way in which censorship law might embrace developments in cultural theory and the Imaginary Domain will be considered again in the final chapter alongside advancements in regulatory theory. Censorship deploys itself spatially and this chapter has explored just four of the ways in which this occurs: through the production of childhood, in regulatory fortressing, through acting as the gatekeeper to public discourse and via the production of the Imaginary Domain which links public and private representational spaces. Where these strategies are deployed across cyberspace, the simple models of power and regulation on which the Australian censorship law is premised on begin to falter.

Censorship in Cyberspace

> Once again porn was demonstrating its power to drive new technology forward while also dragging it through the dirt, ably demonstrating its inadvertent knack of softening up a new and unruly media system for regulation.[235]

Innovations in technological spaces threaten the stability of the existing order, at least until they are assimilated and naturalized. New technologies create or exploit liminal pathways, allowing for intersections of spaces that were once kept discrete. Cyberspaces intercut spaces of home, office, school, pornography shop, strip joint, shopping precinct, government, bedroom and others. Technology creates new sites of anxiety such as the capacity of photo editing software to create faux 'nude celebrity' images or virtual child pornography.

Pornographers frequently lead the way in new technologies: the use of databases in the serving of dynamic content; streaming video; e-commerce and identity verification; expansion of bandwidth and security.[236] Pornography has traditionally led the way with media technologies from advances in anatomical representation to the development of printing and cinema technologies. The relationship between video and pornography lead to a greater uptake of video cassette recorders (at a time when little else was available, exploitation films quickly filled the gaps) and related technology (use of video cameras to create amateur pornography).[237]

However, the spread of technology also mobilizes fear. Public concerns about Internet addiction (particularly to pornographic sites)[238] have not been significantly

---

235 Ibid. at 251.
236 Johnson P (1996) 'Pornography drives Technology: Why not censor the Internet', *Federal Communications Law Journal*, V49(1), 217.
237 O'Toole, op. cit. fn. 77 at 104.
238 Green P (1998) 'Net Addicts Fix at Home', *The Australian*, 29 May.

verified by research. Although there is an indication that some people can develop compulsive disorders around their online habits, most Internet behaviour is part of ordinary practices including sexual exploration.[239]

The anonymous nature of cyberspace interaction has also been a cause of concern, not just because of the difficulty of verifying age. Moral reformers criticized the eighteenth century vogue for masquerades, claiming that anonymity deprived virtue and religion of their last resort – shame.[240] Ethnographic research has revealed complex social structures emerging out of pseudonymous Internet Relay Chat trading groups who swap pornographic images which challenge simple assumptions about anonymity.[241]

It is interesting to compare the 'moral panics' of cyberspace pornography with the anxieties of the Industrial Revolution which influenced Victorian morality movements, themselves influenced by disruptions to imagined sex roles and fear of technological and social change. 'This experience of problematic acceleration was epitomized by the mix of fear and excitement that was unleashed as the railways marched across the land and penetrated into the cities'[242] just as the Internet has penetrated the spaces of the home.

Urbanization has a significant impact on fear of new technologies. Cities were seen as dangerously heterogenous as was evidenced by conflicting languages, customs, religions – the city became a foreign place beyond the reach of traditional governance which could not hope to contain the simmering locales of sexual indulgence.[243]

These fears are reflected in the urbanization of the wired virtual spaces of the Internet discussed in Chapter 4. In that chapter, Lessig suggests that zoning is an effective way of regulating cyberspace, which draws heavily on the spatial metaphor rather than a media/textual one: 'In real space we have all sorts of zonings. Children cannot enter bars, men cannot enter women's bathrooms, the badly dressed cannot enter a trendy club.'[244]

In physical space, regulation is often dependent on verification of identity or aspects of identity either from visual data or from documents of identification. In the early Internet, there was just no effective way to implement this in the code architecture. Methods of online identity verification include passwords, cookies

---

239 Cooper A, Scherer CR, Boies SC and Gordon BL (1999) 'Sexuality on the Internet: From Sexual Exploration to Pathological Expression', *Professional Psychology: Research and Practice*, v30(2), 154, which also contains an excellent review of published material in the area.

240 Hunt, op. cit. fn. 46 at 39.

241 Slater D (1998) 'Trading Sexpics on IRC: Embodiment and Authenticity on the Internet', *Body and Society*, v 4(4), 91.

242 Hunt, op. cit. fn. 46 at 91.

243 Smith-Rosenberg C (1985) *Religion and the Rise of the American City: The New York City Mission Movement, 1812–1870*, Cornell University Press: Ithaca, at 172.

244 Lessig, op. cit. fn. 16 at 28.

and digital certificates.[245] Lessig suggests that cryptography is 'the most important technological breakthrough of the last one thousand years' because it not only protects confidentiality but also, ironically, allows the potential for control through verification of identity.[246]

Lessig uses his four modalities of regulation to examine the regulation of pornography claiming a common end 'to keep porn away from kids while (sometimes) ensuring adults' access to it'.[247]

Lessig goes on the argue that in the real world law prevents children from having access to pornography (through punishment of vendors), social norms do likewise, placing pressure on vendors to behave responsibly, the market keeps pornography too expensive for most children and the architecture of shopping makes it difficult for a child to pretend to be an adult. Lessig does not mention that last factor is backed up by the legal architecture of identity documentation where age is not physically apparent.

Of the different proposed approaches to content regulation, Lessig supports provision of zoning. Of the two proposed zoning alternatives (proving the user is an adult or designating them as a child), he prefers the 'Kids ID' option. Digital certificates can be created as part of the profile of a browser user which limits access to sites designated suitable for children. Lessig argues that this is the most efficient, cheapest, least intrusive mode of regulation.[248] He argues against the PICS labelling system because the architecture allows it to be integrated, seamlessly and invisibly, at any stage in the process. This would allow for impermissible silent censorship, of which the end user is never aware.[249]

Lessig prefers zoning to filtering, an approach which is mirrored in Cornell's approach to the protection of the Imaginary Domain by zoning public space.[250] Filtering is a politically charged concept. It has certain appeal based on the liberal notions of free choice, at least for voluntary filtering. Some have rejected this approach, claiming that a free society is dependent on people not being able to filter out all that is distressing, objectionable or disquieting:

> What will it mean if audiences are increasingly fractioned into social groups with special interests? What will it mean if the agenda of national fads and concerns is no longer effectively set by a few mass media to which everyone is exposed? Such a trend raises for society the reverse problems from those posed by mass conformism. The cohesion and effective functioning of a democratic society depends upon some sort of public agora in which everyone participates

---

245 Ibid. at 34.
246 Ibid. at 35–6.
247 Ibid. at 173
248 Ibid. at 177.
249 Ibid. at 179.
250 Cornell, op. cit. fn. 173.

and where all deal with a common agenda of problems, however much they argue over the solutions.[251]

Citing examples of homeless and impoverished neighbourhoods, Lessig, suggests that society should not be able to expunge unpleasant issues from the public agenda by silencing and removing everything that makes people feel uncomfortable.[252] O'Toole echoes these concerns using distinctly spatial imagery:

> There is no ready-made solution for dealing with differences of opinion in the public domain, for settling the 'boundary disputes' that clog and enrich a society of pluralities. In response to such feelings of distaste and disapproval, arguments are made for being discreet about where pornography is seen or goes on sale. There should be zoning laws, it is suggested, where adult materials are sectioned off from the rest of the community. With porn locked away like this, however, it can easily take on the identity of the bogeyman. Making public spaces porn-exclusion zones, driving adult back to the edge of town, will also help to reaffirm porn's traditional status as a male-only preserve, restricting access to adult material for a lot of women [...] reducing the possibility that women will challenge and remake the porn genre. It is hard, therefore, to support pressure for driving it into the night.[253]

At first gloss, classification based censorship schemes seem to provide a zoning solution, to present a sense of regulatory certainty in the definitions of the media strata and a through legal legitimization of the framework but these simply make more complicated definitions of core terms such as 'offence' and 'community'. Black notes that increases in the complexity of rules frequently increases uncertainty instead and leads to creation of contradictions, loopholes and potential for 'creative compliance' with the letter of the law rather than its spirit.

> Thus the 'precision' of law is more a rhetorical device than a functional asset [...] Precision does not on its own produce certainty. Rather [...] the certainty or uncertainty of norms has little to do with the way they are expressed; it has everything to do with how they are understood and interpreted.[254]

Where the Australian Internet censorship scheme fails is that it neglects to take account of where zoning is already successful, prior to the exercise of law. In

---

251 Ithiel de Sola Pool (1990) *Technologies Without Boundaries: On Telecommunications in a Global Age*, edited by Noam EM, Harvard University Press: Cambridge, MA.
252 Lessig, op. cit. fn. 16 at 180–1.
253 O'Toole, op. cit. fn. 77 at 57.
254 Black J (2002) 'Regulatory Conversations', *Journal of Law and Society*, Volume 29 (1), 163 at 180.

Australia today, pornography is widely available for those who want it, but it is usually kept in discrete spaces. Concepts of symbolic legislation see only part of the picture by failing to subordinate law to broader social regulator practices.

Instead, censorship law seeks to co-opt a sparse model of 'the community' in setting legal standards rather than recognize law in the context of diverse regulatory practices and communities. Law ought to have a role as mediator between different communities but this does not occur without recognition that these communities indeed exist and already perform the bulk of the task in zoning the Imaginary Domain. Censorship law should, like the criminal law, be a resort where all other regulatory apparatus have broken down.

Pornography itself is not a dangerous contagion which threatens the community but, rather, a social space of representation that is connected to other social spaces and sends ripples of influence through adjacent spaces. Pornography cannot be simply reified as a harmful or harmless regulatory object, it is a discursive process which exercises spatial practices in the Imaginary Domain alongside the regulatory practices of censorship. Legal theorist Lasker urges us to see both the practices of pornography and the urban spaces on which it is inscribed as contingent, in flux and available for revision and re-inscription.[255]

The next chapter will examine prominent trends in regulatory theory and make some initial suggestions concerning the multiple regulatory communities which already thrive, despite their exclusion from the monolithic state censorship models. Like Cornell's concept of the Imaginary Domain (which will again prove important), it is argued that a spatial understanding of regulation might facilitate a censorship law model based on conceptualization of diverse regulatory practices and communities and yet operate justly. Through this critical re-imagination it is hoped that a truly co-regulatory model might be envisioned.

---

255 Lasker, op. cit. fn. 32 at 1184.

Chapter 6
Censorship, Power and Regulatory Communities

Despite its appeal as a technique of regulatory flexibility, community is a difficult concept to define. Geographers have tended to use the terms 'community' and 'neighbourhood' synonymously to refer to geographically bounded areas, but have in the last decades begun to also explore imagined communities such as diasporic and gay communities.[1] The communities of cyberspace mentioned in Chapter 4 serve to connect geographically disparate communities in ways which enhance rather than displace localized communities.[2] Can a single subject be said to belong to multiple communities, and is membership of these communities one which must be an exclusive, or at least serial, status?

Interestingly, censorship common law contemplates multiple communities in its focus on specific audiences of media reception. The Australian High Court rejected the 'deprave and corrupt test'[3] and substituted a concept of offence based on community standards. 'Offence' was to be expressed contextually, with regard to the audience to whom or among whom the matter was published, bearing in mind the age group and values of that audience.[4] Thus the test originally contemplated multiple communities of reception and interpretation, before these communities were conflated into the single community of reception and meaning used in current debates.

The policy process elides, too easily, ambivalence to (or even ignorance of or apathy toward) censorship law into 'the support of the community'. Public reviews of censorship laws have had low numbers of public submissions. The 1999 the Office of Film and Literature Classification review of its publications classification guidelines received just 147 submissions, despite 1,400 specific invitations to submit and general newspaper advertisements. Of these, 19 submissions came from community groups (eight religious groups, four women's groups and seven

---

 1 Rothenberg T (1995) '"And She Told Two Friends": Lesbians Creating Urban Social Space', in Bell D and Valentine G (eds) *Mapping Desire: Geographies of Sexualities*, Routledge: London.
 2 New media have also enhanced local community spaces by providing global and local connectivity. Goggin G (2003) 'Digital Rainbows: Inventing the Internet in the Northern Rivers' in Wilson H (ed.) *Belonging in the Rainbow Region: Cultural Perspectives on the NSW North Coast*, Southern Cross University Press: Lismore, NSW.
 3 *R v Hicklin* (1868) LR 3 QB 360.
 4 *Crowe v Graham* (1969) 121 CLR 375.

'special interest' groups), 11 came from industry, 52 were the result of three localized letter-writing campaigns and 19 per cent of the total demonstrated at least one misunderstanding of the guidelines.[5] The OFLC's independent consultant, Professor Peter Sheehan, expressed disappointment at the un-representative nature of the sample.[6] It has been noted that special interest groups, and particularly religious groups, utilize lobbying tactics designed to appear that they represent a wider cross-section of the community than they actually do.[7]

By relying on complaints and simply presenting 'move along' notices to offensive websites (which are free to relocate elsewhere) the Australian Internet regulation scheme produces a regulatory network which is porous, discontinuous and incomplete as well as inconsistent with a unitary model of community. A legal positivist framework[8] would find this situation deeply unsatisfying and perceive a waste of power, directed for little effect. Even if the Act could be considered as 'symbolic legislation', having expectations of purely ideological effects, it would be appear to be an expensive exercise in public edification. Positioned between critiques of excessive power and tyranny on the one hand and ineffectual power and impotence on the other, the *Broadcasting Services Amendment (Online Services) Act 1999* nevertheless appears to have reached an equilibrium point and remains in force without too much dissent, perhaps because it does not have too much effect. Yet, is this the best that an Act of Parliament can hope for?

This chapter examines developments in regulatory theory and theories of power in the context of the spatial arrangements of law, cyberspace and pornography examined in the previous chapters. It will be argued that an examination of the Act, informed by Foucault's theories of power and critical legal geography, answers questions about the nature of regulatory power. This inquiry may challenge legal models of jurisdiction as well as the concept of a unitary regulatory community arranged around the state. Instead, this chapter will conclude with some tentative observations about the network of multiple regulatory communities which regulate and produce media, drawing on three examples as avenues of further research.

Censorship rests on models of regulation and power that focus on the role of the state as a nexus of governance. Censors/regulators position themselves at the thin line between civilization and anarchy, holding back a tide of objectionable material which would otherwise engulf society. This is the ideology of regulatory

---

5   Sheehan P (1999) Report on the Review of OFLC Publications *Guidelines*, obtained by Electronic Frontiers Australia under Freedom of Information Law, extracted at http://www.efa.org.au/publish/oflcpublrev989.html.

6   Ibid.

7   Vnuk H (2003) *Snatched: Sex and Censorship in Australia*, Vintage: Sydney at 229.

8   The concept of law in law reform is premised on liberal pluralist notions of power which, strongly influenced by legal positivism, models power as a resource to be allocated. Hunter R and Johnstone R (1995) 'Explaining Law Reform' in Hunter R, Ingleby R and Johnstone R (eds) *Thinking About Law: Perspectives on the History, Philosophy and Sociology of Law*, Allen and Unwin: St Leonards, NSW.

fortressing. In criminology, this kind of falsified logic is termed 'tiger protection',[9] named after the fable of a man found engaged in chanting tiger protection mantras in Central Park, New York. When asked what he is doing, he replies that the chant protects the citizens from tigers. When the interlocutor responds that there are no tigers in New York City, the man notes with satisfaction that his chant must be working. Belief in the necessity of formal regulation may be misplaced – there may be other reasons which explain the absence of tigers or indeed the orderly distribution of pornographic material outside of general public space.

It is the argument of this book that the formal mechanism of the censor forms but one of a multitude of regulatory communities which constitute and regulate the production and consumption of media, sexual or otherwise. Rather than regulation being situated in opposition to production, the two processes are woven together. The *Broadcasting Services Amendment (Online Services) Act 1999* already contemplates multiple regulatory communities with its co-option of the industry, the various regulatory agencies that have a share of the pie and a community of children constituted through the agency of their parents and commercial filtering services. To establish the importance of these communities, it is necessary to engage with an understanding of how both power and jurisdiction operate.

Regulation and Power

> Political power grows out of the barrel of a gun – Mao Tse-Tung[10]

> Power may be at the end of a gun, but sometimes it is also at the end of the shadow or the image of a gun – Jean Genet[11]

It is difficult to get a precise definition of power as it is used in law reform discourse. Legal positivism[12] is an extremely influential discourse which models power relationships using concepts drawn from scientific positivism which seeks to locate 'the authority of law in some fixed point: rather than seeing the ground of a legal system as continually shifting.'[13]

---

9   Zimring FE and Hawkins CJ (1976) *Deterrence: The Legal Threat in Crime Control*, University of Chicago Press: Chicago.

10 Mao Tse-Tung (1938) *Problems of War and Strategy*, (Speech) 6 November.

11 Genet J (1989) *Prisoner of Love*, trans Bray B, Wesleyan University Press: Hanover, NH.

12 Legal theorists such as Jeremy Bentham, John Austin, H L A Hart and Hans Kelsen are typically described as legal positivists. For further description of each of these see McCoubrey H and White ND (1993) *Textbook on Jurisprudence*, Blackstone Press: London.

13 Davies M (1994) *Asking the Law Question*, The Law Book Company: North Ryde, NSW at 56. Law's use of scientific positivism, including Newtonian models of power, is extremely problematic. Minkkinen P (1998) 'Law, Science and Truth' in Hirvonen A (ed.) *Polycentricity: The Multiple Scenes of Law*, Pluto Press: London.

While censorship law seems to behave in an orderly manner, applying legal rules to evidence, it cannot be separated from the social networks through which representation and meaning are achieved. Inevitably, the judgement of what is obscene becomes reduced to Justice Potter Stewart's famous (but as a positivist rule, uncertain) contention that, while he could provide no fixed definition of obscenity, he knew it when he saw it.[14]

Law reform is considered to be a pragmatic exercise which seldom allows space for reflexive scrutiny of its own practices.[15] Legal theorists identify the importance of liberal ideas such as pluralism in the way that law reform agencies and reports approach power, power relationships and their responsibility to the community.[16] This kind of pluralism relies on mechanistic models of power, expressing power as a resource or commodity which may be owned, stockpiled and divided up.[17] In complicated areas of regulation such as media regulation, the interplay of state censorship, co-regulatory schemes, industry codes of ethics and private morality cannot be neatly modelled as discrete pools of power.

Monolithic and spatially neutral accounts of law are rejected by legal pluralists and by the theory of legal polycentricity – a fluid account of legality that resists the order and hierarchy of rules-based models. This theory is related to legal pluralism but, rather than suggesting multiple sites for different legal systems, polycentricity suggests multiple scenes exist even within the decentred and fragmented framework of legal and regulatory networks. According to its proponents, polycentric theory aims to avoid the totalizing and centralizing effects of legal theory, to reject the model of law as a closed and fixed system of order and meaning, to explore

---

14 'I have reached the conclusion [...] that under the First and Fourteenth Amendments, criminal laws in this area are constitutionally limited to hard-core pornography. I shall not today attempt further to define the kinds of material I understand to be embraced with that shorthand description; and perhaps I could never succeed in intelligently doing so. But I know it when I see it, and the motion picture involved in this case is not that' (Justice Potter Stewart, *Jacoblellis v Ohio*, 378 US 184 [1964] at 197).

15 Simpson and Charlesworth challenge the concept of liberalism which is enshrined in a dichotomy between 'pragmatic' legal training against critical legal academia. Simpson GJ and Charlesworth H (1995) 'Objecting to Objectivity: the Radical Challenge to Legal Liberalism' in Hunter R, Ingleby R and Johnstone R (eds) *Thinking About Law: Perspectives on the History, Philosophy and Sociology of Law*, Allen and Unwin: St Leonards, NSW.

16 Hunter et al, ibid.

17 Critical human geographers have contested the liberal pluralist idea of power that situates the state as the only legitimate site of authority, and describe it a position from where power is divided among competing interest groups. Problems with this perspective include the central position allocated to the state and its role in harnessing legitimacy; the model of power which sees power as a measurable object, the notion of power being 'rooted' in institutions and elites; and the idea that 'community power' is dependent on the openness and accessibility of the state. Sharp JP, Routledge P, Philo C and Paddison R (eds) (2000) *Entanglements of Power: Geographies of Domination/Resistance*, Routledge: London at 4–5.

narratives and myths of the foundation of legal order such as rule of law and to undertake an ontological re-assessment of law.[18]

This theory has much in common with de Sousa Santos' concept of 'interlegality', a phenomenological legal pluralism with describes different legal spaces which are superimposed, interpenetrated and mixed both conceptually and in performance of legality.[19] Both of these theories challenge law's claims of closure and universal operation. This is not necessarily a fatal flaw, for legal institutions, under the polycentric framework law, should be considered rational not despite their indeterminacy, flexibility and adaptability, but because of it.[20]

It is useful to consider Latour's idea of the conceptual 'black box'[21] as a way of understanding the operation of legislation and other schemes of regulation. Drawing on engineering ideas, Latour notes the tendency to model a complex concept (be it scientific, social or otherwise) as a fixed and unified phenomenon: that is, as a 'black box' with a set of inputs and outputs but with little inquiry into its internal components. Theories of regulation which see power in mechanistic ways reify the regulatory instruments themselves as 'laws' with little discussion of the regulatory space in which they operate. But what if power is not that simple? Drawing on the Foucauldian tradition, Black suggests that regulation exists not as a thing but as a set of conversations, a discourse.[22]

The idea of regulatory conversations will be explored more fully in the next section. Before this can happen, it is important to consider some different concepts of power which underpin the theory, particularly the impact of Foucault's discussions of power.[23] Foucault acknowledges the importance of space in describing power[24] and explores further some of Lefebvre's observations about the 'fluid dynamics' of power. Lefebvre's concept of power is a Marxist one, yet it is not necessarily

---

18   Erikssson LD, Hirvonen A, Minkkinen P and Poyhonen J (1998) 'Introduction: A Polytical Manifesto' in Hirvonen A (ed) *Polycentricity: The Multiple Scenes of Law*, Pluto Press: London.

19   de Sousa Santos B (1987) 'Law: A Map of Misreading', *Journal of Law and Society*, v14, 279.

20   Eriksson LD (1998) 'The Indeterminacy of law or Law as a Deliberative Practice', in Hirvonen A (ed.) *Polycentricity: The Multiple Scenes of Law*, Pluto Press: London.

21   Latour B (1987) *Science in Action: How to Follow Scientists and Engineers through Society*, Harvard University Press: Cambridge, MA.

22   Black J (2002a) 'Regulatory Conversations', *Journal of Law and Society*, Vol 29 No 1, 163–96.

23   It should be acknowledge that, like Lefebvre, Foucault's work constitutes an approach rather than a comprehensive methodology. Foucault M (1980a) 'The Confession of the Flesh' in Gordon C (ed.) *Power/Knowledge: Selected Interviews and Other Writings 1972–1977*, Pantheon Books: New York.

24   Rabinow P and Foucault M (1984) 'Space, Knowledge and Power', in Rabinow P (ed.) *The Foucault Reader: An Introduction to Foucault's Thought*, Penguin: London.

inconsistent with a Foucauldian approach.[25] A combination of these two approaches provides a useful way of discussing the ways in which the networks of power are located throughout spaces – real, conceptual and social.[26] Connections between geography and power are key sites of research in the governance field, particularly the dialectic between dominance and resistance,[27] the embodied nature of spatial power[28] and all aspects of cyberspace culture and practices.[29]

Spatial power models help explain the Australian Internet censorship laws and should be actively considered as part of the law reform practices which, instead, remain committed to the idea of power as a resource and to legal positivism. Spatial heterogeneity and sense of place has been silenced in legal discourse in favour of uniform rule of law which constructs power as non-geographic abstract force.[30]

Lukes's 'three dimensional view of power' is perhaps the most useful of the pre-Foucauldian concepts of power which inform law reform discourse and legal positivism generally.[31] It consists of three increasingly complex models of power. The one dimensional view of power is the bare positivist conception: power is owned by an agent who exercises it over an object in order get the object to do something which it would not otherwise do. The two dimensional view of power acknowledges that inaction can be as powerful as action and gives the powerful actor the force of inertia. This is often done in a hegemonic manner, by preventing issues from arising in public discourse altogether. The three dimensional view

---

25 Foucault and Lefebvre can be read together; where Lefebvre refers to 'power' this may be read consistently with Foucault's concept of dominating power. Sharp JP, Routledge P, Philo C and Paddison R, op. cit. fn. 17 at 26.

26 For an exploration of Foucault's notion of governmentality in the context of cyberspace, see Baddeley S (1997) 'Governmentality' in Loader BD (ed.) *The Governance of Cyberspace: Politics, Technology and Global Restructuring*, Routledge: London.

27 Sharp et al., op. cit. fn. 17.

28 Hinchliffe S (2000) 'Entangled Humans: Specifying powers and their spatialities' in Sharp JP, Routledge P, Philo C and Paddison R (eds) *Entanglements of Power: Geographies of Domination/Resistance*, Routledge: London.

29 See the excellent collection of articles in Crang M, Crang P and May J (1999) *Virtual Geographies: Bodies, Space and Relations*, Routledge: London.

30 Legal historian Fraser explores the rise of the 'science of law' in the context of the centralization of power and argues that spatial particularity has been replaced by an abstract model of 'society'. He suggests that the loss sense of place and space, of localized community occurred through the transfer of sovereignty to the state. Because of this, he argues, law has had to invent for itself a new source of meaning; namely, a generic understanding of 'society' and of social causation. Through this imagination the newly ascendant social sciences were introduced into legal discourse as a source of power and explanation of social situations and events. Fraser A (1984) 'Legal Amnesia: Modernism versus the Republican Tradition in American Legal Thought', *Telos*, v 60, 15. On the other hand, the High Court of Australia has acknowledged that the notion of *causation* has an extremely simplified legal meaning, which bears little relation to the notion in physics or philosophy per Mason J in *March v E and EH Stramore Pty Ltd* (1990–91) 171 CLR 546.

31 Lukes S (1974) *Power: A Radical View*, Macmillan: New York.

of power takes this concept further and acknowledges that power is socially and culturally situated and ideologically internalized by 'the masses'.

The 'three dimensional' approach has been very influential in the critique of pornography, anti-pornography feminist MacKinnon seems to have been influenced by Lukes' three dimensional view of power and has adapted it quite successfully to the notion of patriarchy.[32] Both positions have been critiqued for their approach to ideology which renders subjects without agency, the passive objects of regulatory power.[33] Legal theorist Winter challenges the manner in which Lukes's three dimensional model invokes (and reproduces) the metaphor of power as container, located in an abstract Cartesian plane.[34]

Western conceptions of power are shaped by the mechanistic worldview of the Enlightenment which became enshrined in modern legal and political discourse. As Newton's causal models of physics were adopted in the examination of the social world, political theorists such as Hobbes were influenced by the mechanistic concept of force. Hobbes' contribution to theories of power is 'a discursive framework for analysis of power as motion, causality, agency and action.'[35] This framework is reflected in legal positivism which analyses legal activity in relation to whether a regulator owns power as a kind of property and whether it is properly executed in relation to those who have residual interests in that power.

In his comprehensive and post-Foucauldian analysis of 'The "Power" Thing', Winter explains this approach as just part of a historically situated discourse of power which rests on a set of clumsy metaphors: 'power is an object, power is a location (or container), power is a force and control is up.'[36] Thus, power is something which can be seized, amassed, stockpiled, lost, handed out, wasted. This idea of power is deeply embedded in culture and is used to explain events and states of being, even when there is evidence to the contrary. Events, changes to states of being, are all too easily explained in metaphors of causation based on the use or loss of power as property.

Winter notes that power is often seen as both an object and a location: 'the location/container can be filled out with a specific such as a fort or other building'[37] and power is often conceived of in this manner. This explains part of the phenomenon of regulatory fortressing explored in the Chapter 5, where jurisdiction is described as a wall to keep out disorderly and unregulated elements.

Accordingly, power is reified as an object which gives little opportunity for challenge, except for 'seizing it' from its current owners. Instead of these metaphors,

---

32 Winter SL (1996) 'The "Power" Thing', *Virginia Law Review*, v82, 721 at 783–7; Cornell D (1995) *The Imaginary Domain: Abortion, Pornography and Sexual Harassment*, Routledge: New York.
33 Winter, op. cit. fn. 32 at 785–7.
34 Ibid. at 773.
35 Clegg S (1989) *Frameworks of Power*, Sage Publications: Newbury Park, CA at 31.
36 Winter, op. cit. fn. 32 at 745.
37 Ibid. at 748.

Winter urges us to examine Foucault's discussion of power which conceives of power as a shifting network of relationships between agents, spread thin (but not evenly) and operating from the social nexus rather than from hierarchy.

Foucault's ideas of power are the quantum theory of social power, introducing relativity to simple power Newtonian 'force' physics previously employed. Foucault challenges the 'juridico-discursive' model of power as a negative, repressive force maintained and enforced through ideological discourse through rules and prohibitions.[38] The modes and institutions of authority such as the state and the law 'are only the terminal forms power takes',[39] a mere reflection of the actual networks of power. Thus, censorship law is not a mere container for the power of media regulation. It should be displaced from the centre and considered, rather, to be a state institution which is itself locked into and constituted by power networks of media regulation.

Foucault's theory of power is geographical in that it operates in networks and displaces the state from the centre of government.[40] Foucault's spatial/geographical imagination[41] which conceives of power deployed in networks can be read in combination with Latour's Actor-Network theory which explores the nature of network power.[42] Latour's theory challenges the 'cause and effect' imagination of power, preferring a relational and embodied concept of power which rejects the idea of causal power modelled as a geometry of essentialist, pre-rendered objects, a shift from an emphasis on surfaces to filaments.[43]

Foucault's alternative approach is based on a set of observations which defy traditional models of power and the metaphors that they rest on: power and agency

---

38 Foucault M (1978) *The History of Sexuality Volume 1: An Introduction*, Pantheon Books: New York at 82–5.
39 Ibid. at 92.
40 Sharp et al., op. cit. fn. 27 at 16.
41 'A whole history remains to be written of spaces – which would at the same time be the history of powers (both these terms in the plural) – from the great strategies of geopolitics to the little tactics of the habitat [...] passing via economic and political installations.' Foucault M (1980b) 'The Eye of Power' in Gordon C (ed.) *Power/Knowledge: Selected Interviews and Other Writings, 1972–1977*, Pantheon Books: New York, at 149. Foucault also acknowledges the importance of space in power in Rabinow and Foucault, op. cit. fn. 24. Foucault's contention that power circulates and is therefore located within a geographic framework, containing structures of domination and resistance, is explored in Sharp et al., op. cit. fn. 17.
42 'Strength does not come from concentration purity and unity, but from dissemination, heterogeneity and the careful plaiting of weak ties.' Latour B (1997a) 'On Actor-Network Theory: A Few Clarification', Centre for Social Theory and Technology, Keele Univeristy, http://www.keele.ac.uk/depts/stt/staff/jl/pubs–jl2.htm.
43 Hinchcliffe, op. cit. fn. 28.

are not the same things;[44] power is located in the social not in hierarchies;[45] power is dynamic defined by relationships and networks;[46] power is not property to be owned; power is productive, selves are constituted through power;[47] power is diffuse and does not operated in binaries of ruler/ruled, from the top down;[48] power shifts from moment to moment; exercise of power produces resistance and the potential for change.[49]

The discourses by which the *Broadcasting Services Amendment (Online Services) Act 1999* scheme has been presented and critiqued have, largely, relied on models of power as a resource and placed the state at the centre of the model as the originator of that power. The importance of the state and the sanctions it can impose should not be underplayed, but it is nevertheless only one influence and its regulatory role seems more akin to a broker rather than a producer of power. Regulatory power cannot be described by simple 'cause and effect' models which fail to encompass the importance of self regulation beyond that which is motivated by fear of state sanction. In many sites of regulation, there are mechanisms other than legislation which constitute the everyday practices by which people access, read, produce and relate to media.

Regulatory Conversations and Power Networks

In overturning the United States *Communications Decency Act 1996*, Judge Stewart Dalzell described the Internet as 'a never-ending worldwide conversation.'[50] One of the more exciting contentions to arise out of Foucault's unpacking of power is the concept of regulation as discourse, which Julia Black names 'regulatory conversations, the communicative interactions that occur between all involved in the regulatory "space"'.[51] Black fuses discourse analysis with regulatory theory and suggests that regulation is embedded in language and communicative structures operating as conversations, an interactive process rather than a static, fetishized set of rules. This theory is bold and exposes a rich site of interdisciplinary analysis which promises to shape much of future discussion of regulation, law and rules.

---

44 Winter, op. cit. fn. 32 at 802.
45 Foucault M (1983) 'Afterword: The Subject and Power' in Dreyfus HL and Rabinow P *Michel Foucault: Beyond Structuralism and Hermeneutics*, University of Chicago Press: Chicago.
46 Foucault (1980c) 'Power and Strategies' and 'Two Lectures' in Gordon C (ed.) *Power/Knowledge: Selected Interviews and Other Writings, 1972–1977*, Pantheon Books: New York at 98.
47 Foucault 'Two Lectures', ibid.
48 Foucault, op. cit. fn. 38 at 94.
49 Ibid. at 96.
50 *ACLU v Reno*, 1929 F Supp 824 (ED Pa 1996).
51 Black, op. cit. fn. 22.

Regulatory conversations are especially important where the regulator is allowed discretion ('discretion is seen as the space both within and between rules'[52]), where meanings are uncertain and in co-regulatory systems where the regulatory framework expects a broad consensus from a large number of participants.[53] As such, regulatory conversations form a perfect framework for analysis of Australian censorship law.

> Understanding and adopting the argument employed in discourse analysis as to the social and inter-subjective production of meaning, and as to the dialectical relationship between language and agency, has significant potential for understanding regulatory processes, in four respects. First, it provides a theoretical ground for opposing the formalist view of rules and interpretation. Second, it provides a basis for suggesting how and why inter-subjective interpretive communities need to be created around regulatory language and regulatory practices. Third, it provides a basis for understanding how certainty as to language and practices might be produced. Fourth, and developing from the insights above, the coordination required for the production of inter-subjective meaning forms the basis for action by those involved in the regulatory process.[54]

Rather than refer to abstract values of 'the community', regulatory communities formed around sites of regulation are vital in understanding how the practices of governance operate and they impact they have on everyday of life. Within each of these spaces, regulatory conversations occur. But how are these discourses organized in jurispace?

Castells' claim that we are seeing 'The Rise of the Network Society'[55] has had an impact on the way in which the regulation of information technology has been conceived and is relevant to regulatory theory generally. Castells claims that the effects of digitization of information, rapid communications and media convergence have led to quantum shifts in organization, information sharing and governance generally and have challenged conventional notions of organizations and administration.[56] Further, the concept of networks has enabled explorations of the fusion, overlap and ambiguity between public and private regulatory interests.[57]

---

52 Ibid. at 172.
53 Ibid. at 171–3.
54 Ibid. at 175.
55 Castells M (2000) *The Information Ages: Economy, Society and Culture: Volume 1: The Rise of the Network Society*, Blackwell Publishers: Malden.
56 Ibid. at 255–8.
57 Picciotto S (2002) 'Introduction: Reconceptualising Regulation in the Era of Globalisation', *Journal of Law and Society*, Vol 29(1), 1.

Regulatory theory has become interested in networks as organizing concepts for explaining 'patterns of negotiation and mediation [which] could not be adequately defined by formal structures.'[58] Network theory challenges conventional positivist accounts of power as vested in hierarchies and bureaucracy – the abstraction of governance and its model in jurispace away from everyday life and experiences of power.

In a study of British governance mechanisms, Rhodes[59] finds elements of the network approach in different political discourses, manifesting variously as recognition of intermediate institutions, networks of communities, in reinventing the constitution and in concepts of joined-up government. Rejecting any true core of governance, Rhodes suggests that different political traditions use networks in different ways, but usually to resist overly-simplistic positivist models.

The network metaphor sees an intersection of similar concerns across disciplines:[60] information economy,[61] communications,[62] organizational theory, innovation theory,[63] political science[64] and sociology (actor network theory which seeks to explore intersection of human agency and technology, 'life at the edge of chaos'[65]). The variety in network discourse demonstrates 'an enormously diffuse set of relationships, meanings and engagements'[66] which thwart simple reductionist models. Networked governance theories challenge abstract and monolithic models of power and governance. Combining the networked governance concept with Black's concept of regulatory conversations, these concepts provide models of interconnected conversations to replace the monolithic abstract community of censorship.

---

58   International Political Science Association Committee, Structure and Organisation of Government Research (2002) *Knowledge Networks and Joined-Up Government*, http://www.public–policy.unimelb.edu.au/events/IPSA_Conference.html.

59   Rhodes R (2002) 'Decentring British Governance: From Bureaucracy to Networks', *Knowledge, Networks and Joined-Up Government Conference Proceedings*, http://www.public–policy.unimelb.edu.au/events/IPSA_Conference.html.

60   For a survey of these see Considine M (2002) 'Joined at the lip? What does network research tell us about governance?', http://www.public–policy.unimelb.edu.au/events/IPSA_Conference.html.

61   Lipnack J and Stamps J (1994) *The Age of the Network*, John Wiley: New York.

62   Wellman B (2001) 'The Rise of Networked Individualism' in Keeble L (ed.) *Community Networks Online*, Taylor and Francis: London.

63   Valente TW (1995) *Network Models of the Diffusion of Innovations*, Hampton Press: Cresskill, NJ.

64   Streeck W and Schmitter P (1995) 'Community, Market, State and Associations: The Prospective contribution of interest governance to social order' in Streek and Schmitter (eds) *Private Interest Government*, Sage: London.

65   Latour B (1997b) 'Train of thought: Piaget, Formalism and the Fifth Dimension', *Common Knowledge*, Vol 6, 170.

66   Considine, op. cit. fn. 60 at 4.

Black argues for a model of 'decentred regulation' which resists the assumption that governments have monopolies over power and control, a model which engages with 'complexity, the fragmentation and construction of knowledge, the fragmentation of the exercise of power and control, the recognition of the autonomy and interdependence of social actors, the recognition that regulation is the product of complex interactions between social and political actors [...], the collapse of the public/private distinction.'[67]

Just as Black has expanded the discursive terrain of regulation, Lange[68] has suggested that regulatory theory ought to include an understanding of the emotional dimension of regulation in order to properly appreciate the social context in which these practices occur and recognize the 'links between a social and a legal realm.'[69] Indeed, moral regulation of sexual practices cannot be understood if premised on an understanding of sexuality as a set of purely cognitive, opportunistic practices. Law's expulsion of the 'messy individuality' of emotions in favour of abstract rules and cognitive models of behaviour result in skewed models of regulation, compliance and resistance, in cyberspace and elsewhere.

Understanding the *Broadcasting Services Amendment (Online Services) Act 1999* requires a different understanding of power than overly-simple mechanistic models can offer. In relation to pornography, a more sophisticated approach to power moves beyond a simple causal model, the kind criticized by Cornell[70] and others. However, if regulation is a spatialized conversation, it must be asked how this meshes with legal concepts of jurisdiction?

Jurispace, Jurisdiction and Sovereignty

> Governments of the Industrial World, you weary giants of flesh and steel, I come from Cyberspace, the new home of Mind. On behalf of the future, I ask you of the past to leave us alone. You are not welcome among us. You have no sovereignty where we gather.[71]

---

67 Black, op. cit. fn. 22 at 192; Black J (2001) 'Decentring Regulation: The Role of Regulation and Self Regulation in a "Post-Regulatory" World', in Freedman M (ed) *Current Legal Problems*, Oxford University Press: New York; Black J (2002b) 'Critical Reflections on Regulation', *Australian Journal of Legal Philosophy*, v27(1), 46; Scott C (2001) 'Analysing Regulatory Space: Fragmented Resources and Institutional Design', *Public Law*, 329.

68 Lange B (2002) 'The Emotional Dimension in Legal Regulation', *Journal of Law and Society*, v29(1), 197.

69 Ibid. at 198.

70 Cornell, op. cit. fn. 32.

71 Barlow J P (1996) 'Declaration of the Independence of Cyberspace', *Cyber-Rights Electronic List*, 8 February.

Cyber-libertarian arguments, like the one above, argue that cyberspace is a place of liberation beyond the frontier, outside of jurisdictional limits. These arguments echo the history of pirate radio stations where transmitters were placed outside territorial limits, a costly process. Now the Internet allows anyone to effect a similar avoidance of jurisdiction at low cost. It recalls the episode of *The Goodies* where, encouraged by the success of their pirate radio station, a deranged Graeme Garden attempts to move Britain in its entirety outside the five mile limit and beyond the reach of authority.[72]

The concept of jurisdiction is an important starting point to examine the kinds of power and governance that are exercised in cyberspace.[73] Its problems and contradictions suggest exploration of different types of power and urge an understanding of existing regulatory communities that already exist and may even be enhanced by the Internet.

Jurisidiction is a shorthand concept for a bundle of legal concepts: sovereignty, reach of enforcement, range of surveillance and the sense of being before the law. Traditionally, jurisdiction has been attached to concepts of geographical territory, but in a 'glocalized' world this may no longer contemplate the range of relationships that a subject may hold with various legal authorities.

Ties to jurisdiction are, to most subjects, not a question of choice; such connections are no more than a matter of historical happenstance. The 'social contract', one of the great foundational myths of liberalism and law, suggests that presence within a jurisdiction amounts to consent to be governed.[74] Historically, geographical translocation has not been an option for most people, born into a jurisdiction and possessing a social network that they simply cannot abandon, just because they disagree with the laws governing the space in which they live.

Jurisidiction, as a concept based on physical geography, is flawed as a universal concept of governance and sovereignty. It is convenient in many contexts, but it can readily be challenged wherever it is not. The 'legal crises' of cyberspace have proven that the old fixed model of jurisdiction needs to be dismantled and replaced by conditional, fluid ones. But how is this to be achieved?

One apparent application of the Lefebvre's concept of spatial production is the creation and use of legal jurisdiction. In one of the clearest analyses of the historical

---

72 *The Goodies*, episode 'Radio Goodies', first broadcast 20/12/70.

73 Lenk K (1997) 'The challenge of cyberspatial forms of human interaction to territorial governance and policing' in Loader BD (ed.) *The Governance of Cyberspace: Politics, Technology and Global Restructuring*, Routledge: London.

74 Within academic discourses of jurisdiction, Ford isolates two oppositional concepts. First is the concept of jurisdiction as a 'self-validating and foundational unit of government', premised on the choice of individuals to live or otherwise place themselves in the physical territory and therefore before the law (at 848). Second, contrasting with this, is the concept of jurisdiction as a mere technique of government, a method for authority to exercise power and a channel of governance. Ford RT (1999) 'Law's territory (a history of jurisdiction)', *Michigan Law Review*, Vol 97, 843.

and philosophical foundations of jurisdiction, legal historian Ford[75] critiques the surface of realistic pragmatism which has been built over the abstractions of jurisdiction. Rather than being attached to human geography and populations, modern jurisdiction rests on a kind of physical geography, of maps and arbitrary abstract boundaries. This is inscribed in the boundaries of nation states and, more interestingly, in the creation of sub-national territories, either through federalism or through other divisions of human geography.

> The centralization of formal power in national governments is not necessarily inconsistent with the existence of sub-national territorial divisions. In fact [...] the production of local difference can be an effective strategy for consolidating and maintaining centralized power.[76]

By selecting 'cyberspace' and 'childhood' as difficult localized sites of regulation, the concept of jurisdiction is assumed to be a uniform and complete phenomenon outside these troublesome locations. While jurisdiction is concerned with centralization of power and identification of sites of control, it is difficult to find articulation of what jurisdiction is, beyond what it does. Ford suggests that there are four characteristics which are reasonably consistent across the current concepts of jurisdiction, in summary:[77]

- Jurisdiction categorizes elements primarily by area and secondarily (if at all) by type. Therefore, the enforcement area is the baseline, the things within that territory a subsidiary concept to that space.
- Jurisdiction is definitely bounded. Ambiguity is an embarrassment.
- Jurisdiction is abstractly and homogenously conceived.[78]
- Jurisdictional divisions 'produce "gapless" maps of contiguous political territories'.[79] This conceals the margins and unregulated spaces.

Consistent with Black's notion of regulatory conversations, Ford argues that jurisdiction should be perceived in terms of space and also discursively, as a 'bundle of practices'[80] which produce identities through their structure, opportunities, roles or lack thereof. Like Blomley,[81] Ford emphasizes the importance of cartography in the development of contemporary notions of jurisdiction. Echoing Lefebvre,

---

75 Ibid.
76 Ibid. at 844.
77 Ibid. at 848–9.
78 It does not seem to be a coincidence that Ford uses Lefebvre's terms here. He further explains the effect these have on jurisdictional spaces (ibid. at 849).
79 Ibid. at 849.
80 Ibid. at 850.
81 Blomley NK (1994) *Law, Space, and the Geographies of Power*, The Guilford Press: New York, Chapter 3 'Legal Territories and the "Golden Metewand" of the Law'.

this suggests that the more abstract space of maps is more persuasive for the state than maps based on identity or experience. Ironically, to legal practitioners and reformers, the arbitrary and abstract maps can seem more concrete and realistic than the social network and experiences which predate those maps.[82]

Both cartography and jurisdiction are historically produced inventions or techniques of knowledge and control. 'We can tie certain historical developments in the art of government to the availability of jurisdiction as a tool, just as we can tie certain developments in the art of war to the availability of gunpowder.'[83] Implicitly departing from Lefebvre's celebration of differential space, Ford argues that abstraction and difference are connected, that jurisdictional power thrives on labelling and inscribing difference. He invokes Foucault[84] to suggest that repression does more than censor difference, it constitutes and produces difference. Likewise, the process of centralization and abstraction is not challenged by difference, it is enhanced by the creation of typologies and classification of local differences, all 'before' uniformity as the individual subject is before the abstraction of the law. According to Ford, assimilation is effected by positioning difference in relation to the mean:

> [C]entralisation tells only part of the story. Always buried within these narratives of inexorable, unmediated, unmodified centralisation, one finds a glimpse of its opposite: an explosion of differentiation, the production of ever new categories that are represented as 'merely descriptive' mappings. No doubt there was a trend toward centralisation that characterised a significant program of modern government; universalism was imposed, difference was punished and censored. But there was also, and to a significant extent, the opposite phenomena: typology, sorting, differentiation to an ever more 'precise' and infinitesimal degree, a carving up into distinct parts. This too is the legacy of modernity, and of liberal democracy.[85]

Ford is critical of politics which pursue difference as an objective in itself, finding the protection of local difference as an 'empty vessel' which can be used to protect discriminated-against minorities but which can just as easily be used to prop up local systems of apartheid using exactly the same criteria. While the 'politics of difference' may not necessarily be an expression of Lefebvre's differential space, Ford does warn that even localized difference can serve to enhance centralized abstraction.

---

82   Ford (op. cit. fn., 74 at 844) points us to Maine's 'famous historical shift from status to contract was accompanied by an equally significant shift from status to locus'.

83   Ibid. at 854.

84   He uses Foucault M (1977) *Discipline and Punish: The Birth of the Prison*, Penguin: London at 153; Foucault M (1984) 'Governmentality' in Rabinow P (ed) *The Foucault Reader: An Introduction to Foucault's Thought*, Penguin: London; *The History of Sexuality* (op. cit. fn. 38) and 'The Eye of Power' (op. cit. fn. 41).

85   Ford, op. cit. fn. 74 at 882.

Cyberspace is, of course, subject to many different forms of regulation which exercise their own type of 'jurisdiction' in different ways. Recognition that cyberspace regulation is inconsistent, incomplete and heterogenous opens the path to challenge the uniformity of other legal regulatory spaces. Internet regulation, particularly moral regulation, is attempted not in the face of cyberspace's uncontrollability but, rather because of it.

Cyberspace sovereignty is a difficult issue to conceptualize due to the inexactitude of description and metaphors involved. Mitchell (whose work is discussed in Chapter 4) argues that in cyberspace jurisdictional battles 'a new logic has emerged. The great power struggles of cyberspace will be over network topology, connectivity and access – not the geographic borders and chunks of territory that have been fought over in the past.'[86] The perception of cyberspace as an 'elsewhere', a separate space, is misleading and provides an unnecessary conceptual divide between the regulation by code and regulation by law.[87] A 'there vs. here' model is not helpful and denies the embodied aspects of the cyberspace experience.[88]

For some critical legal scholars, the problem of sovereignty is irresolvable as cyberspace is too complex, embraces too many jurisdictions and so, it follows, is impossible to govern.[89] For others, the issue is no different from inter-jurisdictional conflicts of the past: cyberspace, as such, does not exist or at least has no sovereignty attached to it, it is merely a vector along which inter-jurisdictional conflicts have increased in number and frequency.[90] The conflict between these positions arises from different perspectives on what jurisdiction is and how it operates.

Lessig (whose work was also examined in Chapter 4) seeks to explain the problem of cyberspace jurisdiction by integrating both perspectives to some extent. Drawing on the international law 'conflict of laws' doctrine and on federal constitutionalism he asserts that cyberspace does possess its own sovereignty, but that this does not displace a user from embodied space, it is not a legal anathema for a user to occupy two spaces simultaneously.[91]

---

86 Mitchell W (1996) *City of Bits: Space, Place and the Infobahn*, MIT Press, MA at 151.

87 Lessig L (1999) *Code and other Laws of Cyberspace*, Basic Books: New York at 233 and Shapiro AL (1998) 'The Disappearance of Cyberspace and the Rise of Code' *Seton Hall Constitutional Law Journal*, Vol 8, 703.

88 Turkle S (1995) *Life on the Screen: Identity in the Age of the Internet*, Simon and Schuster: New York and Stone S (1991) *Will the Real Body Please Stand Up? Boundary Stories About Virtual Cultures*, MIT Press: Cambridge, MA.

89 See for example Johnson D and Post D (1996) 'Law and Borders: The Rise of Law in Cyberspace', *Stanford Law Review*, Vol 48, 1367.

90 See for example Goldsmith JL (1998) 'Against Cyberanarchy', *University of Chicago Law Review*, Vol 65, 1199.

91 Lessig, op. cit. fn. 87 in Chapter 14.

Lessig points to the ways in which law contemplates people moving between jurisdictions[92] as well as the 'nested' jurisdictions contemplated under American (and Australian) constitutions and notions of federalism. It is already possible to occupy multiple jurisdictions at once (for example national, state and local authorities), and legal tools presently exist to resolve conflicts, deciding which set of rules is supreme. Therefore, a concept of cyberspace as a different jurisdiction should present no problem for law. Lessig does indicate that there may be some transitional issues as 'conflict of laws' tools were designed not for disputes between citizens but between institutions and sophisticated entities such as corporations.[93]

Unlike Lessig's focus on multiple jurisdictions, Blomley challenges the abstraction of federalism, the way in which it contributes to denial of place.[94] A good example of this comes from Lessig himself, who suggests that at its most local level, jurisdiction begins to lose meaning as a mere geographical location, without the ideological appeal of the nation-state:

> At [state or federal] level, the link between entitlement and geography makes sense. But as we work down the hierarchy of 'communities', it makes less sense. As we move down the chain, where I live seems less and less determinative of membership [...] These troubles with geography at the local level are nothing, however, compared with the problem in cyberspace. No one really lives in cyberspace; people who are 'in' cyberspace are always also 'in' real space.[95]

Rather than challenge the importance of place, Lessig's assertion serves rather to challenge the assumption of jurisdiction resting on narrow physical space. Perhaps this uncertainty encourages recognition instead of social or community spaces, constituted in different ways depending on the context.[96] Resisting even the strongest centralization practices, place does have a way of reinstating itself, even within the most totalizing and abstracting of discourses. This is especially true when social networks are explored as places of themselves, with their own

---

92 Lessig uses the example of criminal law; a person abroad is bound by the criminal laws of the country in which they are present. Also in some circumstances they will be bound by domestic laws, such as the 'sex tourism' laws aimed at preventing citizens from engaging in pedophile behaviour in countries where it is legal. The justification Lessig offers for the latter is that the behaviour *does* effect the domestic community by contamination 'they are more likely to carry their norms back to their life here.' Lessig, op. cit. fn. 87 at 191. While this is far from clear, it does suggest a reason why regulation of cyberspace behaviour might be seen as relevant for physical space.

93 Ibid. at 193.

94 Blomley, op. cit. fn. 81.

95 Lessig, op. cit. fn. 87 at 199–200.

96 Anderson suggests that the impossibility of experiencing community means that imaginary communities are important, the 'Imagined Community' concept will be further discussed later in this chapter. Anderson B (rev. edn.) (1983) *Imagined Communities: Reflections on the Origins and Spread of Nationalism*, Verso: London at 7.

laws and regulatory architecture. Beyond the physical–geographically deployed state jurisdiction, there are many social and informal regulatory networks and communities which intersect with the law's jurispace, especially in the governance of cyberspace.

Jurisdiction, Globalization and Challenges to the Sovereignty of the Public Sphere

The global nature of Internet media disrupts the stability of spatial practices of regulatory culture, particularly in the public private divide, concepts of jurisdiction and as sovereign nation states are threatened by globalization generally. Legal geographer Aoki describes the legal strategy of designating public and private spaces as an important element of sovereignty which depend on concepts of property law in order to establish jurisdiction.[97] Trans-border information flows, including the Internet, disrupt this neat dichotomy and challenge both legal sovereignty and jurisdiction, by blurring the line between public and private.[98]

Globalization puts the meaning of the nation-state in flux.[99] The combination of forces of globalization and localization have transformed the ways of being for contemporary subjects[100] and for law itself.[101] Robertson examines the sites where these concepts intersect, the phenomenon of 'glocalization' and the tension it creates between homogeneity and heterogeneity.[102] Appadurai describes this tension as being situated within five domains of global cultural flows: mediascape, ethnoscape, technoscape, finanscape and ideoscape.[103]

> Thus the central feature of global culture today is the politics of the mutual effort of sameness and difference to cannibalize one another and thus to proclaim their successful hijacking of the twin Enlightenment ideas of the triumphantly

---

97 Aoki K (1996) '(Intellectual) Property and Sovereignty: Notes Toward a Cultural Geography of Authorship', *Stanford Law Review*, v48, 1293 at 1311.

98 Ibid. at 1296.

99 Arnason JP (1990) 'Nationalism, Globalization and Modernity', in Featherstone M (ed.) *Global Culture: Nationalism, Globalization and Modernity*, Sage Publications: London.

100 Friedman J (1990) 'Being in the World: Globalization and Localization', in Featherstone M (ed.) *Global Culture: Nationalism, Globalization and Modernity*, Sage Publications: London.

101 Twining W (2000) *Globalisation and Legal Theory*, Butterworths: London.

102 Robertson R (1995) 'Glocalization: Time–Space and Homogeneity–Heterogeneity', in Featherstone M, Lash S and Robertson R (eds) *Global Modernities*, Sage Publications: London.

103 Appadurai A (1990) 'Disjuncture and Difference in the Global Cultural Economy', in Featherstone M (ed.) *Global Culture: Nationalism, Globalization and Modernity*, Sage Publications: London.

universal and the resiliently particular [...] Both sides of the coin of global cultural process today are products of the infinitely varied mutual contest of sameness and difference on a stage characterized by radical disjunctures between different sorts of global flows and the uncertain landscapes created in and through these disjunctures.[104]

The Internet is important and contentious as, under conditions of globalization: it can form a site of political resistance[105] which challenges national sovereignty and legitimacy.[106] Mendilow argues that because of this, the Internet has become an important space, a conceptual place in which the citizens negotiate the concept of government and its expression in the state.[107]

The cyberspace political economy is a 'simulated sovereignty'[108] and its virtual character can be seen to have accelerated the trend which has seen the movement of community interaction out of public spaces[109] as the structure and practices of the Internet resists definition as part of the public sphere.[110] Critical geographer Crang, on the other hand, argues that the public sphere has always been virtual.[111]

---

104 Ibid. at 307.

105 Terranova T (2001) 'Demonstrating the globe: virtual action in the network society' in Holmes D (ed.) *Virtual Globalization: Virtual Spaces/Tourist Spaces*, Routledge: London. This however should be read with Bhabha's discussion of 'third space' in which he describes sites where resistance is never complete, unfractured practice. Practices of resistance are entwined with practices of domination and marginalization, segregation and exile. Bhabha H (1994) *The Location of Culture*, Routledge: London. Globalization is not a unitary process and it is shaped by global forces such as multinational corporations but also social movements, a new 'global public space or forum' has been opened by new media technologies. Cohen R and Rai SM (2000) *Global Social Movements*, The Althone Press: London.

106 Perritt H (1998) 'The Internet as a Threat to Sovereignty? Thoughts on the Internet's Role in Strengthening National and Global Governance', *Indiana Journal of Global Legal Studies*, v5, 423; Sassen S (1998) 'On the Internet and Sovereignty', *Indiana Journal of Global Legal Studies*, v5, 545 and Trachman J (1998) 'Cyberspace, Sovereignty, Jurisdiction and Modernity', *Indiana Journal of Global Legal Studies*, v5, 561.

107 Mendilow J (2001) 'The Internet and the Problem of Legitimacy: A Tocquevillian Perspective', in Ebo B (ed) *Cyberimperialism? Global Relations in the New Electronic Frontier*, Praeger: Westport, CT.

108 Luke TW (1999) 'Simulated Sovereignty, Telematic Territoriality: The Political Economy of Cyberspace', in Featherstone M and Lash S (eds) *Spaces of Culture: City, Nation, World*, Sage Publications: London.

109 Wellman B and Gulia M (1999) 'Virtual communities as communities: Net surfers don't ride alone', in Smith MA and Kollock P (eds) *Communities in Cyberspace*, Routledge: New York.

110 Poster M (1997) 'Cyberdemocracy: The Internet and the Public Sphere', in Porter D (ed.) *Internet Culture*, Routledge: London.

111 Crang M (2001) 'Public space, urban space and electronic space: would the real city please stand up?' in Holmes D (ed.) *Virtual Globalization: Virtual Spaces/Tourist Spaces*, Routledge: London at 85.

Just as the discourses of architecture inform the production of physical public space, therefore digital architecture informs new public spaces.[112]

'The public sphere' has several meanings and can signify a democratic site or an exclusive domain based on identity and exclusion of Others. Public spaces and the public sphere are linked together, disorder in public spaces signifying disorder in the public sphere and therefore demanding regulation.[113] The zoning of public space occurs through formal and informal management techniques, involving the exclusion of undesirable elements.[114]

Cyberspace challenges modernity's division of public and private space, particularly the separation of work and the home.[115] In modernism, the layering of spaces between the body and public sphere were privatized, like layers of clothing. Technology has lead to the collapse of some of these boundaries as bodies and communities mutually constitute each other.[116] Public spaces have become privatized through technologies of surveillance and regulation, the shopping mall being the paradigmatic example.[117] The challenge of virtuality must be considered in the context of other social trends, the public/private divide was also challenged by the birth of identity politics in the 1960s, particularly due to the involvement of the discipline of psychoanalysis and the creation of new role for the cultural and the social.[118]

While the globalization of information technologies has been hailed as 'the end of geography' or 'the death of distance', these technologies actually emphasize sense of place and increase sites of connectivity.[119]

Ultimately, the place of the public sphere is vital for situating citizenship,[120] political action and community. Two extreme arguments figure cyberspace as saviour or represser of the political and of community. Poster argues that cyberspace

---

112   Ibid. at 87.

113   Blomley N, Delaney D and Ford RT (eds) (2001) *The Legal Geographies Reader*, Blackwell: Oxford, UK at 3.

114   Ellickson RC (2001) 'Controlling chronic misconduct in city spaces: Of panhandlers, skid rows, and public-space zoning', in Blomley N, Delaney D and Ford RT (eds) *The Legal Geographies Reader*, Blackwell: Oxford, UK.

115   Dodge M and Kitchin R (2001) *Mapping Cyberspace*, Routledge: London.

116   Stone, op. cit. fn. 88.

117   Shields R (1989) 'Social Spatialization and the Built Environment: The Case of the West Edmonton Mall', *Environment and Planning D*, V7, 147.

118   Zaretsky E (1995) 'The Birth of Identity Politics in the 1960s: Psychoanalysis and the Public/Private Distinction', in Featherstone M, Lash S and Robertson R (eds) *Global Modernities*, Sage Publications: London.

119   Mosco V (2000) 'Webs of Myth and Power: Connectivity and the New Computer Technopolis' in Herman A and Swiss T (eds) *The World Wide Web and Contemporary Cultural Theory*, Routledge: London.

120   Citizenship has become important to debates on globalization as it is a term which seeks to frame the subject in a context which avoids economic commodification. Mosco, ibid.

ruptures/challenges human geography and produces places of difference and resistance to society.[121] On the other hand Sardar claims that cyberspace is little more than 'the American dream' writ large, a technology geared to the erasure of non-Western histories.[122] The Internet is a complex social phenomenon, encompassing both of these perspectives and more besides.

Jurisdiction and Zoning in the Imaginary Domain

Before the relationship between jurisdiction and community can be investigated in detail, it is important to draw some connections between the spatial nature of jurisdiction and the spatial deployment of censorship law. In Chapter 5 the spatial practices of censorship law were discussed, in particular the governance of spaces (cyberspace and physical) and media within those spaces. Feminist legal theorist Drucilla Cornell's theory of the Imaginary Domain proved to be a useful tool for balancing liberal notions of free speech with feminist concerns about the harmful effects of media, particular on those who are involuntarily exposed to images.

Cornell argues that management of spatial boundaries between public and private spaces is essential to protect the self integrity of legal subjects and to provide a space of self constitution. Cautious of the liberal public/private divide which has proven to privilege elite groups and marginalize Others, Cornell shifts the focus to legal protection of an Imaginary Domain as a more useful notion than that of private space. Drawing on Lacan, the Imaginary Domain is a textual space, akin to Lefebvre's 'representational space' which comprises physical, social and mental spaces.

While focussing on feminist issues concerning pornography and sexual imagery in public spaces, Cornell's concept involves a radical re-conceptualization of the role of the censor generally as well as that of the state in regulating media and the Imaginary Domain. Rather than being an arbiter of obscenity the state role shifts to mediating different interests and positions, acting where conflict or need arises. The state is transformed into one of several regulators charged with protection of the Imaginary Domain, a role which cannot simply be performed by force and imposition of rules. The state role is not in policing the domain but helping to protect and nurture it through zoning, addressing power imbalances and blockages in the power flows. Cornell locates the governance of the Imaginary Domain within the practices of everyday life rather than an abstract terrain of legal rules or social science models of human behaviour:

> Part of what I try to challenge is the causality model because I understand fantasy differently from some feminists who have felt that behaviourism – literally

---

[121] Poster, op. cit. fn. 110.
[122] Sardar Z (1995) 'alt.civilisations.faq: Cyberspace and the Darker Side of the West', *Futures*, V27, 777.

behavioural training – could be the solution to this governing fantasy [...] part and parcel of the mainstream heterosexual [...] pornography industry. [...] I think the problem is the causality model, meaning that human beings are just these behavioural objects, and that we can use the law to remake the man, so to speak, by giving him electric shocks when he tries to express those fantasies. [...] We have to involve ourselves in aesthetic re-creation of our own sexuality. And I don't mean just those of us who actually do sexually explicit videos or who write sexually explicit literature. I mean those of us who in our day-to-day lives are struggling to try to come to terms with what it means to be 'a girl', what it means to have a period, what it means to have the bodies we have, and what it means to try to re-conceive of ourselves as whole and not as somebody who is just a fetishistic object in someone else's imaginary.[123]

It is essential to recognize that while the Imaginary Domain is a social space, it is an embodied psychic space and its violation has physical consequences. 'It is because our sense of self, our constitution as a self, turns on the construction and mirroring of others that we can be so severely violated by enforced confrontation with imagistic signifiers.'[124]

The liberal component of Cornell's philosophy demonstrates her suspicion of state power, particularly law. She doubts that law is useful in the regulation of pornography because it entrenches cultural stereotypes of femininity (women as victims, mere subjects or 'fuckees') and because law is a 'force of accommodation' of pluralist interests and does not serve as a vehicle for aspirations, particularly for feminism.[125]

According to Cornell, pornography is an important field of contestation because it is fantasy, because it allows for shifting positions for a reader, 'it is possible for powerful men to fantasize about taking up the position of a dominated Other, and for women to imagine themselves in the positions of phallic agency, as one who 'fucks' back.'[126] Cornell sees the state role not in silencing and suppressing sites of conflict, but in helping to maintain 'level playing fields' of contestation by legally inscribed limits, zones and boundaries. This is a different model of jurisdiction but not necessarily inconsistent with the way that law operates in everyday life.

Cornell argues that censorship mirrors the simplistic and legalistic city zoning which has excluded women from active participation in the sexual spaces of the city, except for those who work in the sex industry. Restrictive zoning practices aim at keeping pornography shops out of the 'decent' parts of town displace them into liminal zones, places where it seems or indeed is dangerous for a woman to be.

---

123 Cornell D and hooks b (1998) 'Dialogue: The Imaginary Domain: A Discussion Between Drucilla Cornell and bell hooks', *Women's Rights Law Reporter*, vol 19, 261 at 264–5.
124 Cornell, op. cit. fn. 32 at 156.
125 Ibid. at 99.
126 Ibid. at 133.

Lasker uses urban semiotics to demonstrate the production of sexual meaning through the zoning of city space.[127] In this way, we can perceive the intersection of spaces – physical, jurispace, erotic spaces – which are isolated through the agency of law. Zoning practices inscribe the erotic as a male domain, dangerous for women who are isolated in domestic (family) spaces[128] where they are protected from being offended. Lasker argues that this denies women fundamental tools in constructing their own sexual identities: 'In much more than a merely metaphorical way, the theory and practice of zoning adult entertainment land uses play a significant role in society's denial of women's access to their bodies and sexualities while continuing to facilitate men's access to both.'[129]

Lasker suggests that urban regulatory discourses have been complicit in this, producing an image of pornography which is linked to urban decay – an image which is a product of zoning practices rather than a natural situation.[130] The veneer of social science[131] provides credibility to a binary of pastoral suburb/jungle city in which morality is lost in misrepresented statistics of crime rates and property values. The recent phenomenon of 'respectable' adult stores, often targeted at couples, may defy the traditional association of pornography and decay.

Cornell's deconstruction and reconstruction of civic space may raise objections[132] both from anti-pornography activists who demand a morally protected public sphere and the protestations of liberal legalists who seek to sustain a traditional division of public and private spheres. While liberalism has protected erotic media as a form of free speech, it is also challenged by transgressive media which threatens the tidy division between public and private – in this way its sense of morality is spatialized. In this manner the liberal legal model of jurisdiction also spatializes morality by defining jurisdictional reach – moralizing the public sphere and protecting private spaces.

One of the most clearly expressed, if perhaps shrillest, expressions of this liberal anxiety is 'Changing Images of the State: The Pornographic State' by

---

127 Lasker S (2002) '"Sex and the City" Zoning "Pornography Peddlers and Live Nude Shows"', *UCLA Law Review*, vol 49, 1139.

128 The family home is also a key site of moral regulation, sustained through the inscription of public and private spaces through architecture. Wigley M (1992) 'Untitled: The Housing of Gender', *Sexuality and Space*, Princeton Papers on Architecture: Princeton, NJ.

129 Lasker, op. cit. fn. 127 at 1144.

130 Ibid. at 1162–3.

131 For example a New York Study of adult establishment contains a quote from a psychiatrist who claims that growth in adult establishments is directly linked to young people becoming addicted to heroin and other drugs. Department of City Planning, City of New York (1994) *Adult Entertainment Study 66.*

132 As yet her work does not seem to have been academically critiqued from either of these perspectives.

Collins and Skover.[133] These authors express an anxiety that the space of public discourse is threatened by a viral pornography that promises to over-run sensible political discourse and spill over into society, contaminating political life and civic society. This contamination is spatialized and constructed as a deviant and viral Pornotopia, a threat to the orderly public/private divide of civic society. Collins and Skover ask: 'Is it any longer possible to distance public good from private self indulgence? [... They warn against the influence of pornography], the potentially corrupting effect of certain forms of private expression on public discourse.'[134]

Collins and Skover claim that the blame for this lies in a convergence of 'forces of self-gratification, mass consumerism, and advanced technology.'[135] Each of these factors contains a conceptual dichotomy: self gratification ('in which the irrational consumes the rational, and in which images dominate discourse'[136]) opposes the valorized self realization of the liberal citizen; mass consumerism opposes an authentic political community; and technology opposes a romantic Thoreauian appeal to simpler times, via Norman Rockwell. Each of these elements bears strongly on the Internet censorship debate. Genuine authentic relationships between 'human beings' are positioned by Collins and Skover in contrast to degraded interactions mediated by technology and through images.

Here Cornell's Imaginary Domain is drawn in stark contrast to liberal conceptions of the private realm. While Cornell draws on key liberal ideas and theorists such as Rawls, her invocation of Lacan is at least partially successful in jettisoning the liberal concept of the private realm and the discrimination this involves regarding gender, sex and sexuality and its ideological reconceptualization of the moral domain. It is only partial because the Imaginary Domain includes the liberal private spaces within its spaces, but also allows for (and encourages) critical oppositions to be situated in the domain. Most importantly these kinds of zoning regulations would extend to the public spaces of the Internet and avoid the need to turn to simple and misleading conceptions of 'private', 'community' and 'offence'.

So far the Imaginary Domain seems a workable model, with an emphasis on discretion and self governance. But does this amount to merely hiding the problem, like the prudish Victorians who covered the suggestive legs of pianos? Cornell herself is wary of moral-based zoning schemes which are predicated on imagined notions such as 'the family' in attempts to keep pornography away from schools and family places.[137] Cornell is emphatic: 'It is extremely important that the kind of zoning that I am recommending be consistent with that kind of sexual tolerance which has, at least in one study, been correlated with a lessening of attitudes of

---

133 Collins RKL and Skover DM (1994) 'Changing Images of the State: The Pornographic State', *Harvard Law Review*, Vol 107, 1374.
134 Ibid. at 1377.
135 Ibid. at 1375.
136 Ibid. at 1375.
137 Cornell, op. cit. fn. 32 at 152.

inequality towards women and a corresponding drop in explicit acts of violence against them.'[138]

The most substantial critique of the Imaginary Domain comes from feminist lawyer Plank who embraces Cornell's remodelling of public/private space but suggests that her modest zoning proposal does not go far enough to protect the Imaginary Domain from the intrusion of heterosexist images which are presently unregulated.[139] Soft core pornography and sexist images in advertising (especially billboards and magazines) may prove to be even more dangerous than hard core images due to their ubiquitous nature and tacit approval of a singular form of desire. 'Such images enable the containment of female subjectivity because, being shown only the woman's exposed breasts and/or pubic hair, the masculine viewer is not threatened with the possibility of the woman's own sexual desire; he is not threatened with the subjectivity, as represented by the image of the clitoris, of the Other.'[140]

Further, Plank targets the intertexual strategies by which soft core images are presented in magazines such as *Playboy* and newspapers such as *The Sun* (Britain).[141] The 'intellectual', news and interview content of these publications is directly juxtaposed against the passive female body, representing a duality of serious 'men's business' and a frivolous fantasy of femininity. 'Here, the world of news and politics is equated with the male world in which women exist simply as objects of male desire and sexual consumption.'[142]

Plank is concerned that as a legal strategy, Cornell's zoning approach leaves open too many imponderables. By governing those selling erotic materials, it does nothing to regulate consumers who bring the material into public spaces, such as reading a pornographic magazine on public transport.[143] The Internet equivalent of this may be the 'pop-up' advertisement for pornographic sites which occur on some websites.

The concept of the Imaginary Domain may not resolve the more difficult issues of censorship and Internet regulation but it presents a site for exploration by challenging the rigid public/private division In formulating the Imaginary Domain, Cornell has attempted to construct a model of media regulation which allows for a critical reception of media by creating sites of contestation and framing some regulations for representation occurring in those spaces. This was done to allow women a space to critique sexism in pornography while engaging with it, but it has ramifications beyond feminist issues. Cornell's model reconceives jurisdiction

---

138   Ibid. at 153. The study she references is Baron L (1990) 'Pornography and Gender Equality: An Empirical Analysis', *Journal of Sex Research*, Vol 27, 3.

139   Plank T (1997) 'Expanding the Feminine Sexual "Imaginary": A Response to Drucilla Cornell's Theory of Zoning Pornography', *Women's Rights Law Reporter*, vol 18, 215.

140   Ibid. at 224–5.
141   Ibid. at 225–7.
142   Ibid. at 225.
143   Ibid. at 226.

by redefining public and private spaces, shifting law's posture from police officer to facilitator and envisioning a variety of connected legal, media and civic spaces, physical or virtual, intertextually connected by the Imaginary Domain.

But what of the people who live in these spaces? How are communities constituted and can 'community values' suggest useful foundations for regulation? If cyberspace can be said to create virtual communities, what happens when their values contradict the values of physical spaces the virtual planes intersect with? The concept of jurisdiction maps the legal networks of power but the places where this interconnects with regulatory communities are difficult to model without resorting to homogenous, imagined communities which may be misconceived or hegemonically distorted.

Constituting Community and Community Values

The entire credibility of the censorship system rests on the ability of the regulatory apparatus to determine community values and assess media texts against this standard. Black argues that 'regulatory interpretive communities' are formed around regulatory schemes and those who create and enforce regulations.[144] These communities may display a degree of heterogeneity – this may be merely on the surface or may involve deeply held shared goals and values. Black argues that regulatory interpretative communities will be filled with conflicts, inconsistencies and trade-offs.

This concept can be taken further. While Black focuses on those going about the 'business' of regulation, it could be argued that regulatory communities arise around the site of regulatory subjects as well, encompassing a flow of regulatory power situated around social spaces and issues. These regulatory communities possess a multiple, discontinuous and shifting nature. Censorship law, on the other hand, seeks to establish one regulatory community which is consistent with the legal and jurisdictional boundaries of the law itself.

The controversy surrounding the United States *Child Online Protection Act 1998* arose in part from its use of 'community standards'. The law was considered in *Ashcroft v ACLU*[145] where the Federal Appeals Court had suggested that such a standard was constitutionally invalid. On appeal, the majority of the Supreme Court ruled that these standards were not, of themselves, in breach of the Constitution's free speech protection and returned the decision to the lower court. Dissenter, Justice John Paul Stevens, argued that in the Internet arena, community standards became a sword rather than a shield and suggested that the standards of a puritan village should not be used to veto material from more liberal places.

The connection between geography and values is noteworthy here. The localized aspect of community has been part of American anti-censorship discourse because

---

144 Black, op. cit. fn. 22 at 177.
145 *Ashcroft v American Civil Liberties Union* 535 US (2002).

of fears that repressive local enclaves could dictate moral policy for more liberal areas.[146] 'Any test that turns on what is offensive to the community's standard is too loose, too capricious, too destructive of freedom of expression to be squared with the First Amendment.'[147] This issue has not arisen significantly in the Australian federal context.

Internet censorship laws raise the question of whose standards are to be used? How is the community determined, particularly given that cyberspace encompasses geographically disparate subjects who may be situated in different jurisdictions? The term 'community' is used frequently in censorship discourse, but it does not explore the complex or comprehensive manner in which communities are constituted.[148] For instance, one critic uses religion and community almost interchangeably as conservative concepts: 'At one extreme of the debate are religious leaders and community groups that want some sort of protection against offensive content on the Internet in a desperate attempt to protect the local community standards.'[149] This statement displays certain problematic assumptions in the Internet censorship debate: it ties community to locality; it associates community (a general term) with religious groups who claim to represent these values; it assumes an abstraction of community values which exists independently of the everyday experiences of members of the community.

Arguing from a feminist stance, legal critic Lacey is wary of the concept of community and the conservative way it is deployed in legal theory,[150] although legal sociologist Cotteral has attempted to provide law with sociologically-informed definitions of community to remedy this trend.[151] Likewise, cyber-culture theorist Bell is troubled by the ease with which the term 'community' is invoked in the context of cyberspace politics for different, often contradictory purposes.[152] While community values may be observable, at least as a general form of consensus while subjects agree and the system is stable, community fragmentation quickly becomes apparent whenever conflict arises. Some critics have doubted that the virtual spaces of cyberspace and of late-capitalism can any longer sustain a concept

---

146   O'Toole L (1998) *Pornocopia: Porn, Sex, Technology and Desire*, Serpent's Tail: London at 9.

147   Per Justice William O Douglas, dissenting in *Roth v United States, 354 U.S. 476* at 512.

148   Lacey N (1998) *Unspeakable Subjects: Feminist Essays in Legal and Social Theory*, Hart Publishing: Oxford.

149   Rodriquez F (2002) *Burning the Village to Roast the Pig: Censorship of Online Media*, a paper for the OSCE workshop 'Freedom of the Media and the Internet' 30 November 2002, p3.

150   Lacey, op. cit. fn. 148, Chapter 5 'Community in Legal Theory: Idea, Ideal or Ideology?'.

151   Cotteral R (1995) *Law's Community: Legal Theory in Sociological Perspective*, Clarendon Press: Oxford.

152   Bell D (2001) *An Introduction to Cybercultures*, Routledge: London, Chapter 6 'Community and Cyberculture'.

of community. It is argued that social life has become atomized, that individuals seek only narcissistic pleasures in the 'placeless' environments of consumer capitalism, but Crang argues that community may exist even there.[153]

Even the Australian censorship regulator, the Office of Film and Literature Classification, has expressed anxieties about the notion of community:

> [T]he operation can no longer be based on the proposition that we are inherently aware of what community standards are. We have to turn to research, to the more traditional marketing tools of focus groups to monitor how our decisions are going.[154]

In 2002 the conservative Australian Federal Government changed the definition of 'aggrieved person' under the *Classification (Publication, Films and Computer Games) Act 1995* to allow organizations, most likely moral and religious groups, to apply directly to the Classification Review Board without the intervention of the Attorney General or their Members of Parliament. Only organizations whose 'activities relate to the contentious aspects of theme or subject matter'[155] are allowed standing, opening the door for moral groups but effectively excluding free speech advocate groups whose interests, the government claims are too broad.[156]

According to Australian Democrat Senator Brian Grieg: '[the government is] opening the door to every lunatic fringe, nutter organisation and individual in this country to complain about every film that they want to. And let us be clear about this: they will not hold back ... They must be salivating at the thought of having this tremendous opportunity.'[157] Grieg seems to be suggesting that these are the

---

153 Crang, op. cit. fn. at 81.

154 Dickie J (1997) 'Challenges for Classifiers', paper presented at the conference: *Violence, Crime and the Entertainment Media*, Australian Institute of Criminology, 4–5 December.

155 The *Classification (Publication, Films and Computer Games) Amendment Act (No 1) 2001* inserted the following subclause into Schedule 5 cl 16 of the original Act:

> (2) Without limiting paragraph (1)(e), if the classification referred to in that paragraph is a restricted classification, the following persons or bodies are taken to be persons aggrieved by the classification:
>
> (a) a person who has engaged in a series of activities relating to, or research into, the contentious aspects of the theme or subject matter of the Internet content concerned;
> (b) an organisation or association, whether incorporated or not, whose objects or purposes include, and whose activities relate to, the contentious aspects of that theme or subject matter.

156 Marr D (2001) 'Daryl Williams QC at the Chauvel', http://libertus.net/censor/odocs/marr0110ag.html (viewed 7/4/03). Williams noted that film critics would not get standing, that having 'an interest in film' was not enough.

157 quoted in ibid.

kinds of groups that by default represent the 'attitudes the community' under the complaints mechanism of the *Broadcasting Services Amendment (Online Services) Act 1999* regulatory scheme.

The term 'community' can be challenged for imposing conservative, heteronormative views of sexuality[158] and as being a highly politicized attempt to scapegoat those cast outside its bounds and the result of political expedience rather than good policy making.[159] Fulcher points out the problem of the concept of community in public discourse is that it is either too broad or too narrow, and that the government model of community is conceived on three axes, perceptual (sense of belonging), functional (the ability to meet with reasonable economy) and political (the connection between the elected body and the members).[160]

Community is often taken for granted but it reflects a variety of factors: gender, class, ethnicity, history, solidarity, conservatism – all of which are spatially located and connected with a sense of place from which individual identities are drawn.[161]

> Community is a relational rather than a categorical concept, defined both by material social relations and symbolic meanings. Communities are context dependent, contingent and defined by power relations; the boundaries are created by mechanisms of inclusion and exclusion. Although these mechanisms may change and so boundaries alter over time, communities are necessarily bounded entities.[162]

In *The Politics of Environmental Discourse* (a 1995 work), Hajer stresses the importance of communities in constituting self and identity, the dialogic formation of spaces in which issues are discussed which he refers to as implicit in the creation of 'storylines'.[163] These storylines are narratives which simplify complex issues into a format which can be conceptualized and debated. As storylines develop, they become ritualized and accepted as a specific approach to what appears to be

---

158 In Australia this occurs especially in the exclusion of fetish material, Albury K (1999) 'NVE and Australian Community Standards: Whose community are we talking about?', *Adult Industry Review*, Vol 2(3), archived at http://libertus.net/censor/odocs/alburynve.html (viewed 7/4/03).

159 Graham I (2000b) 'Not the Community's Guidelines: The history of the film classification guidelines that banned "Romance"', http://libertus.net/censor/rdocs/history_filmgd1.html (viewed 7/4/03).

160 Fulcher H (1989) *The Concept of Community of Interest: A Discussion Paper Which Explores the Concept of Community of Interest as it Applies to Local Government Boundaries*, South Australian Department of Local Government: Adelaide.

161 McDowell L (1999) *Gender, Identity and Place: Understanding Feminist Geographies*, Polity Press: London at 100.

162 Ibid. at 100.

163 Hajer M (1995) *The Politics of Environmental Discourse: Ecological Modernization and the Policy Process*, Oxford University Press: New York.

a coherent problem. Individual actors define their own identity in relation to these storylines which do not just form networks of understanding, they discursively produce those who locate themselves within or against them. So 'libertarianism' or 'anti-pornography feminism' are much more than rhetorical positions, they are storylines engaged by regulatory communities which constitute the identity to those who share those narratives, as well as those who oppose to them.

The imagination of community is not necessarily an abusive exercise of power (although history has demonstrated that it easily can be put to such ends) and communities will engage in this inscription and policing project in order to gain a sense of solidarity. For smaller, well-defined communities, this can allow scope for a balance of individual identity within community, but this becomes problematic when 'the community' is a totalizing abstraction such as is the case in its use in censorship law.

Regulatory Communities

'The Australian government, in adapting existing regulatory paradigms to the Internet, has overlooked the informal communities who live, work and play within the virtual world of cyberspace.'[164] In criticizing Australia's Internet content censorship scheme, Chen raises the problem of monolithic models of community standards and observes that a pluralistic community by definition will not have 'standards'.[165] Further, the minimum requirements for the IIA codes of practice support the erroneous concept of a singular monolithic community.[166] Likewise, Lyon argues that cyberspace is but one aspect of a much larger exploration of social theory:

> The question of a sociology of cyberspace is part of a much larger debate. Without mentioning cyberspace [it is possible to discuss] the shift in social theory from fixed accounts of self and agency, [to] conceiving of the self as having multiple and contradictory identities, community affiliations, and social interests. Cyberspace becomes a further vehicle for just such debates.[167]

Similarly, Wellman and Gulia link discussion of virtual community to larger debates about community and the social changes which have occurred through technology

---

164 Chen P (1999) 'Community without Flesh: First Thoughts on the New Broadcasting Services Amendment (Online Services) Bill 1999', *M/C: A Journal of Media and Culture 2.3*, http://english.uq.edu.au/mc/9905/bill (viewed 1/10/01) at 4.
165 Ibid. at 2.
166 Ibid. at 3.
167 Lyon D (1997) 'Cyberspace sociality: controversies over computer-mediated relationships' in Loader BD (ed.) *The Governance of Cyberspace: Politics, Technology and Global Restructuring*, Routledge: London.

– in bureaucratization, industrialization, urbanization and in capitalism. They describe how different arguments describe the effects of change, having variously: 'led communities to (1) fall apart, (2) persevere as village-like shelters from mass society, or (3) be liberated from the clasp of traditional solidarity groups.'[168]

The concept of community is often invoked, but difficult to pin down. Pundits frequently substitute a pastoralist myth of community for any actual investigation of how community is experienced.[169] Elsewhere, critics like Friese and Wagner have warned that sociology can no longer rely on related concepts such as 'culture' or 'society' as stable and coherent concepts.[170] Similarly, Hampton and Wellman seek to displace the mid twentieth century sociological treatment of community as a locality. Rather they argue that community should be considered a social network rather than a bounded group.[171]

Postcolonial theorist Anderson conceives of the 'imagined community' as an important aspect of nationalist discourse. He argues that nation is imagined as limited (with coherent borders), sovereign (which comes from an Enlightenment rejection of nobility and religion) and as a community (with horizontal equality, despite real power imbalances).[172] Anderson's concept of 'imagined communities' has become very influential in discussions of the online context.[173]

Working from this perspective, Cooks uses postcolonial analysis to explore the construction of nationalism in virtual space, particularly in diasporic communities. She invokes Bhabha's notion of the gathering and 'border ethnography' to suggest that local knowledges are always indeterminate, fragmented and these knowledges derive meaning from the subject's relationships to borders rather than fixed position in space.[174] By displacing the self and community from a fixed geography, she demonstrates that sense of place and sense of community derives from within self, not from an external referent.[175]

Anderson's concept of 'imagined communities' is used by Appadurai to describe cultural imperialism in cyberspace, particularly Westernization/Americanization. He claims that one person's imagined community is another's prison.[176]

---

168 Wellman and Gulia, op. cit. fn. 109 at 174.
169 Ibid.
170 Friese H and Wagner P (1999) 'Not All that is Solid Melts into Air: Modernity and Contingency', in Featherstone M and Lash S (eds) *Spaces of Culture: City, Nation, World*, Sage Publications: London.
171 Hampton KN and Wellman B (2002) 'The Not So Global Village of Netville', in Wellman B and Haythornthwaite C (eds) *The Internet in Everyday Life*, Blackwell Publishing: Oxford, UK.
172 Anderson, op. cit. fn. 96 at 7.
173 Trend D (ed.) (2001) *Reading Digital Culture*, Blackwell Publishers: Oxford at 4.
174 Cooks L (2001) 'Negotiating National Identity and Social Movement in Cyberspace: Natives and Invaders on the Panama-L Listserv', in Ebo B (ed) *Cyberimperialism? Global Relations in the New Electronic Frontier*, Praeger: Westport, CT.
175 Ibid.
176 Appadurai, op. cit. fn. 103 at 307.

The reception of Internet technology has seen the projection of a binary opposition between the virtual and the real and fear that virtuality comes at the expense of genuine community. Similarly, the introduction of the technologies of the motor vehicle and television created fear that these technologies would harm the community.[177] Wellman and Gulia compare real and virtual communities and find that both form aspects of glocalized social networks. They argue that constituting community is not a 'zero sum game' – one does not necessarily detract from the other. Like real life, virtual relationships are intermittent, specialized and varying in strength.[178]

Rheingold problematizes the contention that virtual communities erode real life community. 'What do we expect from the word 'community', and for whom, precisely do we expect it? Are there more usefully specific terms than 'community' to describe human relationships in the alphabet–printing–press–telephone–Internet–enabled era?'[179]

Katz and Rice examined fears that the Internet lead to a weakening of private community, a decline in public community and a disengagement from community. Through their ethnographic research they found no proof that Internet use leads to a decline in civic involvement and did find positive social and interpersonal consequences.[180] Ethnographic research has also demonstrated the Internet activity has lead to an enhanced sense of belonging across ethnically marked residential zones in Los Angeles[181] and that online activity supplements participation in voluntary organizations and politics.[182]

There have been several moral panics concerning the disappearance of public space throughout the twentieth century, but each of these rely on unproblematic models of public space, concepts which in Western society have been used to marginalize Others and exclude them from political discourse.[183]

---

177 Stein M (1960) *The Eclipse of Community*, Princeton University Press: Princeton, NJ.

178 Wellman and Gulia, op. cit. fn. 109.

179 Rheingold H (2002) 'Foreword: The Virtual Community in the Real World', in Wellman B and Haythornthwaite C (eds) *The Internet in Everyday Life*, Blackwell Publishing: Oxford, UK at xxviii.

180 Katz JE and Rice RE (2002) 'Syntopia: Access, Civic Involvement, and Social Interaction on the Net', in Wellman B and Haythornthwaite C (eds) *The Internet in Everyday Life*, Blackwell Publishing: Oxford, UK at 292.

181 Matei S and Ball-Rokeach SJ (2002) 'Belonging in Geographic, Ethnic, and Internet Spaces', in Wellman B and Haythornthwaite C (eds) *The Internet in Everyday Life*, Blackwell Publishing: Oxford, UK.

182 Quan-Haase A and Wellman B with Witte JC and Hampton KN (2002) 'Capitalising on the Net: Social Contact, Civic Engagement, and Sense of Community', in Wellman B and Haythornthwaite C (eds) *The Internet in Everyday Life*, Blackwell Publishing: Oxford, UK.

183 Light J (1999)'From City Space to Cyberspace' in Crang M, Crang P and May J (eds) *Virtual Geographies*, Routledge: London.

Instead of a single monolith abstract community, it is possible to recognize a diversity of smaller regulatory communities arise around media issues and practices. A community is framed by discourse and discourse is the foundation of regulation. These communities are located in everyday life, not the abstract and taxonomically pure world that censorship jurispace offers. Rheingold has written extensively on virtual communities[184] and it is clear that many of these will be regulatory in nature and in practice.

The image of regulation formulated through conventional theories of power suggests a system of governance whereby the state formulates an ideal model of behaviour which is then applied, more or less successfully, to society. This image not only misses the subtle nuances of power but also lacks perspective where regulation is concerned.

The state is not the centre of regulatory behaviour, nor should it be. The state, through its notion of jurisdiction, attempts to set up boundaries, to manage the edges of where social problems emerge, but this should not be mistaken for control. Control is never complete and pursuing control is an unending addiction, never satisfied. The state should be displaced from the centre of a concept of moral order.[185]

Even within state regulatory discourse the incompleteness of state power is recognized through use of 'the community' to annex community regulatory systems in a kind of co-regulatory arrangement. Unfortunately the universal term 'community' raises more problems than it solves and contains no easy way to conceptualize the relationship between the individual and the community, let alone provide a guide to balancing their interests. All too often use of community standards collapses into a kind of bare majoritarianism with the regulator normalizing its own interests.

Power finds its expression through space. Foucault claims that the history of either would also be a history of the other.[186] It becomes necessary to reject the abstracting, totalizing notion of 'the community', a practice which expels Others to the margins. Instead, a multiplicity of communities needs to be embraced, each constituted by networks of power. These networks may be transitory or may replicate themselves over time. One individual may be networked into different communities in complex, even paradoxical ways.

What happens when one community intrudes on the space of another? How is public space to be shared? Cornell's notion of the Imaginary Domain gives us some guidance here, replacing the old liberal notion of the private with a more sophisticated space of self actualization.

A hypothetical person decides to set up a 'Bananas in Pyjamas' fan site for the television show that they enjoy with their children. The same person also creates a site for another of their passions, hard core bondage pornography. Is this person

---

184   Rheingold (1994) *The Virtual Community*, Secker and Warburg: London.
185   Hunt A (1999) *Governing Morals: A Social History of Moral Regulation*, Cambridge University Press: Cambridge, UK.
186   Foucault, op. cit. fn. 41.

going to mix the content of these sites together through hyperlinks between the two? If not, why not? Is it because of fear of the law? Is it because to do so would contravene the abstract censor's taxonomies of content classification? Rather, the choices that the hypothetical web master makes reflect many the regulatory communities of which they are a member and in which they are actively, discursively involved.

Clearly there is an extensive social network of regulation that co-exists with the legal one. Departing from Lessig's typology which privileges law, it seems that the legal regulatory system can be conceived of as just another social network, perhaps not the most effectual but one with extensive spatial coverage within its jurisdiction, and significant powers of enforcement and coercion. Nevertheless, having the biggest stick does not necessarily make you the most effective regulator.

The shorthand terms of 'the community', 'offence', 'community standards', 'obscenity', long the mainstays of censorship regulatory discourse seem to provide a kind of certainty, as long as the producers of media are content to self regulate. These terms become highly problematic in dealing with a diverse and complex media terrain.

The study of regulatory communities is a large undertaking and this book can merely sketch some outlines of how a study might proceed. In the next section three different regulatory communities, each with their own approach to sexually explicit material, are drawn in broad strokes.

In brief, these are the Capalert community (an online network of Christians who classify films under their own scheme of guidelines), secondly, the irregular community of pornography fans drawn from the many consumer fanbases of different pornographic genres and, thirdly, the loose networks of parents who regulate their children's consumption of and access to media. Each of these communities regulates media in different ways but without state intervention and draws on collective experiences when engaged in regulatory discourse. These groups are quite different and constituted in different ways, but are not mutually exclusive. It would, in theory, be possible to be a member of all three simultaneously, even if this created some ideological tension. Shifting identity is an unavoidable part of shifting contextual spaces – online and off.[187]

Significantly. the Internet has become an important vehicle for communication for each of the communities explored here. In the Internet regulation debate, each of the communities has been constructed as a stereotype (moral activists, pornography consumers, parents) and further investigation of these communities and their practices should displace these assumptions somewhat.

---

187 For an exploration of the links between identity and intersecting spaces in cyberspace, see Shields R (1996) 'CyberPunk Cinderella? Contextual Illness and Subjectivation', in Juul-Christensen (ed.) *The Meeting of the Waves*, Scandanavian University Press: Copenhagen.

The Capalert Project: Mirror of the State?

One of the more ambitious community regulation projects to develop out of the Internet is www.capalert.com, a network of Christian activists who have undertaken to review and classify films, primarily American films, according to their own classification standards.

This community is constituted by volunteers and represents a significant mobilisation of self-governing power. Its readership is not confined to those who conform to the community's ideological premises; many netizens read the Capalert pages for reasons other than moral edification, to inform themselves of conservative fundamentalist values, to get annoyed, or even just for fun.[188]

Spatially, the community of contributors is located primarily across the US but it is viewed worldwide. The diversity of readership would make it difficult to make generalizations, especially since many interact with the site in ways unintended by the authors.

The site provides a summary of each film, an analysis based on a fundamentalist Christian reading of the Bible and a quantified 'thermometer' of six key elements of classification, forming the WISDOM acronym:

- Wanton Violence/Crime (W)
- Impudence/Hate (I)
- Sex/Homosexuality (S)
- Drugs/Alcohol (D)
- Offence to God (O)
- Murder/Suicide (M)

The rating scale is accumulative and does not make allowance for mitigating factors or exculpatory good intentions: 'We make no attempt to quantify the "artistic" or "redeeming" values of entertainment. These matters are up to you. The CAP Analysis model makes no allowances for trumped-up "messages" to excuse for manufacturing of justification for aberrant behaviour or imagery.'[189]

Capalert receive a good amount of abusive email accusing it of censorship.[190] This is a signficant misreading of the site's purpose, signficant because it shows just how sensitive people are to state classification schemes which purport not to

---

188 The 'Capalert Bingo' game represents an interesting reading against the grain. Those participating in this informal game view a film, and try to make predictions regarding the WISDOM scale, as well as guessing what specific things the reviewers will take issue with. While the WISDOM scale is more explicit and certain than most state schemes, there is always room for interpretive uncertainty which gives the game a sense of challenge.

189 ChildCare Action Project (CAP) *Christian Analysis of American Culture: Frequently Asked Questions*, http://www.capalert.com/faqpage.htm (viewed 14/4/03).

190 Ibid.

function as censorship. Like Paretsky's 'Protocols of the Elders of Feminism',[191] it is all too easy to read too much into critique, to conflate the critic with the coercive actions of the state.

While it is possible to dispute many of Capalert's readings of texts and their analyses of their meaning, this is not the point. Capalert opens a space for discussion, even if you vehemently disagree; indeed, especially if you do. Because its classification process is argued at length and backed up with both observational and dogmatic argument, it forms an interesting counterpoint to censorship – simultaneously more accountable and more arbitrary than state regulation.

Capalert provides a remarkable model of a regulatory community and represents an attempt to structure Imaginary Domain and does not, of itself, represent a significant incursion into the space of others (except the children of fundamentalist Capalert readers, which is another issue). The reviewer's willingness to engage in a detailed manner with texts themselves represents a subtle shift in position from the classification system's neat taxonomies.

Since it relies heavily on volunteer labour, it remains to be seen if the Capalert project can be maintained over time. It presents an important opportunity for investigation of regulatory communities as the community members are actively and overtly engaged in building regulatory structures. The other two examples which will be explored next represent regulatory communities which are more loosely structured and whose regulatory practices are less overt.

Pornography Fans:[192] Consumption of Desire

One of the prevalent images of anti-pornography discourse is the unbridled capitalism of the pornography industry. Some critics even conflate moral restriction with a kind of basic liberalism or anticapitalism, Skover and Collins argue that 'we forbid the sale of men and women, but often allow the sale of their sex divorced from their persons.'[193] Consumers of any media are actively and critically engaged with the texts that they read and consume. This does not refute the influence of the market in selling, advertising and encouraging consumption but, rather, acknowledges that consumers have agency in governing and even resisting industry interests.

---

191 Paretsky S (1994) 'The Protocols of the Elders of Feminism', *Law/Text/Culture*, v1, 16.

192 The term 'fan' rather than 'consumer' is used here to acknowledge that not all pornography is of commercial character, there is a good deal of amateur pornography, particularly on the Internet. The regulatory community of those consuming pornography is not necessarily structured by market architecture, but this does have an important influence.

193 Collins and Skover, op. cit. fn. 133 at 1379.

Until recently, the pornography consumer was such a secretive and obscured figure that aggregate sales figures were the main kind of feedback that the pornography producers had available. Unfortunately this encouraged deceptive practices, for example video cover models who did not match the film performers. With the emergence of independently published 'zines'[194] and, later, with Internet discussion groups, forums and chat, consumers have become more visible despite (or indeed because of) anonymity.[195]

The consumers of pornography are traditionally difficult to represent, outside of very broad stereotypes. One significant spatial aspect is the interest or fetish groupings which organize media and social interaction. Sexual identities and genres are extremely self regulating without any influence of law having to occur.[196] Heterosexual and gay male porn do not overlap at all, but heterosexual porn permits girl/girl action as a part of normalized heterosexuality.[197] While many of these generic categories are extremely rigid, sexual identities are surprisingly fluid though and it is possible for one person to negotiate different texts and streams of discourse from a pornographic smorgasbord of different genres, not be entirely bound and constituted by a singular uniform identity based on a singular sexual identity. Online identity is especially fluid[198] and in this way technology facilitates exploration of sexuality identity.

Some cultural pundits have enthusiastically embraced technology's role in the future of sex, lauding the potential of teledildonics.[199] Other critics are more cautious, fearing the eroticization of technology. For these writers, the Internet is linked with fear of isolation, loss of community and authentic human selves; the human is estranged from nature by the machine and virtual subjects are isolated from real experience and relationships.[200]

> The Delphic injunction of the Madisonian free speech guarantee is 'know thyself'; the Dionysian maxim of the pornotopian First Amendment is 'feel thyself.' The primary appeal of self-realization in deliberative democracy is to

---

194 O'Toole, op. cit. fn. 146 at 285.
195 Slater D (1998) 'Trading Sexpics on IRC: Embodiment and Authenticity on the Internet', *Body and Society*, v 4(4), 91.
196 Williams argues that pornographic genre is extremely regulatory. Williams L (1999) *Hard Core: Power, Pleasure, and the 'Frenzy of the Visible'*, University of California Press: Berkeley at 128.
197 Williams explains that girl/girl sexuality in heterosexual male pornography was originated by censorship practices which forbade representation of erect penises. Williams, ibid. at 97.
198 Turkle, op. cit. fn. 88.
199 Creed B (2003) *Media Matrix: Sexing the New Reality*, Allen and Unwin: Sydney, Chapter 7 'Cybersex'.
200 O'Toole points to McLuhan, JG Ballard, Cronenberg and 'cybersceptic' Mark Dery as key critics in of the intersection of sexuality and technology – O'Toole, op. cit. fn. 146 at 295.

master oneself; the 'primary appeal' of self gratification in the pornographic state is 'to lose one's self, lose it utterly'. [...] It concocts a pseudo-world in which all too frequently decent talk among men and women succumbs to indecent views of men and women; togetherness surrenders to selfness; and contact and communication between the sexes yield to auto-eroticization.[201]

Even Palmer, whose *Cultures of Darkness: Night Travels in the Histories of Transgression* (2000)[202] is a paeon to night spaces and night people rejects pornography as an inauthentic site of expression and subjectivity:

> It was on its way to 'pornotopia', that state of alienated sexuality where the erotic is hived off from the rest of life. In the dark night of libidinal need the lonely masturbatory hand, incapable of reaching out its loving caress to another human being with whom it is possible to share both sensually and politically, grasps at representational straws, all of which have the same tedious form and identical boring content.[203]

Further, Palmer suggests, lamenting the loss of political libertine underpinnings of pornography that:

> Pornography as it is known at the end of the twentieth century, is a one-dimensional, unidirectional, eminently finite experience, never speaking directly to larger personal or social issues. It is an exercise in commodification. Contemporary pornography does of course illuminate wider matters of power, difference, and human negotiations of freedom and the forbidden. Some of this is not unrelated to transgressive impulses.[204]

By consolidating pornography into one monolithic form of expression, Palmer rejects the political spaces of pornography. This discounts the intersection with erotic art, the potential to challenge, of amateurs taking their own control of media. These may not dominate the discourse, but are significant elements which even commercial pornographers respond to by mass producing their own 'amateur' titles. Palmer particularly neglects queer experience, especially those for whom early experiences of surreptitious consumption of pornography forms the only

---

201 Collins and Skover, op. cit. fn. 133 at 1380. See also Masters KW (1992) 'Law in the Electronic Brothel: How Postmodern Media Affect First Amendment Obscenity Doctrine', *University of Puget Sound Law Review*, Vol 15, 415.

202 Palmer BD (2000) *Cultures of Darkness: Night Travels in the Histories of Transgression*, Monthly Review Press: New York.

203 Ibid. at 92, see similar themes in LaHaye T (1991) 'The Mental Poison', in Baird and Rosenbaum (eds) *Pornography: Private Right or Public Menace?*, Prometheus: Buffalo as well as in public discourses on pornography addiction and Internet addiction.

204 Palmer, op. cit. fn. 202 at 76.

manner of exploring their sexuality and experimenting with identity. All this is not to suggest that pornography is a universally positive influence, to foreclose debate with any one universal reading of pornography is extremely premature.

In contrast to these stories of alienation, O'Toole suggests that there is another 'less heralded, less quantifiable tale of connectivity', the emergence of online communities where they can access materials and belong to a community of others with similar interests.[205]

> [Cyberspace] is a safe space in which to explore the forbidden and the taboo. It offers the possibility for genuine, unembarrassed conversations about accurate as well as fantasy images of sex.[206]

Critics such as O'Toole argue that the experience of pornography is under-represented and lacking in study: 'studies are meagre and too preoccupied with attaching gizmos to gonads, with measuring tumescence and blood flows, rather than subjective experiences.'[207] From work of Freud, through to social scientists such as Kinsey[208] and sexual radicals like Reich and Marcuse,[209] through to Foucault and feminist critical theorists like Linda Williams,[210] queer ethnographists[211] and critical sexual geographers,[212] there has been a steady stream of research concerning sexuality.

In *The Reader, The Author, His Woman and Her Lover* (1998), Hardy attempts to expand scholarship on pornography by using discourse analysis in order to formulate a model of readership for heterosexual men.[213] O'Toole attempts to sketch out some preliminary observations in this under-researched area, based on his ethnographic research derived from interviews and Internet postings.[214] Accepting the methodological limitations, some interesting observations emerge:

---

205   O'Toole, op. cit. fn. 146 at 274.
206   Carlin Meyer, New York Law School quoted in O'Toole, ibid. at 294.
207   Ibid. at 297.
208   Gathorne-Hardy J (1998) *Alfred Kinsey: Sex the Measure of All Things: A Biography*, Chatto and Windus: London.
209   Robinson PA (1972) *The Sexual Radicals*, Paladin: London.
210   Williams, op. cit. fn. 196, see also Hardy who uses discourse analysis. Hardy S (1998) *The Reader, The Author, His Woman and Her Lover: Soft-core Pornography and Heterosexual Men*, Cassell: London.
211   Weston K (1999) *Slow Burn: Sexualities and Social Science*, Routledge: London.
212   Bell D and Valentine G (eds) (1995) *Mapping Desire: Geographies of Sexualities*, Routledge: London.
213   Hardy, op. cit. fn. 210.
214   O'Toole, op. cit. fn. 146, Chapter 9.

1. There is no such thing as an average pornography user.
2. More women use porn than otherwise assumed,[215] and more couples use it. There were until recently few venues to discuss this, although lesbians generally were more vocal than heterosexual women.
3. Sexual fantasy is a complex interactive experience, with the user's fantasies, stories and memories interacting with the image, cutting and cross-cutting like fast edits.
4. Readings of pornographic texts are never simple and do not necessarily involve a straight projection of identification onto one performer. Men do not necessarily put themselves in the place of the male actor. A curious kind of cross-subjectivity may actually occur, which can be multiple and shifting. Despite otherwise fixed sexual identity, viewers may fantasize about different participants, or adopt a detached voyeuristic standpoint. Some heterosexual men report that they attempt to identify with female experience. Desire is unpredictable.
5. Desire is complex and not necessarily skin deep. Arousal can occur through situations, expressions, feelings the actors are conveying (although performers' skill at representing emotion is another matter), again intersecting with the reader's experience. It is not just 'looking at dirty pictures'. Images are staging points for more complex fantasies. Information is 'compressed' into a set of codes which the reader is actively engaged with manipulating and receiving.[216]

The Internet has opened a space for discussion, safe differential space free of some of the regulatory code which governs real space discourse about sexuality,[217] yet it is still situated within regulatory networks. This includes sex sites constructed for and by women which are of a different character to those directed at men, 'many of them have erotic fiction, articles, message boards, surveys and chat rooms, creating

---

215 Williams describes the creation of a market for women's pornography, gentrified adult stores, pornographic cable channels and self-help books and magazines which have all assisted in 'taming sex' for women. Williams, op. cit. fn. 196 at 283. She argues that as pornography enters the home it adapts itself to women's spaces (at 272).

216 O'Toole, op. cit. fn. 146 at 310 uses Barthes notion of 'punctum' the instant, primal and unreflected aesthetic experience of a photograph, 'this element which rises from the scene, shoots out of it like an arrow, and pierces me'. Barthes R (1993) *Camera Obscura*, Vintage: London.

217 These new technologically mediated sexual strategies are arguably appealing to women as they involve less exposure to dangerous spaces. Furthermore, the use of Internet pseudonyms also allows experimentation with identity. MacDougall A (1999) '"And the word was made flesh and dwelt among us ...": Towards pseudonymous life on the Internet', *M/C: A Journal of Media and Culture 2.3*, http://www.uq.edu.au/mc/9905/life.html (viewed 1/10/01). Slater's ethnographic research into trading of erotic images through Internet relay chat found a community arising because of this flexibility of identity, rather than in spite of it. Slater, op. cit. fn. 195.

a community atmosphere like a group meeting for coffee and discussing sex.'[218] The Internet creates a meeting space for people over large geographical areas, especially if their area of erotic interest is specific or unusual. The combination of website, mail and chat allows someone to find others with common interests – O'Toole interviewed a balloon fetishist who was surprised to discover that others were aroused by the same fetish and was pleased to explore his sexuality in a safe environment rather than be ashamed.[219]

The notion of 'restricted access systems' under the Australian legislation does allow for a kind of pluralistic self-regulating community even if it is one driven by commerce. On the one hand this may be considered repressive, a community which is permitted 'provided they keep well away from the public gaze. A ghetto without physical walls'.[220] Alternatively this might be considered a prudent strategy for governing the Imaginary Domain and preventing accidental exposure.

There are a great many important issues which need to be explored in the context of pornography. The danger of censorship is that it prematurely forecloses debate and does not allow informed contribution, leaving the discussion framed by stereotypes and assumptions. Active engagement in this discourse is predicated on the media literacy skills of participants. Motivated by a variety of ideological concerns, from liberal free speech to radical anti-consumerism to religious self governance, the movement for media literacy seeks to equip learners with the skills to engage discursively with texts. This is presented as an alternative to censorship which is fundamentally concerned with denial of the autonomy of the regulatory subject.[221] The focus of these educational programs tends to be on empowerment rather than silencing.

Regulatory communities are essential to the media literacy movement, providing a set of different discursive spaces and storyline narratives which readers can critically engage with, contest or endorse. Through media literacy autonomy might be achieved, enhancing the freedom to constitute the self, in differential space and the Imaginary Domain. Understanding more about pornography, erotic media and fans/consumers disrupts the binary of obscene or on/scene[222] imposed by censorship law. Further investigation of the regulatory communities which are generated around sites of pornography reception will, it is suggested, provide

---

218   Vnuk, op. cit. fn. 2 at 49.
219   O'Toole, op. cit. fn. 146 at 294.
220   Chen, op. cit. fn. 164 at 3.
221   Heins M and Cho C (2002) *Media Literacy: An Alternative to Censorship*, Free Expression Policy Project: New York.
222   Williams describes practices of 'On/scenity', a gesture by which a culture brings the hidden into the public sphere. She gives the example of the public investigation into President Clinton's penis. On/scene practices involve the politicization of sexuality and the proliferation of sexual discourses by which 'sex speaks'. Williams, op. cit. fn. 196 at 282.

more information about how informal regulatory communities are constituted and how networks of power are experienced.[223]

The Governance of Childhood: Informal Parenting Networks

The first two regulatory communities which have been suggested, the Capalert community and the informal networks of pornography consumers, are actively constituted by people who seek out spaces to discuss media and the representation of sexuality. The third community suggested by this book, parenting networks, is much more informally constituted and takes many different forms.

When a parent governs their children's access to media (even if the decision is to permit entirely free access) they engage with many different networks, contexts, media and issues. These include the state regulatory ratings, advertising, media reviews, children's educators, 'self help' and advice books, their own experiences as both a parent and a child and informal discussion with others. These networks occur in cyberspace for some parents, as well as through storytelling and traditional media for most.

As a regulatory community, parenting networks are much more disparate and difficult to map than the two examples mentioned previously. Nevertheless, the rhetoric of the Internet regulation debate speaks of 'parents' as a uniform set of interests and presumes the governance of childhood to be a uniform, discrete and continuous set of practices. Legal discourse has little formal contact with childhood development discourse although there are several sites of interaction.[224] It is because of mismatch between abstract model and complex experience that this regulatory community demands thorough exploration, and this book can do no more than frame a few questions for consideration.

Sexually explicit material is not the only sexually-themed media available to children. Many texts which are expressly branded for children, ostensibly purged of all sexual content engage in sexual ideology in a way far more subtle than explicit depictions. Disney's *The Lion King* (1994), by linking sun-king mythology with anthropomorphized lions presented a very specific image of male dominated sexuality and naturalized it as part of the 'circle of life'.

What role does the state have in regulating this process? How are children themselves engaged in these governance practices? As a group, children face the risk of being entirely objectified as mere aspects of parental legal subjectivity. How is the Imaginary Domain of a child constituted and how far does the parent have access or policing powers? The law's transference of a child's autonomy to their parents must be challenged where relationships are abusive or where children

---

223   McKee A, Albury K and Lumby C (2008) *The Porn Report*, Melbourne University Press: Melbourne.

224   These would include family law, social welfare, criminal law and, of course, censorship law.

are growing up queer in heterosexist households. These are core issues of identity and development of the Imaginary Domain, not peripheral to growing autonomy and selfhood.

Childhood is a significant site of social conflict and discourse and it ought to be considered as such, not foreclosed by abstract models and stereotypes. Multimedia artist L Dement links censorship discourse to complex and troublesome issues of childhood silences, situating censorship within the governance of the parent rather than the child:

> This was the first censorship. A child expresses something of the way it is with them. An adult sees it and can't cope. It shatters their idea of the way the world is and should be. They respond by denying. They say 'It isn't. It doesn't. That can't be true ...', over and over with their eyes shut. [...] Silenced incest children draw pictures of genitals, behave obscenely with their little friends, misbehave in school, get fat, get depressed, take drugs, fuck around, cut their own flesh. But things can't really be silenced. [...] The paternal kindness of censorship, protecting us from damage and evil, is actually a protection of pater himself, his position, his power, his pleasures. [...] It's an act of violence by the powers that be, to try to contain representations that threaten their continued comfort [...] They panic over their failing hold on women and children and queers and blacks and technologies and information and everything, everything. They try to reclaim something by banning one more story while a hundred more have been created and we've already been to the websites. Fucken pathetic.[225]

This book can do no more than suggest that the governance of the spaces of childhood is an important site of ethnographic exploration for further research into regulatory communities. The multiple, fragmentary and dynamically constituted regulatory communities that parents and children engage with cannot be as clearly mapped as the Capalert community, or even the more disparate communities which are discursively situated around pornography consumption. The complexity of parenting networks is in stark contrast to the ease with which overly-simplistic models of parents and children are represented in debates concerning Internet regulation. The three communities considered in this chapter refuse any easy invocation of a singular and uniform community as the source of censorship power. Is it possible to substitute the replace the singular with the plural, to model regulation across multiple sites, networks, communities and subject positions?

---

225 Dement L (1998) 'Dying Frightened Gasps of Old Men in Suits', *Artlink*, V 18(3), 17 at 17–21.

Classification: One Community or Many?

> State law does take identity by deriving support from other social forms [...] But in the constitution and maintenance of its identity, state law stands in opposition to and in asserted domination over social forms that support it. There exists a contradictory process of mutual support and opposition.[226]

Black's notion of regulatory conversations provides support for a model of regulatory power deployed spatially through the discourses of regulatory communities, but she acknowledges that law takes an active, ideological role in denying the importance of other regulatory communities: 'Control over interpretation is thus control over a central power resource.'[227]

Critical geographer Sabrina Williams[228] argues that spatial concepts determine the models of community participation in urban policy making. Many of her observations have clear ramifications for the way in which community is constructed in censorship discourses. Williams is concerned with the production of meaning in everyday life; policies that are meaningful for residents and which require meaningful participation in the policy making process, incorporating local structures of interpretation. To Williams, place and community are interdependently linked concepts,[229] which suggests why strategies of exclusion are self defeating for censors in their project of imagining community.

Williams cites Marx and discusses how local narratives are commodified, appropriated by the state in processes similar to commodity fetishism.[230] The contest for ownership and over appropriation of meaning has become a key object of political struggle.[231] In censorship law the abstract and universal community represents a fetishization of legitimate community narrative, and denies the idea of localized regulatory communities, each with their own practices and structures of interpretation. However, these communities persist, each attached to a place, a site of regulation which may be physical (sexist billboards in train stations), a space of flows (the Internet) or may be attached to a place of human geography (such as childhood).

Communities and their legal/regulatory apparatus emerge from a place built on practices and experiences of that place constructing local knowledges.[232] The

---

226 Fitzpatrick P (1984) 'Law and Societies', *Osgoode Hall Law Journal*, v22, 115 at 116.
227 Black, op. cit. fn. 22 at 194.
228 Williams SL (2001) 'On Blues, Marx and Elvis: Why We need a Meaningful Participation Model to Frame Spatial Theory', *Margins*, v1, 103.
229 Ibid. at 112.
230 Ibid. at 104.
231 Ibid. at 106.
232 Geertz C (1983) *Local Knowledge: Further Essays in Interpretive Anthropology*, Basic Books: New York.

smaller, the more bounded an area, the more certainty with which community can be spoken of. Abstract, society-wide notions of community are at best unhelpful and at worst a politically coercive method of inducing conformity. If analysis of regulatory community is to have meaning, it must be connected to a notion of regulatory place and space.

Rather than be located in abstract space of national identity, regulatory communities generate a sense of place, of locality, through the practices of everyday life. Both Lefebvre[233] and de Certeau[234] have investigated everyday life as a site of self constitution and resistance to abstract narratives that project models of universal human experience, transforming human subjects into mere objects of study. Similarly, author Kurt Vonnegut challenges objectification and instrumentalism in fictional conventions and its impact on policy making:

> I thought [the author] had joined hands with other old-fashioned storytellers to make people believe that life had leading characters, minor characters, significant details, insignificant details, that it had lessons to be learned, tests to be passed, and a beginning, a middle and an end.
>
> As I approached my fiftieth birthday, I had become more and more enraged and mystified by the idiot decisions made by my countrymen. And then I had come suddenly to pity them, for I understood how innocent and natural it was for them to behave so abominably, and with such abominable results: They were doing their best to live like people invented in story books. This was the reason Americans shot each other so often: It was a convenient literary device for ending short stories and books.
>
> Why were so many Americans treated by their government as though their lives were as disposable as paper facial tissues? Because that was the way authors customarily treated bit-part players in their made-up tales.[235]

In 1936, legal sociologist Ehrlich suggested that study of law should extend beyond the abstract principles enshrined in legislation and books, and should embrace 'the living law':

> To attempt to imprison the law of a time or of a people within the sections of a code is about as reasonable as to attempt to confine a stream within a pond. The water that it put in the pond is no longer a living stream, but a stagnant pool, and but little water can be put in the pond. Moreover, if one considers that the

---

233 Lefebvre H (1991b) *Critique of Everyday Life Volume 1*, Verso: London (originally published in French in 1947).
234 De Certeau M (1984) *The Practice of Everyday Life*, University of California Press: California.
235 K Vonnegut (1974) *Breakfast of Champions*, Jonathan Cape: London, at 194–5.

living law had already overtaken and grown away from the each one of these codes at the very moment the latter were enacted, and is growing away from the more and more every day, one cannot but realise the enormous extent of this as yet unplowed an unfurrowed field of activity which is being pointed out to the modern legal investigator.[236]

In some ways Ehrlich presages Foucault by describing the study of legal history, metaphorically, in the same manner that a palaeontologist studies fossils, by reference and comparison to living animals. He urges attention to the concrete not the abstract,[237] and looks to everyday practices such as business and marriage rather than in the legal documentation of contracts and marriage certificates, or the narrow slice of facts legally admissible as evidence. This engagement with lived experience is mirrored in de Certeau's explanation of the operation of state law:

> There is no law that is not inscribed on bodies. Every law has a hold on the body. The very idea of an individual that can be isolated from the group was established along with the necessity, in penal justice, of having a body that could be marked by punishment, and in matrimonial law, of having a body that could be marked with a price in transactions among collectivities. From birth to mourning after death, law 'takes hold of' bodies in order to make them into text. Through all sorts of initiations (in rituals, at school, etc.), it transforms them into tables of the law, into living tableaux of rules and customs, into actors in the drama organized by a social order.[238]

Censorship concerns the body located in space – physical, social and mental space. In censorship it is the desiring body, the erotic body, practices of mutual and self gratification that are inscribed with a hierarchical models of legitimate and illegitimate pleasures, along with a wide transgressive border between the two. Sexuality pervades everyday life and is enshrined in structures such as the concept of privacy, inscribed both socially and physically in architecture.[239] Regulatory communities of sexuality are deployed spatially via erogenous zones and fetishes, good touches and bad touches, age restraints on consumption and expression of the erotic, normal and deviant practices, good health and compulsive sex addiction. According to Dement, censorship is connected to these spatial practices: 'A boundary is established between what is an acceptable representation and what is not. Censorship is the enforcing and patrolling of that boundary, the removal and suppression of material that exceeds it.'[240]

---

236 Ehrlich E (1936) *Fundamental Principles of the Sociology of Law*, (trans 2002 Walter J Moll), Transaction Publishers: New Jersey, at 488.
237 Ibid. at 501.
238 de Certeau, op. cit. fn. 234, at 139.
239 Wigley, op. cit. fn. 128.
240 Dement, op. cit. fn. 225 at 17.

Philosopher and historian de Certeau insists on a 'street-level' viewpoint of everyday life and reject the 'summit-level' or 'god's-eye' positions adopted by many social and regulatory discourses. Kaplan invokes this approach, insisting on the importance of new media literacy to distribute and access tools of governance.[241] Inverting the customary concept that space precedes place, de Certeau argues that space is produced out of the practices of place.[242] Therefore cyberspace can be conceptualized as an extension of the sense of place generated by individuals and communities occupying and practicing in the many places of Internet media.

There have been some attempts to apply de Certeau's approach to everyday life within the discipline of law. Ewick and Sibley's *The Common Place of Law*[243] suggests that the everyday experience of law is the compilation of multiple sites of accommodation and resistance and that law itself is constituted out of an accretion of these experiences, not through grand narratives of justice. This approach seeks to incorporate the relationship between structure and agency, where state authority and local action encounter, where law, self and social practice are mutually constituted.

Ewick and Sibley's approach is to research stories, narratives from hundreds of subjects in order to identify broad trends in experiences of law. Unfortunately, the scope of that investigation proved to be just too large and as a result too little could be said of the relationship between specific experiences of law and legal abstraction. In particular *The Common Place of Law* was not able to demonstrate how specific experiences are filtered through culture and eventually become reified as legal rules which either enshrine or oppose local practices. Critic Mezey argues that: 'The fact of the matter is we still don't know much about how the individual shells of experience and perception become the coral reef of culture.'[244]

Similarly, the practices of censorship gloss over the transition from individual experiences of media reception to universal rules of depiction and representation of sexuality, violence and other content. By preferring a singular monolithic model of community and by using the power to ban (or 'refuse classification' of) difficult texts, the Australian censor excludes from public discourse and marginalizes other regulatory communities.

Chen argues that no real sense of community values have been incorporated into the *Broadcasting Services Amendment (Online Services) Act 1999*[245] and

---

241   Kaplan N (2000) 'Literacy Beyond Books: Reading When All the World's a Web' in Herman A and Swiss T (eds) *The World Wide Web and Contemporary Cultural Theory*, Routledge: London.
242   de Certeau, op. cit. fn. 234 at 117.
243   Ewick P and Sibley SS (1998) *The Common Place of Law: Stories from Everyday Life*, University of Chicago Press: Chicago.
244   Mezey N (2001) 'The Common Place of Law Out of the Ordinary: Law, Power, Culture, and the Commonplace', *Law and Social Inquiry*, v26, 145 at 160.
245   Chen P (2002) 'Australia: Where forward co-regulation?', paper presented at *Growing Australia Online*, 3–4 December, Canberra at 1.

presents an alternative model of governance in which the government's role is not censorious, but rather acts as a central focussing point in debates, a clearing house of regulatory practices and strategies. According to Chen, an effective content regulation scheme would need to identify and resolve four issues: effectiveness (the ability to address segments of population and communities of interest); flexibility (adapting to change); stakeholder engagement (commitment from the industry); and positive intervention without arbitrary paternalism (public diversity must be recognized and internalized).[246]

Using online media itself to facilitate electronic democracy,[247] Chen suggests a model which cuts across existing institutional boundaries under which 'the emphasis on risks […] will have to give way to a positive educational experience […] Users need, not dire warnings about the hostile environment they face, but positive and protective messages about what can be achieved online (be that political, social, or economic).'[248]

Classification, of itself, presents less of a problem than outright censorship, especially when an industry is self regulating and applying classification labels as consumer advice. While this merely displaces many of the problems to private venues, it transforms the role of the state into one where it oversees the process as a watchdog, not as a paternalistic authority.[249] Stronger regulation may be justified where aggressive marketing results in breaches of the rules of the Imaginary Domain, such as the control of spam email (pornographic or otherwise),[250] but this is predicated on the rules of open conversation and respect, not on moral control.

Are Regulatory Communities an Answer?

It is difficult to maintain faith in 'other people', especially in the face of news media which deliver a concentrated dose of bad faith, cruelty and narratives which portray uncontrolled objects crying out for regulation; when spaces of difference are presented as fearful, unregulated spaces; when people are afraid of participating in the Imaginary Domain and seek to prevent others from doing so.

The *Broadcasting Services Amendment (Online Services) Act 1999* is poised between success and failure because, as a legislative instrument, it incorrectly

---

246   Ibid. at 17.
247   See also Frissen P (1997) 'The virtual state: postmodernisation, informationisation and public administration' in Loader BD (ed.) *The Governance of Cyberspace: Politics, Technology and Global Restructuring*, Routledge: London.
248   Chen, op. cit. fn. 245 at 18.
249   This is pertinent since the Australian OFLC re-classifies films which have *already* been classified by the self regulatory bodies. This seems an unnecessary and wasteful duplication of effort, particularly when areas of dispute are relatively rare.
250   See National Office for the Information Economy (2003) *SPAM: Final Report of the NOIE Review of the Spam Problem and How it can be Countered*, NOIE: Canberra.

positions itself in authority over its regulatory objects and misconceives regulatory power as force to be exercised, rather than a flow to be directed in fragmented, incomplete and discontinuous regulatory spaces. By replicating the censorship law's ambition for inscribing moral order, the scheme will inevitably fail in that it does not take account of the mutual relationship between censorship and media nor the fact that both are themselves constituted by diverse regulatory networks and communities.

Nevertheless, the Act contains within it a contradictory narrative which speaks implicitly of other regulatory communities. Even though it speaks of the community as a monolithic abstract interest, the co-regulatory scheme also recognizes regulatory communities beyond the state, in annexing the 'Internet industry', in engaging with commercial filtering services, in promoting self-governance strategies for Internet users, even in the concept of 'community values' itself allows for a counter position to the perspective of the state.

What can regulatory communities hope to achieve? Elmer discusses the various Internet 'awards' communities (by which websites are reviewed, rated and classified), including Freebie Awards and Totally Cool Queer Sites, as examples of multiple regulatory communities engaged in classification practices and using the interactive Internet technology itself to achieve their regulatory aims.[251] These regulatory communities cannot be said to provide the sense of closure, consistency and certainty that legal regulation promises but, then again, legal regulation cannot deliver on that promise either. Regulatory structures are messy, discontinuous networks of practices which deserve fuller exploration and better understanding than the overly simplistic model produced, and often made the object of regulatory fortressing, in jurispace.

A regulatory theory which is not premised on respect for the regulated subjects, which treats them as mere objects, cannot succeed. A paternalistic and authoritarian regulator who operates without a suitably articulated model of regulatory theory cannot hope to perform their function at all. Rather than imposing abstract and conformist order on complex regulatory spaces, the role of the regulator ought to be in recognizing different regulatory communities, respecting their views and practices, facilitating spaces for discussion and engagement and protecting the Imaginary Domain.

But how are these regulatory communities to be known and how are they to be incorporated into regulatory theory? It is the responsibility of the regulator, the policy maker, the public interest researcher to seek out regulatory communities in order to understand their regulatory practices and explore their regulatory spaces. It is hoped that this book takes some preliminary steps in that direction.

---

251 Elmer G (2000) 'The Economy of Cyberpromotion: Awards on the World Wide Web' in Herman A and Swiss T (eds) *The World Wide Web and Contemporary Cultural Theory*, Routledge: London.

Bibliography

Legislation and Regulations

Broadcasting Services Act 1992
Broadcasting Services Amendment (Online Services) Act 1999 (Cth)
Censorship Act 1996 (WA)
Child Online Protection Act 1998 (US)
Child Pornography Prevention Act 1996 (US)
Chidren's Internet Protection Act 2000 (US)
Classification of Computer Games and Images Act 1995 (Qld)
Classification of Films Act 1991 (Qld)
Classification (Markings for Films and Computer Games) Determination 2007
Classification of Publications Act 1991 (Qld)
Classification of Publications, Films and Computer Games Act 1996 (NT)
Classification (Publications, Films and Computers Games) Act 1995 (Cth)
Classification (Publications, Films and Computer Games) Act 1995 (SA)
Classification (Publications, Films and Computer Games) Amendment Bill 2007
Classification (Publications, Films, Computer Games) Enforcement Act 1995 (ACT)
Classification (Publications, Films and Computer Games) Enforcement Act 1995 (NSW)
Classification (Publications, Films, Computer Games) Enforcement Act 1995 (Tas)
Classification (Publications, Films and Computer Games) (Enforcement) Act 1995 (Vic)
Classification (Publications, Films and Computer Games) (On-Line Services) Amendment Bill 2002 (SA)
Communications Act 1934 (US)
Communications Decency Act 1996 (US)
Communications Legislation Amendment Bill 2002 (Cth)
Communications Legislation Amendment (Content Services) Bill 2007
Crimes Act 1900 (ACT)
Crimes Act 1900 (NSW)
Crimes Act 1958 (Vic)
Criminal Code 1899 (Qld)
Criminal Code 1999 (NT)
Criminal Code Act 1924 (Tas)
Criminal Code (R.S.C. 1985, c. C-46) (Canada)

Customs Act 1876 (UK)
National Classification Code, Classification (Publications, Films and Computer Games) Act 1995 (Cth)
Obscene Publications Act 1959 (UK)
Post Office Act 1953 (UK)
Summary Offences Act 1953 (SA)
Telecommunications Act 1996 (US)
Video Recordings Act 1984 (UK)

Cases

ACLU v Reno 1929 F Supp 824 (ED Pa 1996)
Ashcroft v American Civil Liberties Union 535 US (2002)
Australian Capital Television Pty Ltd v The Commonwealth (no 2) (1992) 177 CLR 106
Crowe v Graham (1968) 121 CLR 375
Electronic Frontiers Australia v Australian Broadcasting Authority (Q2000/979)
Ginsberg v New York 390 US 629 (1968)
Glad Day Bookshop v The Queen, Toronto 619/90 (Ontario Court, General Division), 14 July 1992 (unreported)
Gutnick v Dow Jones and Co Inc (2002) HCA 56
Harrods v Dow Jones (2003) EWHC 1162 (QB)
Hepburn v TCN Channel Nine Pty Ltd (1983) 2 NSWLR 682 at 694
Hughes Tool Co. v Motion Picture Ass'n of America, Inc 66 F. Supp, 1006 (S.D. N.Y. 1946)
Jacoblellis v Ohio 378 US 184 (1964)
Knuller v DPP (1973) AC 435
Lange v Australian Broadcasting Corporation (1997) 190 CLR 520
Little Sisters Book and Art Emporium v Canada (Minister of Justice) 2000 SCC 69, File No 26858, unreported
Mabo v Qld (No 2) (1992) 175 CLR 1
March v E & M H Stramore Pty Ltd (1990-91) 171 CLR 546
Miller v California 413 US 15, 24 (1973)
Nationwide News Pty Ltd v Wills (1992) 175 CLR 1
New York v Ferber 458 US 747 (1982)
R v Butler (1992) 1 SCR 452 (SCC)
R v Close (1948) VLR 445
R v Hicklin (1868) LR 3 QB 360
Roth v United States 354 US 476 (1957)
Steve Jackson Games Inc v United States Secret Service, unreported decision of the United States District Court, Western District of Texas, Austin Division 12 March 1993, archived at http://www.eff.org/legal/cases/SJG/decision.sjg (viewed 19/8/01)

United States v Thomas 74 F.3d 701 (6th Cir. 1996)
Young v New Haven Advocate 315 F 3d 256 (4th Cir. 2002)

News and Press Releases

ABC News Online (2003) *Author takes Gutnick decision to UCHR*, 19 April, http://www.abc.net.au/news/newsitems/s835716.htm.

Adult Video News (1996) 'Positive legal decisions in Colorado, New York and more', September, 46.

Alston R (1999) 'Regulation is not Censorship', *The Australian*, 13 April.

Australian Broadcasting Authority News Release (1999a) ABA decides on adult verification systems for users who wish to access R-rated Internet content, NR 130/1999, 8 December.

Australian Broadcasting Authority News Release (1999b) *International research on attitudes to the Internet*, NR 71/1999, 24 August.

Calcutt A (1994) 'Exposed: Computer Porn Scandal in Commons', *Living Marxism*, 22 April.

Clausing J (1998) 'New Rules of Internet Content Fuel the Battle Over Filters', *New York Times Cybertimes*, 6 January.

CSIRO Media Release (1999) *Content Blocking on the Internet*, 14 April.

Department of Communications and the Arts (1997) Media Release on Principles for a Regulatory Framework for On-line Services in the Broadcasting Services Act 1992.

Department of Communications, Information Technology and the Arts Media Release (1999a) *Internet Content Advisory Board Announced*, 26 November.

Department of Communications, Information Technology and the Arts Media Release (1999b) *Regulation of Objectionable Online Material*, 5 October.

Department of Communications, Information Technology and the Arts Media Release (1999c) *New Guide Helps Families Manage Net Access*, 22 December.

Department of Communications, Information Technology and the Arts Media Release (1999d) *Senate Passes Internet Content Legislation*, 26 May.

Electronic Frontiers Australia Media Release (1999) *Australians Reject Net Censorship*, 29 August, http://www.efa.org.au/Publish/PR9908s9.html (viewed 27/7/01).

Findlaw (2003a) *New Offences to Clamp Down on Internet Child Pornography*, 7 April, via http://www.findlaw.com/news (viewed 7/4/03).

Findlaw (2003b) *Amendments to Regulation the Publication of Prohibited Internet Content Passed by Senate*, 11 September, http://www.findlaw.com.au/news/default.asp?task=read&id=16567&site=LE (viewed 22/9/03).

Forbes M (1999) 'Porn sites head offshore to beat law', *Sydney Morning Herald*, 9 June.

Green P (1998) 'Net Addicts Fix at Home', *The Australian*, 29 May.

Guilliatt R and Casimir J (1996) 'The Return of the Wowsers', *Sydney Morning Herald*, 6 July.

Hamilton C (2002) 'Admit it: The left has lost its way', *The Age*, 14 May.

Hamilton C (2003) 'Kids' exposure to porn must be curbed', *The Canberra Times*, 7 March.

Harmon A (1995) 'On-Line Service Provider Draws Protest in Censor Flap', *LA Times*, 12 December.

Hayes S (2000) 'ABA fails to stop porn site', *Australian IT*, 8 June.

Marr D (2002) 'Opinion: The letter that dare not speak its name', *Sydney Morning Herald*, 2 January.

Martin L (2002) 'Opinion: Alston's X files: the secret truth about Internet censorship', *Sydney Morning Herald*, 21 January.

New Scientist (2002) 'Peekabooty aims to banish internet censorship' 19 February.

Quittner J (1997) 'Empire State Censorship', *The Netly News*, 4 March.

Reichel B (1996) 'New Directions in Censorship', *Artlines*, Issue 1(1), 1.

Reuters News (2003) 'Net Censorship Debate Rages as POW Pictures Pulled', http://www.reuters.com/newsArticle.jhtml?type=internetNewsstoryID=2446564 (viewed 1/4/03).

Rocks D (2000) 'Cyber Skin', *Business Week*, Issue 3667, p10.

Rollins A (1999) 'Alston Brands Lesbians "Not Normal"', *The Age*, 26 May.

Scheeres J (2002) 'When Kid Porn Isn't Kid Porn', *Wired News*, 8 May, http://www.wired.com/news/business/0,1367,52345,00.html (viewed 9/5/02).

Shiff G (1997) 'Internet Censorship in Australia', *Metro Magazine*, No 108, 21.

Sinclair J (1999a) 'Net censorship under fire', *The Age*, 24 August.

Sinclair J (1999b) 'Sex sites and the gov.au connection', *Fairfax IT*, 7 June.

Sydney Morning Herald (2003a) 'Kids drawn into vile web porn as '60s generation sits on its hands', 3 March (viewed online 4/3/03).

Sydney Morning Herald (2003b) 'We've seen it all before, say teen surfers', 3 March (viewed online 4/3/03).

The Age (2003a) 'Net porn traps unsuspecting', 3 March (viewed online 4/3/03).

The Age (2003b) 'Regulations fail to protect children', 4 March (viewed online 4/3/03).

The Age (2003c) 'Soaring Premiums Take their Toll on Festivals', 4 January, http://www.theage.com/articles/2003/01/03/1041566224854.html (viewed 6/1/03).

Time Magazine (1995) 'Cyberporn issue', 3 July.

Uninews (1999) 'Internet Censorship Laws Condemned', (Vol.8 No.30), 30 August.

Verkaik R (2002) 'Libel laws used to curb web protests', *Independent.co.uk*, 18 December, http://news.independent.co.uk/digital/news/story/story.jsp?story=362634.

Vnuk H (2003) 'X-rated? Outdated', *The Age*, 20 September at 8.

Wakeley (1996) 'The New Stranger Danger on the Net', *The Age*, 14 May.

Wardill S (2002) 'Code to push Internet out of reach', *Courier Mail*, 13 May.

ZDNet (2001) *Australian censorship leads Web filter market growth*, 18 September, http://www.zdnet.com.au/newstech/enterprise/story/0,2000025001, 20260515,00.htm.

ZDNet Australia (1999a) *Australia joins net censorship club*, 26 May, http://www.zdnet.com.au/newstech/news/story/0,2000025345,20103417,00.htm.

ZDNet Australia (1999b) *Gay community lashes Net censorship proposal*, 5 May, http://www.zdnet.com.au/newstech/news/story/0,200002534,20103359,00.htm.

ZDNet Australia (2001a) *Taming the Web*, 20 April, http://www.zdnet.com.au/newstech/ebusiness/story/0,2000024981,20216841,00.htm.

ZDNet Australia (2001b) *GTA3 officially banned in Australia*, 13 December, http://www.zdnet.com.au/newstech/enterprise/story/0,2000025001,20262360,00.htm.

ZDNet Australia (2001c) *New Australian Net censorship laws condemned*, 19 November, http://www.zdnet.com.au/newstech/security/story/0,2000024985, 20261920,00.htm.

ZDNet Australia (2001d) *Hackers to unleash anti-censorship tool*, 6 May, http://www.zdnet.com.au/newstech/security/story/0,2000024985,20220053,00.htm.

ZDNet (2001e) *Australian censorship leads Web filter market growth*, 18 September, http://www.zdnet.com.au/newstech/enterprise/story/0,2000025001, 20260515,00.htm.

ZDNet Australia (2002a) *Net censorship? AOL bans independent news source*, 24 January, http://www.zdnet.com.au/newstech/ebusiness/story/0,20000, 24981,20263129,00.htm.

ZDNet Australia (2002b) *SA pollies debate Net censorship bill*, 8 July, http://www.zdnet.com.au/newstech/security/story/0,20000,24985,20266592m00.htm.

ZDNet Australia (2002c) *Exclusive: Alston Hits Back*, 27 November, http://www.zdnet.com.au/newstech/communications/story/0,2000024993,20270255,00.htm.

ZDNet Australia (2002d) *EFA: Alston covering tracks on Net censorship failure*, 22 July, http://www.zdnet.com.au/newstech/security/story/0,2000024985, 20266815,00.htm.

ZDNet Australia (2002e) *Will NSW opt for Net censorship?*, 11 March, http://www.zdnet.com.au/newstech/communications/story/0,2000024993,20263957,00.htm.

Books and Articles

2600 Australia (2000a) 'Evading the *Broadcasting Services Amendment (Online Services) Act 1999*', http://www.2600.org.au/censorship-evasion.html, updated 4 January 2000.

2600 Australia (2000b) 'Response to Shake Communication's paper on censorship', http://www.2600.org.au/shake-response.html.

Albury K (1999) 'NVE and Australian Community Standards: Whose community are we talking about?', *Adult Industry Review*, Vol 2(3), archived at http://libertus.net/censor/odocs/alburynve.html (viewed 7/4/03).

Altman D (2001) *Global Sex*, Allen and Unwin: Sydney.

American Library Association (1996) *Statement on Labelling – An Interpretation of the Library Bill of Rights*, http://www.ala.org/oif/labeling.html (viewed 27/7/01).

Anderson B (1983) *Imagined Communities: Reflections on the Origins and Spread of Nationalism* (rev. edn.), Verso: London.

Aoki K (1996) '(Intellectual) Property and Sovereignty: Notes Toward a Cultural Geography of Authorship', *Stanford Law Review*, v48, 1293.

Appadurai A (1990) 'Disjuncture and Difference in the Global Cultural Economy', in Featherstone M (ed.) *Global Culture: Nationalism, Globalization and Modernity*, Sage Publications: London.

Arcand B (1993) *The Jaguar and the Anteater: Pornography Degree Zero*, Verso: New York.

Argyle K and Shields R (1996) 'Is There a Body in the Net?' in Shields R (ed.) *Cultures of the Internet: Virtual Spaces, Real Histories and Living Bodies*, Sage: London.

Arnason JP (1990) 'Nationalism, Globalization and Modernity', in Featherstone M (ed.) *Global Culture: Nationalism, Globalization and Modernity*, Sage Publications: London.

Ashworth GJ, White PE and Winchester HPM (1988) 'The red-light district in the West European city: a neglected aspect of the urban landscape', *Geoforum*, v19(2), 201–212.

Assister A (1988) 'Romance Fiction: Porn for Women?' in Day G and Bloom C (eds) *Perspectives on Pornography: Sexuality in Film and Literature*, St Martin's Press: New York.

Assister A (1989) *Pornography, Feminism and the Individual*, Pluto Press: London.

Attorney General's Commission on Pornography (1986) *Final Report Vols 1 and 2*, Washington, DC ('The Meece Commission').

Australian Broadcasting Authority (1995) *Issues Paper on the Investigation into the Content of On-Line Services*, ABA: Canberra.

Australian Broadcasting Authority (1996) *Investigation into the Content of On-Line Services*, ABA: Canberra.

Australian Broadcasting Authority (1999a) *Restricted Access Systems Declaration (No. 1) made under the Broadcasting Services Act 1992*, 7 December, ABA: Canberra.

Australian Broadcasting Authority (1999b) *Online services content regulation: background/history of regulatory scheme*, http://www.aba.gov.au/what/online/background.htm.

Australian Broadcasting Authority (1999c) *Online services content regulation: Internet and some international regulatory issues relating to content*, http://www.aba.gov.au/what/online/unesco_report.htm.

Australian Broadcasting Authority (1999d) *Online services content regulation: Ministers directions*, http://www.aba.gov.au/what/online/ministers_directions.htm.

Australian Broadcasting Authority (1999e) *Online services content regulation: Overview of regulatory scheme*, http://www.aba.gov.au/what/online/overview.

Australian Broadcasting Authority (1999f) *Online services content regulation: Research*, http://www.aba.gov.au/what/online/research.htm.

Australian Broadcasting Authority (2000) *Australian Families Guide to the Internet*, http://www.aba.gov.au/family (viewed 29/2/00).

Australian Broadcasting Authority (2001) *The Internet at Home: A Report on Internet Use in the Home*, ABA: Sydney.

Australian Law Reform Commission (1986) *The Recognition of Aboriginal Customary Laws, Report no 31*, AGPS: Canberra.

Australian Law Reform Commission (1991a) *Film and Literature Censorship Procedure, Report no 55*, National Capital Printing: Canberra.

Australian Law Reform Commission (1991b) *Censorship Procedure. Discussion Paper 47*, AGPS: Canberra.

Baddeley S (1997) 'Governmentality' in Loader BD (ed.) *The Governance of Cyberspace: Politics, Technology and Global Restructuring*, Routledge: London.

Balkin JM (1998) *Cultural Software: A Theory of Ideology*, Yale University Press: New Haven.

Balkin JM, Noveck BS and Roosevelt K (1999) *Filtering the Internet: A Best Practices Model*, Bertelsmann Foundation Publishers: Gütersloh.

Barlow JP (1994) 'The Economy of Ideas', *Wired* 2.03, 84.

Barlow JP (1996) 'Declaration of the Independence of Cyberspace', *Cyber-Rights Electronic List*, 8 February.

Baron L (1990) 'Pornography and gender equality: an empirical analysis', *Journal of Sex Research*, vol 27(3), 363.

Barthes R (1974) *S/Z*, trans Miller R, Hill and Wang: New York.

Barthes R (1993) *Camera Obscura*, Vintage: London.

Batty M (1997) 'Virtual Geography', *Futures*, 29, 4/5, 337.

Baumann Z (1992) 'A Sociological Theory of Postmodernity' in *Intimations of Postmodernity*, Routledge: London.

Beattie S (1997) 'Is Mediation a real Alternative to Law? Pitfalls for Aboriginal Participants', *Australian Dispute Resolution Journal*, v8(1), 57.

Beattie S (unpublished) 'Contents Under Pressure: Interactive Media and the Return of Political Censorship'.

Beck U (1992) *Risk Society: Towards a New Modernity*, trans. Ritter M, Sage: London.

Bell D (1995) 'Perverse Dynamics, Sexual Citizenship and the Transformation of Intimacy' in Bell D and Valentine G (eds) *Mapping Desire: Geographies of Sexualities*, Routledge: London.

Bell D (2001) *An Introduction to Cybercultures*, Routledge: London, Chapter 6 'Community and Cyberculture'.

Bell D and Valentine G (eds) (1995) *Mapping Desire: Geographies of Sexualities*, Routledge: London.

Bell V (1995) 'Bio-politics and the Spectre of Incest: Sexuality and/in the Family', in Featherstone M, Lash S and Robertson R (eds) *Global Modernities*, Sage Publications: London.

Benedetti P and Detlart N (eds) (1970) *Forward Through the Rearview Window: Reflections on and by Marshall McLuhan*, MIT Press: Cambridge, MA.

Benedict M (ed.) (1991) *Cyberspace: First Steps*, MIT Press: Cambridge. MA.

Benjamin J (1986) 'A Desire of One's Own: Psychoanalytic Feminism and Intersubjective Space', in de Laurentis T (ed.) *Feminist Studies/Critical Studies*, Indiana University Press: Bloomington.

Bensley L and Van Eeenwyk J (2001) 'Video Games and Real-Life Aggression: Review of the Literature', *Journal of Adolescent Health*, Vol 29, 244.

Bernstein A (1997) 'How to Make a New Tort: Three Paradoxes', *Texas Law Review*, v75, 1539.

Bertelsmann Foundation (1999a) *Comments on the Bertelsmann Foundation Recommendations*, Bertelsmann Foundation Publishers: Gütersloh.

Bertelsmann Foundation (1999b) *Risk Assessment and Opinions concerning the Control of Misuse on the Internet*, Bertelsmann Foundation Publishers: Gütersloh.

Bertelsmann Foundation (1999c) *Self-Regulation for Responsibility and Control on the Internet*, Bertelsmann Foundation Publishers: Gütersloh.

Bertelsmann Foundation (1999d) *Self-regulation of Internet Content*, Bertelsmann Foundation Publishers: Gütersloh.

Bey H (1996) 'The Information War' in Druckery T (ed.) *Electronic Culture: Technology and Virtual Representation*, Aperture: New York.

Bhabha H (1990) *Nation and Narration*, Routledge: London.

Bhabha H (1994) *The Location of Culture*, Routledge: London.

Bijker and Law (eds) (1992) *Shaping Technology/Building Society: Studies in Sociotechnical Change*, MIT Press: Cambridge, MA.

Bingham N (1999) 'Unthinkable complexity? Cyberspace otherwise', in Crang M, Crang P and May J (eds) *Virtual Geographies: Bodies, Space and Relations*, Routledge: London.

Black J (2001) 'Decentring Regulation: The Role of Regulation and Self Regulation in a "Post-Regulatory" World', in Freedman M (ed.) *Current Legal Problems*, Oxford University Press: New York.

Black J (2002a) 'Regulatory Conversations', *Journal of Law and Society*, Volume 29 (1), 163.

Black J (2002b) 'Critical Reflections on Regulation', *Australian Journal of Legal Philosophy*, v27(1), 46.
Blake W (1984) *Songs of Innocence and Experience*, Dover: New York (originally published 1826).
Blomley NK (1994) *Law, Space, and the Geographies of Power*, The Guilford Press: New York.
Blomley NK, Delaney D and Ford RT (eds) *The Legal Geographies Reader*, Blackwell: Oxford, UK.
Bloom C (1988) 'Grinding with the Bachelor: Pornography in a Machine Age', in Day G and Bloom C (eds) *Perspectives on Pornography: Sexuality in Film and Literature*, St Martin's Press: New York.
Bonnett A (1989) 'Situationism, Geography and Poststructuralism', *Environment and Planning D: Society and Space*, v7, 131.
Borden I (2001) *Skateboarding, Space and the City: Architecture and the Body*, Berg: Oxford.
Boyle J (1996) *Shamans, Software, and Spleens: Law and the Construction of the Information Society*, Harvard University Press: Cambridge, MA.
Boyle J (1997) *Foucault in Cyberspace*, http://www.law.duke.edu/boylesite/foucault.htm (viewed 27/7/01).
Brand JE (2002) *A Review of the Classification Guidelines for Films and Computer Games*, prepared for the OFLC, 11 February, OFLC: Canberra.
Brooks J and Boa I (eds) (1995) *Resisting the Virtual Life*, City Light Books: San Francisco.
Brown M (1996) 'The Portrayal of Violence in the Media: Impacts and Implications for Policy', *Trends and Issues in Criminal Justice No 55*, Australian Institute of Criminology: Canberra.
Brown W (1995) *States of Injury: Essays on Power and Freedom in Late Modernity*, Princeton University Press: Princeton.
Burk DL (1997) 'Jurisdiction in a World without Borders', *Virginia Journal of Law and Technology*, Vol 1, 3.
Burroughs WS (1979) *Ah Pook is Here and Other Texts*, John Calde: London.
Burrows R (1997) 'Virtual culture, urban social polarisation and social science fiction' in Loader BD (ed.) *The Governance of Cyberspace: Politics, Technology and Global Restructuring*, Routledge: London.
Busby K (1994) 'LEAF and Pornography: Litigating on Equality and Sexual Representations', *Canadian Journal of Law and Society*, vol 9.1, 165.
Calcutt A (1994) 'Exposed: Computer Porn Scandal in Commons', *Living Marxism*, 22 April.
Carol A (1993) *Fake Science and Pornography*, Libertarian Alliance: London.
Carter A (1993) *The Sadeian Woman: An Exercise in Cultural History*, Virago: London.
Carter J and Miller D (eds) (1998) *Virtualism and its Discontents*, Berg: Oxford.
Carter P (1988) *The Road to Botany Bay: An Exploration of Landscape and History*, Knopf: New York.

Cassell J and Jenkins H (eds) (1999) *From Barbie to Mortal Combat: Gender and Computer Games*, MIT Press: Cambridge, MA.

Castells M (1996) *The Information Age: Economy, Society and Culture Vol 1: The Rise of the Network Society*, Blackwell: Oxford.

Castells M (2001) *The Internet Galaxy: Reflections on the Internet, Business and Society*, Oxford University Press: Oxford.

Castronova E (2001) *Virtual Worlds: A First Hand Account of Market and Society on the Cyberian Frontier*, http://papers.ssrn.com/abstract=294828.

Chalmers R (2002) 'Regulating the Net in Australia: Firing Blanks or Silver Bullets?', *E Law – Murdoch University Electronic Journal of Law*, Vol 9(3), http://www.murdoch.edu.au/elaw/issues/v9n3/chalmers93_text.html (viewed 7/4/03).

Chauncey G (1994) *Gay New York: Gender, Urban Culture, and the Making of the Gay Male World 1890–1940*, Basic: New York.

Chen P (1999) 'Community without Flesh: First Thoughts on the New Broadcasting Services Amendment (Online Services) Bill 1999', *M/C: A Journal of Media and Culture* 2.3, http://english.uq.edu.au/mc/9905/bill (viewed 1/10/01).

Chen P (2000a) *Australia's Online Censorship Regime: The Advocacy Coalition Framework and Governance Compared*, PhD Thesis, Australian National University.

Chen P (2000b) 'Pornography, Protection, Prevarication: The Politics of Internet Censorship', *University of NSW Law Journal*, v6 (1), http://www.austlii.edu.au/cgi-bin/disp.pl/au/other/unswlj/forum/2000/vol6n1/Chen.html?query=%7e+chen (viewed 6/3/01).

Chen P (2002) 'Australia: Where forward co-regulation?', paper presented at *Growing Australia Online*, 3–4 December, Canberra.

Chernaik L (1999) 'Transnationalism, technoscience and difference: the analysis of material-semiotic practices', in Crang M, Crang P and May J (eds) *Virtual Geographies: Bodies, Space and Relations*, Routledge: London.

Christensen NB (1999) *Inuit in Cyberspace: Embedding Offline Identity and Culture Online*, http://home.worldonline.dk/nbc/arcus.html (viewed 2/5/01).

Clark D (2001) 'The guidelines and Advertising Review and how they affect the film industry', speech at *Australian International Movie Convention*, 16 August.

Clark D (2003) 'Film Classification and Harmonisation in Australia', speech delivered at *ShowCanada*, 30 April.

Clark D (2005) 'Launch of New OFLC Classification Markings: "Managing Content in a World of Borderless Entertainment"', 6 June, 1–4.

Clark D (2007) 'Address to the Conference', *International Ratings Conference*, 26 February.

Clark GL (1981) 'Law, the state and the spatial integration of the United States', *Environment and Planning A*, 13(10), 1189–1322.

Clark GL (1985) *Judges and the Cities: Interpreting Local Autonomy*, University of Chicago Press: Chicago.

Clark GL (1989a) 'The context of federal regulation: propaganda in the US union elections', *Transactions of the Institute of British Geographers*, NS 14, 59–73.
Clark GL (1989b) 'Law and the interpretive turn in the social sciences' *Urban Geography*, 10(3), 209–228.
Clark GL (1989c) *Unions and Communities under Siege: American Communities and the Crisis of Organised Labour*, Cambridge University Press: Cambridge.
Clark GL (1989d) 'The Geography of Law' in Peet R and Thrift N (eds) *New Models in Human Geography*, Unwin Hyman: London.
Clark GL (1992) 'Problematic status of corporate regulation in the United States: towards a new moral order', *Environment and Planning A*, 24, 704–725.
Clark GL (1993) 'The legitimacy of judicial decision making in the context of Richmond v Croson', *Urban Geography*, 13(3), 205–229.
Classification Review Board (2001) *Review of GTA3*, 40th Meeting, 11 December.
Clegg S (1989) *Frameworks of Power*, Sage Publications: Newbury Park, CA.
Cohen R and Rai SM (2000) *Global Social Movements*, The Althone Press: London.
Cohen S (1972) *Folk Devils and Moral Panics: The Creation of the Mods and Rockers*, Oxford University Press: Oxford.
Coleman P (2000) *Obscenity, Blasphemy, Sedition: The Rise and Fall of Literary Censorship in Australia* (rev. edn.), Duffy and Snellgrove: Sydney.
Collins RKL and Skover DM (1994) 'Changing Images of the State: The Pornographic State', *Harvard Law Review*, Vol 107, 1374.
Colomina B (ed) (1992) *Sexuality and Space*, Princeton Architectural Press: New York.
Commission on Child Online Protection (COPA) (2000) *Report to Congress*, 20 October.
Committee of Australian University Directors of Information Technology (CAUDIT) (1997) *Code of Practice*, CAUDIT: Canberra.
Computer Professionals for Social Responsibility (1999) *One Planet, One Net: Principles for the Internet Era*, http://www.cpsr.org/program/nii/onenet.html.
Connett London D and Henley Helsinki J (1996) 'These men are not paedophiles – they are Internet abusers', *The Observer*, 25 August, 19.
Considine M (2002) *Joined at the Lip? What does Network Research Tell us about Governance?*, http://www.public-policy.unimelb.edu.au/events/IPSA_Conference.html.
Cooks L (2001) 'Negotiating National Identity and Social Movement in Cyberspace: Natives and Invaders on the Panama-L Listserv', in Ebo B (ed.) *Cyberimperialism? Global Relations in the New Electronic Frontier*, Praeger: Westport, CT.
Cooper A, Scherer CR, Boies SC and Gordon BL (1999) 'Sexuality on the Internet: From Sexual Exploration to Pathological Expression', *Professional Psychology: Research and Practice*, v30(2), 154.

Cornell D (1993) *Transformations: Recollective Imagination and Sexual Difference*, Routledge: New York.

Cornell D (1995) *The Imaginary Domain: Abortion, Pornography and Sexual Harassment*, Routledge: New York.

Cornell D and hooks b (1998) 'Dialogue: The Imaginary Domain: A Discussion Between Drucilla Cornell and bell hooks', *Women's Rights Law Reporter*, vol 19, 261.

Cotteral R (1986) 'Law and Sociology: Notes on the Confrontation of Disciplines', *Journal of Law and Society*, Vol 13(1), 9–34.

Cotteral R (1995) *Law's Community: Legal Theory in Sociological Perspective*, Clarendon Press: Oxford.

Court JH (1984) 'Sex and violence: a ripple effect', in Malamuth NM and Donnerstein E (eds) *Pornography and Sexual Aggression*, Academic Press: London.

Coyne R (1999) *Technoromanticism: Digital Narrative, Holism and the Romance of the Real*, The MIT Press: Cambridge, MA.

Crang M (2001) 'Public space, urban space and electronic space: would the real city please stand up?' in Holmes D (ed.) *Virtual Globalization: Virtual Spaces/ Tourist Spaces*, Routledge: London.

Crang M, Crang P and May J (eds) (1999) *Virtual Geographies: Bodies, Space and Relations*, Routledge: London.

Crang M and Thrift N (eds) (2000) *Thinking Space*, Routledge: London.

Creed B (2002) *Media Matrix: Sexing the New Reality*, Allen and Unwin: Sydney.

CSIRO (1998) *Blocking Content on the Internet: A Technical Perspective*, June 1998.

CSIRO (2001) *Effectiveness of Internet Filtering Software Products*, report prepared for the Australian Broadcasting Authority, September.

Curry M (1995) 'On Space and Spatial Practice in Contemporary Geography', in Earle C, Mathewson K and Kezer M (eds) *Concepts in Human Geography*, Rowman and Littlefield Publishers: Lanham.

Dahl G (1999) 'The Anti-Reflexivisit Revolution: On the Affirmationism of the New Right', in Featherstone M and Lash S (eds) *Spaces of Culture: City, Nation, World*, Sage Publications: London.

Davies M (1994) *Asking the Law Question*, The Law Book Company: North Ryde, NSW.

Davies M (1999) *Gangland: Cultural Elites and the New Generationalism* (2nd edn.), Allen and Unwin: St Leonards, NSW.

Davies M (2000) *Asking the Law Question* (2nd edn.), The Law Book Company: North Ryde, NSW.

Day G (1988) 'Looking at Women: Notes toward a Theory of Porn', in Day G and Bloom C (eds) *Perspectives on Pornography: Sexuality in Film and Literature*, St Martin's Press: New York.

Day G and Bloom C (eds) (1988) *Perspectives on Pornography: Sexuality in Film and Literature*, St Martin's Press: New York.
de Certeau M (1984) *The Practice of Everyday Life*, trans. Rendall S, University of California Press: Berkeley.
de Sade (1990) *120 Days of Sodom and Other Writings*, trans Wainhouse, Arrow Books: London.
de Sousa Santos B (1987) 'Law: A Map of Misreading', *Journal of Law and Society*, v14, 279.
Debord G (1967) *The Society of the Spectacle*, Black Spot Press.
Deleuze G and Guattari F (1987) *A Thousand Plateaus: Capitalism and Schizophrenia*, translated by Massumi B, University of Minnesota Press: Minneapolis.
Dement L (1998) 'Dying Frightened Gasps of Old Men in Suits', *Artlink*, V 18(3), 17–21.
Department of City Planning, City of New York (1994) *Adult Entertainment Study 66*.
Department of Communications and the Arts (1990) *BBS Task Force*.
Department of Communications and the Arts (1997) *Principles for a Regulatory Framework for On-line Services in the Broadcasting Services Act 1992*.
Department of Communications, Information Technology and the Arts (1999) *Frequently Asked Questions*, http://www.noie.gov.au/legrev/content/ContentFAQ_16July.htm.
Department of Communications Information Technology and the Arts (2002) *A Review of the Operation of Schedule 5 to the Broadcasting Services Act 1992*, September.
Dibbell J (1998) *My Tiny Life: Crime and Passion in a Virtual World*, Fourth Estate: London.
Dickie J (1997) 'Challenges for Classifiers', paper presented at the conference: *Violence, Crime and the Entertainment Media*, Australian Institute of Criminology, 4–5 December.
Dickinson T (2003) 'Cognitive Dissident: An Interview with John Perry Barlow', *Mother Jones*, 3 February, http://www.motherjones.com/news/99/2003/06/we_26_01.html (viewed 3/5/03).
Dodge M and Kitchin R (2001) *Mapping Cyberspace*, Routledge: London.
Drazen P (2002) *Anime Explosion: The What? Why? and Wow! of Japanese Animation*, Stonebridge Press: Berkeley, CA.
Druckery T (ed.) (1996) *Electronic Culture: Technology and Virtual Representation*, Aperture: New York.
Duncanson K (2001) 'Tracing the Law Through The Matrix', *Griffith Law Review*, v10(2), 16.
Durkin K and Aisbett K (1999) *Computer Games and Australians Today*, OFLC: Sydney.
Dworkin A (1981) *Pornography: Men Possessing Women*, Women's Press: London.

Dworkin A (1987) *Intercourse*, Secker and Warburg: London.

Dworkin A (1988) 'Pornography is a Civil Rights Issue for Women', *University of Michigan Journal of Law*, Vol 21, 55.

Dworkin A and MacKinnon C (1988) *Pornography and Civil Rights: A New Day for Women's Equality*, Organizing Against Pornography: Minneapolis.

Dyer R (1985) 'Male Gay Porn: Coming to Terms', *Jump Cut: A Review of Contemporary Media*, V30 (March), 27.

Dyson E, Gilder G, Keyworth G and Toffler A (1996) 'Cyberspace and the American Dream: A Magna Carta for the Knowledge Age', *The Information Society*, No 12, 295–308.

Eagleton T (1983) *Literary Theory: An Introduction*, University of Minnesota Press: Minneapolis.

Eberwein R (1999) *Sex Ed: Film, Video, and the Framework of Desire*, Rutgers University Press: New Brunswick.

Ebo B (ed.) (2001) *Cyberimperialism? Global Relations in the New Electronic Frontier*, Praeger: Westport, CT.

Edelman M (1971) *Politics as Symbolic Action: Mass Arousal and Quiescence*, Markham: New York.

Ehrenreich B, Hess E and Jacobs G (1986) *Re-Making Love: The Feminization of Sex*, Anchor Books: New York.

Ehrlich E (1936) *Fundamental Principles of the Sociology of Law*, (trans 2002 Walter J Moll), Transaction Publishers: New Jersey.

Electronic Frontiers Australia (1997) *International Censorship Issues*, http://www.efa.org.au/Issues/Censor/cens3.html, updated 4 July 1997.

Electronic Frontiers Australia (1998) http://www.efa.org.au/Publish/publrev9805.html (viewed 8/5/99).

Electronic Frontiers Australia (1999a) *Internet Regulation in Australia*, http://www.efa.org.au/Issues/Censor/cens1.html, updated 27 June 1999.

Electronic Frontiers Australia (1999b) *Classification: Censorship by another Name*, http://www.efa.org.au/Issues/Censor/cens5.html, updated 15 November 1999.

Electronic Frontiers Australia (1999c) *Content Rating and Filtering*, http://www.efa.org.au/Issues/Censor/cens2.html, updated 20 June 1999.

Electronic Frontiers Australia (1999d) *Electronic Frontiers Australia Response to IIA Draft Code of Conduct, Version 5.0*, http://www.efa.org.au/Publish/iiacode5.htm.

Electronic Frontiers Australia (1999e) *Submission Draft Model State/Territory Legislation On-Line Content Regulation*, updated 29 September 1999.

Electronic Frontiers Australia (2002) *Internet Censorship: Law and Policy around the World*, http://www.efa.org.au/Issues/Censor/cens3.html.

Elkin-Koren N (1996) 'Public/Private and Copyright Reform in Cyberspace', *Journal of Computer Mediated Communication*, 2, 2. http://www.ascusc.org/jcmc/vol2/issue2/elkin.html.

Ellickson RC (2001) 'Controlling chronic misconduct in city spaces: Of panhandlers, skid rows, and public-space zoning', in Blomley N, Delaney D and Ford RT (eds) *The Legal Geographies Reader*, Blackwell: Oxford, UK.

Ellis R (1988) 'Disseminating Desire: Grove Press and "The End(s) of Obscenity"', in Day G and Bloom C (eds) *Perspectives on Pornography: Sexuality in Film and Literature*, St Martin's Press: New York.

Elmer G (2000) 'The Economy of Cyberpromotion: Awards on the World Wide Web' in Herman A and Swiss T (eds) *The World Wide Web and Contemporary Cultural Theory*, Routledge: London.

Emes C (1997) 'Is Mr Pac Man Eating our Children? A Review of the Effect of Video Games on Children', *Canadian Journal of Psychiatry*, Vol 42, 409.

Eriksson LD (1998) 'The Indeterminacy of law or Law as a Deliberative Practice', in Hirvonen A (ed.) *Polycentricity: The Multiple Scenes of Law*, Pluto Press: London.

Eriksson LD, Hirvonen A, Minkkinen P and Poyhonen J (1998) 'Introduction: A Polytical Manifesto' in Hirvonen A (ed.) *Polycentricity: The Multiple Scenes of Law*, Pluto Press: London.

Ewald F (1991) 'Norms, Discipline and Law' in Post R (ed.) *Law and the Order of Culture*, University of California Press: Berkeley.

Ewick P and Sibley SS (1998) *The Common Place of Law: Stories from Everyday Life*, University of Chicago Press: Chicago.

Featherstone M (ed) (1990) *Global Culture: Nationalism, Globalization and Modernity*, Sage Publications: London.

Featherstone M and Lash S (eds) (1999) *Spaces of Culture: City, Nation, World*, Sage Publications: London.

Findlay M and Duff P (1998) *The Jury Under Attack*, Butterworths: Sydney.

Fink-Eitel H (1992) *Foucault: An Introduction*, Pennbridge Books: Philadelphia.

Finkelstein S (2000) *SmartFilter – I've Got A Little List*, http://setf.com/anticensorware/smartfilter/gotalist.php (viewed 6/3/01).

Fish S (1983) *Is There a Text in this Class? The Authority of Interpretive Communities*, Harvard University Press: Cambridge, MA.

Fitzpatrick P (1984) 'Law and Societies', *Osgoode Hall Law Journal*, v22, 115 at 127.

Flood M and Hamilton C (2003a) *Discussion Paper Number 52: Youth and Pornography in Australia: Evidence on the extent of exposure and likely effects*, The Australia Institute: Canberra.

Flood M and Hamilton C (2003b) *Discussion Paper Number 53: Regulating Youth Access to Pornography*, The Australia Institute: Canberra.

Ford R T (1999) 'Law's territory (a history of jurisdiction)', *Michigan Law Review*, Vol 97, 843 at 847.

Foucault M (1972) *The Archaeology of Knowledge*, Tavistock: London.

Foucault M (1977) *Discipline and Punish: The Birth of the Prison*, Penguin: London.

Foucault M (1978) *The History of Sexuality Volume I: An Introduction*, Penguin: London.

Foucault M (1980a) 'The Confession of the Flesh' in Gordon C (ed.) *Power/ Knowledge: Selected Interviews and Other Writings 1972–1977*, Pantheon Books: New York.

Foucault M (1980b) 'The Eye of Power' in Gordon C (ed.) *Power/Knowledge: Selected Interviews and Other Writings, 1972–1977*, Pantheon Books: New York.

Foucault M (1980c) 'Power and Strategies' Gordon C (ed.) *Power/Knowledge: Selected Interviews and Other Writings, 1972–1977*, Pantheon Books: New York.

Foucault M (1980d) 'Two Lectures' in Gordon C (ed.) *Power/Knowledge: Selected Interviews and Other Writings, 1972–1977*, Pantheon Books: New York.

Foucault M (1982) 'The Subject and Power' in Dreyfus HL and Rabinow P *Michel Foucault: Beyond Structuralism and Hermeneutics*, University of Chicago Press: Chicago, p 208–26.

Foucault M (1983) 'Afterword: The Subject and Power' in Dreyfus HL and Rabinow P *Michel Foucault: Beyond Structuralism and Hermeneutics*, University of Chicago Press: Chicago.

Foucault M (1984) 'Governmentality' in Rabinow P (ed.) *The Foucault Reader: An Introduction to Foucault's Thought*, Penguin: London.

Foucault M (1985) *The Use of Pleasure: The History of Sexuality: 2*, Penguin: London.

Foucault M (1986) *The Care of the Self: The History of Sexuality: 3*, Penguin: London.

France A (1894) *The Red Lily*, Project Gutenberg, http://www.gutenberg.org/etext/3922.

Fraser A (1984) 'Legal Amnesia: Modernism versus the Republican Tradition in American Legal Thought', *Telos*, v 60, 15.

Frasier DK (1990) *Russ Meyer – the Life and Films*, McFarland and Co: Jefferson, New York.

Free Expression Policy Project (2001) *Identifying What is Harmful or Inappropriate for Minors: White Paper Submitted to the Committee on Tools and Strategies for Protecting Kids from Pornography and their Applicability to other Inappropriate Internet Content*, http://www.fepproject.org/whitePapers/NRCwhitePapers.html (viewed 3/3/02).

Freedman J (2002) *Media Violence and its Effects on Aggression: Assessing the Scientific Evidence*, University of Toronto Press: Toronto.

Friedman J (1990) 'Being in the World: Globalization and Localization', in Featherstone M (ed.) *Global Culture: Nationalism, Globalization and Modernity*, Sage Publications: London.

Friese H and Wagner P (1999) 'Not All that is Solid Melts into Air: Modernity and Contingency', in Featherstone M and Lash S (eds) *Spaces of Culture: City, Nation, World*, Sage Publications: London.

Frissen P (1997) 'The virtual state: postmodernisation, informationisation and public administration' in Loader BD (ed.) *The Governance of Cyberspace: Politics, Technology and Global Restructuring*, Routledge: London.

Fuery P (1995) *Theories of Desire*, Melbourne University Press: Melbourne.

Fulcher H (1989) *The Concept of Community of Interest: A Discussion Paper Which Explores the Concept of Community of Interest as it Applies to Local Government Boundaries*, South Australian Department of Local Government: Adelaide.

Gaitenby A (1996) 'Law's Mapping of Cyberspace: The Shape of New Social Space', *Technological Forecasting and Social Change*, v 52, 135.

Galanter M (1981) 'Justice in many rooms: Courts, private ordering and indigenous law', *Journal of Legal Pluralism*, 19, 1–47.

Gathorne-Hardy J (1998) *Alfred Kinsey: Sex the Measure of All Things: A Biography*, Chatto and Windus: London.

Geertz C (1973a) *The Interpretation of Cultures*, Fontana Press: New York.

Geertz C (1973b) 'Ideology as a Cultural System' in *The Interpretation of Cultures: Selected Essays*, Basic Books: New York.

Geertz C (1983) *Local Knowledge: Further Essays in Interpretive Anthropology*, Basic Books: New York.

Genet J (1989) *Prisoner of Love*, trans. Bray B, Wesleyan University press: Hanover, NH.

Giddens A (1984) *The Constitution of Society*, University of California Press: Berkeley.

Girard R (1977) *Violence and the Sacred*, Johns Hopkins University Press: Baltimore.

Girard R (1984) *Deceit, Desire and the Novel, Self and Other in Literary Structure*, Johns Hopkins University Press: Baltimore.

Global Internet Liberty Campaign (1999) *Australian Government Internet Censorship Proposals Criticised*, http://www.gilc.org/speech/australia.gilc-statement-399.html.

Godwin M (1998) *CyberRights*, Time Books: New York.

Goggin G (2003) 'Digital Rainbows: Inventing the Internet in the Northern Rivers' in Wilson H (ed.) *Belonging in the Rainbow Region: Cultural Perspectives on the NSW North Coast*, Southern Cross University Press: Lismore, NSW.

Goldsmith JL (1998) 'Against Cyberanarchy', *University of Chicago Law Review*, Vol 65, 1199.

Goode E and Ben-Yehuda N (1994) *Moral Panics: The Social Construction of Deviance*, Blackwell: Oxford.

Goodrich P (1990) *Languages of Law: From Logics of Memory to Nomadic Masks*, Weidenfeld and Nicholson: London.

Goodrich P (1998) 'The Laws of Love: Literature, History and the Governance of Kissing', *New York University Review of Law and Social Change*, v24, 183.

Gordon C (ed) (1980) *Power/Knowledge: Selected Interviews and Other Writings 1972–1977*, Pantheon: New York.

Gordon RW (1981) 'Historicism in Legal Scholarship', *Yale Law Journal*, Vol 90, 1017.

Gordon W (1990) 'Toward a Jurisprudence of Benefits: The Norms of Copyright and the Problem of Private Censorship' *University of Chicago Law Review*, Vol 57, 1009.

Graham I (1999a) *Blinded by Smoke: The Hidden Agenda of the Online Services Bill 1999*, http://rene.efa.org.au/liberty/blinded.html.

Graham I (1999b) *The Debate: Government Control or Individual Responsibility*, http://rene.efa.org.au/liberty/debate.html (viewed 22/4/00).

Graham I (2000a) *The Net Labelling Delusion: Saviour or Devil*, http://rene.efa.org.au/liberty/label.htm.

Graham I (2000b) *Not the Community's Guidelines: The History of the Film Classification Guidelines that Banned 'Romance'*, http://libertus.net/censor/rdocs/history_filmgd1.html (viewed 7/4/03).

Graham I (2000c) *The PICS Risk*, http://rene.efa.org.au/liberty/picsrisk.html.

Grbich JE (1992) 'The Body in Legal Theory', *University of Tasmania Law Review*, v11, 26.

Greenfield P, Rickwood P, Tran HC (2001) *Effectiveness of Internet Filtering Software Products*, CSIRO Mathematical and Information Sciences.

Griffin S (1981) *Pornography and Silence: Culture's Revenge against Nature*, The Women's Press: London.

Griffith G (2002) *Censorship in Australia: Regulating the Internet and other Recent Developments, NSW Parliament Briefing Paper*, http://www.parliament.nsw.gov.au/prod/web/PHWebContent.nsf/PHPages/ResearchBf043003?OpenDocument (viewed 7/4/03).

Grillo T (1991) 'The Mediation Alternative: Process Dangers for Women', *Yale Law Journal*, v100(6), 1545.

Gunkel DJ (2001) 'The Empire Strikes Back Again: The Cultural Politics of the Internet', in Ebo B (ed.) *Cyberimperialism? Global Relations in the New Electronic Frontier*, Praeger: Westport, CT.

Gustafsson G (1983) 'Symbolic and Pseudo Policies as Responses to Diffusion of Power', *Policy Sciences*, Vol 15, 269.

Hafner K and Lyon M (1996) *Where Wizards Stay up Late: The Origins of the Internet*, Touchstone Press: New York.

Hajer M (1995) *The Politics of Environmental Discourse: Ecological Modernization and the Policy Process*, Oxford University Press: New York.

Halewood P (1996) 'Law's Bodies: Disembodiment and the Structure of Liberal Property Rights', *Iowa Law Review*, Vol 81, 1331.

Hamilton C and Flood M (2003) *Parents' Attitudes to Regulation of Internet Pornography*, The Australia Institute: Canberra.

Hampton KN and Wellman B (2002) 'The Not So Global Village of Netville', in Wellman B and Haythornthwaite C (eds) *The Internet in Everyday Life*, Blackwell Publishing: Oxford, UK.

Handsley E and Biggins B (2000) 'The sheriff rides into town: a day for rejoicing by innocent westerners', *University of New South Wales Law Journal*, v23, 257.

Harden I and Lewis N (1986) *The Noble Lie*, Hutchinson: London.

Hardy S (1998) *The Reader, The Author, His Woman and Her Lover: Soft-core Pornography and Heterosexual Men*, Cassell: London.

Harpold T and Philip K (2000) 'Of Bugs and Rats: Cyber-Cleanliness, Cyber-Squalor, and the Fantasy-Spaces of Informational Globalization', *Postmodern Culture*, v11.1, http://muse.jhu.edu/journals/pmc/v011/11.1harpold.html (viewed 5/1/01).

Harvey D (1989) *The Condition of Postmodernity*, Johns Hopkins University Press: Baltimore, MD.

Haste C (1994) *Rules of Desire: Sex in Britain, World War I to the Present*, Pimlico: London.

Heath S (1982) *The Sexual Fix*, Macmillan: London.

Heim M (1994) 'The Erotic Ontology of Cyberspace' in *The Metaphysics of Virtual Reality*, Oxford University Press: New York.

Heins M (1997) 'Indecency: The Ongoing American Debate Over Sex, Children, Free Speech, and Dirty Words', *Paper Series on Art, Culture and Society, Paper Number 7*, The Andy Warhol Foundation for the Visual Arts.

Heins M (2001) *Not in Front of the Children: 'Indecency', Censorship, and the Innocence of Youth*, Hill and Wang: New York.

Heins M and Cho C (2001) *Internet Filters: A Public Policy Report*, http://www.ncac.org/issues/internetfilters.html.

Heins M and Cho C (2002) *Media Literacy: An Alternative to Censorship*, Free Expression Policy Project: New York.

Heitman K (2000) 'Vapours and Mirrors', *University of New South Wales Law Journal*, v23, 246.

Herman A and Swiss T (eds) (2000) *The World Wide Web and Contemporary Cultural Theory*, Routledge: London.

Hermer J and Hunt A (1996) 'Official Graffiti of the Everyday', *Law and Society Review*, v30 (5), 455.

Hinchliffe S (2000) 'Entangled Humans: Specyifying powers and their spatialities' in Sharp JP, Routledge P, Philo C and Paddison R (eds) *Entanglements of Power: Geographies of Domination/Resistance*, Routledge: London.

Hirvonen A (ed.) (1998) *Polycentricity: The Multiple Scenes of Law*, Pluto Press: London.

Holmes D (ed.) (2001) *Virtual Globalization: Virtual Spaces/Tourist Spaces*, Routledge: London.

Howell P (2000) 'Victorian sexuality and the moralisation of Cremorne Gardens' in Sharp JP, Routledge P, Philo C and Paddison R (eds) *Entanglements of Power: Geographies of Domination/Resistance*, Routledge: London.

Howitt D and Cumberbatch G (1990) *Pornography: Its Impacts and Influences, a Review of the Available Research Evidence on the Effects of Pornography*, HMSO: London, commissioned by the Home Office Research and Planning Unit, UK.

Hubbard P (2002) 'Pulp Fictions: Mapping the Sexual Landscape', *Journal of Psychogeography and Urban Research*, Vol 1(2) formerly available at: http://www.psychogeography.cok.uk/v1_n2/pulp.htm (viewed 26/2/02).

Human Rights and Equal Opportunity Commission (2002) *Race Hate and the Internet: Background Paper for Cyber-racism Symposium*, HREOC: Sydney.

Hunt A (1992) 'Foucault's Expulsion of Law', *Law and Society Inquiry*, vol 17, 1–38.

Hunt A (1996) *Governance of the Consuming Passions: A History of Sumptuary Regulation*, Macmillan: London.

Hunt A (1999) *Governing Morals: A Social History of Moral Regulation*, Cambridge University Press: Cambridge, UK.

Hunt A and Wickham G (1994) *Foucault and Law: Towards a Sociology of Law as Governance*, Pluto Press: London.

Hunt L (1993) *The Invention of Pornography: Obscenity and the Origins of Modernity 1500–1800*, Zone Books: New York.

Hunter N (1993) 'Identity, Speech, and Equality', *Virginia Law Review*, v79, 1695.

Hunter R and Johnstone R (1995) 'Explaining Law Reform' in Hunter R, Ingleby R and Johnstone R (eds) *Thinking About Law: Perspectives on the History, Philosophy and Sociology of Law*, Allen and Unwin: St Leonards, NSW.

Imken O (1999) 'The convergence of virtual and actual in the Global Matrix: artificial life, geo-economics and psychogeography', in Crang M, Crang P and May J (eds) *Virtual Geographies: Bodies, Space and Relations*, Routledge: London.

Inquiry of the Senate Select Committee on Community Standards Relevant to the Supply of Services Utilising Electronic Technologies (1997), Australian Commonwealth Government: Canberra.

International Political Science Association Committee, Structure and Organisation of Government Research (2002) *Knowledge Networks and Joined-Up Government*, http://www.public-policy.unimelb.edu.au/events/IPSA_Conference.html.

Internet Industry Association (1998) *IIA Industry Code of practice*, Version 4.2.

Internet Industry Association (1999a) *Internet Industry Codes of Practice*, December 1999.

Internet Industry Association (1999b) *About the IIA*, http://www.iia.net.au/join.html.

Internet Industry Association (2000) *Guide for Internet Users: Information about Online Content*, http://www.iia.net.au/guideuser.html.

Irigiray L (1986) *The Speculum of the Other Woman* (Gill GC trans), Cornell University Press: Ithaca, NY.

Irvine JM (1995) 'Regulated Passions: The Invention of Inhibited Sexual Desire and Sexual Addiction' in Terry J and Urla J (eds) *Deviant Bodies: Critical Perspectives on Difference in Science and Popular Culture*, Indiana University Press: Bloomington.

Ithiel de Sola Pool (1990) *Technologies Without Boundaries: On Telecommunications in a Global Age*, edited by Noam EM, Harvard University Press: Cambridge, MA.

Jain SS (1998) 'Inscription Fantasies and Interface Erotics: A Social-Material Analysis of Keyboards, Repetitive Strain Injuries and Products Liability Law', *Hastings Women's Law Journal*, v9, 219.

Jew B (1999) *Cyberjurisdiction – Emerging Issues and Conflicts of Law when Overseas Courts Challenge your Web,* Gilbert and Tobin Publications, http://gtlaw.com.au/templates/publications/default.jsp?puid=76.

Johnson A (1999) *Key Legal and Technical Problems with the Broadcasting Services Amendment (Online Services) Bill 1999*, http://www.securitysearch.net/search/papers/bsaprobs.htm.

Johnson DR and Post DG (1996) 'Law and Borders – The Rise of Law in Cyberspace', *Stanford Law Review*, v 48, 1367.

Johnson P (1996) 'Pornography Drives Technology: Why Not Censor the Internet', *Federal Communications Law Journal*, v49 (1), 217.

Johnson S (2001) *Emergence: The Connected Lives of Ants, Brains, Cities and Software*, Scribner: New York.

Joint Select Committee on Video Material (1988) *Report of the Joint Select Committee on Video Material*, AGPS.

Jordan T (1999) *Cyberpower: The Culture and Politics of Cyberspace and the Internet*, Routledge: London.

Kahn B and Nesson C (eds) (1997) *Borders in Cyberspace: Information Policy and the Global Information Infrastructure, MIT Press*: Cambridge, MA.

Kaplan N (2000) 'Literacy Beyond Books: Reading When All the World's a Web' in Herman A and Swiss T (eds) *The World Wide Web and Contemporary Cultural Theory*, Routledge: London.

Katz JE and Rice RE (2002) 'Syntopia: Access, Civic Involvement, and Social Interaction on the Net', in Wellman B and Haythornthwaite C (eds) *The Internet in Everyday Life*, Blackwell Publishing: Oxford, UK.

Kellerman J (1999) *Savage Spawn – Reflections of Violent Children*, Ballantine: New York.

Kelman M (1987) *A Guide to Critical Legal Studies*, Harvard University Press: Cambridge, MA.

Kelsen H (1967) *Pure Theory of Law*, University of California Press: Berkeley, CA.

Kendall CN (2001) 'The Harms of Gay Male Pornography: A Sex Equality Perspective Post Little Sisters Book and Art Emporium', *Gay and Lesbian Law Journal*, Vol 10, 43.

Kendall G and Wickham G (1999) *Using Foucault's Methods*, Sage: London.

Kendrick W (1987) *The Secret Museum: Pornography in Modern Culture*, Viking: New York.

Kerekes D and Slater D (1995) *Killing for Culture*, Creation Books: San Francisco.

Kim AJ (1998) 'Killers Have More Fun', *Wired* 6.05, http://wired.com/archive/6.05/ultima_pr.html.

King L (1985) 'Censorship and law reform: will changing the law mean a change for the better', in Burstyn V (ed.) *Women against Censorship*, Douglas and McIntyre: Toronto.

Kipnis L (1993) 'She-male fantasies and the aesthetics of pornography', in Church Gibson P and Gibson R (eds) *Dirty Looks: Women, Pornography, Power*, British Film Institute: London.

Kitchin R (1998) *Cyberspace*, Wiley: Chicksfer.

Kraidy MM (2001) 'From Imperialism to Glocalization: A Theoretical Framework for the Information Age', in Ebo B (ed.) *Cyberimperialism? Global Relations in the New Electronic Frontier*, Praeger: Westport, CT.

Kropotkin P (1885) 'What geography ought to be', *Nineteenth Century*, 18, 940–956.

Kropotkin P (1886) 'Law and Authority', in Baldwin RM (ed.) (1970) *Kropotkin's Revolutionary Pamphelets*, Dover: New York.

Kropotkin P (1903) *The State: Its Historic Role*, Freedom Press: London.

Kutchinsky B (1990) 'Pornography and rape: Theory and practice? Evidence from crime data in four countries where pornography is easily available', *International Journal of Law and Psychiatry*, v 14, 47.

Lacey N (1998) *Unspeakable Subjects: Feminist Essays in Legal and Social Theory*, Hart Publishing: Oxford.

LaHaye T (1991) 'The Mental Poison', in Baird RM and Rosenbaum SE (eds) *Pornography: Private Right or Public Menace?*, Prometheus: Buffalo.

Lange B (2002) 'The Emotional Dimension in Legal Regulation', *Journal of Law and Society*, v29 (1), 197.

Laqueur TW (2003) *Solitary Sex: A Cultural History of Masturbation*, Zone Books: New York.

Lasker S (2002) '"Sex and the City" Zoning "Pornography Peddlers and Live Nude Shows"', *UCLA Law Review*, vol 49, 1139.

Latour B (1987) *Science in Action: How to Follow Scientists and Engineers through Society*, Harvard University Press: Cambridge, MA.

Latour B (1997a) *On Actor-Network Theory: A Few Clarifications*, Centre for Social Theory and Technology, Keele Univeristy, http://www.keele.ac.uk/depts/stt/staff/jl/pubs-jl2.htm.

Latour B (1997b) 'Train of thought: Piaget, Formalism and the Fifth Dimension', *Common Knowledge*, Vol 6, 170.

Law Meme (2002) 'The Future of Virtual Kiddie Pr0n and Other Notes on *Ashcroft v Free Speech*', 18 April, http://research.yale.edu/lawmeme/modules.php?name=News&file=article&sid=186.

Lefebvre H (1991a) *The Production of Space*, Blackwell: Oxford (originally published in French, 1976).
Lefebvre H (1991b) *Critique of Everyday Life Volume 1*, Verso: London (originally published in French in 1947).
Lenk K (1997) 'The challenge of cyberspatial forms of human interaction to territorial governance and policing' in Loader BD (ed.) The *Governance of Cyberspace: Politics, Technology and Global Restructuring*, Routledge: London.
Lessig L (1998) *Governance, Keynote*: CPSR Conference on Internet Governance 10 October 1998, http://www.cpsr.org.conferences/annmtg98/.
Lessig L (1999) *Code and Other Laws of Cyberspace*, Basic Books: New York.
Levinson P (1997) *The Soft Edge: A Natural History and Future of the Information Revolution*, Routledge: New York.
Light J (1999) 'From City Space to Cyberspace' in Crang M, Crang P and May J (eds) *Virtual Geographies*, Routledge: London.
Linz D, Malamuth NM and Beckett K (1992) 'Civil Liberties and Research on the Effects of Pornography' in Suedfeld P and Tetlock PE (eds) *Psychology and Social Policy*, Hemisphere: New York.
Lipnack J and Stamps J (1994) *The Age of the Network*, John Wiley: New York.
Livingstone KT (1996) *The Wired Nation Content: The Communication Revolution and Federating Australia*, Oxford University Press: Melbourne.
Lizard (1998) 'Kill Bunnies, Sell Meat, Kill More Bunnies', *Wired* 6.05, http://wired.com/archive/6.05/bunnies_pr.html.
Loader BD (ed.) (1997) *The Governance of Cyberspace: Politics, Technology and Global Restructuring*, Routledge: London.
Luke TW (1995) 'New World Order or Neo-World Orders: Power, Politics and Ideology in Informationalising Glocalities', in Featherstone M, Lash S and Robertson R (eds) *Global Modernities*, Sage Publications: London.
Luke TW (1999) 'Simulated Sovereignty, Telematic Territoriality: The Political Economy of Cyberspace', in Featherstone M and Lash S (eds) *Spaces of Culture: City, Nation, World*, Sage Publications: London.
Lukes S (1974) *Power: A Radical View*, Macmillan: New York.
Lutz CA and Collins JL (1993) *Reading National Geographic*, The University of Chicago Press: Chicago.
Lyon D (1997) 'Cyberspace sociality: controversies over computer-mediated relationships' in Loader BD (ed.) *The Governance of Cyberspace: Politics, Technology and Global Restructuring*, Routledge: London.
MacDougall A (1999) '"And the word was made flesh and dwelt among us ...": Towards pseudonymous life on the Internet', *M/C: A Journal of Media and Culture* 2.3, http://www.uq.edu.au/mc/9905/life.html (viewed 1/10/01).
MacKenzie D and Wajcman J (eds) (1999) *The Social Shaping of Technology* (2nd edn.), Open University Press: Buckingham, UK.
MacKinnon C (1989) *Towards a Feminist Theory of the State*, Harvard University Press: Cambridge, MA.

MacKinnon C (1993a) *Only Words*, Harvard University Press: Cambridge, MA.
MacKinnon C (1993b) 'Turning Rape into Pornography', *Ms*, July–August, 24–40.
MacKinnon CA (1995) 'Vindication and Resistance: A Response to the Carnegie Mellon Study of Pornography in Cyberspace', *Georgetown Law Journal*, v83, 1959.
MacKinnon CA and Dworkin A (1997) *In Harm's Way: The Pornography Civil Rights Hearings*, Harvard University Press: Boston.
Manchester C (1999) 'Obscenity, Pornography and Art', *Media and Arts Law Review*, v4 (2), 65.
Mao Tse-Tung (1938) *Problems of War and Strategy*, (Speech) 6 November.
Marcus S (1966) *The Other Victorians: A Study of Sexuality and Pornography in Mid-Nineteenth Century England*, New American Library: New York.
Marcuse H (1955) *Eros and Civilisation: A Philosophical Inquiry into Freud*, Beacon Books: Boston.
Marcuse H (1964) *One Dimensional Man*, Beacon Hill Press: Boston.
Marr D (2001) *Daryl Williams QC at the Chauvel*, http://libertus.net/censor/odocs/marr0110ag.html (viewed 7/4/03).
Masters KW (1992) 'Law in the Electronic Brothel: How Postmodern Media Affect First Amendment Obscenity Doctrine', *University of Puget Sound Law Review*, Vol 15, 415.
Matei S and Ball-Rokeach SJ (2002) 'Belonging in Geographic, Ethnic, and Internet Spaces', in Wellman B and Haythornthwaite C (eds) *The Internet in Everyday Life*, Blackwell Publishing: Oxford, UK.
Mathews R and Phyne J (1988) 'Regulating the Newfoundland inshore fishery: Traditional values versus state control in the regulation of a common property resource', *Journal of Canadian Studies*, 23(1,2), 158–76.
McCafferey L (ed.) (1991) *Storming the Reality Studio: A Casebook of Cyberpunk and Postmodern Science Fiction*, Duke University Press: Durham.
McCallum D (2001) *Personality and Dangerousness: Genealogies of Antisocial Personality Disorder*, Cambridge University Press: New York.
McChesney R (2000) 'So much for the magic of technology and the free market: The World Wide Web and the corporate media system', in Herman A and Swiss T (eds) *The World Wide Web and Contemporary Cultural Theory*, Routledge: London.
McClintock A (1995) *Imperial Leather: Race, Gender and Sexuality in the Colonial Contest*, Routledge: London.
McCoubrey H and White ND (1993) *Textbook on Jurisprudence*, Blackstone Press: London.
McDonald A (1998) 'The Noble Lie: Constitutionalism, Criticised', in Hirvonen A (ed.) *Polycentricity: The Multiple Scenes of Law*, Pluto Press: London.
McDowell L (1999) *Gender, Identity and Place: Understanding Feminist Geographies*, Polity Press: London.
McKee A, Albury K and Lumby C (2008) *The Porn Report*, Melbourne University Press: Melbourne.

Mendilow J (2001) 'The Internet and the Problem of Legitimacy: A Tocquevillian Perspective', in Ebo B (ed.) *Cyberimperialism? Global Relations in the New Electronic Frontier*, Praeger: Westport, CT.

Metcalf JT (1996) 'Obscenity Prosecutions in Cyberspace: The Miller Test Cannot "Go Where No (Porn) Has Gone Before"', *Washington University Law Quarterly*, v74, 481.

Meyrowitz J (1985) *No Sense of Place*, Oxford University Press: New York.

Mezey N (2001) 'The Common Place of Law Out of the Ordinary: Law, Power, Culture, and the Commonplace', *Law and Social Inquiry*, v26, 145.

Miller D (1998) 'A theory of virtualism' in Carter J and Miller D (eds) *Virtualism and its Discontents*, Berg: Oxford.

Miller L (1995) 'Women and Children First: Gender and the Settling of the Electronic Frontier', in Brooks J and Boa I (eds) *Resisting the Virtual Life*, City Light Books: San Francisco.

Mills J (2001) *The Money Shot: Cinema, Sin and Censorship*, Pluto Press: Annandale, NSW.

Minister for Communications and the Arts (1995) *First Direction for Online Services, Direction No.1 of 1995*, Australian Commonwealth Government: Canberra.

Minister for Communications and the Arts (1997) *Second Direction for Online Services*, Australian Commonwealth Government: Canberra.

Minister for Communications, Information Technology and the Arts (2000) *Six Month Report on Co-Regulatory Scheme for Internet Content Regulation*, tabled September, Australian Commonwealth Government: Canberra.

Minister for Communications, Information Technology and the Arts (2001) *Six Month Report on Co-Regulatory Scheme for Internet Content Regulation: July to December 2000*, tabled April, Australian Commonwealth Government: Canberra.

Minister for Communications, Information Technology and the Arts (2002a) *Six Month Report on Co-Regulatory Scheme for Internet Content Regulation: January to June 2001*, tabled February, Australian Commonwealth Government: Canberra.

Minister for Communications, Information Technology and the Arts (2002b) *Six Month Report on Co-Regulatory Scheme for Internet Content Regulation: Reporting Period 4: July to December 2001*, tabled August, Australian Commonwealth Government: Canberra.

Minkkinen P (1998) 'Law, Science and Truth' in Hirvonen A (ed.) *Polycentricity: The Multiple Scenes of Law*, Pluto Press: London.

Mitchell FJ, Finkelhor D and Wolak J (2003) 'The Exposure of Youth to Unwanted Sexual Material on the Internet: A National Study of Risk, Impact and Prevention', *Crimes Against Children Research Center, University of New Hampshire*, http://www.unh.edu/ccrc/pdf/exposure_risk.pdf (viewed 20/5/03), also published in *Youth and Society*, v34(3), 330–358.

Mitchell W (1996) *City of Bits: Space, Place and the Infobahn*, MIT Press: Cambridge, MA.

Mitchell WJ (ed.) (1983) *The Politics of Interpretation*, University of Chicago Press: Chicago.

Morgan R (1980) 'Theory and Practice: Pornography and Rape' in Lederer L (ed.) *Take Back the Night: Women on Pornography*, William Morrow: New York.

Mort F (2000) 'The Sexual Geography of the City' in Bridge G and Watson S (eds) *A Companion to the City*, Blackwell: Oxford.

Mosco V (2000) 'Webs of Myth and Power: Connectivity and the New Computer Technopolis' in Herman A and Swiss T (eds) *The World Wide Web and Contemporary Cultural Theory*, Routledge: London.

Nathan D (1995) *Satan's Silence: Ritual Abuse and the Making of a Modern American Witch Hunt*, Basic Books: New York.

National Coalition Against Censorship (1999a) *Sex and Censorship: Dangers to Minors and Others?: A Background Paper*, http://www.ncac.org/issues/sex_censorship.html.

National Coalition Against Censorship (1999b) *Issue #73: Children's Bodies: What Are We Afraid of?*, http://www.ncac.org/cen_news/cn73childrensbodies.html (viewed 1/7/00).

National Office for the Information Economy (2003) *SPAM: Final Report of the NOIE Review of the Spam Problem and how it can be Countered*, NOIE: Canberra.

National Research Council, Computer Science and Telecommunications Board (2002) *Youth, Pornography and the Internet*, National Academy Press: Washington, DC, http://www.nap.edu/books/0309082749.html, Executive Summary.

National Telecommunications and Information Administration (2000) *Falling Through the Net: Toward Digital Inclusion: A Report on Americans' Access to Technology Tools*, US Department of Commerce, October.

Nedelsky J (1990) 'Law, boundaries and the bounded self', *Representations*, 30, 162–89.

Nesson C and Marglin D (1996) 'The Day the Internet Met the First Amendment: Time and the Communications Decency Act', *Harvard Journal of Law and Technology*, 10, 113.

Netalert (2000) *Netalert Limited: Report for the Period 6 December 1999 to 30 June 2000*, Netalert: Hobart.

Netalert (2003) *How to Deal with Pornography and Pop-Ups on the Internet*, http://www.netalert.net.au/Files/00719_HowDoIStopPornandPopUps.asp (viewed 14/7/03).

Nieuwenheizen J (1997) *Asleep at the Wheel: Australia on The Superhighway*, Australian Broadcasting Corporation.

NSW Standing Committee on Social Issues (2002) *Classification Bill – Final Report*, 6 June, Australian Commonwealth Government: Canberra.

O'Callaghan J (1995) '"Under the Influence": Pornography and Alcohol – Some Common Themes', *Akron Law Review*, Vol 29, 35.
OFLC (1992) *Report on Activities 1991–92*, Australian Commonwealth Government: Canberra.
OFLC (1998) *Classification Board and Classification Review Board Annual Report 1996–97*, National Capital Printing: Canberra.
OFLC (1999a) *Guidelines for the Classification of Films and Videotapes (Amendment No.2)*, Australian Commonwealth Government: Canberra.
OFLC (1999b) *Classification Board and Classification Review Board Annual Report 1998–99*, National Capital Printing: Canberra.
OFLC (2001) *Review of the Classification Guidelines for Films and Computer Games – Discussion Paper*, http://www.oflc.gov.au/PDFs/rev class.pdf.
OFLC (2002) *2001–2002 Annual Report*, National Capital Printing: Canberra.
OFLC (2003) *Guidelines for the Classification of Films and Computer Games*, OFLC: Canberra.
OFLC (2005a) *Classification Study*, Australian Commonwealth Government: Canberra.
OFLC (2005b) *Review of Consumer Advice for Films and Computer Games*, Australian Commonwealth Government: Canberra.
Ogborn M (1992) 'Love-state-ego: "centres" and "margins" in 19th century Britain', *Environment and Planning D: Society and Space*, v10, 287–305.
Orwell G (1964) *1984*, New American Library, New York.
O'Toole L (1998) *Pornocopia: Porn, Sex, Technology and Desire*, Serpent's Tail: London.
Pacillo EL (1994) 'Getting a Feminist Foot in the Courtroom Door: Media Liability for Personal Injury Caused by Pornography', *Suffolk University Law Review*, v28, 123.
Palmer BD (2000) 'Cultures of Darkness: Night Travels in the Histories of Transgression', *Monthly Review Press*: New York.
Paretsky S (1994) 'The Protocols of the Elders of Feminism', *Law/Text/Culture*, v1, 14.
Paterson K et al. (1993) *Classification Issues: Film, Video and Television*, Office of Film and Literature Classification: Sydney.
Paul Calvert, Liberal Senator for Tasmania, Senate Select Committee on Information Technologies (1999) *Senate Proof Committee Hansard*, 28 April, 74.
Paul P (2005) *Pornified: How Pornography is Transforming Our Lives, Our Relationships and Our Families*, Times Books: New York.
Peller G (1985) 'The Metaphysics of American Law', *California Law Review*, v73, 1152–1290.
Penabad C (1998) 'Tagging or Not? The Constitutionality of Federal Labelling Requirements for Internet Web Pages', *UCLA Entertainment Law Review*, Vol 5, 355.

Perritt H (1998) 'The Internet as a Threat to Sovereignty? Thoughts on the Internet's Role in Strengthening National and Global Governance', *Indiana Journal of Global Legal Studies*, v5, 423.

Pfohl S (1998) 'Theses on the cyberotics of HIStory: Venus in Microsoft, remix', in Broadhurst Dixon J and Cassidy EJ (eds) *Virtual Futures: Cyberotics, Technology and Post-Human Pragmatism*, Routledge: London.

Picciotto S (2002) 'Introduction: Reconceptualising Regulation in the Era of Globalisation', *Journal of Law and Society*, Vol 29(1), 1.

Plank T (1997) 'Expanding the Feminine Sexual "Imaginary": A Response to Drucilla Cornell's Theory of Zoning Pornography', *Women's Rights Law Reporter*, vol 18, 215.

Plato (1974) *The Republic*, trans Lee D, Penguin: London.

Pope P (2002–2003) *100%*, v 1–5, Vertigo Comics: New York.

Poster M (1997) 'Cyberdemocracy: The Internet and the Public Sphere', in Porter D (ed.) *Internet Culture*, Routledge: London.

Powell B and Wickre K (1995) *Atlas to the World Wide Web*, Ziff-Davis Press: Emeryville, CA.

Poyhonen J and Reunanen S (1998) 'Law and Mimesis' in Hirvonen A (ed.) *Polycentricity: The Multiple Scenes of Law*, Pluto Press: London.

Price ME and Verhulst SG (1999) *The Concept of Self Regulation and the Internet*, Bertelsmann Foundation Publishers: Gütersloh.

Pue WW (1990) 'Wrestling with law: (Geographical) specificity vs (legal) abstraction', *Urban Geography*, 11 (6), 566–85.

Quan-Haase A and Wellman B with Witte JC and Hampton KN (2002) 'Capitalising on the Net: Social Contact, Civic Engagement, and Sense of Community', in Wellman B and Haythornthwaite C (eds) *The Internet in Everyday Life*, Blackwell Publishing: Oxford, UK.

Raab CD (1997) 'Privacy, Democracy, Information' in Loader BD (ed.) *The Governance of Cyberspace: Politics, Technology and Global Restructuring*, Routledge: London.

Rabinow P and Foucault M (1984) 'Space, Knowledge and Power', in Rabinow P (ed.) *The Foucault Reader: An Introduction to Foucault's Thought*, Penguin: London.

Reckless WC (1967) *The Crime Problem* 4th edn., Meredith: New York.

Reid E (1999) 'Hierarchy and power: social control in cyberspace', in Smith MA and Kollock P (eds) *Communities in Cyberspace*, Routledge: New York.

Reidenberg JR (1997) 'Governing Networks and Rule-Making in Cyberspace' in Kahn B and Nesson C (eds) *Borders in Cyberspace: Information Policy and the Global Information Infrastructure*, MIT Press: Cambridge, MA.

Reisman J (2007) 'Cho's Erototoxin Addiction', *World Net Daily*, 23 April.

Rembar C (1969) *The End of Obscenity: The Trials of 'Lady Chatterley', 'The Tropic of Cancer' and 'Fanny Hill'*, Random House: New York.

Resnick P (1999) *PICS-Interest@w3.org, Moving On*, http://www.lists.w3.org/Archives/Public/pics-interest/1999Jan/000.html (viewed 13/5/99).

Reynolds Technology (1999) *Project 1984*, http://www.rts.com.au/projects/1984.
Rheingold H (1994) *The Virtual Community*, Secker and Warburg: London.
Rheingold H (1996) *Democracy is About Communication*, http://www.well.com/user/hir/texts/democracy.html (viewed 27/7/01).
Rheingold H (2002) 'Foreword: The Virtual Community in the Real World', in Wellman B and Haythornthwaite C (eds) *The Internet in Everyday Life*, Blackwell Publishing: Oxford, UK.
Rhodes R (2002) 'Decentring British Governance: From Bureaucracy to Networks', *Knowledge, Networks and Joined-Up Government Conference Proceedings*, http://www.public-policy.unimelb.edu.au/events/IPSA_Conference.html.
Rimm M (1995) 'Marketing Pornography on the Information Superhighway: A Survey of 917,410 Images, Descriptions, Short Stories and Animations Downloaded 8.5 Million Times by Consumers in over 2,000 Cities in Forty Countries, Provinces, and Territories', *Georgetown University Law Journal*, 83, 1849, also at http://www.TRFN.pgh.pa.us/guest/mrtext.html (viewed 10/8/99).
Roberts D (1997) 'The Jurisprudence of Ratings Symposium Part I: On The Plurality of Ratings', *Cardozo Arts and Entertainment Law Journal*, vol 15, 105.
Robertson R (1995) 'Glocalization: Time-Space and Homegeneity-Heterogeneity', in Featherstone M, Lash S and Robertson R (eds) *Global Modernities*, Sage Publications: London.
Robinson PA (1972) *The Sexual Radicals*, Paladin: London.
Rodriquez F (2002) *Burning the Village to Roast the Pig: Censorship of Online Media*, A paper for the OSCE workshop 'Freedom of the Media and the Internet' 30 November 2002.
Rolph D (2002) 'The Message, Not the Medium: Defamation, Publication and the Internet in *Dow Jones and Co Inc v Gutnick*', *Sydney Law Review*, v24, 263.
Rose N and Valverde M (1998) 'Governed by Law?', *Social and Legal Studies*, vol 7, 569–79.
Ross J (1993) *The Incredibly Strange Film Book: An Alternative History of Cinema*, Simon and Schuster: New York.
Rothenberg T (1995) '"And She Told Two Friends": Lesbians Creating Urban Social Space', in Bell D and Valentine G (eds) *Mapping Desire: Geographies of Sexualities*, Routledge: London.
Rusciano FL (2001) 'The Three Faces of Cyberimperialism', in Ebo B (ed.) *Cyberimperialism? Global Relations in the New Electronic Frontier*, Praeger: Westport, CT.
Rushdie S (1990) *Haroun and the Sea of Stories*, Granta Books: London.
Ryan S (1994) 'Inscribing the Emptiness: Cartography, exploration and the construction of Australia', in Tiffin C and Lawson A (eds) *De-Scribing Empire: Post-colonialism and Textuality*, Routledge: London.
Said E (1978) *Orientalism*, Pantheon Books: New York.

Sardar Z (1995) 'alt.civilisations.faq: Cyberspace and the Darker Side of the West', *Futures*, V27, 777.

Sassen S (1998) 'On the Internet and Sovereignty', *Indiana Journal of Global Legal Studies*, v5, 545.

Schuijer J and Rossen B (1992) 'The Trade in Child Pornography', *IPT Forensics*, v4, http://www.ipt-forensics.com/journal/volume4/4_2_1.htm (viewed 27/4/98).

Scott B (1999a) *An Essential Guide to Internet Censorship in Australia*, http://www.gtlaw.com.au/pubs/essentialguidecensorship.html viewed (27/9/99).

Scott B (1999b) *The Dawn of a New Dark Age – Censorship and Amendments to the Broadcasting Services Act*, http://www.gtlaw.com.au/pubs/newdarkage.html.

Scott C (2001) 'Analysing Regulatory Space: Fragmented Resources and Institutional Design', *Public Law*, 329.

Scutt J (1991) 'Incorporating the Dworkin/MacKinnon Approach into Australian Law', *Inkwell*, Vol 5, 3.

Segal L (1987) *Is the Future Female? Troubled Thoughts on Contemporary Feminism*, Virago: London.

Segal L (1993) 'Does pornography cause violence? The search for evidence' in Church Gibson P and Gibson R (eds) *Dirty Looks: Women, Pornography, Power*, BFI: London.

Segal L (1994) *Straight Sex: The Politics of Pleasure*, Virago: London.

Seiden J (2001) 'Scream-ing for a Solution: Regulating Hollywood Violence; An Analysis of Legal and Legislative Remedies', *University of Pennsylvania Journal of Constitutional Law*, v3, 1010.

Senate Select Committee on Community Standards Relevant to the Supply of Services Utilising Electronic Technologies (1997) *Report on Regulation of Computer On-line Services*, Australian Commonwealth Government: Canberra.

Senate Select Committee on Information Technologies (1998) *Issues Paper – Self Regulation in the Information and Communication Industries*, Australian Commonwealth Government: Canberra.

Senate Select Committee on Information Technologies (1999) *Report on the Broadcasting Services Amendment (Online Services) Bill 1999*, Australian Commonwealth Government: Canberra.

Shapiro AL (1998) 'The Disappearance of Cyberspace and the Rise of Code' *Seton Hall Constitutional Law Journal*, Vol 8, 703.

Sharp JP, Routledge P, Philo C and Paddison R (eds) (2000) *Entanglements of Power: Geographies of Domination/Resistance*, Routledge: London.

Sheehan P (1999) *Report on the Review of OFLC Publications Guidelines*, obtained by Electronic Frontiers Australia under Freedom of Information Law, extracted at http://www.efa.org.au/publish/oflcpublrev989.html.

Shields R (1989) 'Social Spatialization and the Built Environment: The Case of the West Edmonton Mall', *Environment and Planning D*, V7, 147.

Shields R (1996) 'CyberPunk Cinderella? Contextual Illness and Subjectivation', in Juul-Christensen (ed.) *The Meeting of the Waves*, Scandanavian University Press: Copenhagen.

Shields R (ed.) (1996) *Cultures of the Internet: Virtual Spaces, Real Histories and Living Bodies*, Sage: London.

Shields R (2000) 'Hypertext Links: The Ethic of the Index and its Space-Time Effects' in Herman A and Swiss T (eds) *The World Wide Web and Contemporary Cultural Theory*, Routledge: London.

Shirow M (1995) *The Ghost in the Shell*, English edition, Dark Horse Comics: Milwaukee, OR.

Shirow M (2005) *Man/Machine Interface*, Dark Horse Comics: Milwaukee, OR.

Simon W (1996) *Postmodern Sexualities*, Routledge: London.

Simpson GJ and Charlesworth H (1995) 'Objecting to Objectivity: the Radical Challenge to Legal Liberalism' in Hunter R, Ingleby R and Johnstone R (eds) *Thinking About Law: Perspectives on the History, Philosophy and Sociology of Law*, Allen and Unwin: St Leonards, NSW.

Slater D (1998) 'Trading Sexpics on IRC: Embodiment and Authenticity on the Internet', *Body and Society*, v 4(4), 91.

Smith MA (1998) *Voices from the WELL: The Logic of the Virtual Commons*, http://www.sscnet.ucla.edu/soc/csoc/papers/voices/Voices.htm (viewed 9/8/00).

Smith MA (1999) 'Invisible Crowds in Cyberspace: Mapping the social structure of the Usenet', in Smith MA and Kollock P (eds) *Communities in Cyberspace*, Routledge: New York.

Smith MA (2000) 'Some Social Implications of Ubiquitous Wireless Networks', *ACM Mobile Computing and Communications Review*, Vol 4(2).

Smith MA and Kollock P (eds) (1999) *Communities in Cyberspace*, Routledge: New York.

Smith N (1993) 'Homeless/global: Scaling Places' in Bird J, Curtis B, Putnam T, Robertson G and Tickner L (eds) *Mapping the Future: Local Cultures, Global Change*, Routledge: London.

Smith-Rosenberg C (1985) *Religion and the Rise of the American City: The New York City Mission Movement, 1812–1870*, Cornell University Press: Ithaca.

Spigel L (1992) 'The Suburban Home Companion: Television and the Neighbourhood Ideal in Postwar America', in Colomina B (ed.) *Sexuality and Space*, Princeton Architectural Press: New York.

Spinell M (1996) 'Radio Lessons for the Internet', *Postmodern Culture*, v6:2, http://muse.jhu.edu/journals/postmodern_culture/v006/6.2spinelli.html (viewed 20/9/01).

Squire SJ (1996) 'Re-territorializing Knowledge(s): Electronic Spaces and Virtual Geographies', *Area*, V28, 101.

Staple GC (1995) 'Notes on Mapping the New: From Tribal Space to Corporate Space', *Telegeography '95*, http://www.telegeography.com/Publications/mapping.html.

Stefik M (1999) *The Internet Edge: Social, Technical and Legal Challenges for a Networked World*, MIT Press: Cambridge, MA.

Stein J (1999) 'The telephone: its social shaping and public negotiation in late nineteenth- and early twentieth-century London', in Crang M, Crang P and May J (eds) *Virtual Geographies: Bodies, Space and Relations*, Routledge: London.

Stein M (1960) *The Eclipse of Community*, Princeton University Press: Princeton, NJ.

Stephenson N (1992) *Snowcrash*, Roc: London.

Stone AS (1991) 'Will the Real Body Please Stand-up?: Boundary Stories About Virtual Cultures', in Benedikt M (ed.) *Cyberspace: First Steps*, MIT Press: Cambridge, MA.

Stotltenberg J (1990) *Refusing to be a Man*, Meridian: New York.

Streeck W and Schmitter P (1995) 'Community, Market, State and Associations: The Prospective contribution of interest governance to social order' in Streek W and Schmitter PC (eds) *Private Interest Government*, Sage: London.

Strossen N (1996) *Defending Pornography: Free Speech, Sex, and the Fight for Women's Rights*, Abacus: London.

Stychin C (1992) 'Exploring the Limits: Feminism and the Legal Regulation of Pornography', *Vermont Law Review*, 857.

Stychin CF (1995) *Law's Desire: Sexuality and the Limits of Justice*, Routledge: London.

Summers M (trans) (1971) *The Malleus Malificarum of Heinrich Kramer and James Sprenger*, Dover: New York.

Tadros V (1998) 'Between Governance and Discipline: The Law and Michel Foucault', *Oxford Journal of Legal Studies*, vol 18, 74–103.

Taylor B (1999) *Prairie Dog: The Cutest Internet Watchdog*, http://www.prairie-dog.net/.

Taylor B (2000a) *The Bernadette List: Australian Government Viewing Porn*, http://www.prairie-dog.net/Blist.htm (viewed 22/4/00).

Taylor B (2000b) *How to Anonymise Yourself*, http://www.prairie-dog.net/anonymise.htm.

Taylor B (2000c) *They're Still Looking*, http://www.prairie-dog.net/cgi-bin/dynamic.pl.

Terranova T (2001) 'Demonstrating the globe: Virtual action in the network society', in Holmes D (ed.) *Virtual Globalization: Virtual Spaces/Tourist Spaces*, Routledge, London.

Thompson B (1994) *Soft Core: Moral Crusades against Pornography in Britain and America*, Cassell: London.

Tofts D and McKeich M (1998) *Memory Trade: A Prehistory of Cyberculture*, Interface: North Ryde, Australia.

Tom Hingston Studio (2003) *Porn?*, Vision on Publishing: London.

Trachman J (1998) 'Cyberspace, Sovereignty, Jurisdiction and Modernity', *Indiana Journal of Global Legal Studies*, v5, 561.

Trend D (ed.) (2001) *Reading Digital Culture*, Blackwell Publishers: Oxford.
Turkle S (1995) *Life on the Screen: Identity in the Age of the Internet*, Simon and Schuster: New York.
Twining W (2000) *Globalisation and Legal Theory*, Butterworths: London.
Valente TW (1995) *Network Models of the Diffusion of Innovations*, Hampton Press: Cresskill, NJ.
Vnuk H (2003) *Snatched: Sex and Censorship in Australia*, Vintage Books: Sydney.
Wakeford N (1999) 'Gender and the landscapes of computing in an Internet Café', in Crang M, Crang P and May J (eds) *Virtual Geographies: Bodies, Space and Relations*, Routledge: London.
Waldron J (1991) 'Homelessness and the issue of freedom', *UCLA Law Review*, 30, 395–42.
Waters J (1991a) *Bad Taste: A Tasteful Book about Bad Taste*, Fourth Estate: London.
Waters J (1991b) *Shock Value*, Fourth Estate: London.
Webster R (1990) *A Brief History of Blasphemy*, The Orwell Press: London.
Wellman B (2001) 'The Rise of Networked Individualism' in Keeble L (ed.) *Community Networks Online*, Taylor and Francis: London.
Wellman B and Gulia M (1999) 'Virtual communities as communities: Net surfers don't ride alone', in Smith MA and Kollock P (eds) *Communities in Cyberspace*, Routledge: New York.
Wertheim M (1999) *The Pearly Gates of Cyberspace: A History of Space from Dante to the Internet*, Doubleday: Sydney.
Wesson M (1991) 'Sex, Lies and Videotape: The Pornographer as Censor', *Washington Law Review*, v66, 913.
Western Australian Internet Association (1999a) *DCITA Internet Regulation*, http://www.waia.asn.au/Issues/Regulation/DCITA/.
Western Australian Internet Association (1999b) *WAIA submission regarding draft framework for proposed Commonwealth legislation*, http://www.waia.asn.au/Issues/Regulation/DCA-framework-response.html.
Weston K (1999) *Slow Burn: Sexualities and Social Science*, Routledge: London.
Wigley M (1992) 'Untitled: The Housing of Gender, Sexuality and Space', *Princeton Papers on Architecture*, Princeton, NJ.
Williams D (1997) 'From Censorship to Classification: An Address by the Attorney-General the Hon Daryl Williams AM QC', *E Law – Murdoch University Electronic Journal of Law*, v4 (4), http://www.murdoch.edu.au/elaw/issues/v4n4/will441.html (viewed 7/4/03).
Williams L (1993) 'Second thoughts on hard core: American obscenity law and the scapegoating of deviance', in Church Gibson P and Gibson R (eds) *Dirty Looks: Women, Pornography, Power*, British Film Institute: London.
Williams L (1999) *Hard Core: Power, Pleasure, and the 'Frenzy of the Visible'*, University of California Press: Berkeley.

Williams L (ed.) (2004) *Porn Studies*, Duke University Press: London and Durham.

Williams SL (2001) 'On Blues, Marx and Elvis: Why We need a Meaningful Participation Model to Frame Spatial Theory', *Margins*, v1, 103.

Wilson E (1992) 'Feminist fundamentalism: the shifting politics of sex and censorship' in Segal L and McIntosh M (eds) *Sex Exposed: Sexuality and the Pornography Debate*, Virago: London.

Winter A (2007) 'Antiporn Activist says Porn Addiction Drove Virginia Tech Killings', *XBiz News Report*, 25 April.

Winter SL (1996) 'The "Power" Thing', *Virginia Law Review*, v82, 721.

Yamaguchi I (2002) 'Beyond De Facto Freedom: Digital Transformation of Free Speech Theory in Japan', *Stanford Journal of International Law*, Vol 38, 109.

Yee D (1999a) *The Internet is not Television*, http://www.anatomy.usyd.edu.au/danny/freedom/99/convergence.html.

Yee D (1999b) *The Effects on Content Providers*, http://www.anatomy.usyd.edu.au/danny/freedom/99/content-providers.html.

Yee D (1999c) *Consumer Rights*, http://www.anatomy.usyd.edu.au/danny/freedom/99/consumers.html.

Yee D (1999d) *Classification and 'Collateral Damage'*, http://www.anatomy.usyd.edu.au/danny/freedom/99/classification.html.

Zaretsky E (1995) 'The Birth of Identity Politics in the 1960s: Psychoanalysis and the Public/Private Distinction', in Featherstone M, Lash S and Robertson R (eds) *Global Modernities*, Sage Publications: London.

Zimring FE and Hawkins CJ (1976) *Deterrence: The Legal Threat in Crime Control*, University of Chicago Press: Chicago.

Index

2600 Australia 80

Actor-network theory 198
Age verification service 59
Aggrieved person 218
Alston, Senator Richard 8, 33, 52, 72, 134, 158
American Psycho 170
Anderson, Benedict 221
Anonymity 186
Anonymous remailer 13
Anti-pornography feminism 169, 171
Aoki, Keith 208
Ashcroft v American Civil Liberties Union 30, 181, 216
Australia Institute, The 12
Australian Communications and Media Authority (ACMA) 50, 57, 61, 62, 72, 74

Baise-Moi 157
Beazley, Kim 11
Benjamin, Walter 147
Black box 195
Black, Julia 188, 195, 199, 202, 216, 234
Blake, William 166
Blomley, Nicholas 97, 204, 207
Body, the 145, 147, 236
Borden, Iain 102
Boyle, James 129
British Board of Film and Video Classification (BBFVC) 21, 165
Broadcasting 29
Broadcasting Services Amendment (Online Services) Act 1999 9, 13, 39, 47, 52, 167, 192
  Complaints mechanism 55
  Industry Code of Practice 55, 60
  Objectives 53
  Takedown notice 56, 72
Butler's case 30, 172

Calvert, Senator Paul 12
Canadian Charter of Rights and Freedoms 30
Capalert 225
Carter, Angela 183
Cartesian space 103
Cartography 205
Castells, Manuel 200
Censorship 138
  Artistic Merit 24, 35, 154
  Arts Funding 27
  Australia 33
  Mitigating Factors 38
  Private censorship 85
  Scientific Merit 24, 35, 154, 156
  Self censorship 152
  United Kingdom 20
  United States 22
Chen, Peter 87, 126, 237
Child Online Protection Act 2000 29, 216
Child pornography 164, 184
Child Pornography Prevention Act 196 29
Children 180, 184
  Childhood 163, 204, 232
Children's Internet Protection Act 2000 29
Civil and political rights 66
Clark, Gordon 99
Classification 145, 151, 153, 160
  MA Rated 36
  Refused classification 18, 38, 58, 137
  R Rated 37, 58, 59, 84
  X rated 14, 37, 57, 58
Classification (Publications, Films and Computer Games) Act 1995 35, 218
Code 122, 126, 140
Colombine Shootings 11
Common Law Censorship 19
Communications Decency Act 1996 28, 199
Community 7, 49, 89, 118, 188, 189, 191, 200, 219, 224
Community Standards 24, 33, 82, 96, 130, 156, 167, 191

Community values 89, 156, 158, 216, 239
Cornell, Drucilla 175, 183, 187, 211, 213
Critical legal geography 89, 99, 100, 140
Crowe v Graham 33
Cultural flows 208
Cybergovernance 94
Cyberlibertarian 128, 203
Cyberspace 9, 93, 94, 106, 116, 119, 132, 185, 204, 206, 210, 220
Cyborg 122, 125

de Certeau, Michel 134, 147, 234, 236, 237
Decentred regulation 202
Degradation 177
Deprave and corrupt 156
Desire 147, 226, 230
Dworkin, Andrea 30, 170, 171

Ehrlich, Eugen 235
Electronic democracy 238
Electronic Frontiers Australia (EFA) 19, 43, 66, 71, 73, 79, 180
Entertainment Software Rating Board (ESRB) 27
Erotica 155
Everyday life 117, 234, 237
Exploitation films 167, 179
Exploitative 35

Filtering 19, 40, 83, 187, 239
    Approved Filter 64
Fish, Stanley 129
Ford, Richard Thomson 204
Foucault, Michel 104, 143, 195, 198, 205
Free speech, Australia 67
Freedom of Information 53, 83

Games 114
Ginsberg principle 26
Globalisation 208
Glocalisation 208
Graham, Irene 43, 69, 71, 75, 83, 133
Grand Theft Auto 3 33
Gratuitous 35
Guidelines for the Classification of Films and Videotapes 35
Gutnick case 94

Hardy, Simon 183, 229
Harm 181
Harradine, Senator Brian 10, 69
Hayes Production Code 23
Helsingius, Johan 13
Henry – Portrait of a Serial Killer 158
Hobbes, Thomas 197
Home 18, 185
Human geography 98
Hunchback of Notre Dame, the 158
Hunt, Alan 150, 153, 161, 164, 167
Hypertext 79

Identity 219, 224, 226
Imaginary domain 175, 183, 187, 211, 214, 231, 238
Imagined community 221
In a Glass Cage 158
Indecency 20
Indigenous customary law 111
Information flows 106, 121
Interlegality 195
Internet Industry Association 47, 53, 60, 75
    Internet Industry Codes of Practice 63
Internet Watch Foundation 22
Interpretative communities 216

Jurisdiction 49, 95, 109–110, 202, 203
Jurispace 105, 119, 139, 202, 239

Ken Park 138
Kendall, Christopher 31

Labelling 40, 44, 85
    Eye-T 41
    PICs 41
    RSACi 41, 44
Lasker, Stephanie 213
Latour, Bruno 195, 198
Lefebvre, Henri 101, 107, 132, 147, 170, 205, 234
Legal geographies 96
Legal pluralism 194
Legal polycentricity 194
Legal positivism 193
Legal reification 79

Legend of Zelda: The Ocarina of Time, The 115
Lessig, Larry 28, 122, 126, 186, 206, 224
Liberal democracy 205
Liminal spaces 110, 142, 212
Little Sisters case 31
Living Law, the 235
Lukes, Steven 196

MacKinnon, Catharine 30, 170, 171, 197
Majoritarianism 223
Marcuse, Herbert 144
Mardi Gras Film Festival 158
Marginal spaces 113, 137
Matrix, The 90, 132, 135, 143
McLuhan, Marshall 120
Media literacy 65, 178
Media spaces 138
Mediascape 139, 208
Meece Commission 32
Meyer, Russ 23
Middle Australia 48, 96
Miller Test 24
Mitchell, William 121, 167, 206
Moral panic 18, 145, 161, 163, 186
Moral regulation 153
Motion Picture Association of America (MPAA) 23, 26

Nation 221
Netalert 65, 72
Network power 198
Network society 200
Network theory 201
Networked governance 201
Networks 131
Night, the 142, 228
Non-space 125
Nudity 164, 179, 184

O'Toole, Laurence 154, 166, 172, 188
Obscenity 20, 23, 24
Offence 224
Offensive 35, 176, 188
Office of Film and Literature Classification (OFLC) 8, 34, 38, 72, 155, 178, 191, 218
    Classification Board 8, 34, 55, 160
    Classification Review Board 8, 34, 159, 218
    Community Assessment Panels 160
    OFLC Classification Guidelines 180
Other, the 158, 166, 212, 215, 222

Paretsky, Sara 170
Patriarchy 197
Peer to peer networks 81
Place 114, 207, 210, 237
Plank, Tonya 215
Policy Networks 87
Porno-anomie 156
Pornography 15, 147, 228
    Hard core 24, 175, 179, 183
    Soft core 175, 183, 215
Pornoland 143
Pornotopia 4, 143, 214, 228
Pornscape 143
Power 193, 197
Prairie Dog List 70
Privacy 71, 176
Private space 146, 150
Production of Space, The 101, 103, 112
    Abstract space 108
    Consumerism 108
    Differential Space 110, 205
    Representational spaces 104
    Representations of space 104
    Spatial practice 104
Public space 93, 137, 146, 150, 187, 209, 222
Public sphere 175, 208, 210
Public/private divide 86, 176, 208, 210
Publication 49
Pue, Wes 98, 101

Realism 179
Rear view regulation 50, 120
Regulatory communities 141, 193, 220, 238
Regulatory conversations 195, 199, 234
Regulatory fortressing 2, 18, 86, 134, 143, 167, 185, 239
Regulatory networks 239
Regulatory space 90
Restricted access system 59
Rheingold, Howard 67, 222

Rice, Anne 174
RICO Laws 25
Rimm, Marty 27
Roth's Case 23, 24
Royale, Candida 173
Rule of law 89, 100

Salo 157
Scott, Brendan 69, 77
Self governance 162
Self gratification 214
Sexploitation 23
Simulated sovereignty 209
Snowcrash 91
Social hygiene 160
Social Networks 129
Social space 104
Spatial ecology 170
Stephenson, Neal 91
Steve Jackson Games case 25
Storylines 219
Stychin, Carl 31
Symbolic legislation 86, 167, 192

Teenager.com.au 74
Television 93
Terra nullius 90
Theories of space 94
Tiger protection 193
Tobacco 162
Transgressive spaces 151

Video nasties 20
Videodrome 144
Violence 179
Virtual communities 216, 217, 220, 222
Vonnegut, Kurt 235

Wigley, Mark 146
Williams, Linda 170, 183, 229
Williams, Sabrina 234

Yee, Danny 50, 71, 74

Zee, Ona 173
Zoning 187, 212, 214